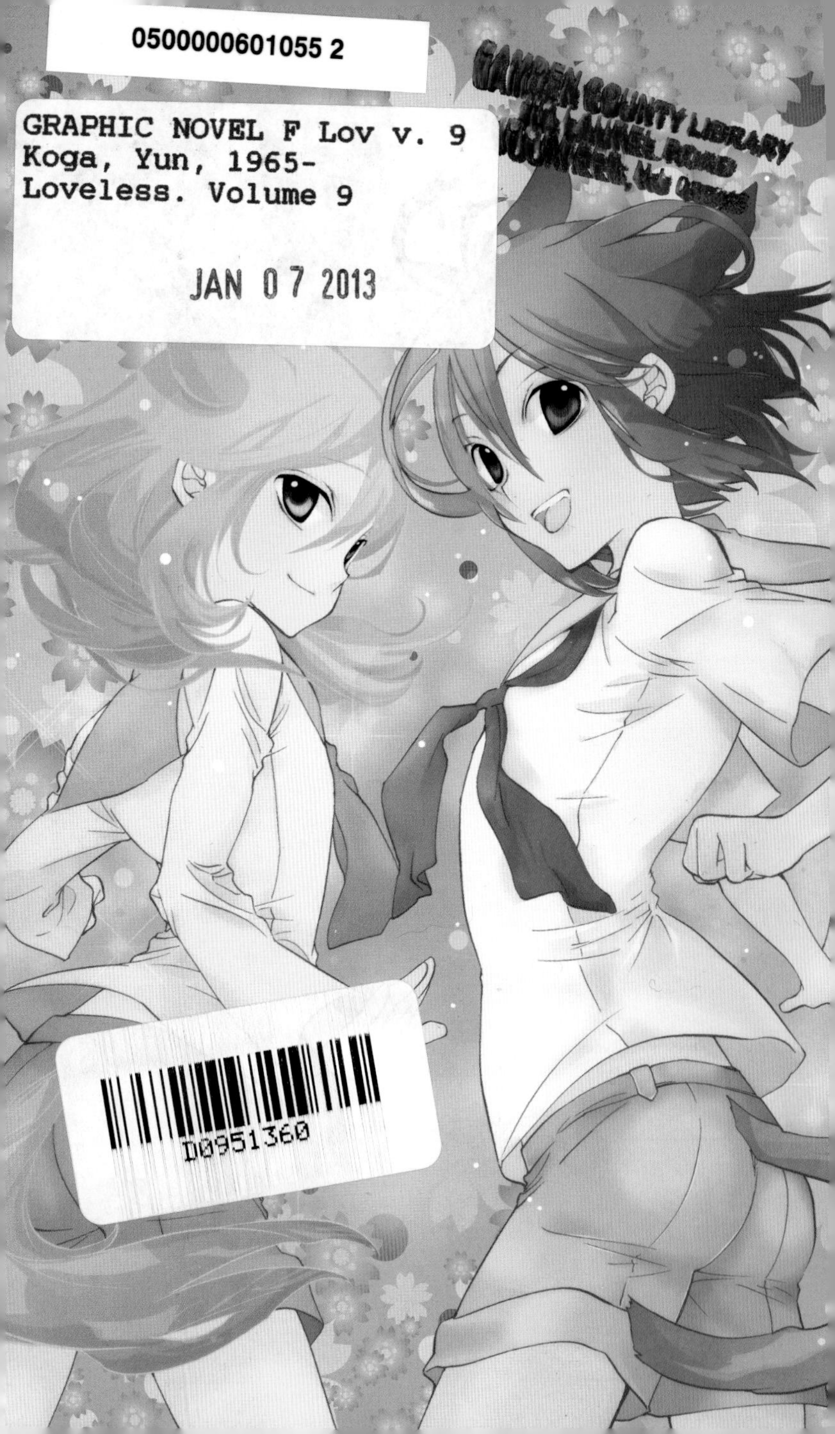

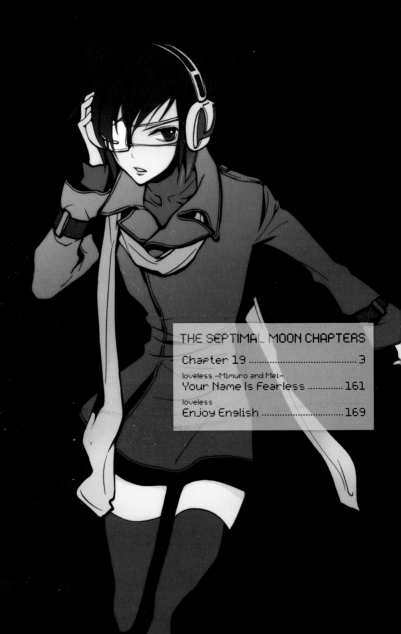

THE SEPTIMAL MOON CHAPTERS

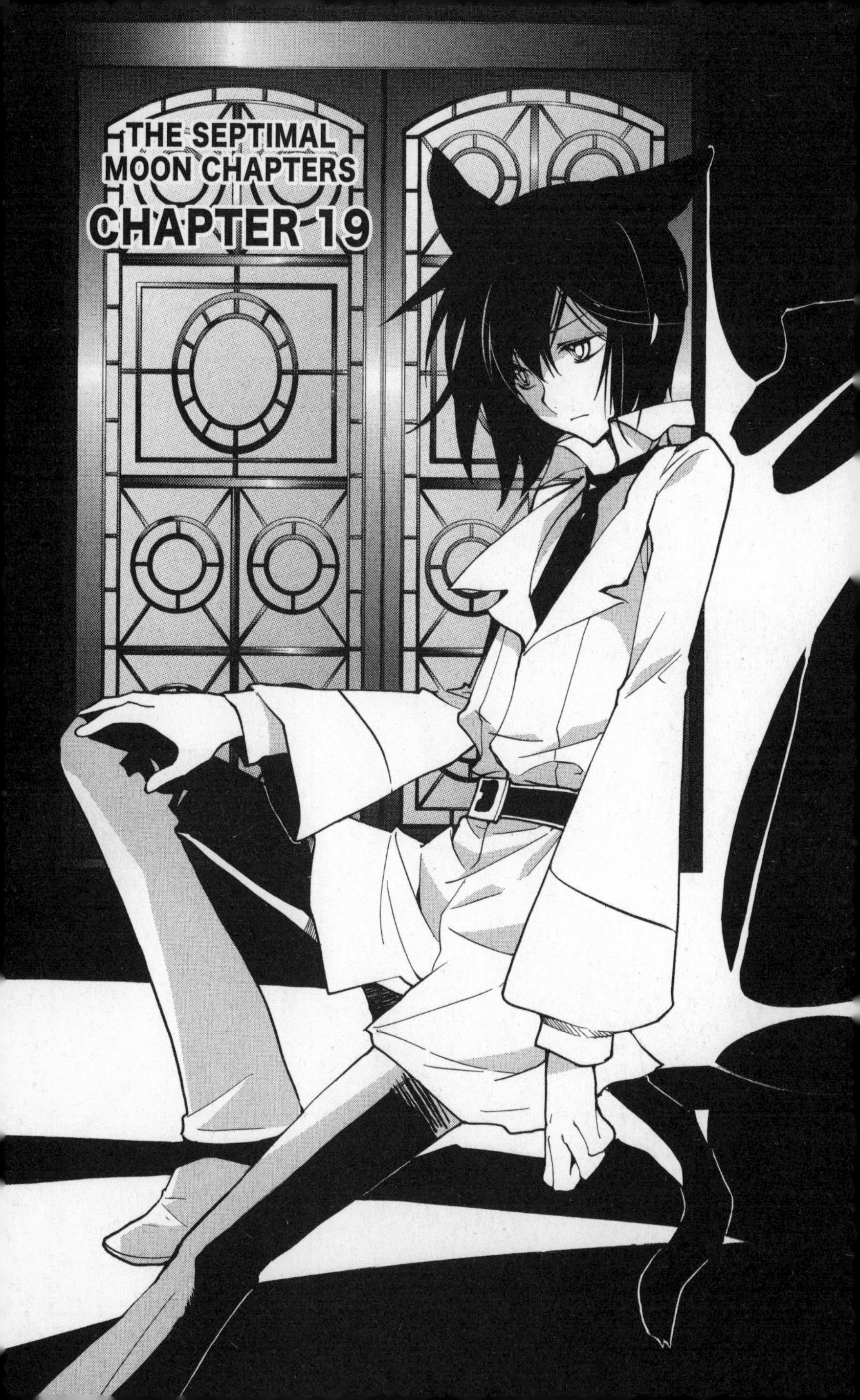
THE SEPTIMAL MOON CHAPTERS
CHAPTER 19

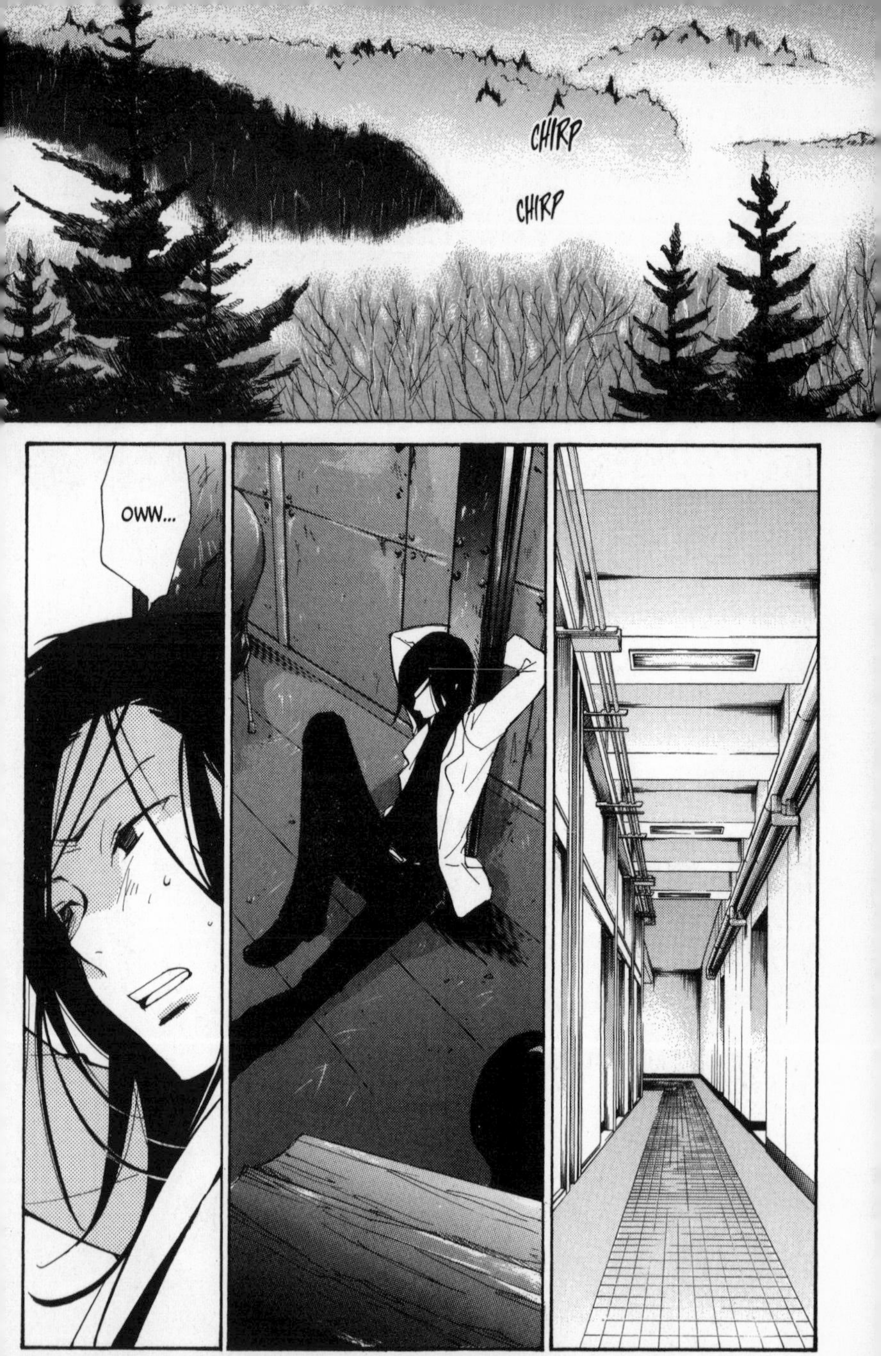
CHIRP
CHIRP
OWW...

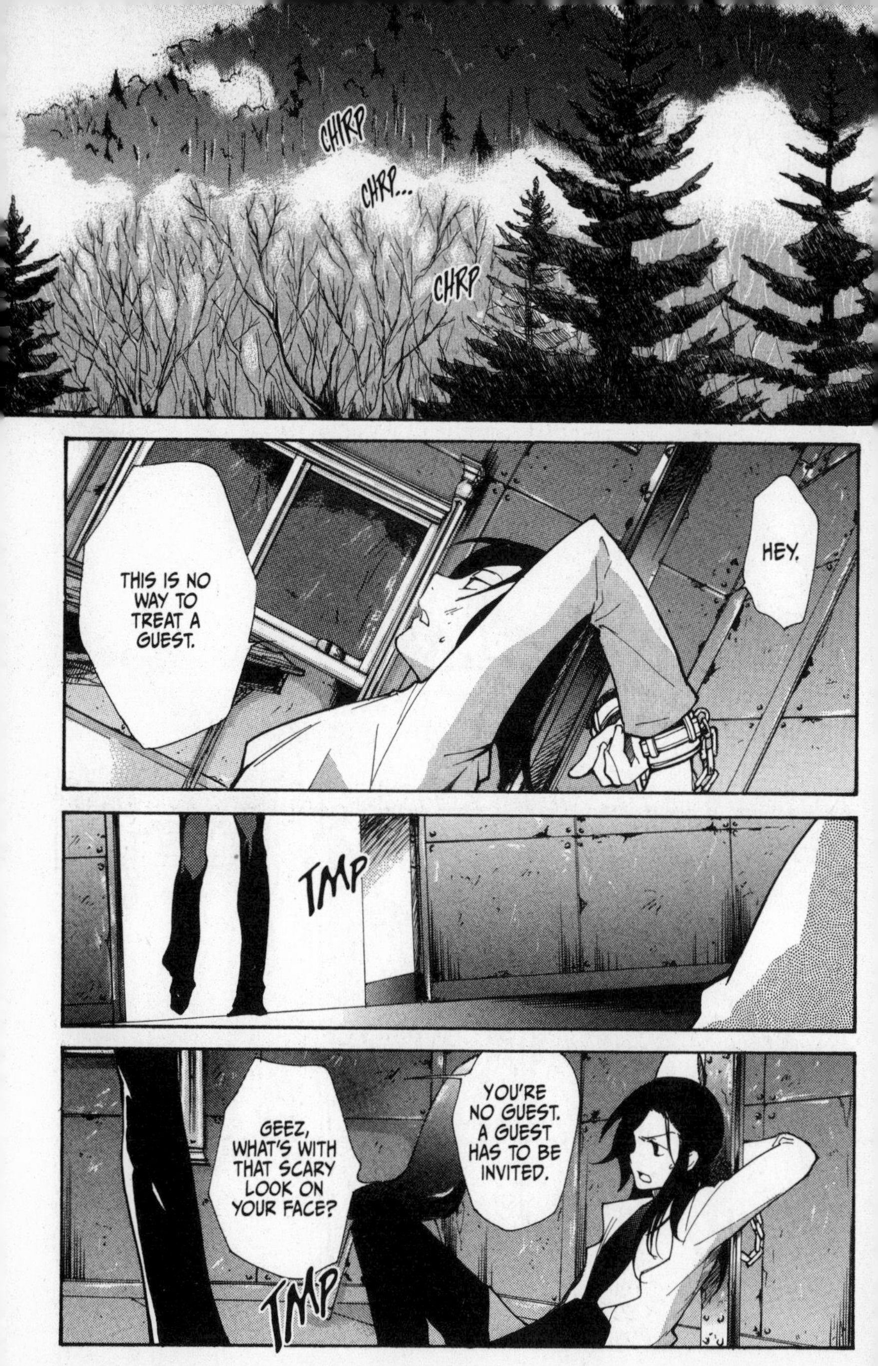
CHRP
CHRP...
CHRP
HEY.
THIS IS NO WAY TO TREAT A GUEST.
TMP
YOU'RE NO GUEST. A GUEST HAS TO BE INVITED.
GEEZ, WHAT'S WITH THAT SCARY LOOK ON YOUR FACE?
TMP

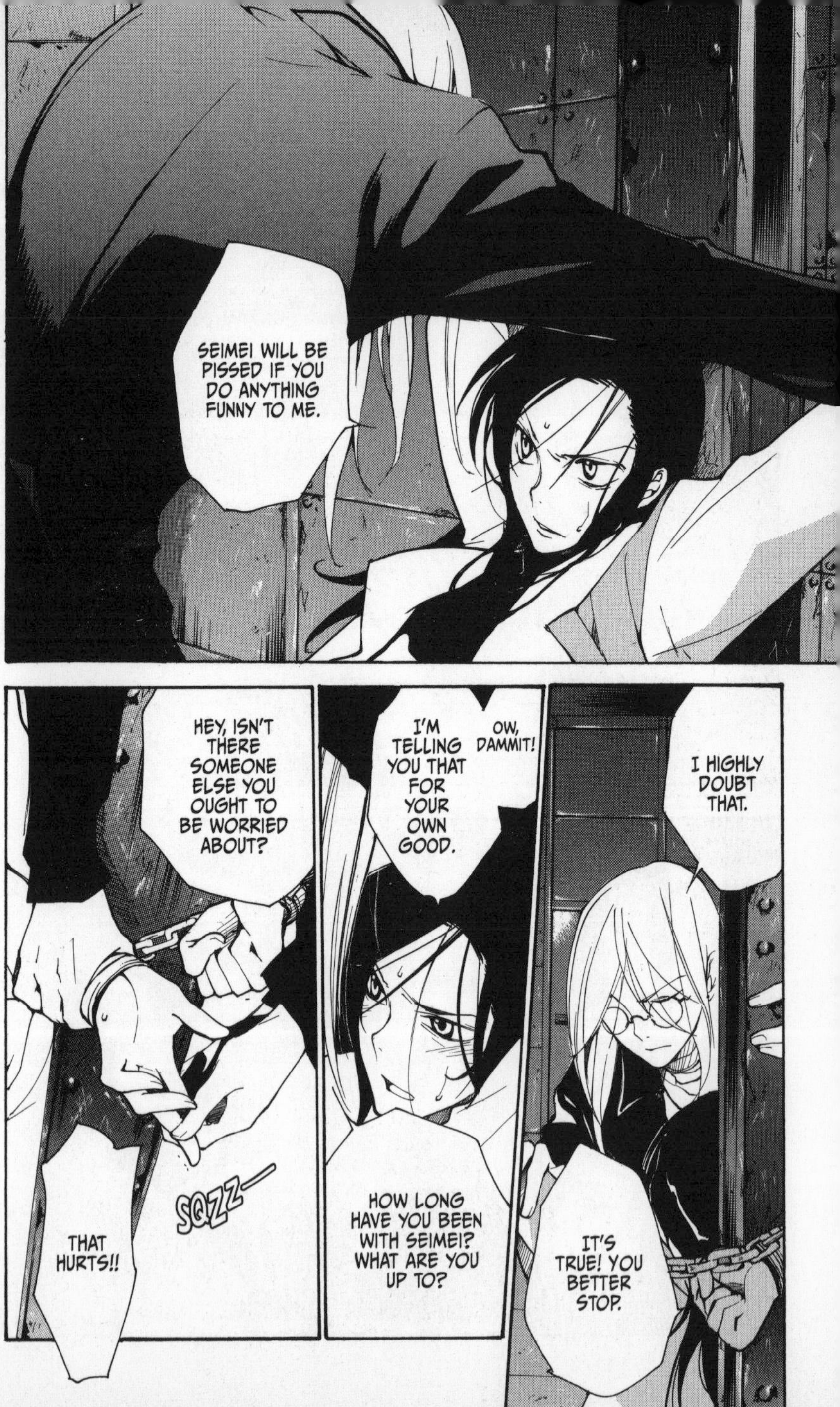
SEIMEI WILL BE PISSED IF YOU DO ANYTHING FUNNY TO ME.
I HIGHLY DOUBT THAT.
IT'S TRUE! YOU BETTER STOP.
OW, DAMMIT!
I'M TELLING YOU THAT FOR YOUR OWN GOOD.
HOW LONG HAVE YOU BEEN WITH SEIMEI? WHAT ARE YOU UP TO?
HEY, ISN'T THERE SOMEONE ELSE YOU OUGHT TO BE WORRIED ABOUT?
SQZZ—
THAT HURTS!!

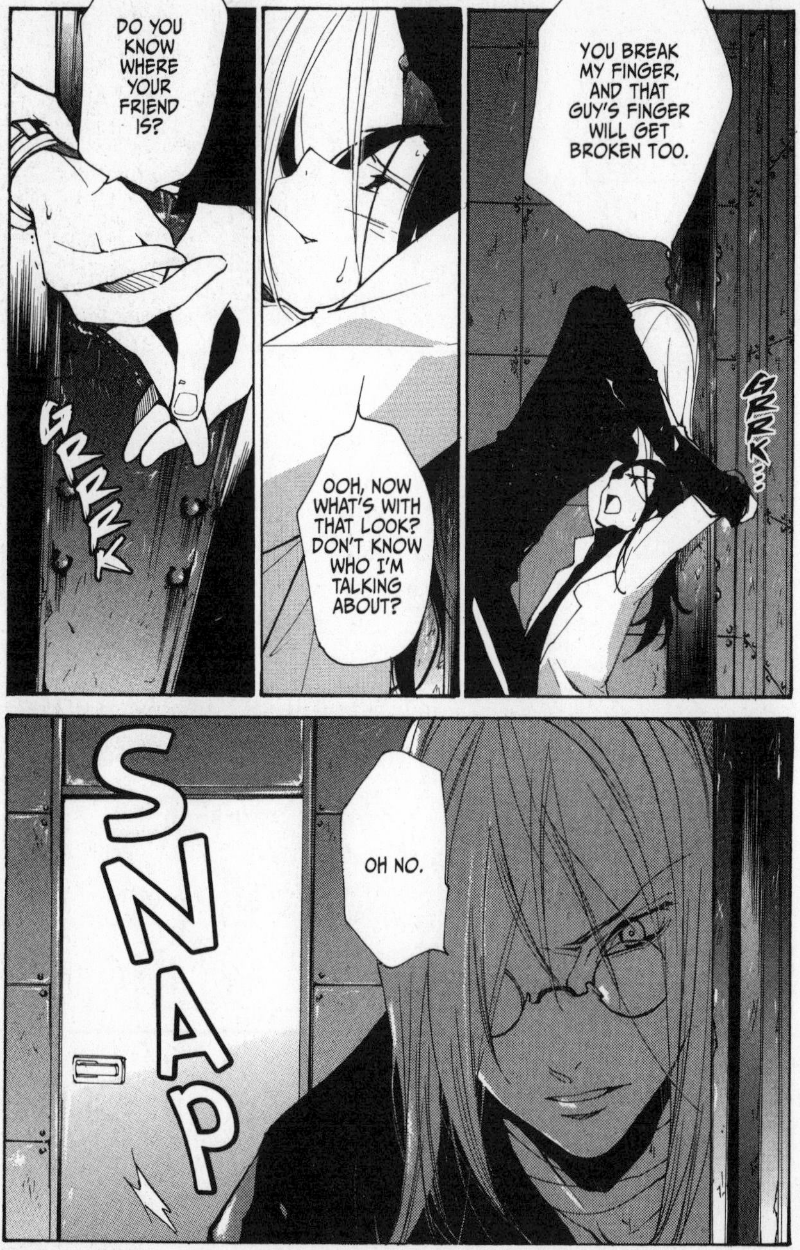
YOU BREAK MY FINGER, AND THAT GUY'S FINGER WILL GET BROKEN TOO.
GRRRK...
OOH, NOW WHAT'S WITH THAT LOOK? DON'T KNOW WHO I'M TALKING ABOUT?
DO YOU KNOW WHERE YOUR FRIEND IS?
GRRRK
OH NO.
SNAP

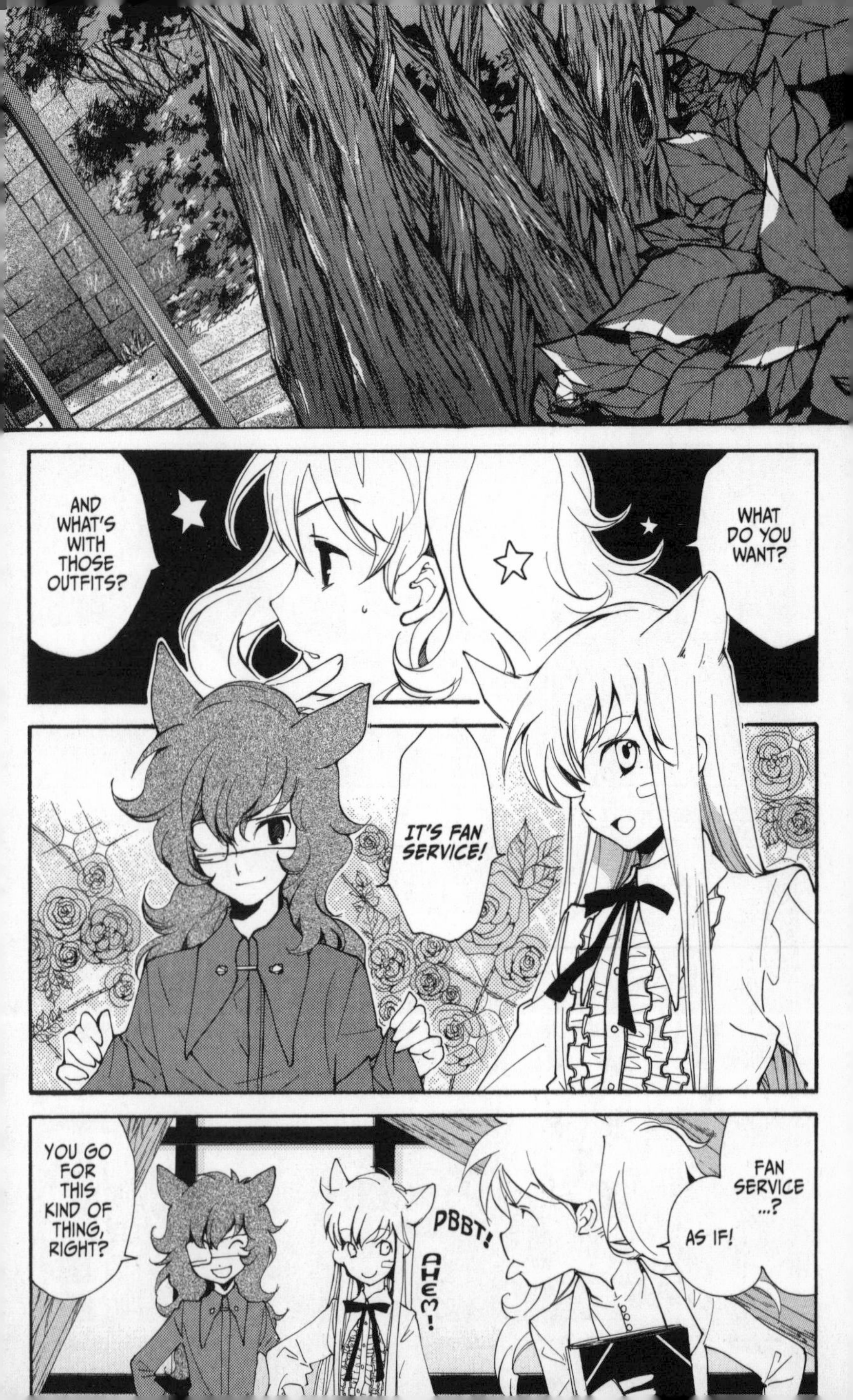
WHAT DO YOU WANT?
AND WHAT'S WITH THOSE OUTFITS?
IT'S FAN SERVICE!
FAN SERVICE ...?
AS IF!
PBBT!
AHEM!
YOU GO FOR THIS KIND OF THING, RIGHT?

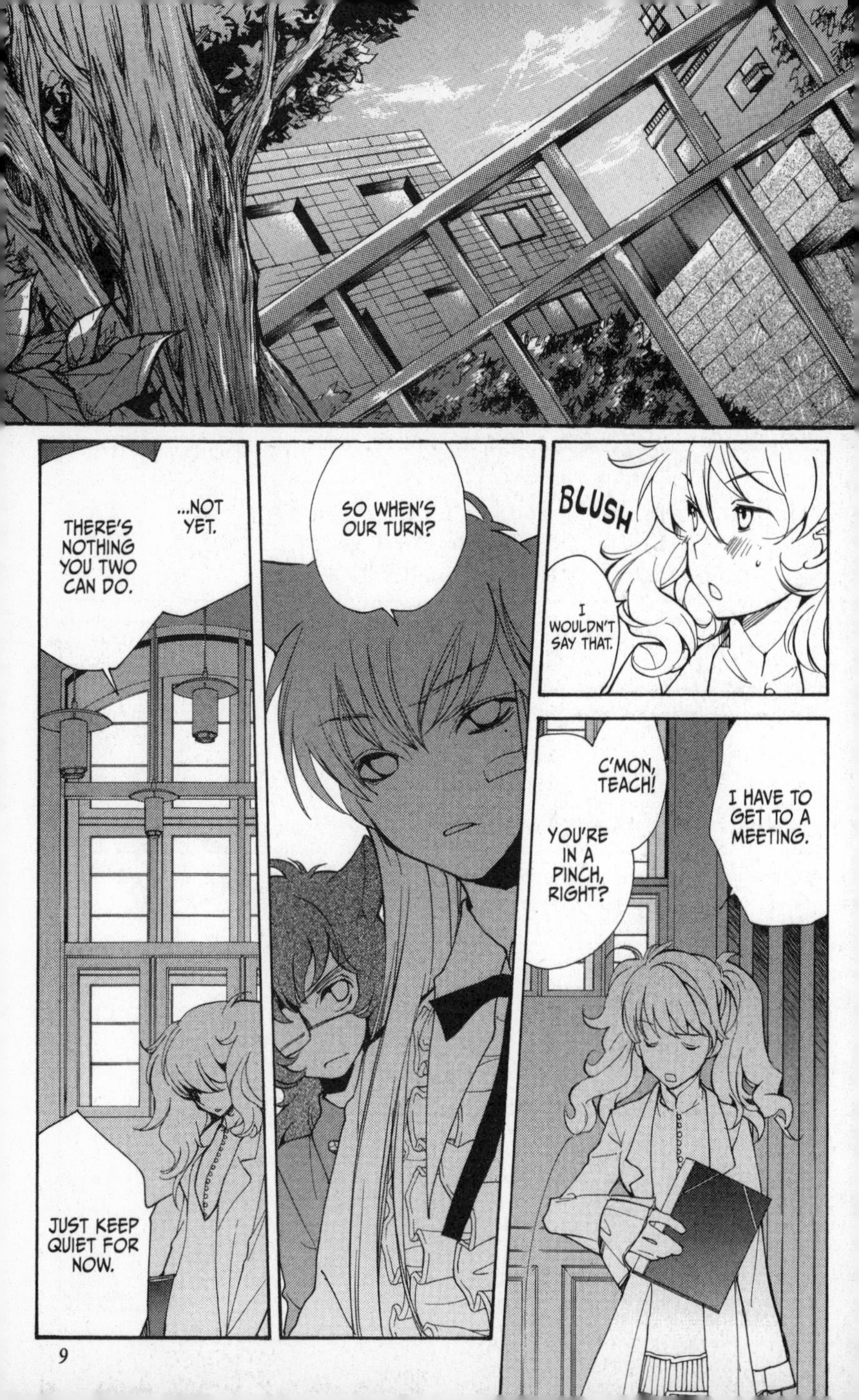
BLUSH
I WOULDN'T SAY THAT.
I HAVE TO GET TO A MEETING.
C'MON, TEACH!
YOU'RE IN A PINCH, RIGHT?
SO WHEN'S OUR TURN?
...NOT YET.
THERE'S NOTHING YOU TWO CAN DO.
JUST KEEP QUIET FOR NOW.

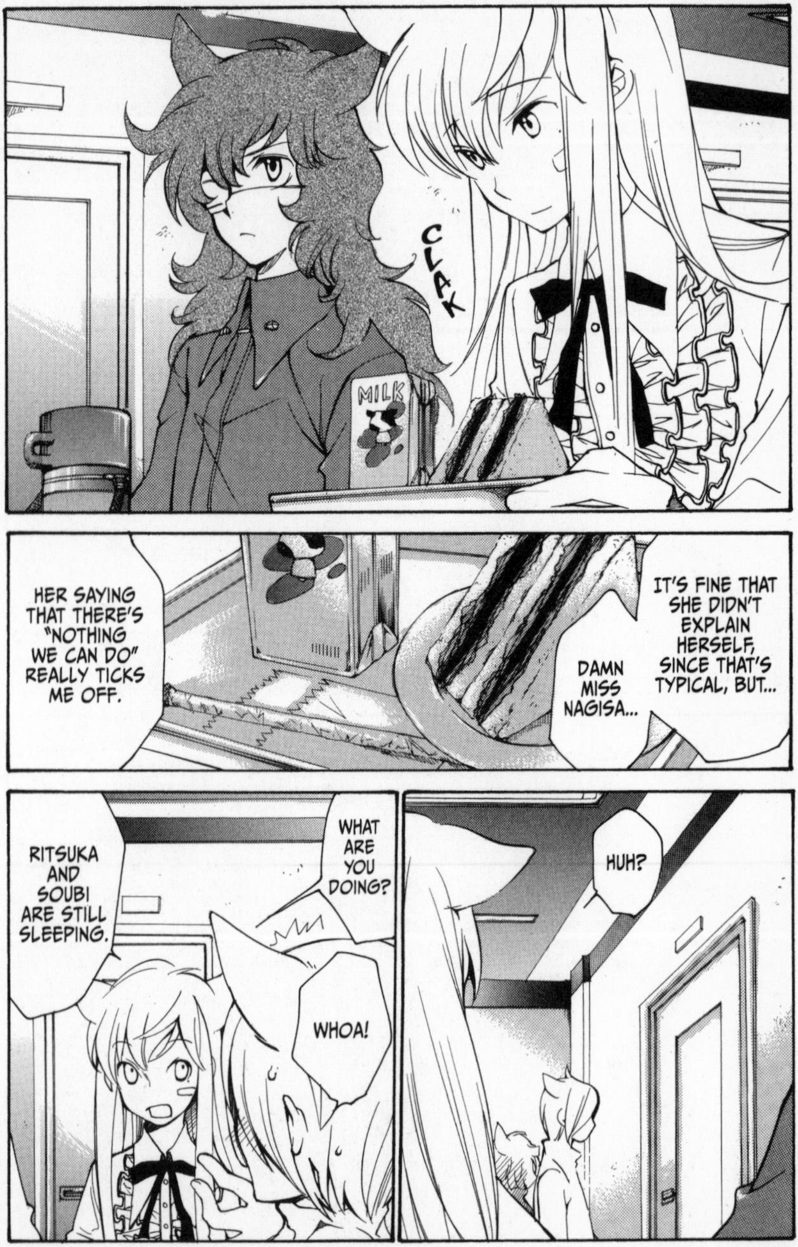
CLAK
IT'S FINE THAT SHE DIDN'T EXPLAIN HERSELF, SINCE THAT'S TYPICAL, BUT...
DAMN MISS NAGISA...
HER SAYING THAT THERE'S "NOTHING WE CAN DO" REALLY TICKS ME OFF.
HUH?
WHAT ARE YOU DOING?
RITSUKA AND SOUBI ARE STILL SLEEPING.
WHOA!
MILK

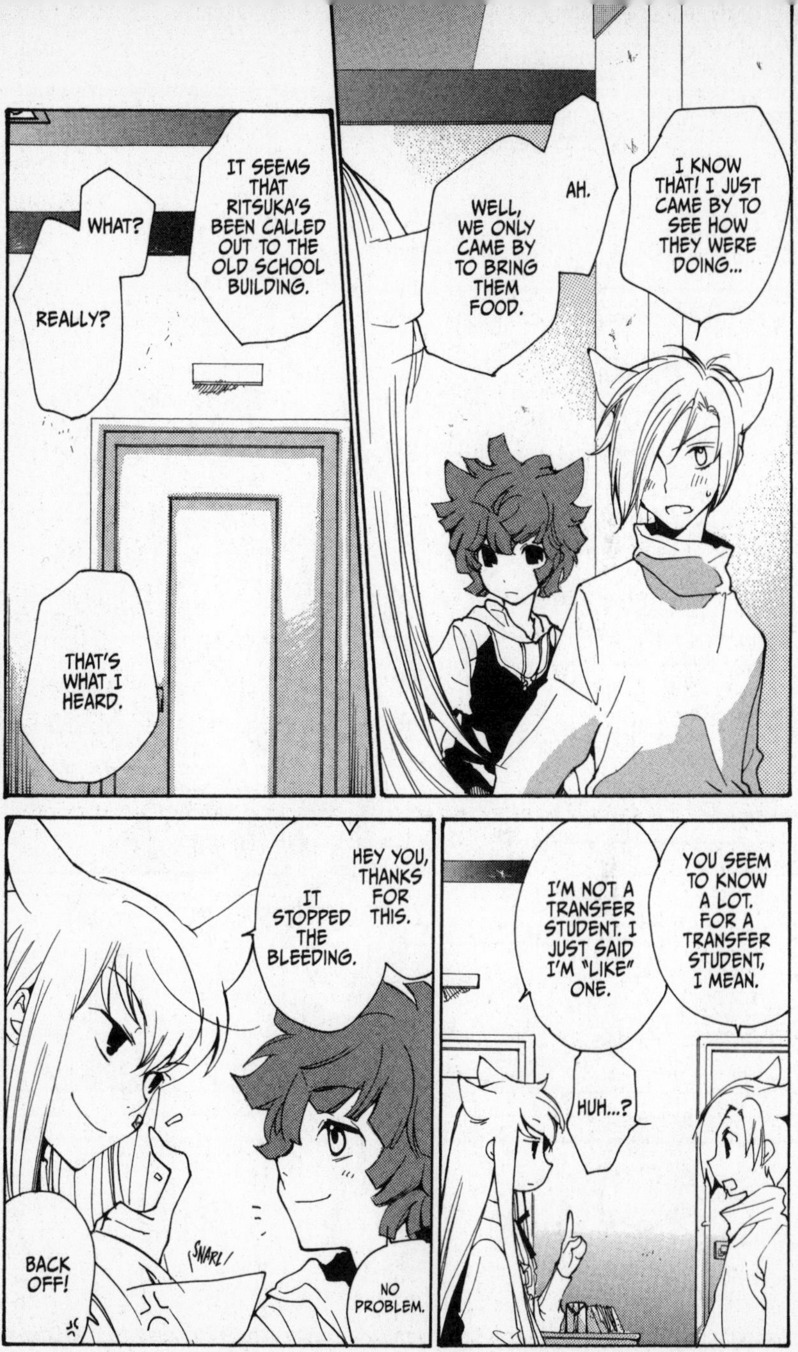
I KNOW THAT! I JUST CAME BY TO SEE HOW THEY WERE DOING...
AH. WELL, WE ONLY CAME BY TO BRING THEM FOOD.
IT SEEMS THAT RITSUKA'S BEEN CALLED OUT TO THE OLD SCHOOL BUILDING.
WHAT? REALLY?
THAT'S WHAT I HEARD.
YOU SEEM TO KNOW A LOT. FOR A TRANSFER STUDENT, I MEAN.
I'M NOT A TRANSFER STUDENT. I JUST SAID I'M "LIKE" ONE.
HUH...?
HEY YOU, THANKS FOR THIS. IT STOPPED THE BLEEDING.
NO PROBLEM.
SNARL!
BACK OFF!

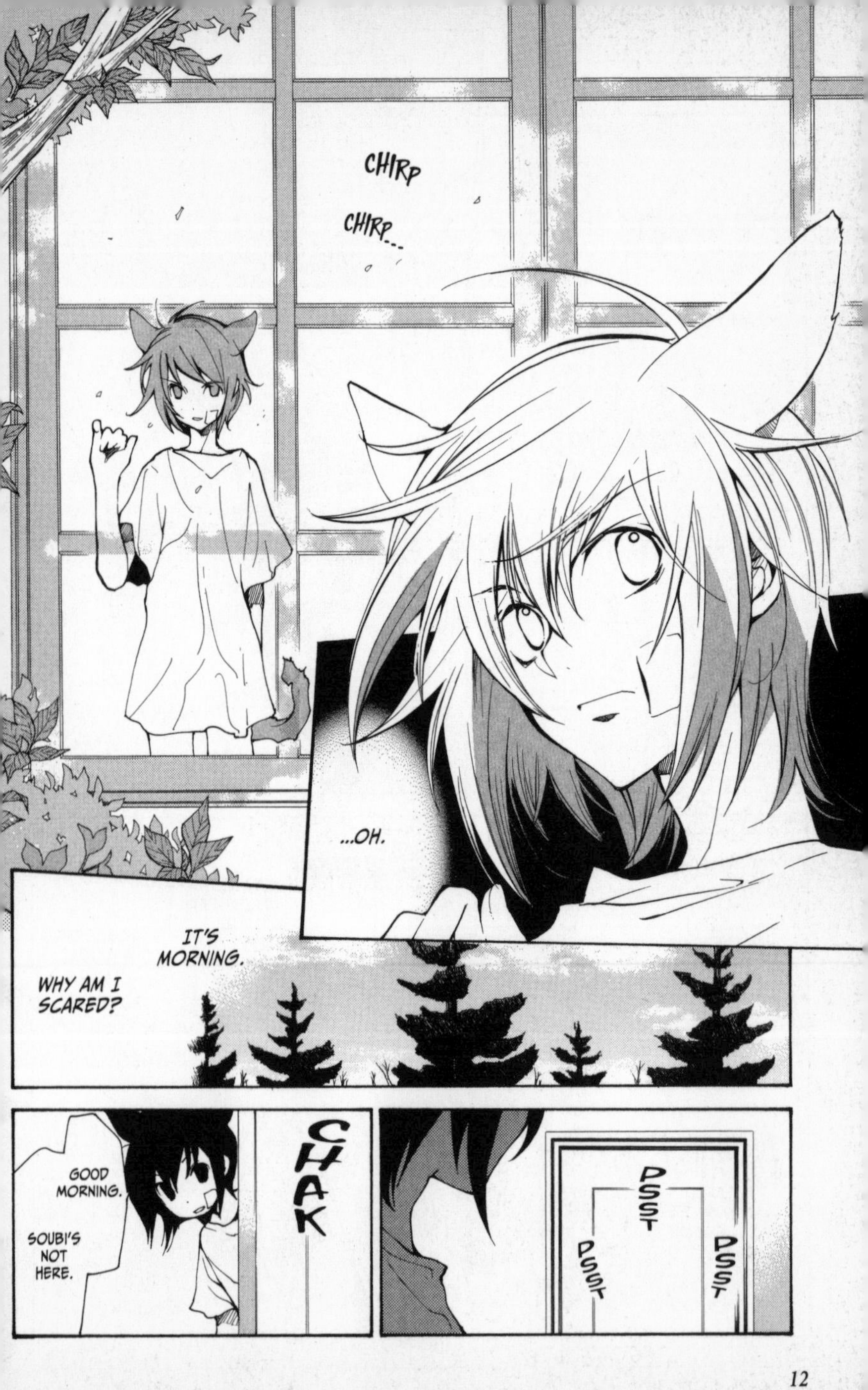

CHIRP
CHIRP...
...OH.
IT'S MORNING.
WHY AM I SCARED?
PSST
PSST
PSST
CHAK
GOOD MORNING.
SOUBI'S NOT HERE.

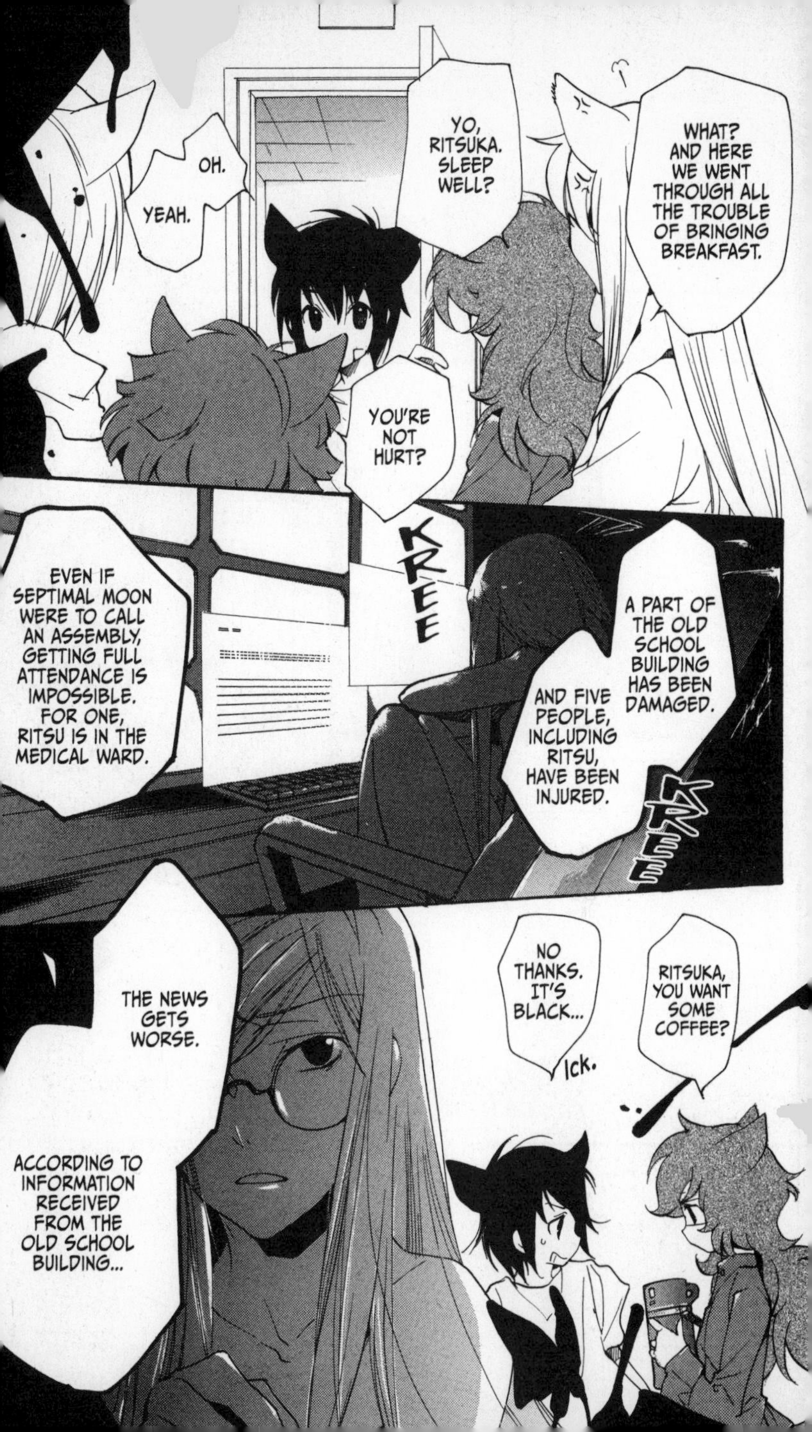
WHAT? AND HERE WE WENT THROUGH ALL THE TROUBLE OF BRINGING BREAKFAST.
YO, RITSUKA. SLEEP WELL?
OH.
YEAH.
YOU'RE NOT HURT?
KREE
A PART OF THE OLD SCHOOL BUILDING HAS BEEN DAMAGED.
KREE
AND FIVE PEOPLE, INCLUDING RITSU, HAVE BEEN INJURED.
EVEN IF SEPTIMAL MOON WERE TO CALL AN ASSEMBLY, GETTING FULL ATTENDANCE IS IMPOSSIBLE. FOR ONE, RITSU IS IN THE MEDICAL WARD.
RITSUKA, YOU WANT SOME COFFEE?
NO THANKS. IT'S BLACK...
Ick.
THE NEWS GETS WORSE.
ACCORDING TO INFORMATION RECEIVED FROM THE OLD SCHOOL BUILDING...

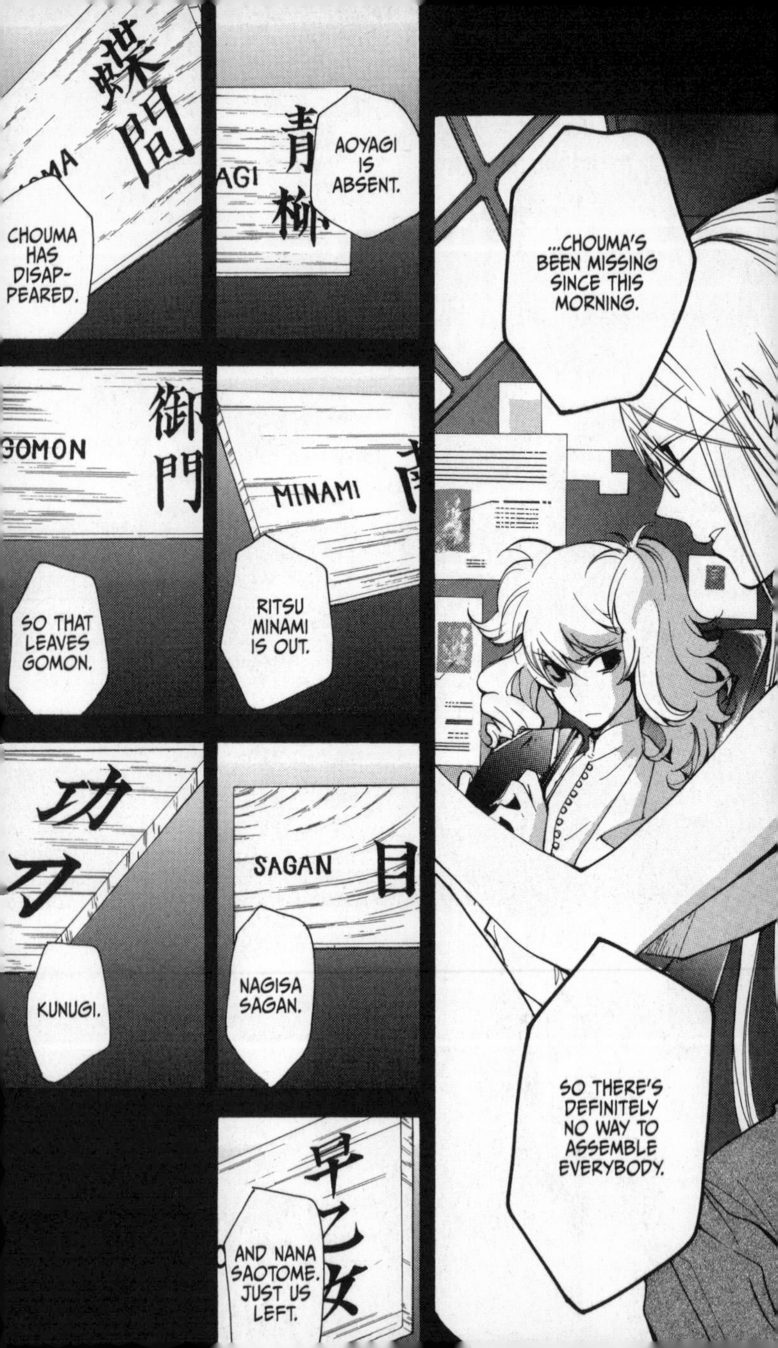
...CHOUMA'S BEEN MISSING SINCE THIS MORNING.
SO THERE'S DEFINITELY NO WAY TO ASSEMBLE EVERYBODY.
青柳
AGI
AOYAGI IS ABSENT.
蝶間
OMA
CHOUMA HAS DISAP-PEARED.
MINAMI
RITSU MINAMI IS OUT.
御門
GOMON
SO THAT LEAVES GOMON.
目
SAGAN
NAGISA SAGAN.
功刀
KUNUGI.
早乙女
AND NANA SAOTOME. JUST US LEFT.

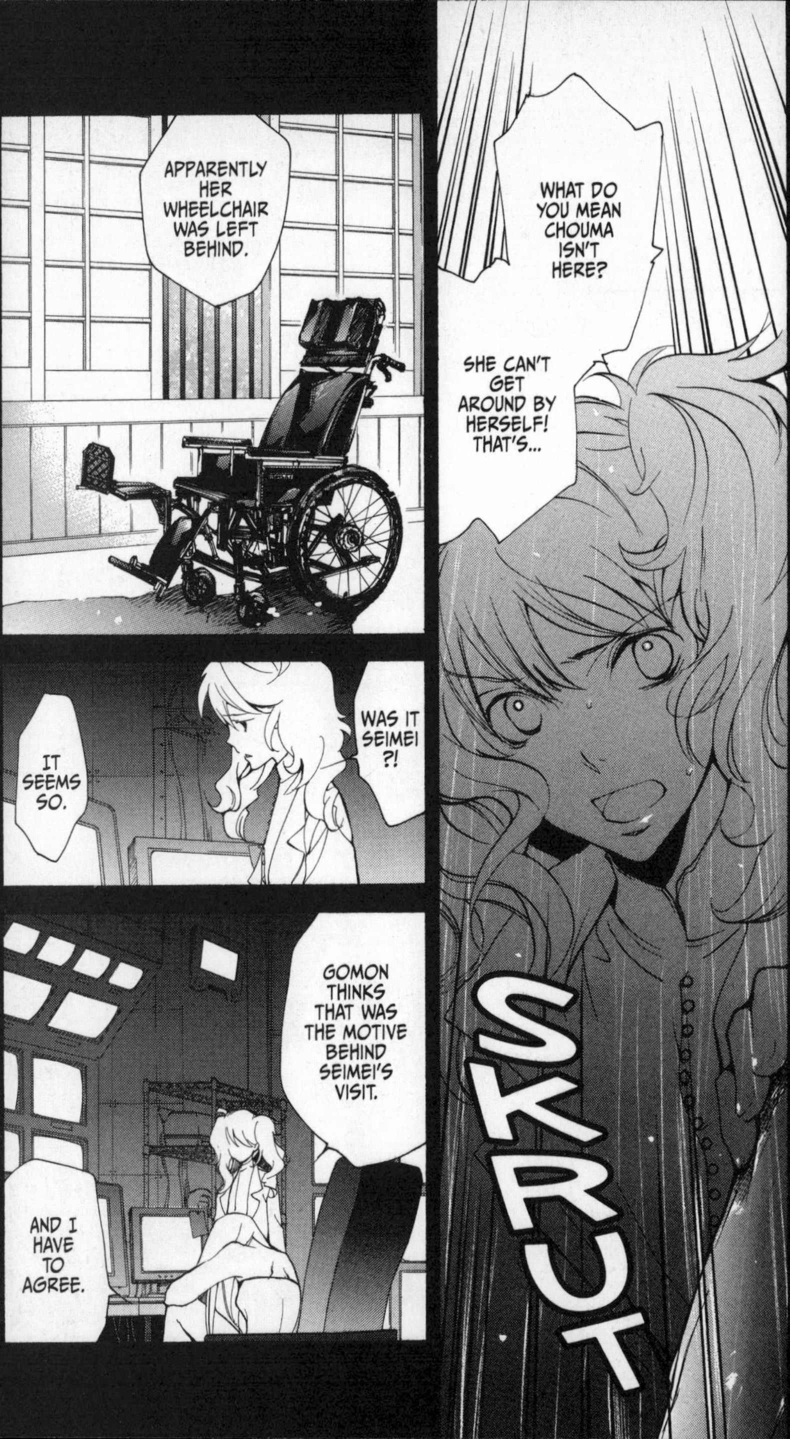
WHAT DO YOU MEAN CHOUMA ISN'T HERE?
SHE CAN'T GET AROUND BY HERSELF! THAT'S...
SKRUT
APPARENTLY HER WHEELCHAIR WAS LEFT BEHIND.
WAS IT SEIMEI?!
IT SEEMS SO.
GOMON THINKS THAT WAS THE MOTIVE BEHIND SEIMEI'S VISIT.
AND I HAVE TO AGREE.

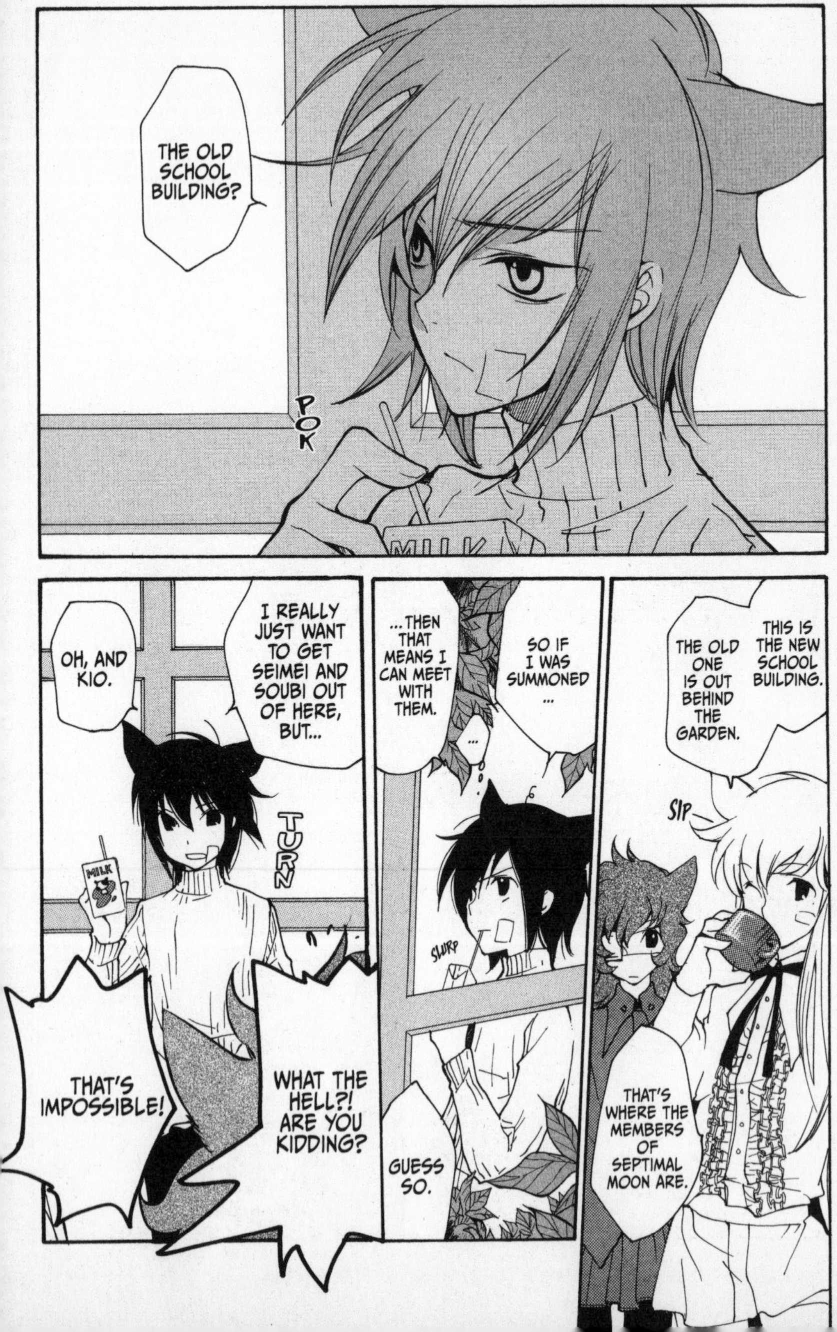
THE OLD SCHOOL BUILDING?
POK
THIS IS THE NEW SCHOOL BUILDING.
THE OLD ONE IS OUT BEHIND THE GARDEN.
SIP
THAT'S WHERE THE MEMBERS OF SEPTIMAL MOON ARE.
SO IF I WAS SUMMONED ...
...THEN THAT MEANS I CAN MEET WITH THEM.
...
SLURP
GUESS SO.
I REALLY JUST WANT TO GET SEIMEI AND SOUBI OUT OF HERE, BUT...
OH, AND KIO.
TURN
MILK
WHAT THE HELL?! ARE YOU KIDDING?
THAT'S IMPOSSIBLE!

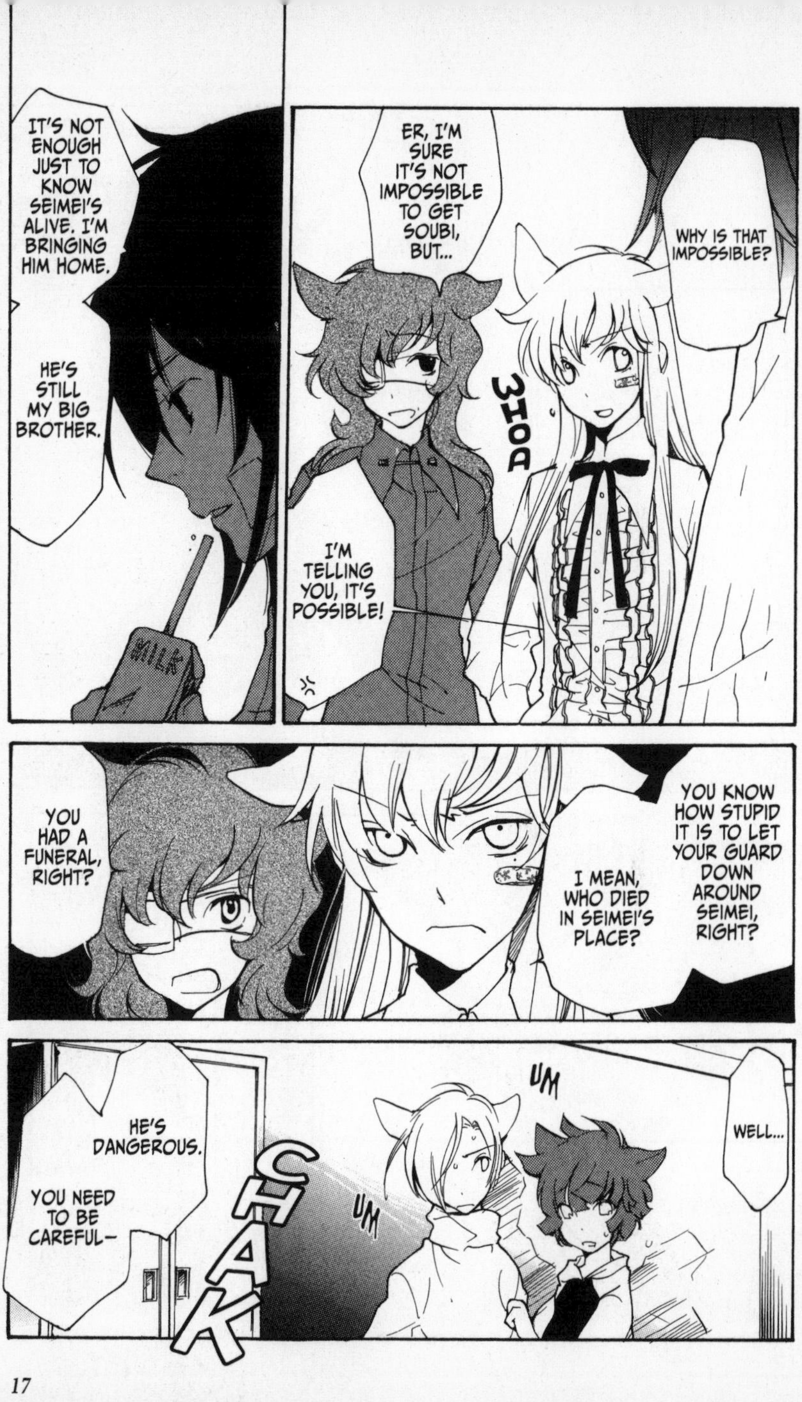
WHY IS THAT IMPOSSIBLE?
ER, I'M SURE IT'S NOT IMPOSSIBLE TO GET SOUBI, BUT...
WHOA
I'M TELLING YOU, IT'S POSSIBLE!
IT'S NOT ENOUGH JUST TO KNOW SEIMEI'S ALIVE. I'M BRINGING HIM HOME.
HE'S STILL MY BIG BROTHER.
MILK
YOU KNOW HOW STUPID IT IS TO LET YOUR GUARD DOWN AROUND SEIMEI, RIGHT?
I MEAN, WHO DIED IN SEIMEI'S PLACE?
YOU HAD A FUNERAL, RIGHT?
WELL...
UM
UM
CHAK
HE'S DANGEROUS.
YOU NEED TO BE CAREFUL–

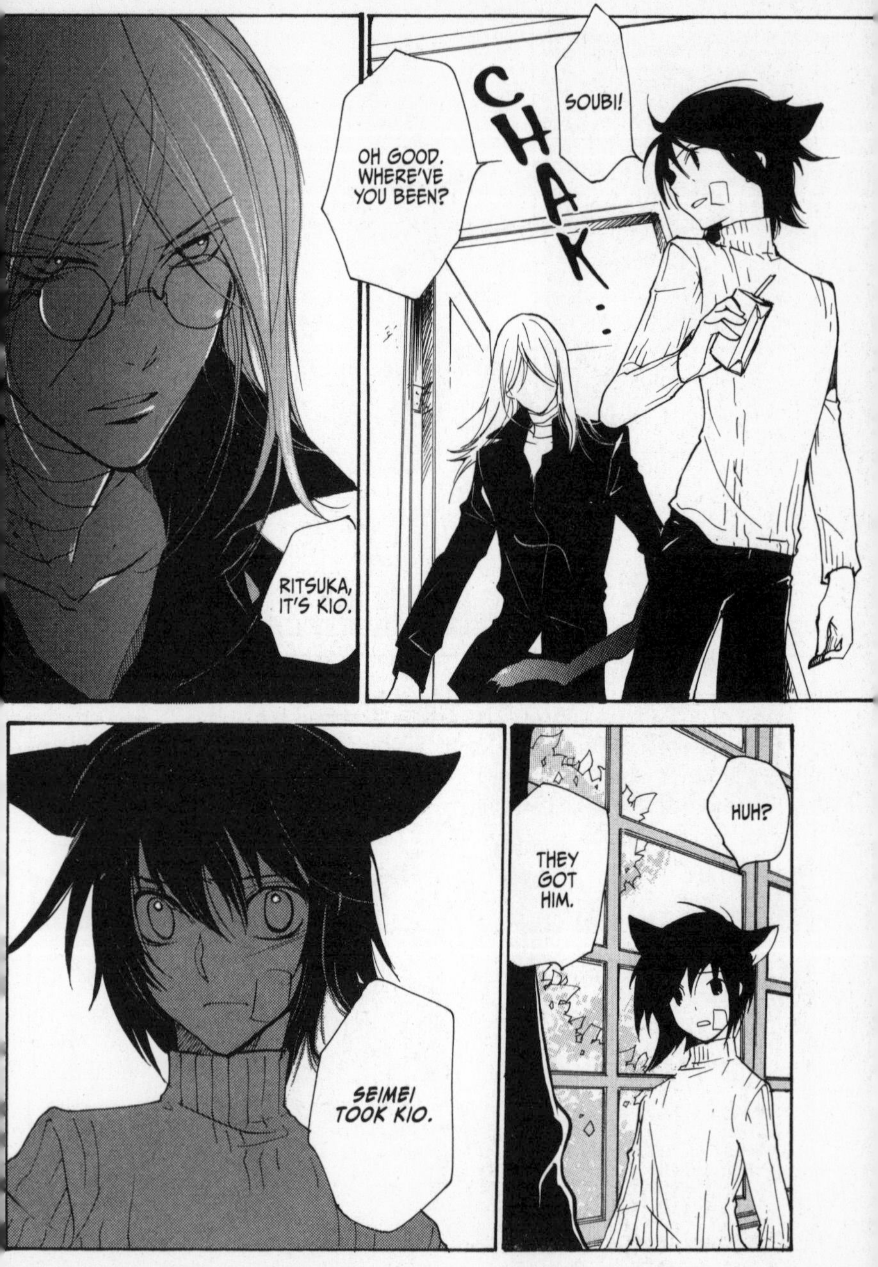
SOUBI!
CHAK...
OH GOOD. WHERE'VE YOU BEEN?
RITSUKA, IT'S KIO.
HUH?
THEY GOT HIM.
SEIMEI TOOK KIO.

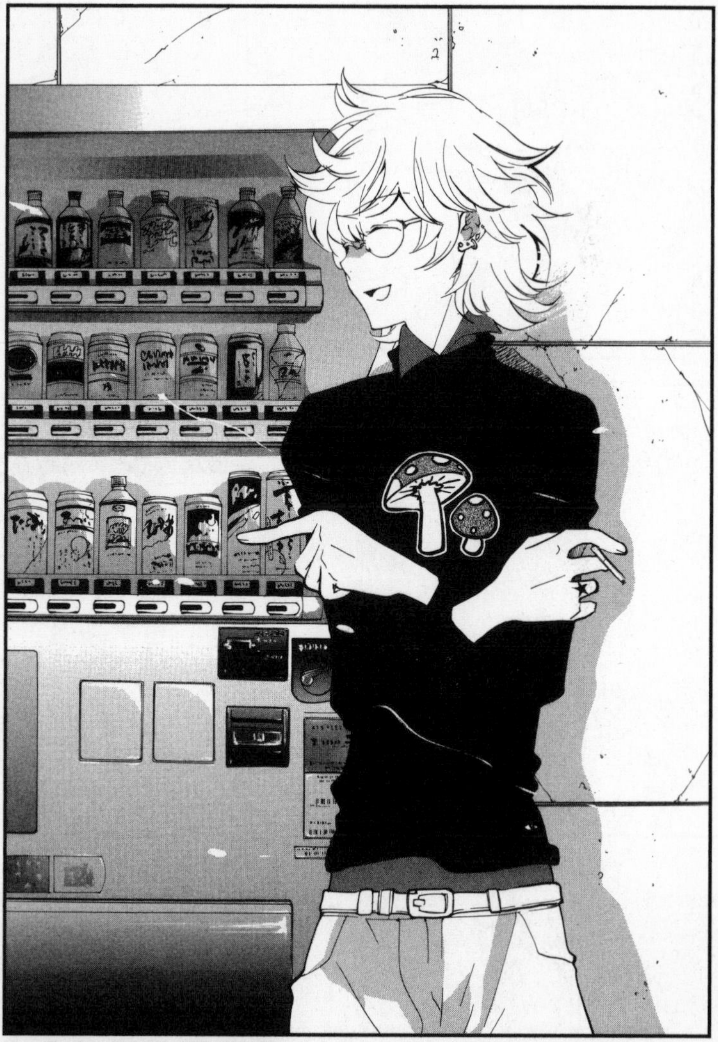

LOVELESS

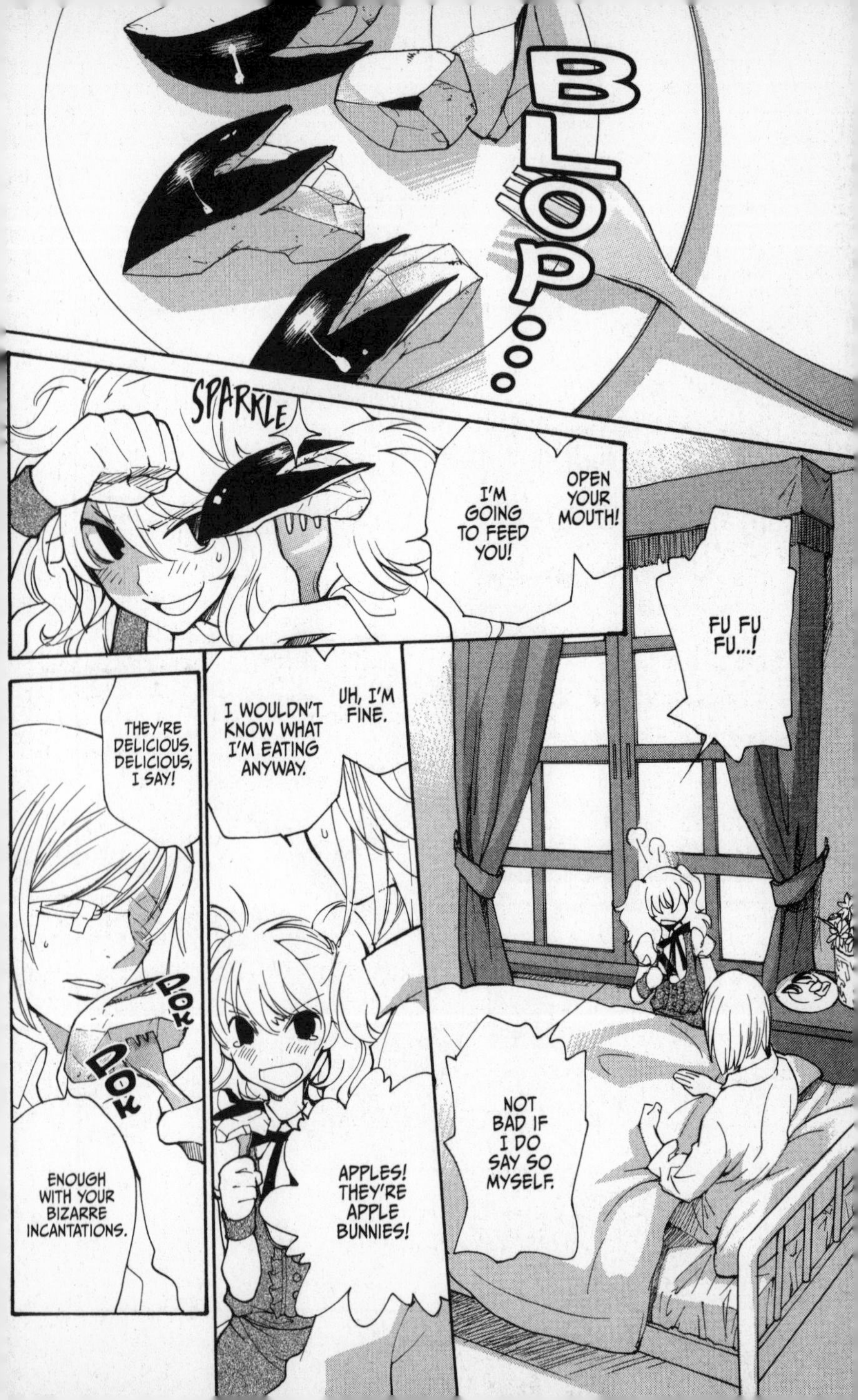
BLOP...
FU FU FU...!
NOT BAD IF I DO SAY SO MYSELF.
SPARKLE
OPEN YOUR MOUTH!
I'M GOING TO FEED YOU!
UH, I'M FINE.
I WOULDN'T KNOW WHAT I'M EATING ANYWAY.
APPLES! THEY'RE APPLE BUNNIES!
THEY'RE DELICIOUS. DELICIOUS, I SAY!
POK
POK
ENOUGH WITH YOUR BIZARRE INCANTATIONS.

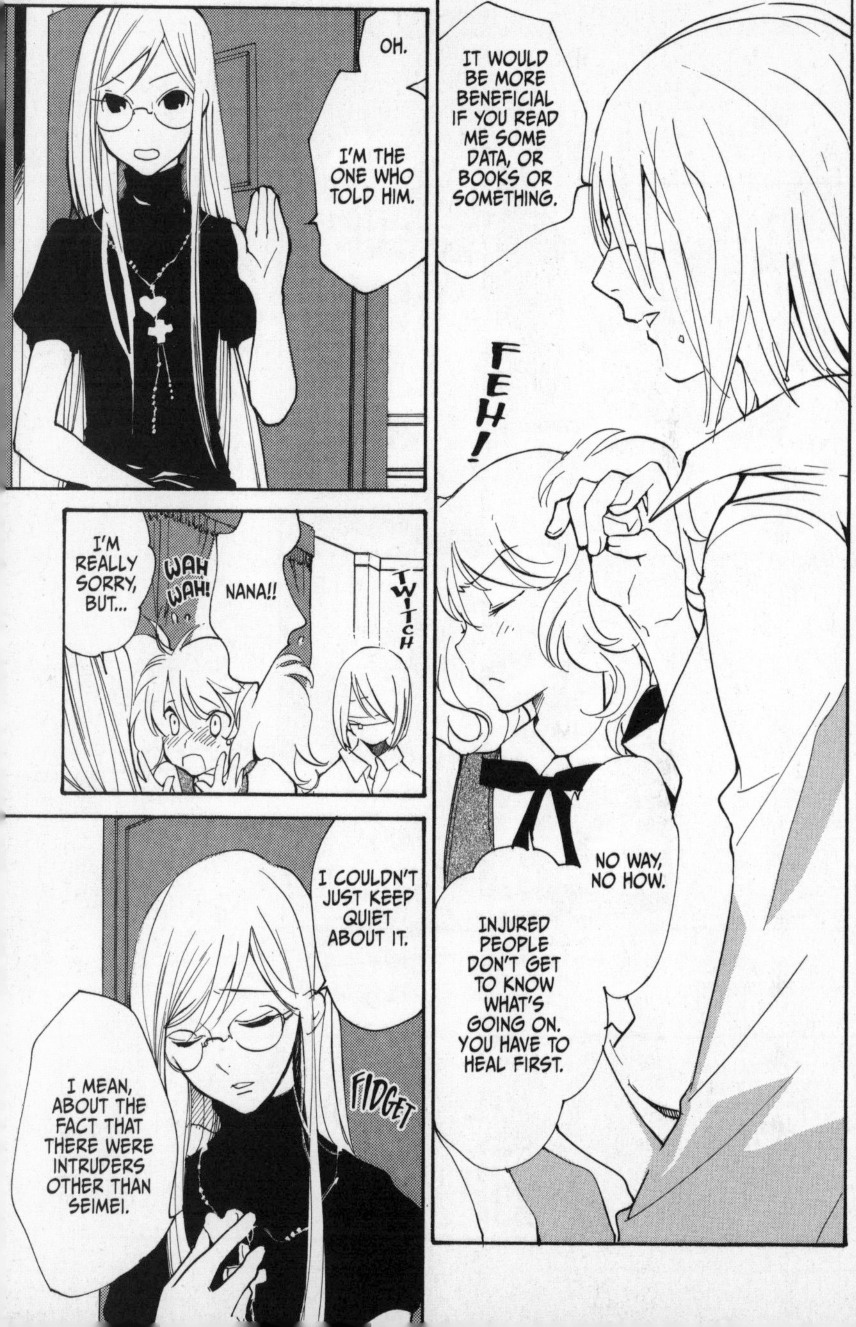
IT WOULD BE MORE BENEFICIAL IF YOU READ ME SOME DATA, OR BOOKS OR SOMETHING.
FEH!
NO WAY, NO HOW.
INJURED PEOPLE DON'T GET TO KNOW WHAT'S GOING ON. YOU HAVE TO HEAL FIRST.
OH.
I'M THE ONE WHO TOLD HIM.
NANA!!
TWITCH
WAH WAH!
I'M REALLY SORRY, BUT...
I COULDN'T JUST KEEP QUIET ABOUT IT.
FIDGET
I MEAN, ABOUT THE FACT THAT THERE WERE INTRUDERS OTHER THAN SEIMEI.

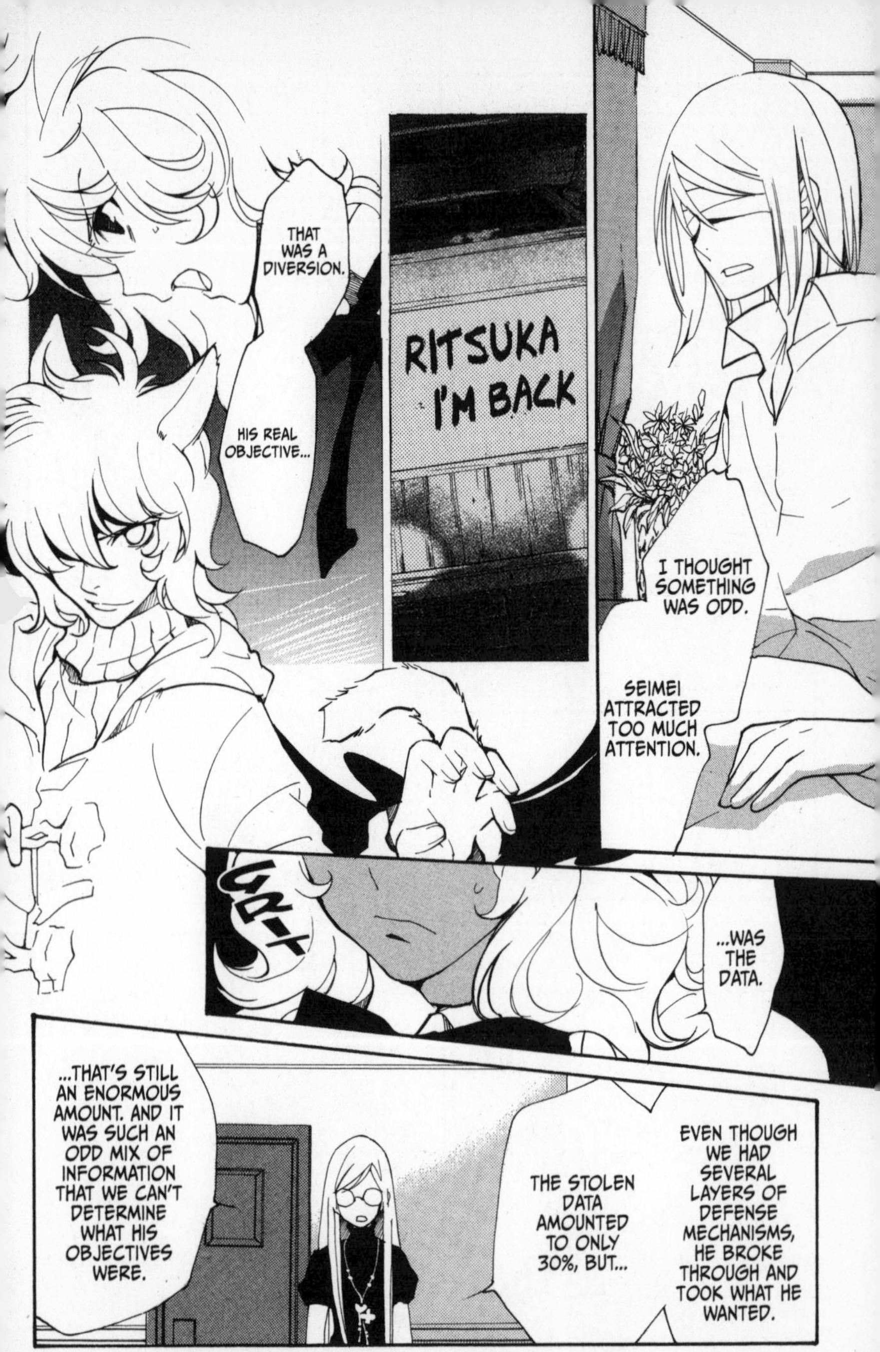
I THOUGHT SOMETHING WAS ODD.
SEIMEI ATTRACTED TOO MUCH ATTENTION.
RITSUKA I'M BACK
THAT WAS A DIVERSION.
HIS REAL OBJECTIVE...
GRIT
...WAS THE DATA.
EVEN THOUGH WE HAD SEVERAL LAYERS OF DEFENSE MECHANISMS, HE BROKE THROUGH AND TOOK WHAT HE WANTED.
THE STOLEN DATA AMOUNTED TO ONLY 30%, BUT...
...THAT'S STILL AN ENORMOUS AMOUNT. AND IT WAS SUCH AN ODD MIX OF INFORMATION THAT WE CAN'T DETERMINE WHAT HIS OBJECTIVES WERE.

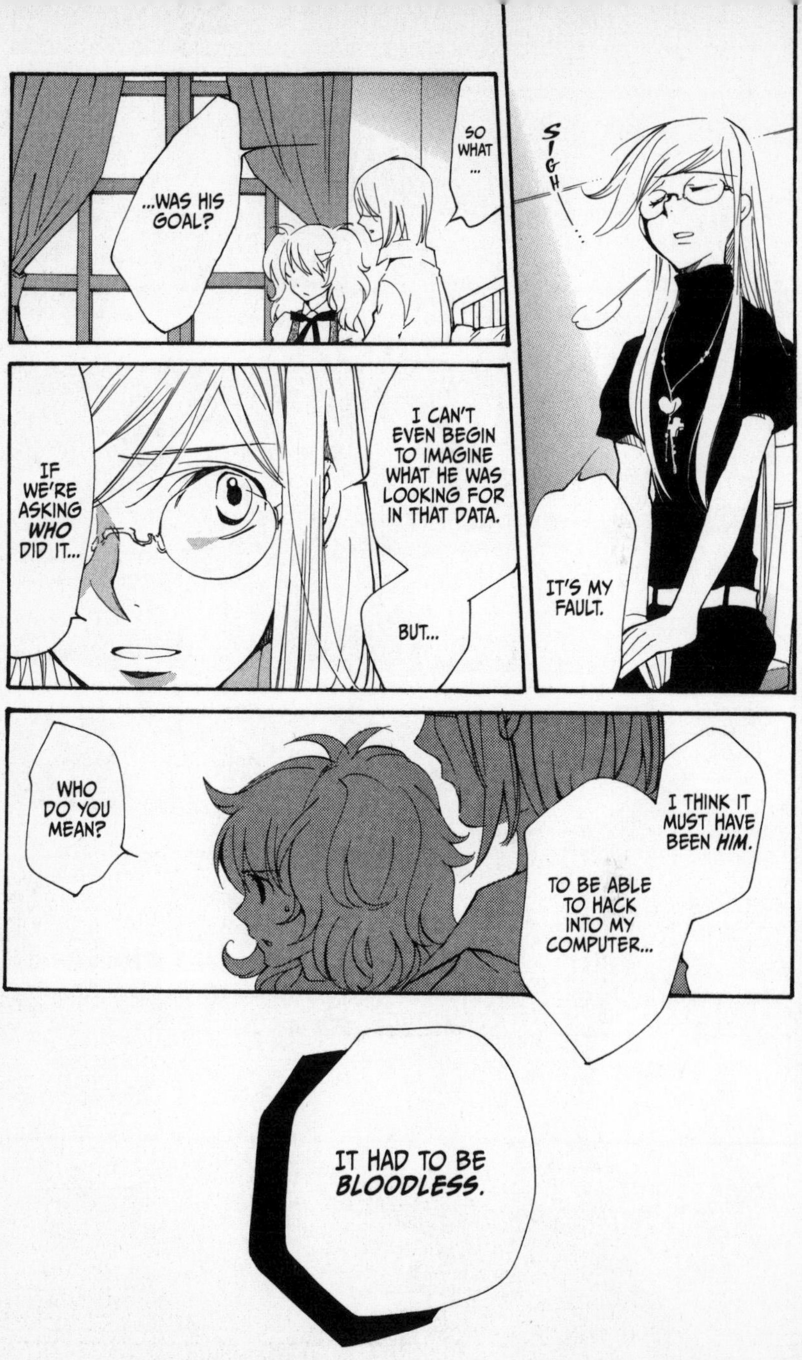
SIGH
IT'S MY FAULT.
SO WHAT...
...WAS HIS GOAL?
I CAN'T EVEN BEGIN TO IMAGINE WHAT HE WAS LOOKING FOR IN THAT DATA.
BUT...
IF WE'RE ASKING *WHO* DID IT...
I THINK IT MUST HAVE BEEN *HIM*.
TO BE ABLE TO HACK INTO MY COMPUTER...
WHO DO YOU MEAN?
IT HAD TO BE *BLOODLESS*.

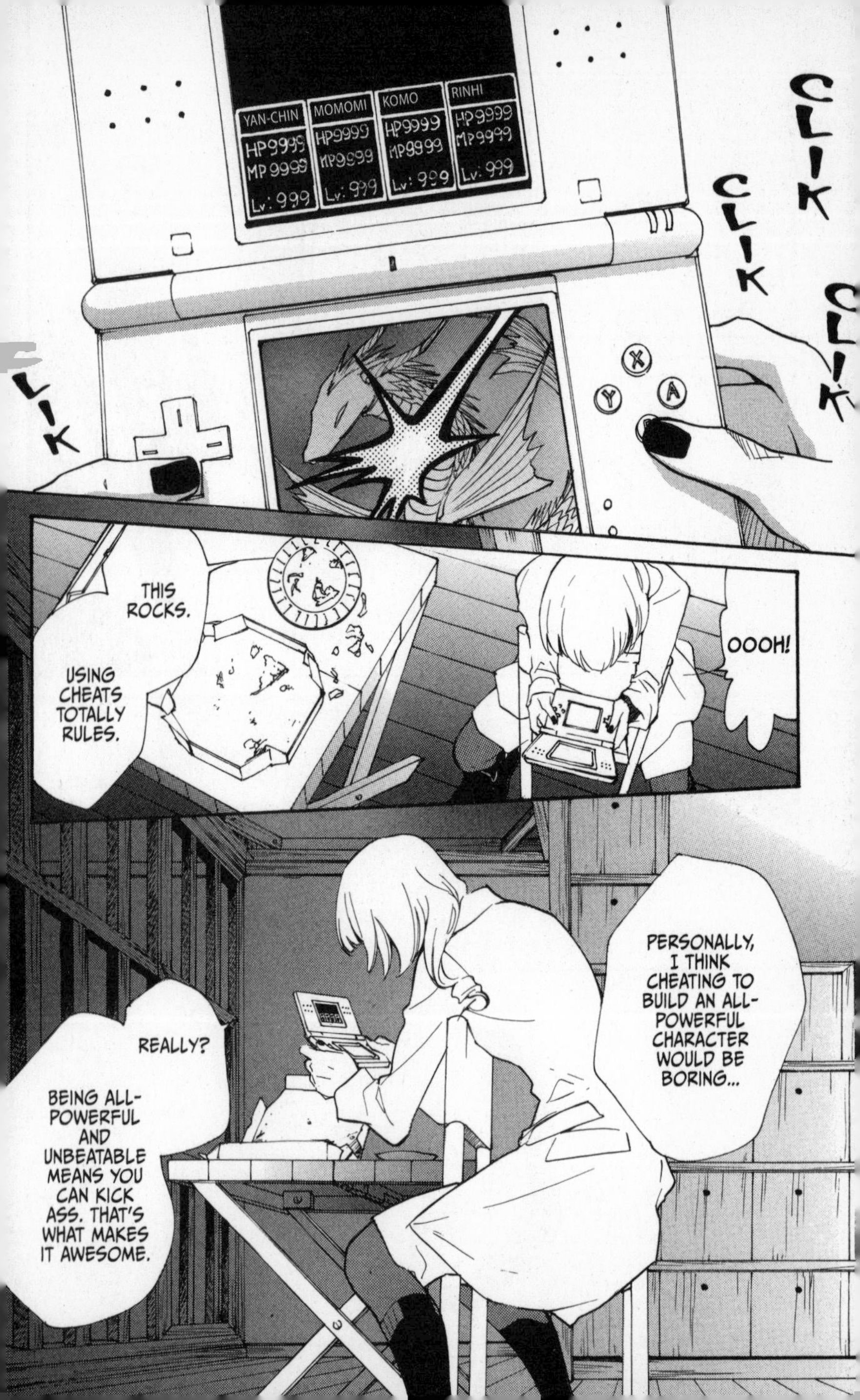
CLIK
CLIK
CLIK
YAN-CHIN
HP9999
MP 9999
Lv: 999
MOMOMI
HP9999
MP9999
Lv: 999
KOMO
HP9999
MP9999
Lv: 999
RINHI
HP9999
MP9999
Lv: 999
LIK
OOOH!
THIS ROCKS.
USING CHEATS TOTALLY RULES.
PERSONALLY, I THINK CHEATING TO BUILD AN ALL-POWERFUL CHARACTER WOULD BE BORING...
REALLY?
BEING ALL-POWERFUL AND UNBEATABLE MEANS YOU CAN KICK ASS. THAT'S WHAT MAKES IT AWESOME.

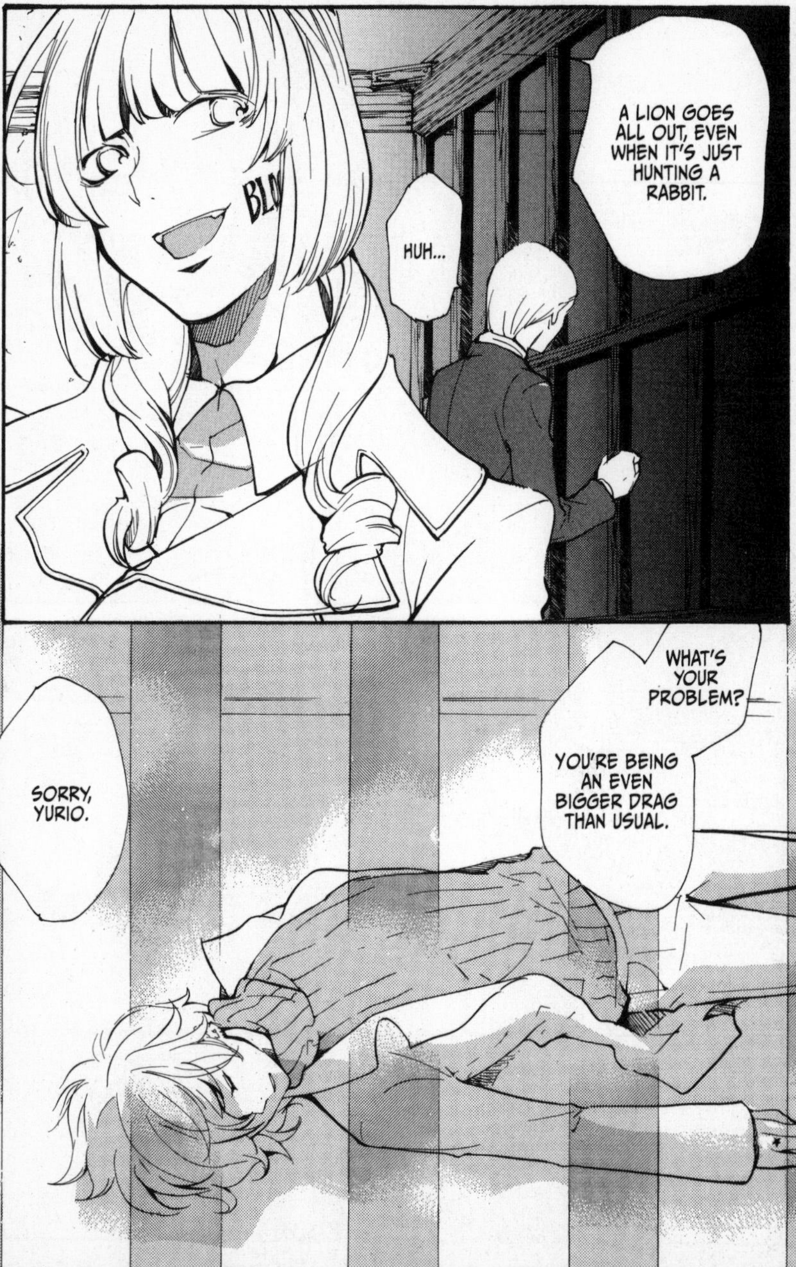
A LION GOES ALL OUT, EVEN WHEN IT'S JUST HUNTING A RABBIT.
HUH...
WHAT'S YOUR PROBLEM?
YOU'RE BEING AN EVEN BIGGER DRAG THAN USUAL.
SORRY, YURIO.

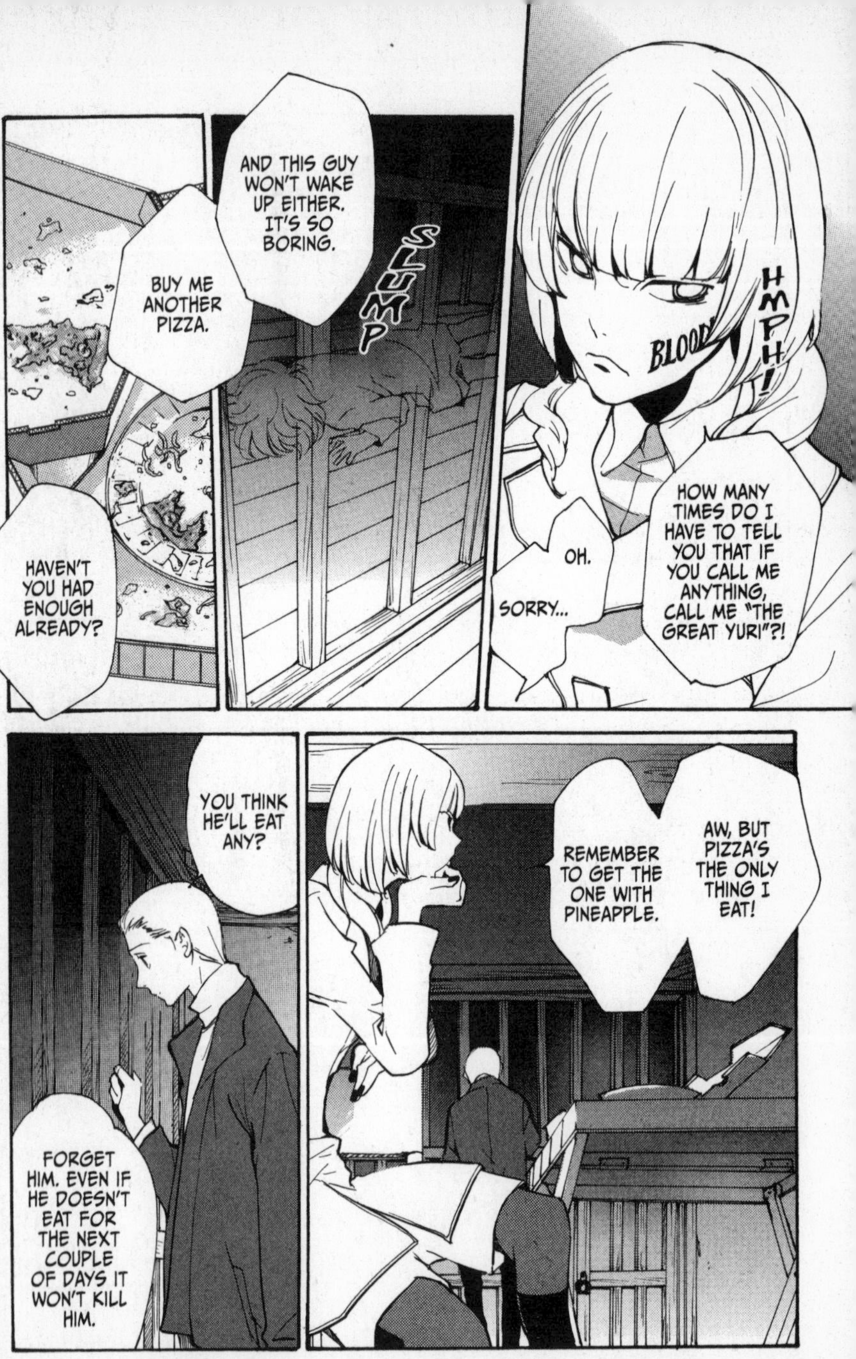
HMPH!
BLOOD
HOW MANY TIMES DO I HAVE TO TELL YOU THAT IF YOU CALL ME ANYTHING, CALL ME "THE GREAT YURI"?!
OH. SORRY...
AND THIS GUY WON'T WAKE UP EITHER. IT'S SO BORING.
SLUMP
BUY ME ANOTHER PIZZA.
HAVEN'T YOU HAD ENOUGH ALREADY?
AW, BUT PIZZA'S THE ONLY THING I EAT!
REMEMBER TO GET THE ONE WITH PINEAPPLE.
YOU THINK HE'LL EAT ANY?
FORGET HIM. EVEN IF HE DOESN'T EAT FOR THE NEXT COUPLE OF DAYS IT WON'T KILL HIM.

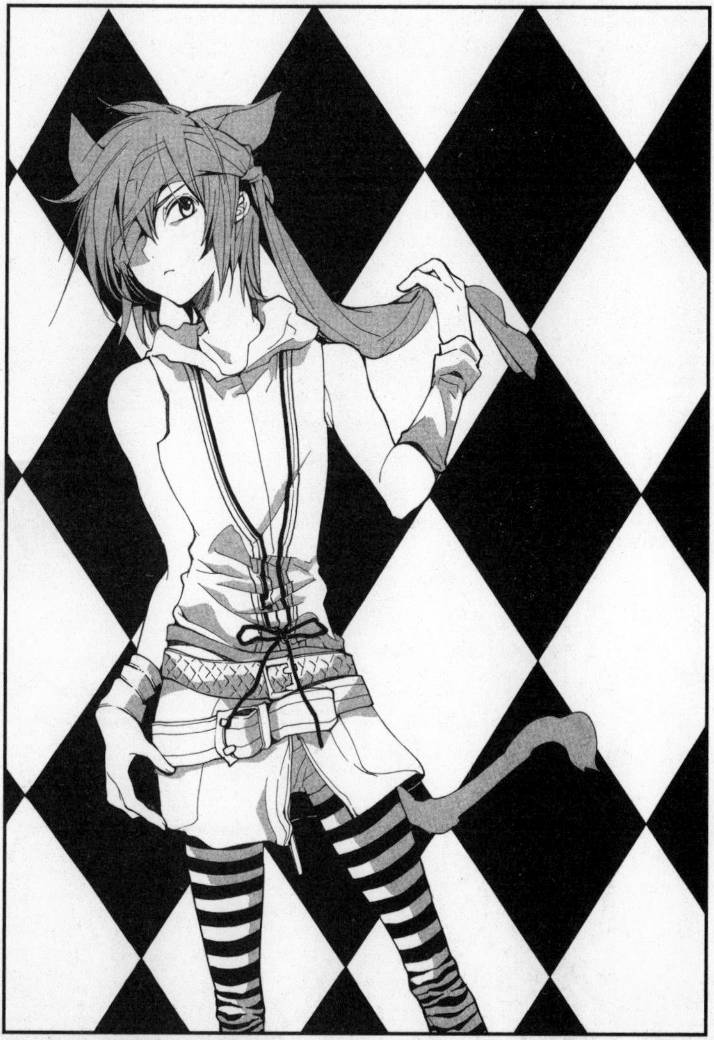

LOVELESS

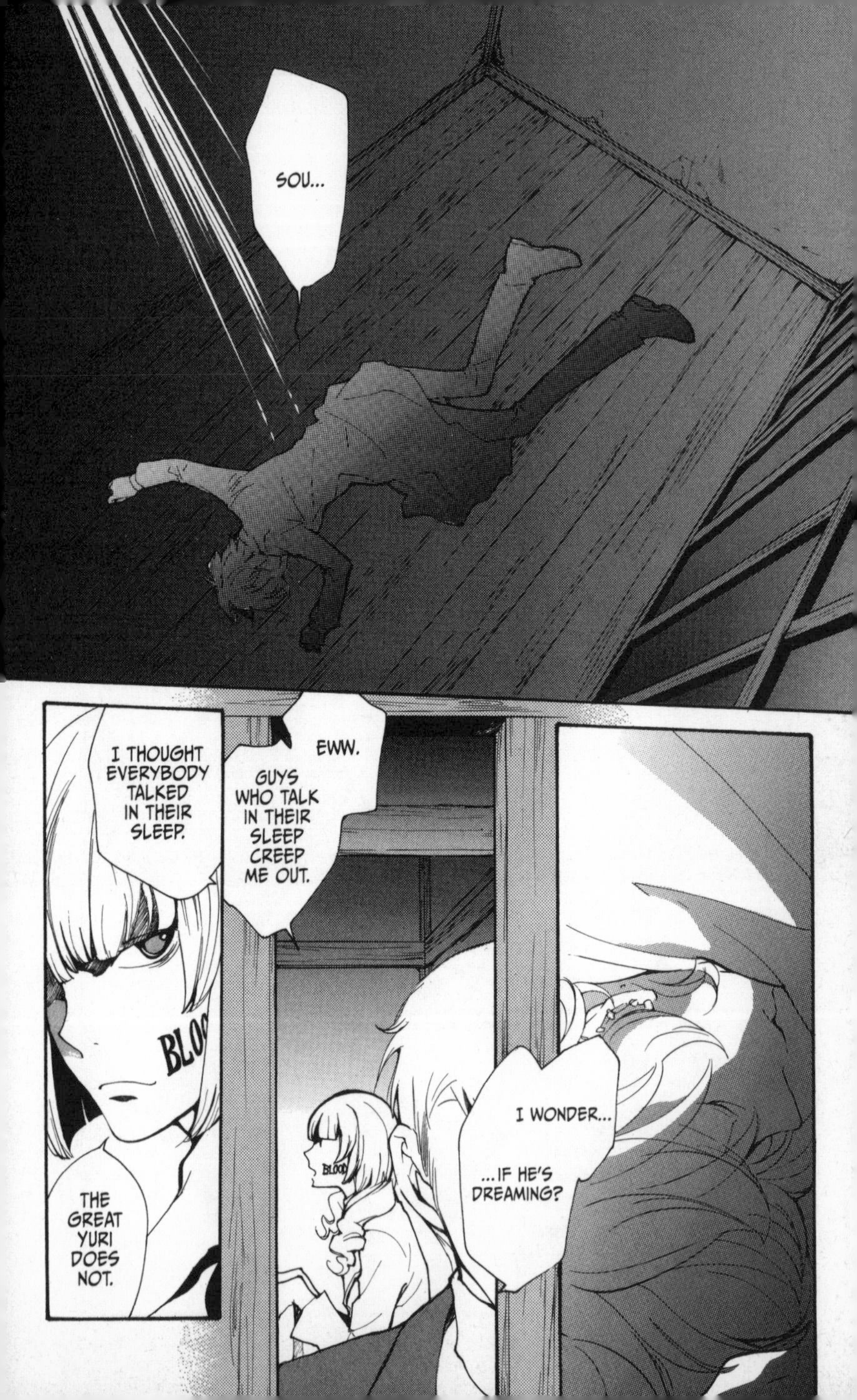
SOU...
I WONDER...
...IF HE'S DREAMING?
EWW.
GUYS WHO TALK IN THEIR SLEEP CREEP ME OUT.
BLOOD
I THOUGHT EVERYBODY TALKED IN THEIR SLEEP.
THE GREAT YURI DOES NOT.

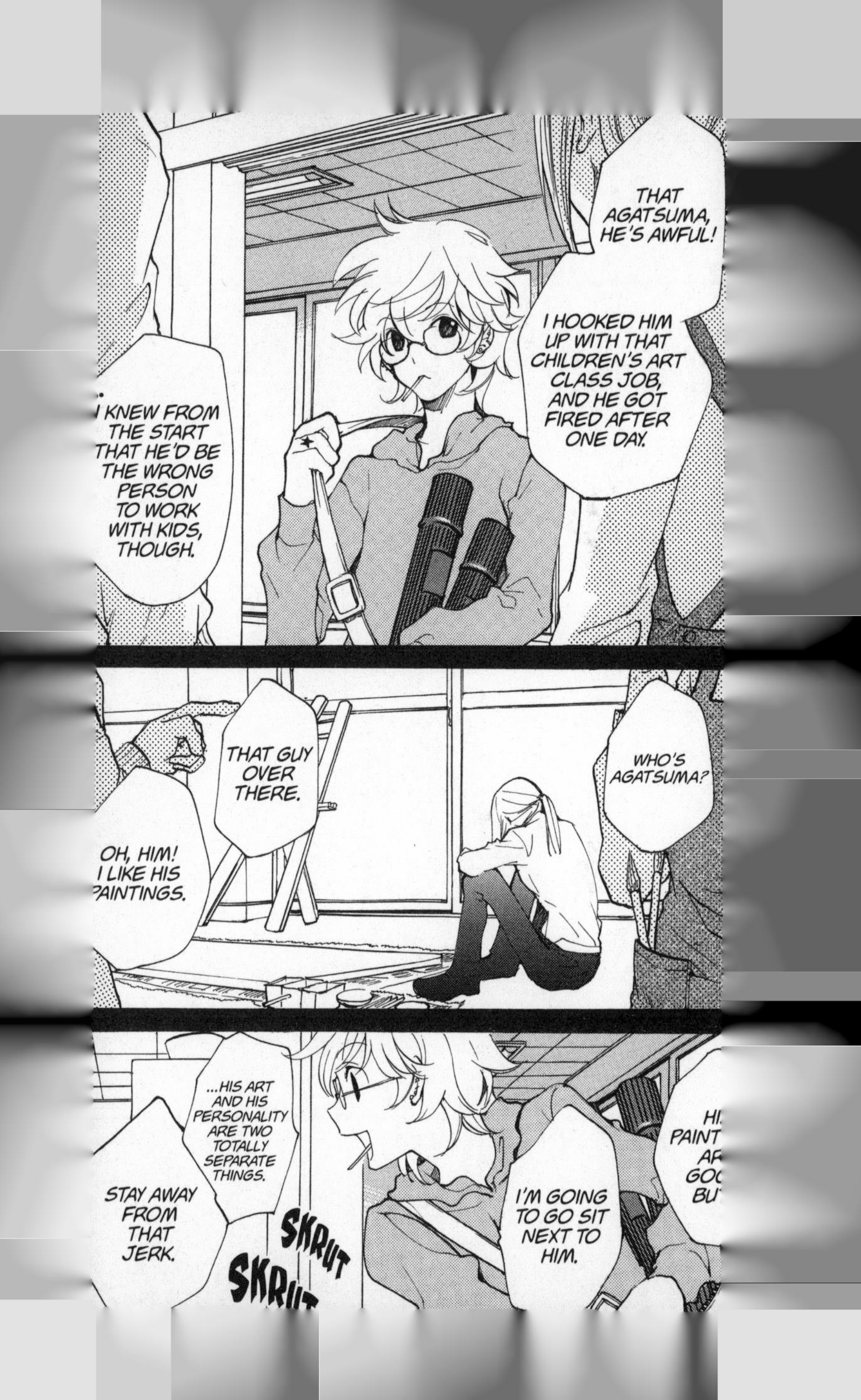
THAT AGATSUMA, HE'S AWFUL!
I HOOKED HIM UP WITH THAT CHILDREN'S ART CLASS JOB, AND HE GOT FIRED AFTER ONE DAY.
I KNEW FROM THE START THAT HE'D BE THE WRONG PERSON TO WORK WITH KIDS, THOUGH.
WHO'S AGATSUMA?
THAT GUY OVER THERE.
OH, HIM! I LIKE HIS AINTINGS.
HI PAINT AR GOO BU
...HIS ART AND HIS PERSONALITY ARE TWO TOTALLY SEPARATE THINGS.
STAY AWAY FROM THAT JERK.
I'M GOING TO GO SIT NEXT TO HIM.
SKRUT
SKRU

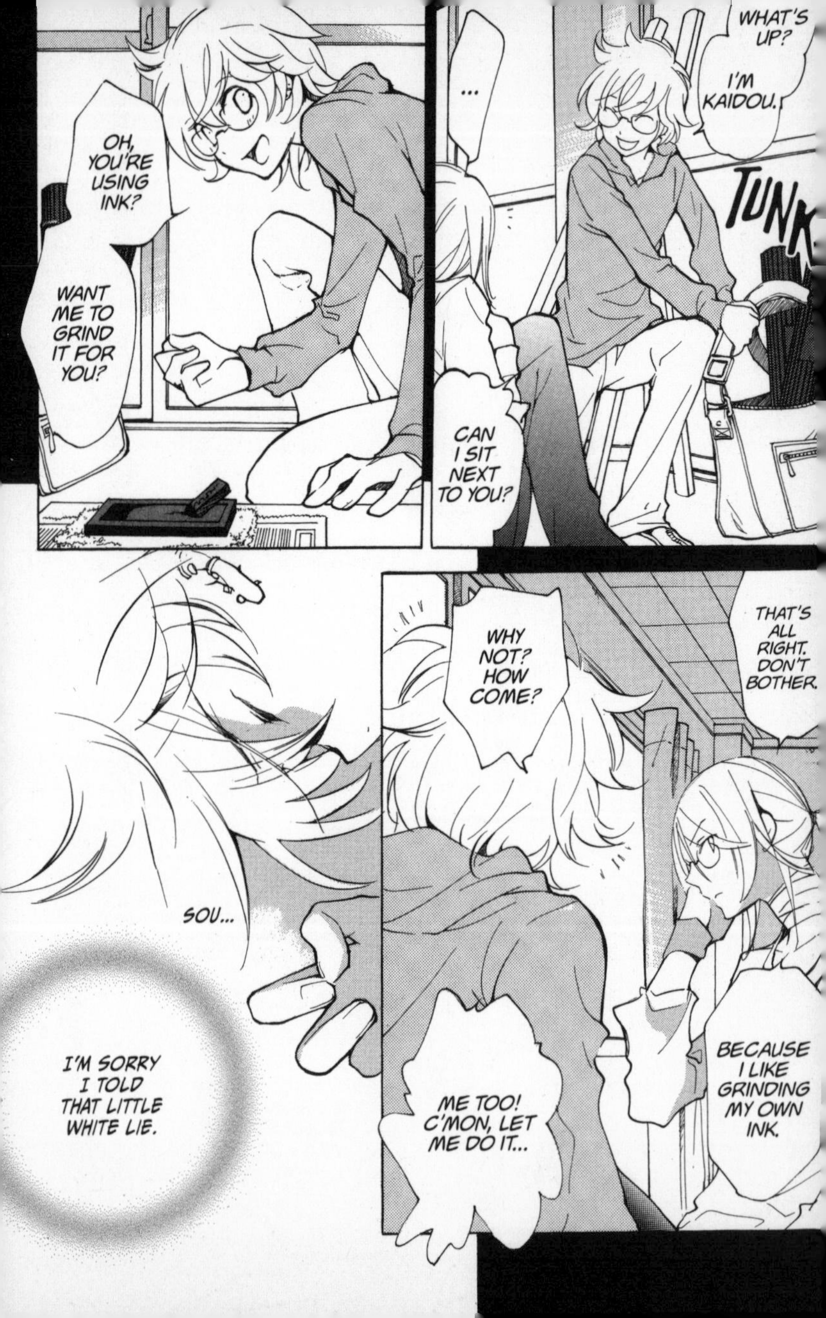
WHAT'S UP? I'M KAIDOU.
TUNK
...
CAN I SIT NEXT TO YOU?
OH, YOU'RE USING INK?
WANT ME TO GRIND IT FOR YOU?
THAT'S ALL RIGHT. DON'T BOTHER.
WHY NOT? HOW COME?
BECAUSE I LIKE GRINDING MY OWN INK.
ME TOO! C'MON, LET ME DO IT...
SOU...
I'M SORRY I TOLD THAT LITTLE WHITE LIE.

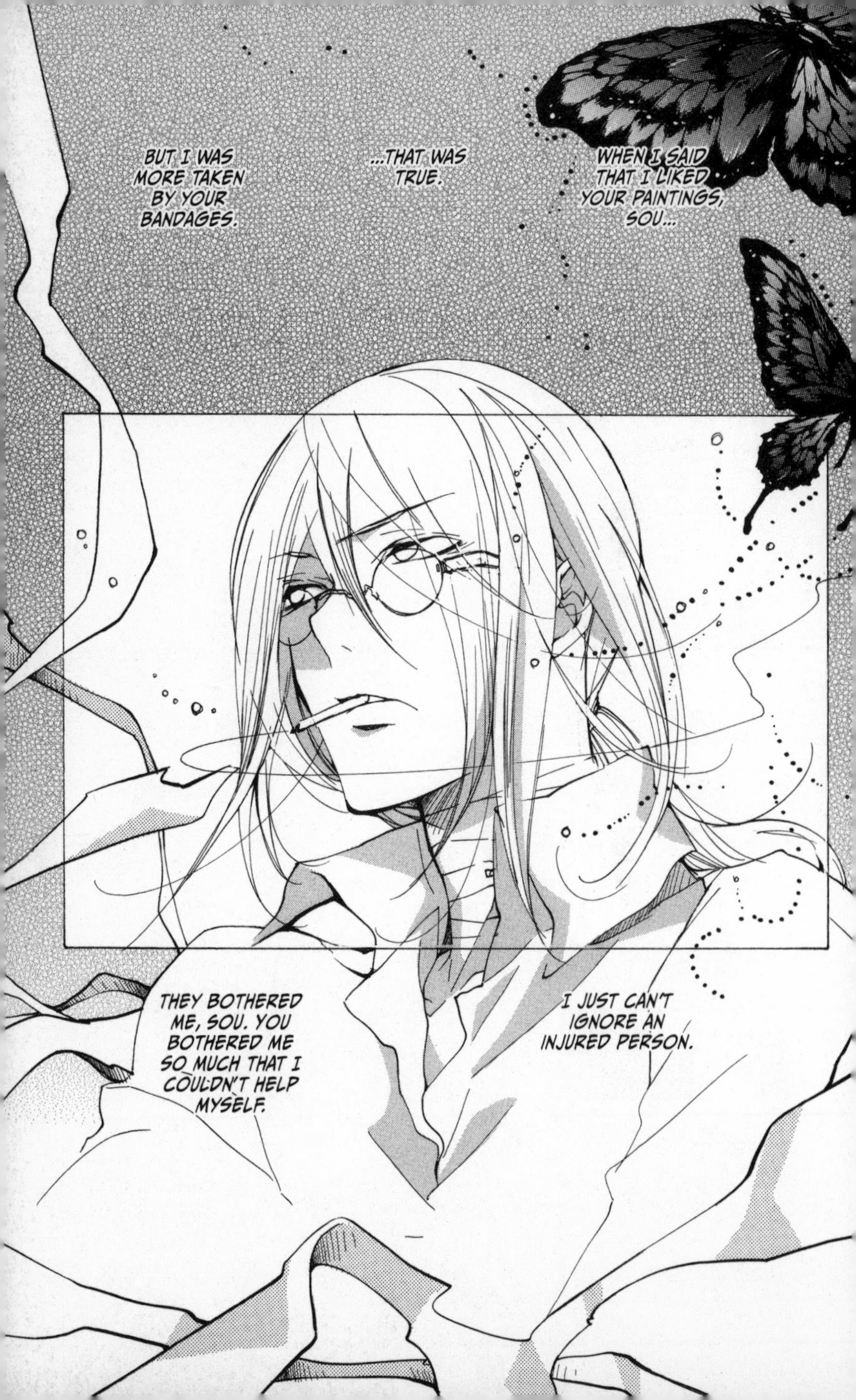
WHEN I SAID THAT I LIKED YOUR PAINTINGS, SOU...
...THAT WAS TRUE.
BUT I WAS MORE TAKEN BY YOUR BANDAGES.
I JUST CAN'T IGNORE AN INJURED PERSON.
THEY BOTHERED ME, SOU. YOU BOTHERED ME SO MUCH THAT I COULDN'T HELP MYSELF.

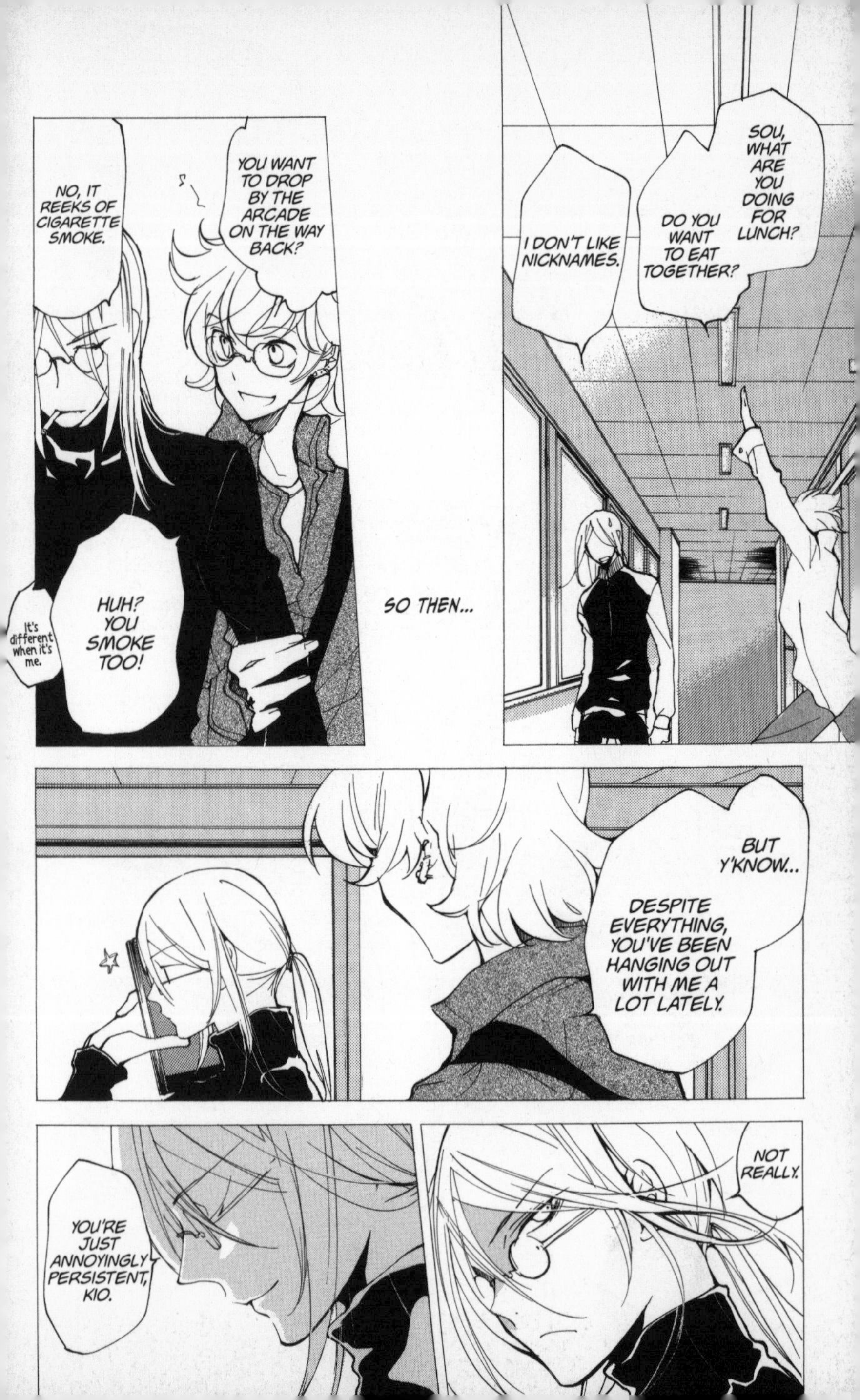
SOU, WHAT ARE YOU DOING FOR LUNCH?
DO YOU WANT TO EAT TOGETHER?
I DON'T LIKE NICKNAMES.
SO THEN...
YOU WANT TO DROP BY THE ARCADE ON THE WAY BACK?
NO, IT REEKS OF CIGARETTE SMOKE.
HUH? YOU SMOKE TOO!
It's different when it's me.
BUT Y'KNOW...
DESPITE EVERYTHING, YOU'VE BEEN HANGING OUT WITH ME A LOT LATELY.
NOT REALLY.
YOU'RE JUST ANNOYINGLY PERSISTENT, KIO.

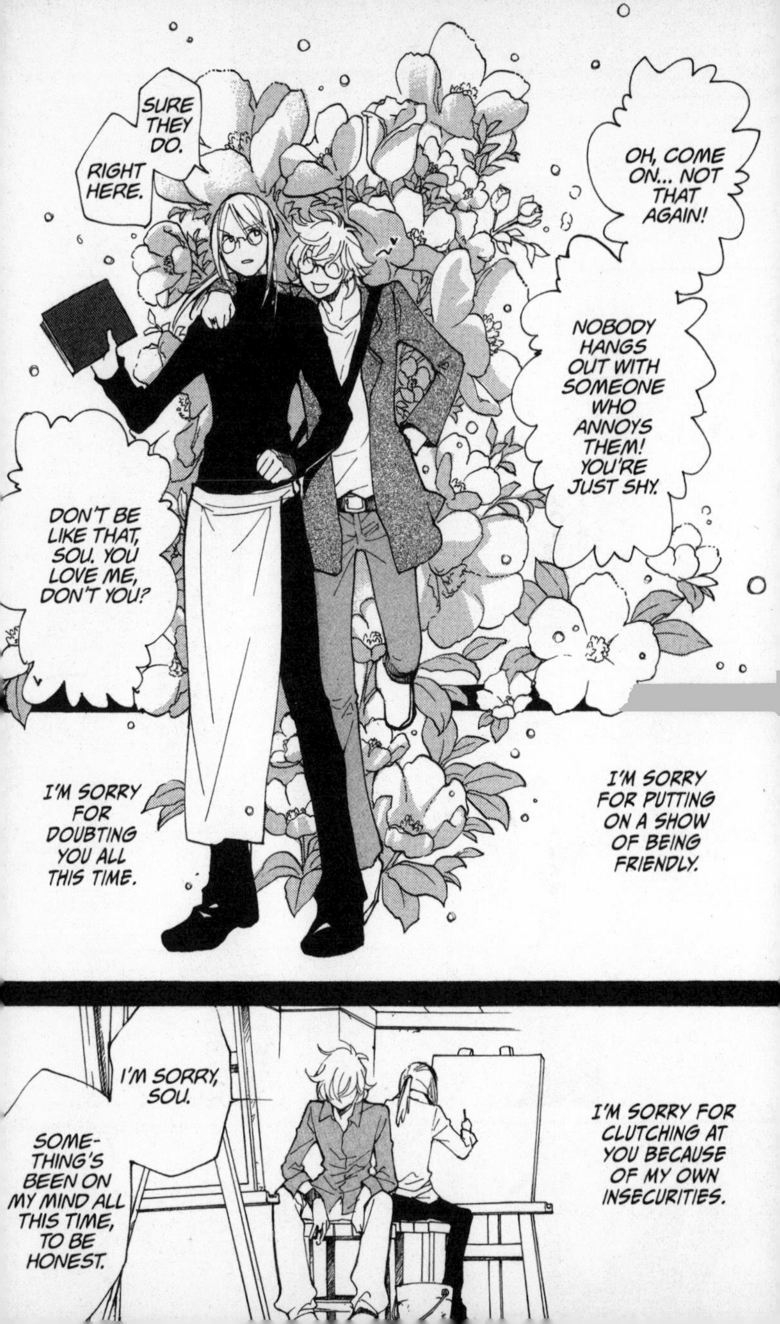
OH, COME ON... NOT THAT AGAIN!
NOBODY HANGS OUT WITH SOMEONE WHO ANNOYS THEM! YOU'RE JUST SHY.
SURE THEY DO. RIGHT HERE.
DON'T BE LIKE THAT, SOU. YOU LOVE ME, DON'T YOU?
I'M SORRY FOR PUTTING ON A SHOW OF BEING FRIENDLY.
I'M SORRY FOR DOUBTING YOU ALL THIS TIME.
I'M SORRY FOR CLUTCHING AT YOU BECAUSE OF MY OWN INSECURITIES.
I'M SORRY, SOU.
SOME-THING'S BEEN ON MY MIND ALL THIS TIME, TO BE HONEST.

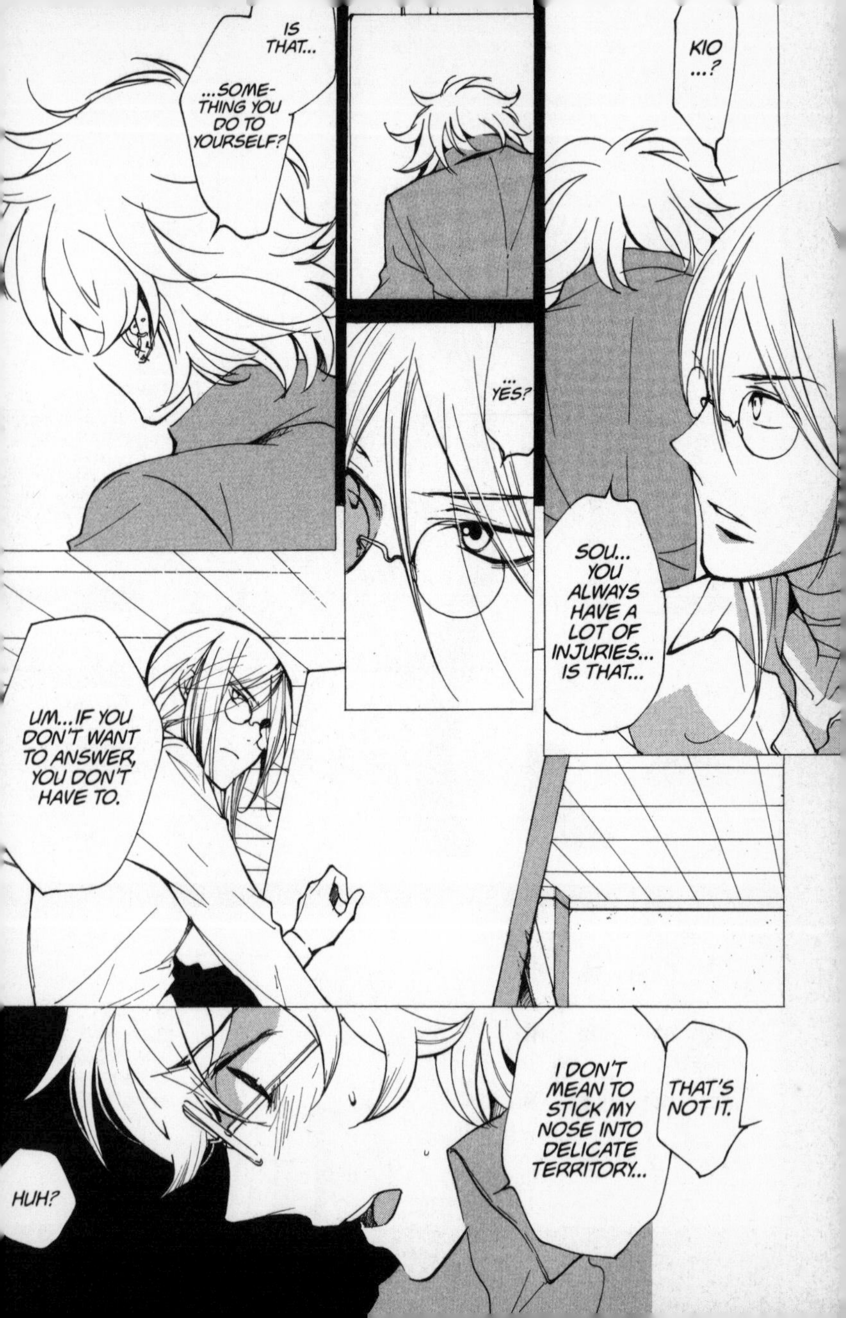
KIO ...?
SOU... YOU ALWAYS HAVE A LOT OF INJURIES... IS THAT...
... YES?
IS THAT...
...SOME-THING YOU DO TO YOURSELF?
UM... IF YOU DON'T WANT TO ANSWER, YOU DON'T HAVE TO.
THAT'S NOT IT.
I DON'T MEAN TO STICK MY NOSE INTO DELICATE TERRITORY...
HUH?

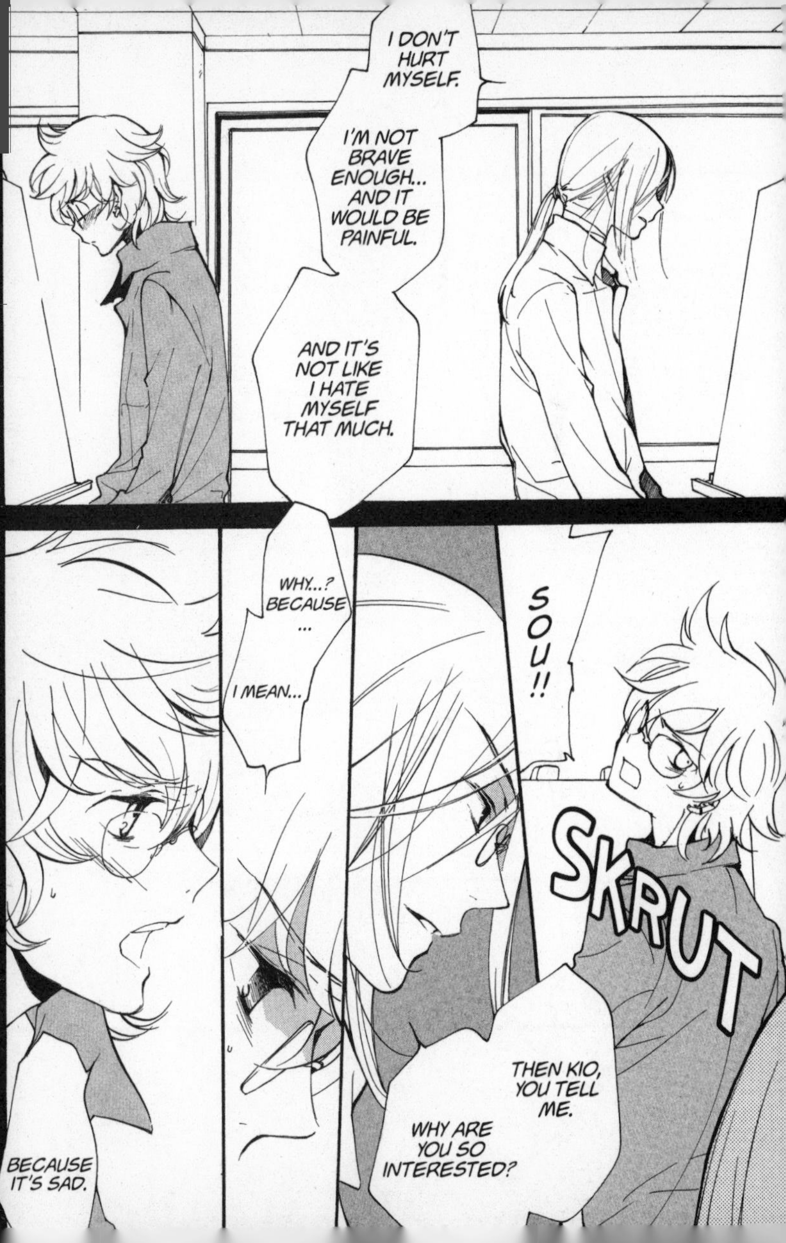
I DON'T HURT MYSELF.
I'M NOT BRAVE ENOUGH... AND IT WOULD BE PAINFUL.
AND IT'S NOT LIKE I HATE MYSELF THAT MUCH.
SOU!!
SKRUT
THEN KIO, YOU TELL ME.
WHY ARE YOU SO INTERESTED?
WHY...? BECAUSE ...
I MEAN...
BECAUSE IT'S SAD.

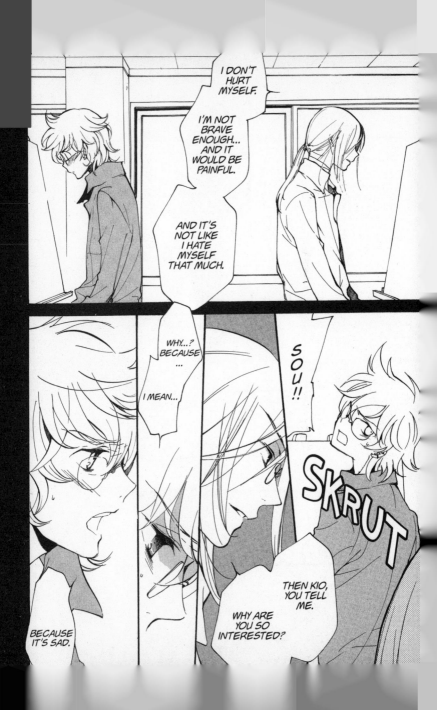

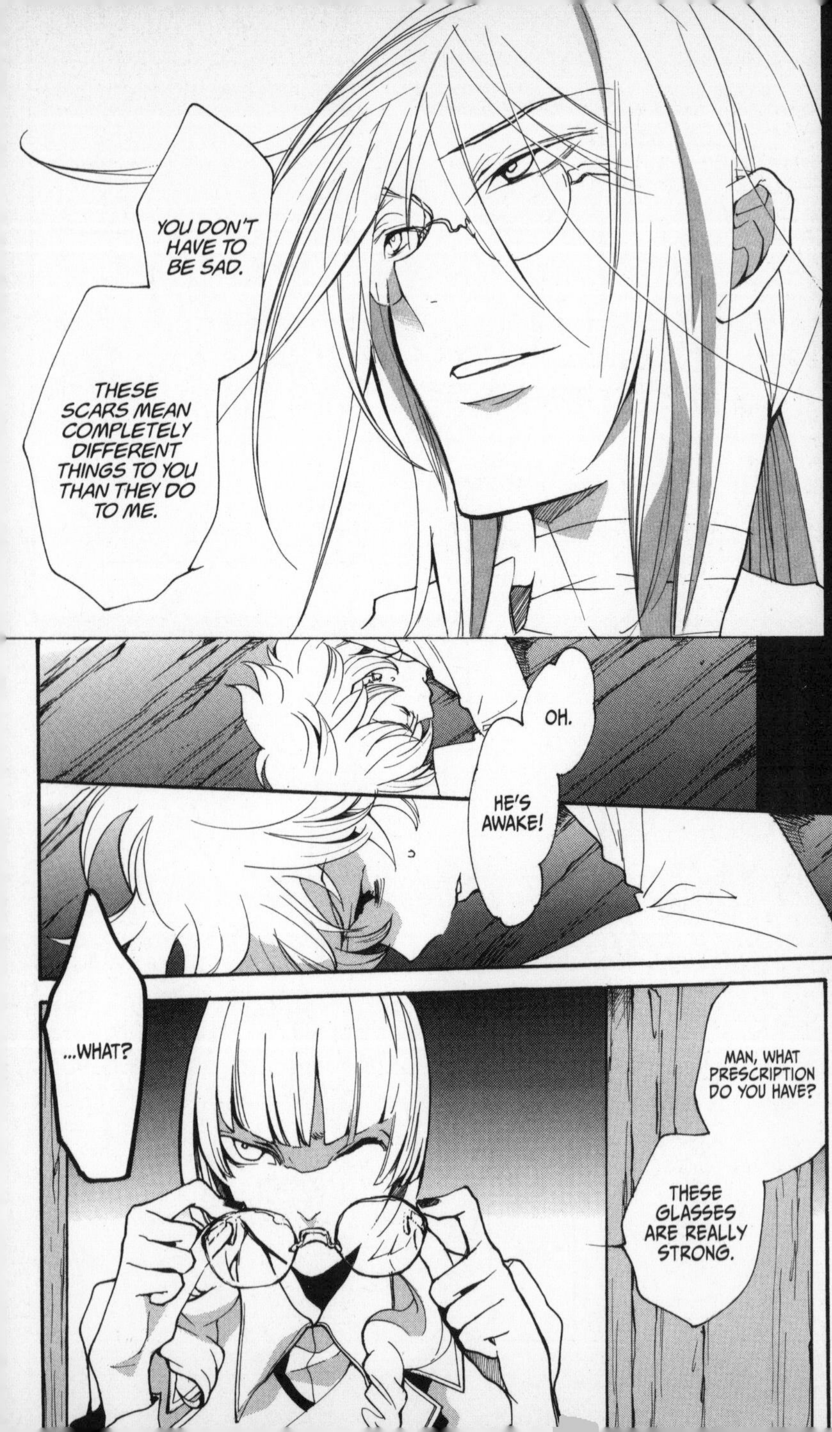
YOU DON'T HAVE TO BE SAD.
THESE SCARS MEAN COMPLETELY DIFFERENT THINGS TO YOU THAN THEY DO TO ME.
OH.
HE'S AWAKE!
...WHAT?
MAN, WHAT PRESCRIPTION DO YOU HAVE?
THESE GLASSES ARE REALLY STRONG.

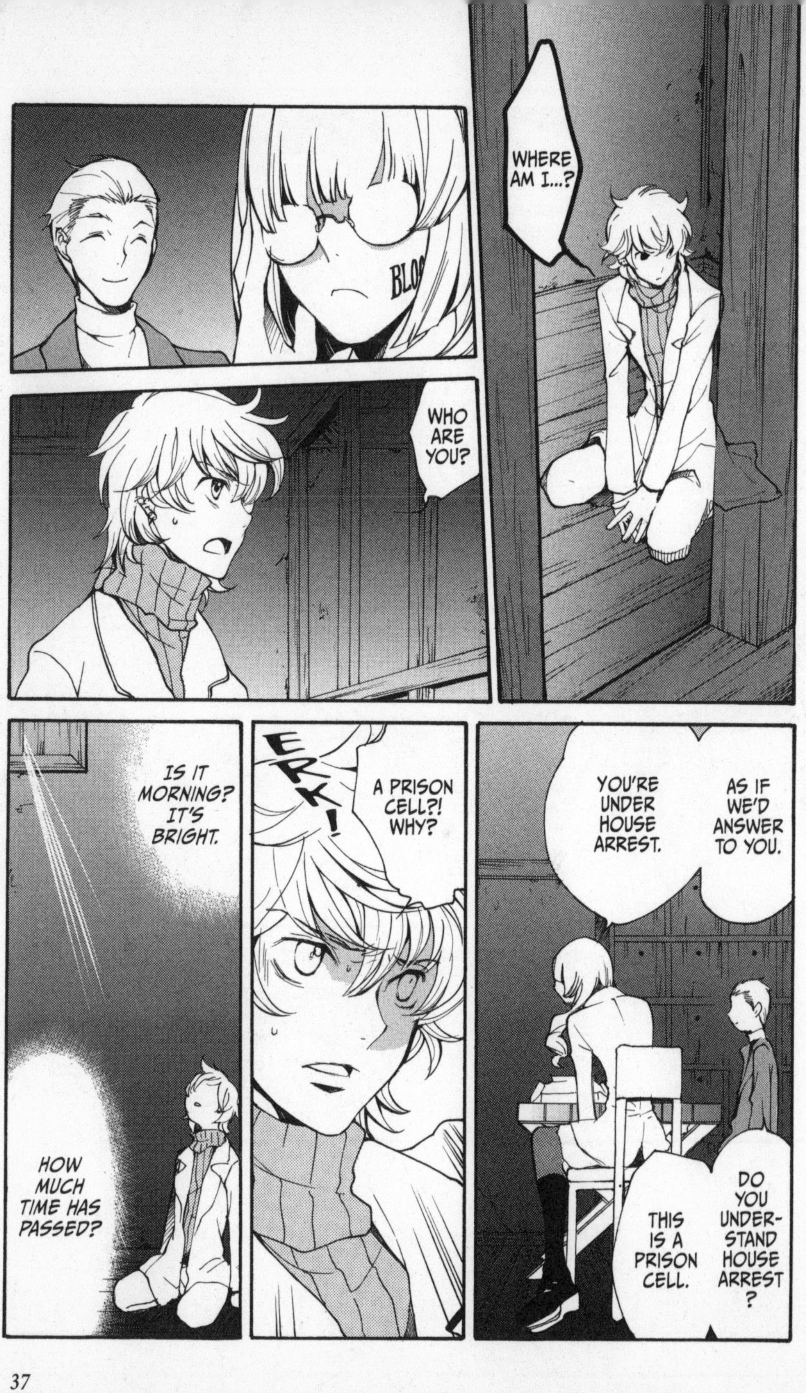
WHERE AM I...?
WHO ARE YOU?
AS IF WE'D ANSWER TO YOU.
YOU'RE UNDER HOUSE ARREST.
DO YOU UNDER-STAND HOUSE ARREST?
THIS IS A PRISON CELL.
ERK!
A PRISON CELL?! WHY?
IS IT MORNING? IT'S BRIGHT.
HOW MUCH TIME HAS PASSED?

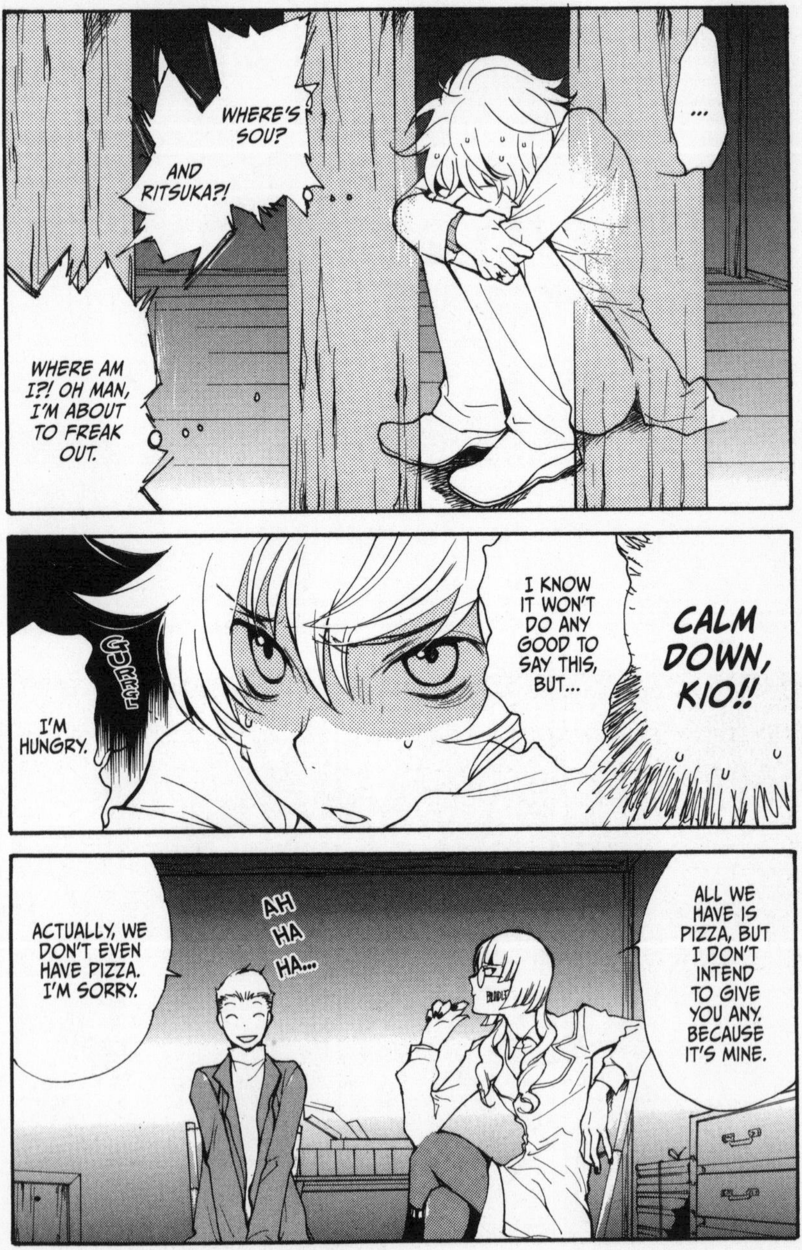
...
WHERE'S SOU?
AND RITSUKA?!
WHERE AM I?! OH MAN, I'M ABOUT TO FREAK OUT.
CALM DOWN, KIO!!
I KNOW IT WON'T DO ANY GOOD TO SAY THIS, BUT...
GURGLE
I'M HUNGRY.
ALL WE HAVE IS PIZZA, BUT I DON'T INTEND TO GIVE YOU ANY. BECAUSE IT'S MINE.
AH HA HA...
ACTUALLY, WE DON'T EVEN HAVE PIZZA. I'M SORRY.

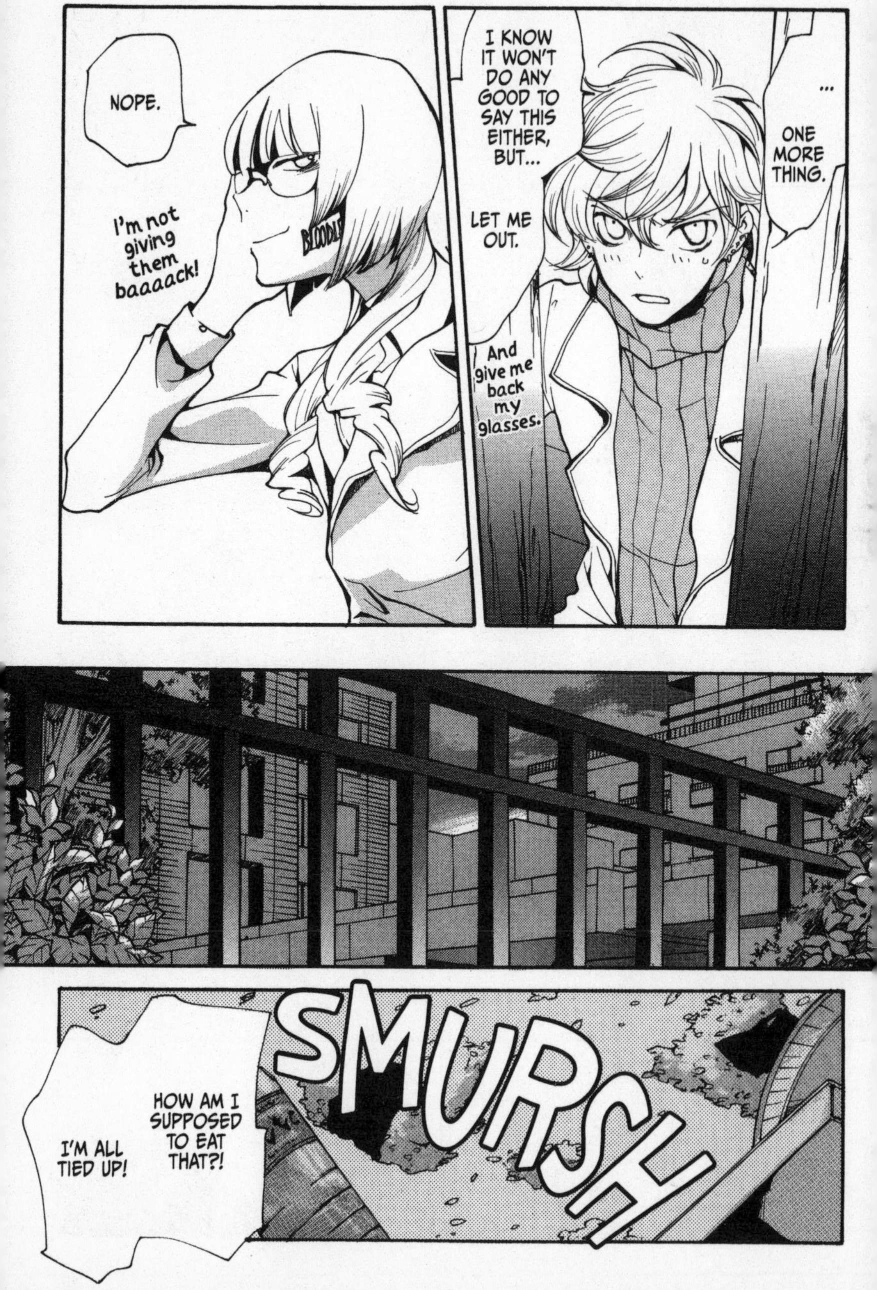
...
ONE MORE THING.
I KNOW IT WON'T DO ANY GOOD TO SAY THIS EITHER, BUT...
LET ME OUT.
And give me back my glasses.
NOPE.
I'm not giving them baaaack!
SMURSH
HOW AM I SUPPOSED TO EAT THAT?!
I'M ALL TIED UP!

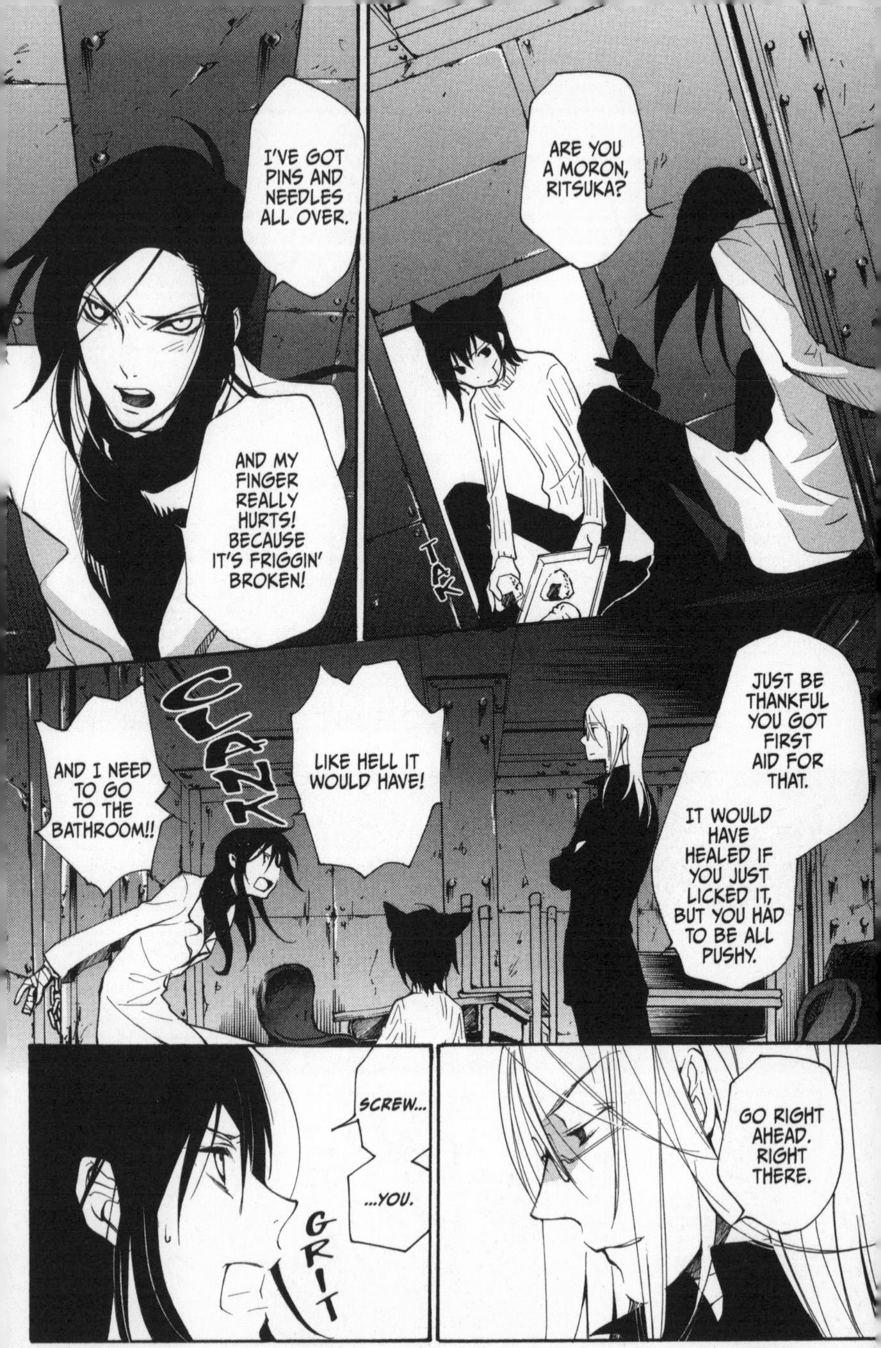
ARE YOU A MORON, RITSUKA?
TAK
I'VE GOT PINS AND NEEDLES ALL OVER.
AND MY FINGER REALLY HURTS! BECAUSE IT'S FRIGGIN' BROKEN!
JUST BE THANKFUL YOU GOT FIRST AID FOR THAT.
IT WOULD HAVE HEALED IF YOU JUST LICKED IT, BUT YOU HAD TO BE ALL PUSHY.
LIKE HELL IT WOULD HAVE!
CLANK
AND I NEED TO GO TO THE BATHROOM!!
GO RIGHT AHEAD. RIGHT THERE.
SCREW...
...YOU.
GRIT

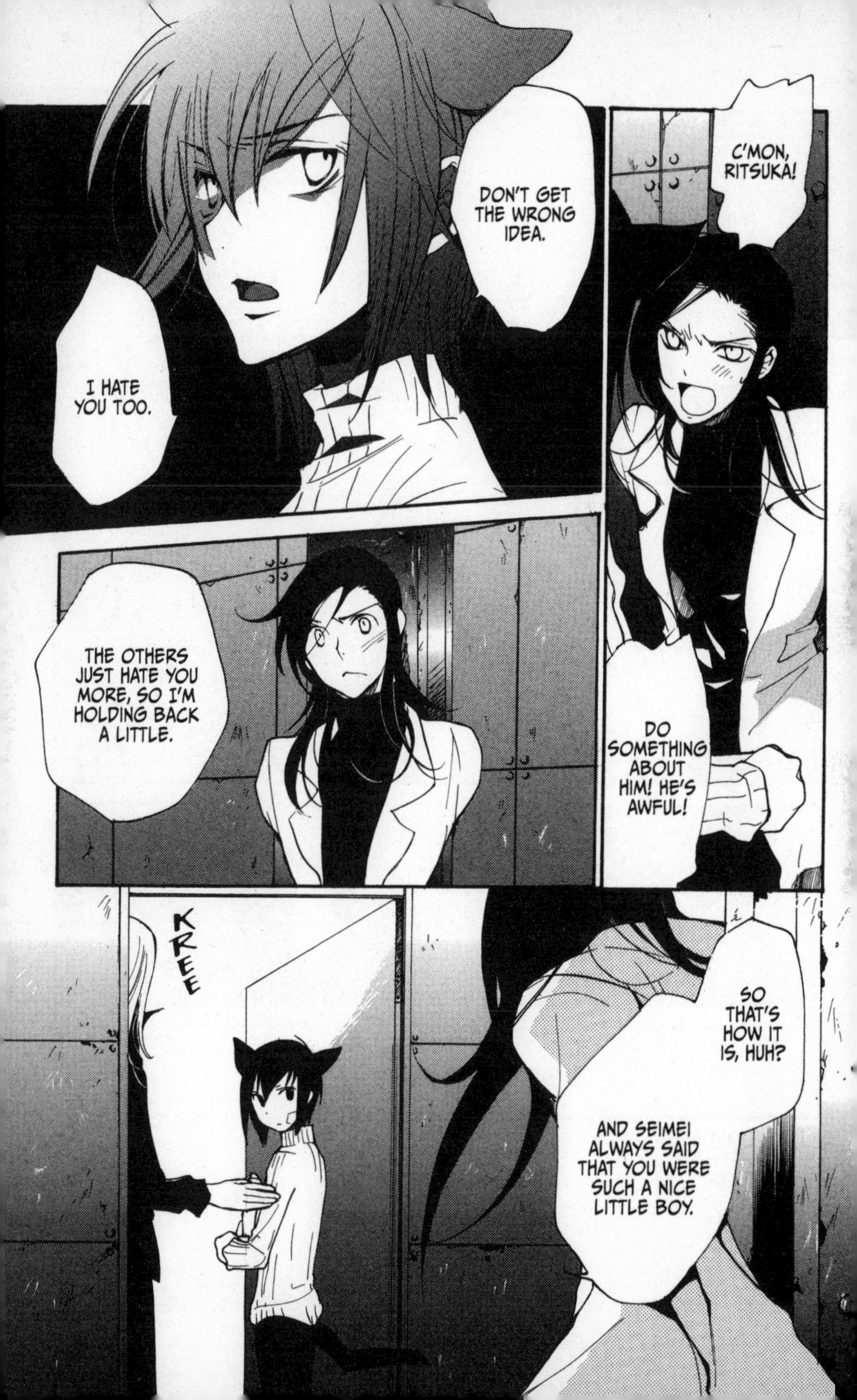
C'MON, RITSUKA!
DO SOMETHING ABOUT HIM! HE'S AWFUL!
DON'T GET THE WRONG IDEA.
I HATE YOU TOO.
THE OTHERS JUST HATE YOU MORE, SO I'M HOLDING BACK A LITTLE.
SO THAT'S HOW IT IS, HUH?
AND SEIMEI ALWAYS SAID THAT YOU WERE SUCH A NICE LITTLE BOY.
KREE

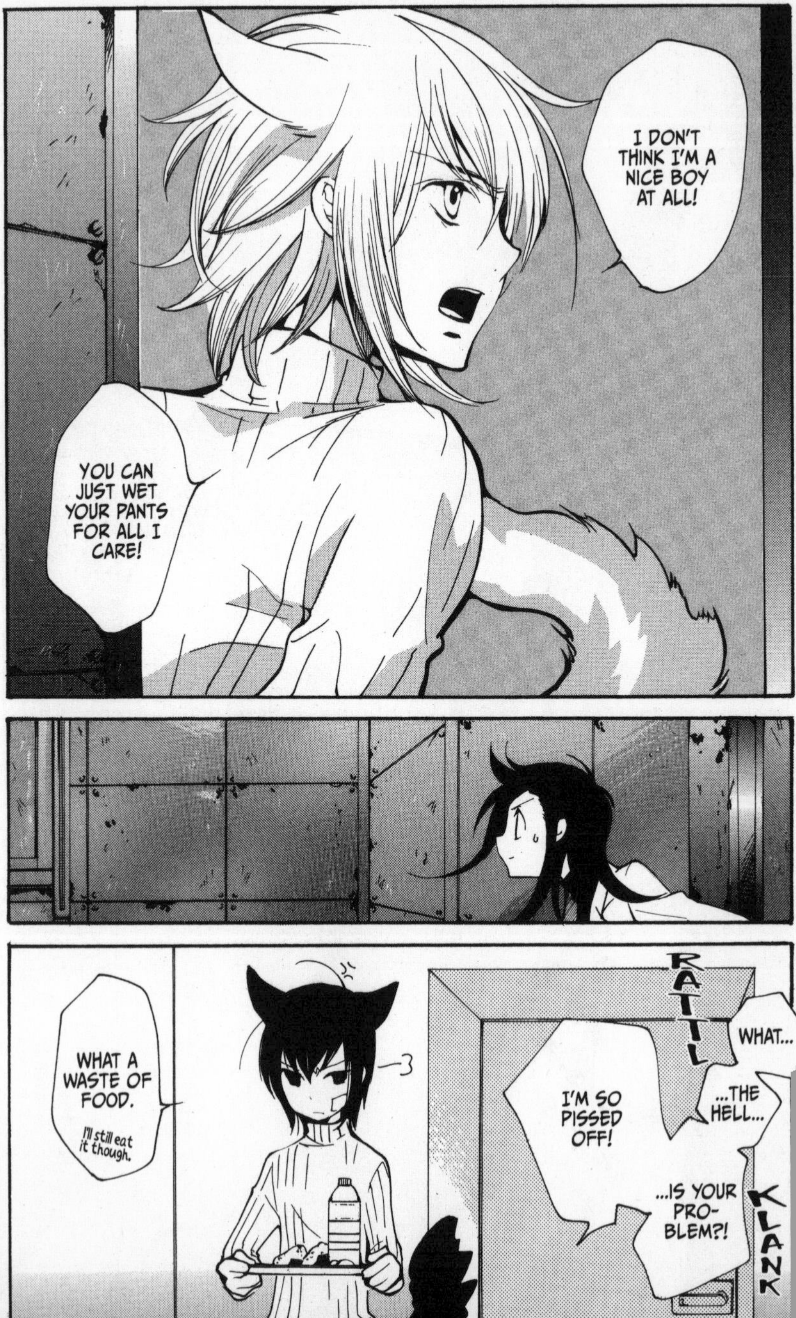
I DON'T THINK I'M A NICE BOY AT ALL!
YOU CAN JUST WET YOUR PANTS FOR ALL I CARE!
RATTL
WHAT...
I'M SO PISSED OFF!
...THE HELL...
...IS YOUR PRO-BLEM?!
KLANK
WHAT A WASTE OF FOOD.
I'll still eat it though.

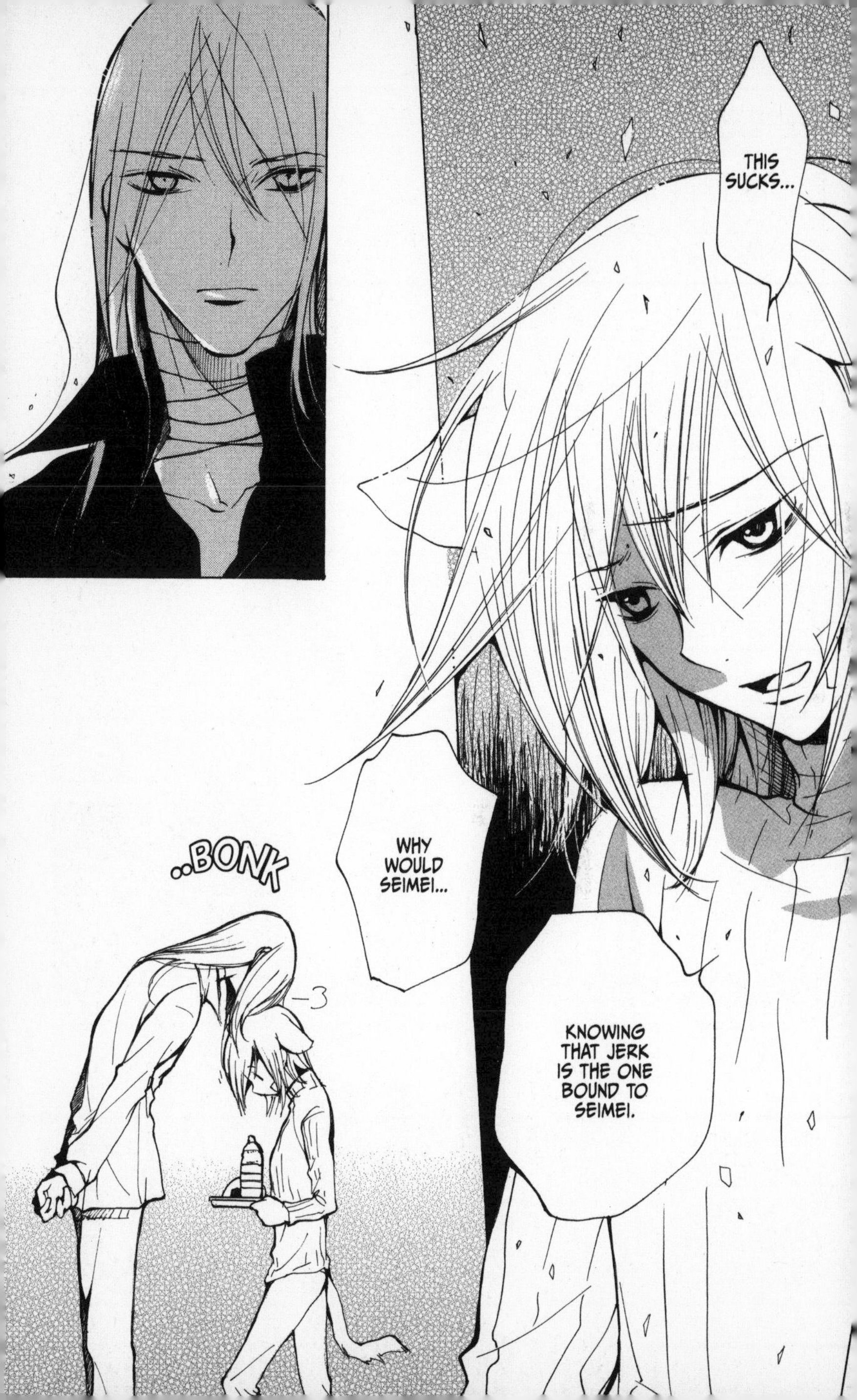
THIS SUCKS...
WHY WOULD SEIMEI...
KNOWING THAT JERK IS THE ONE BOUND TO SEIMEI.
..BONK

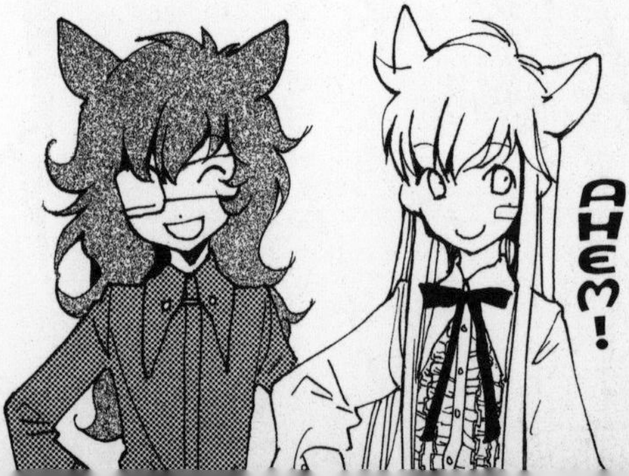
AHEM!

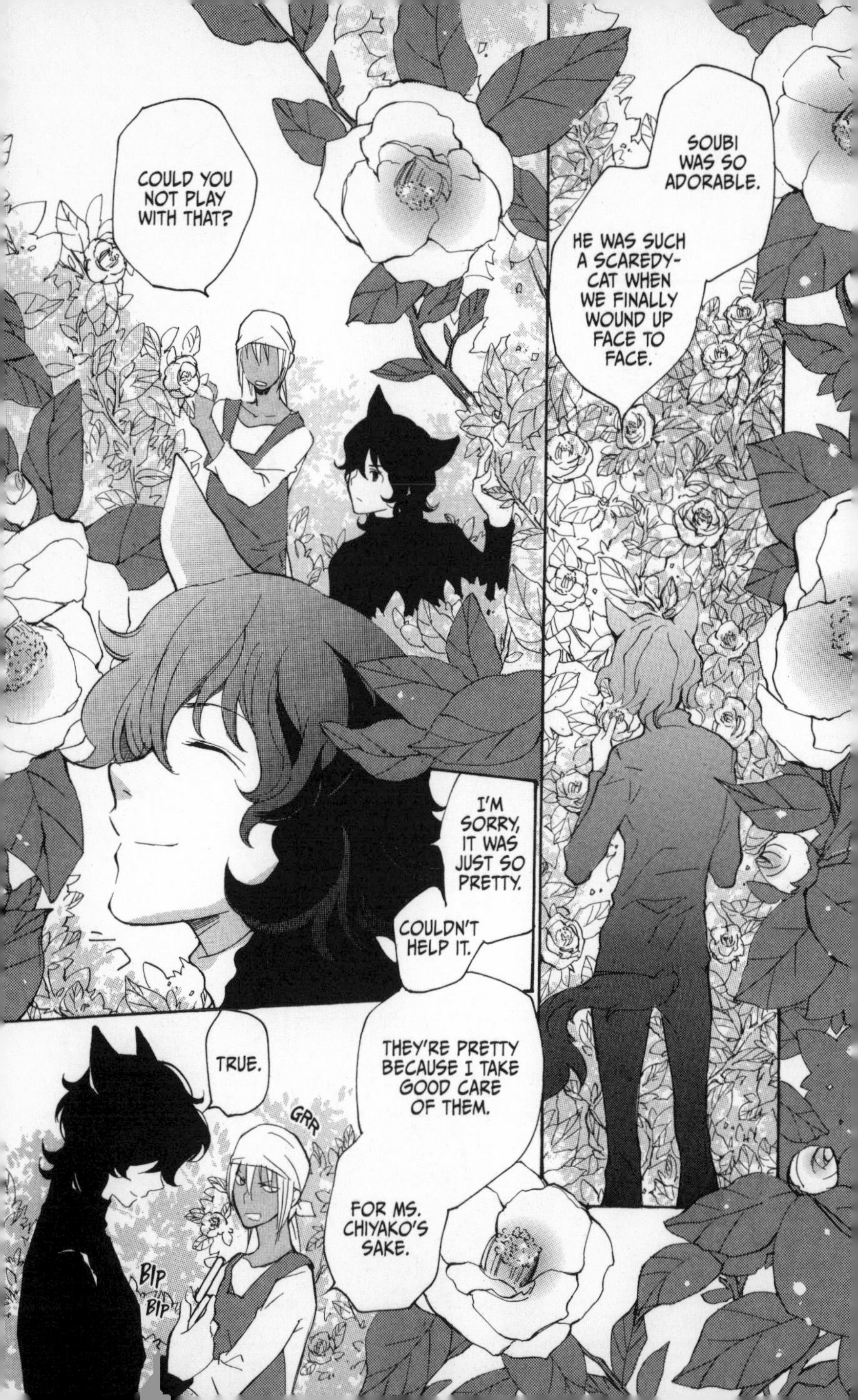
SOUBI WAS SO ADORABLE.
HE WAS SUCH A SCAREDY-CAT WHEN WE FINALLY WOUND UP FACE TO FACE.
COULD YOU NOT PLAY WITH THAT?
I'M SORRY, IT WAS JUST SO PRETTY.
COULDN'T HELP IT.
THEY'RE PRETTY BECAUSE I TAKE GOOD CARE OF THEM.
TRUE.
GRR
FOR MS. CHIYAKO'S SAKE.
BIP
BIP

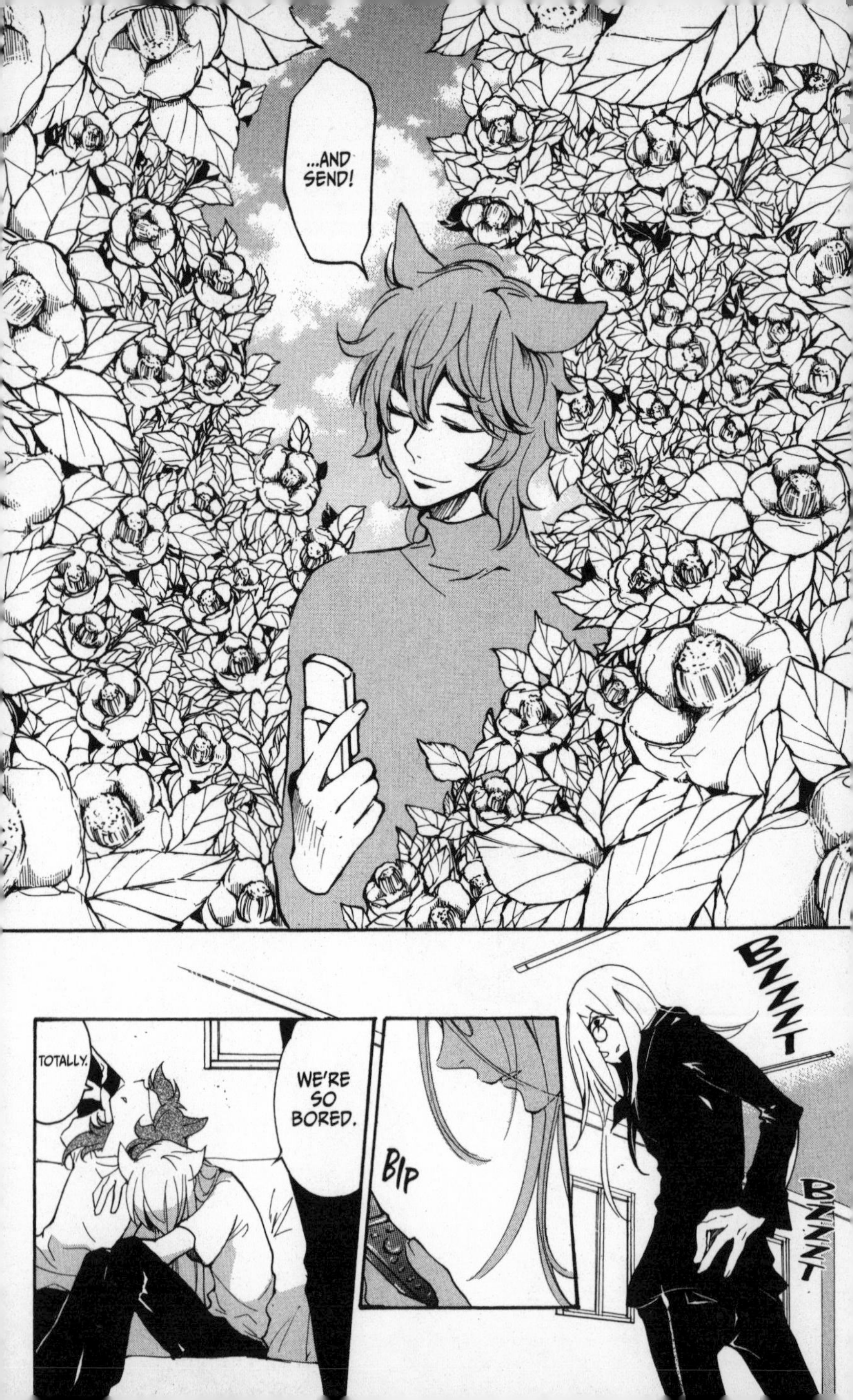
...AND SEND!
BZZZT
BZZZT
BIP
WE'RE SO BORED.
TOTALLY.

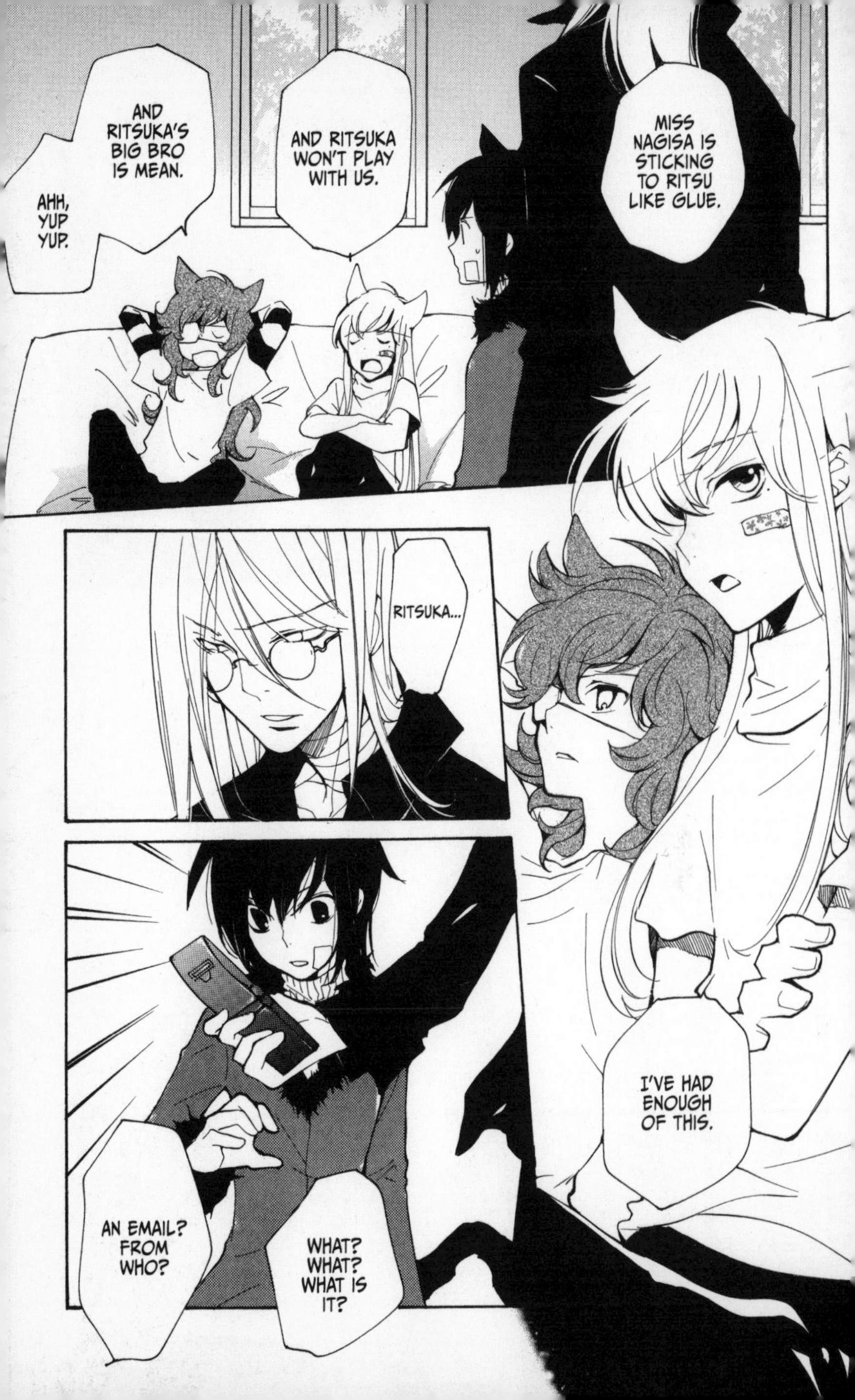
MISS NAGISA IS STICKING TO RITSU LIKE GLUE.
AND RITSUKA WON'T PLAY WITH US.
AND RITSUKA'S BIG BRO IS MEAN.
AHH, YUP YUP.
I'VE HAD ENOUGH OF THIS.
RITSUKA...
WHAT? WHAT? WHAT IS IT?
AN EMAIL? FROM WHO?

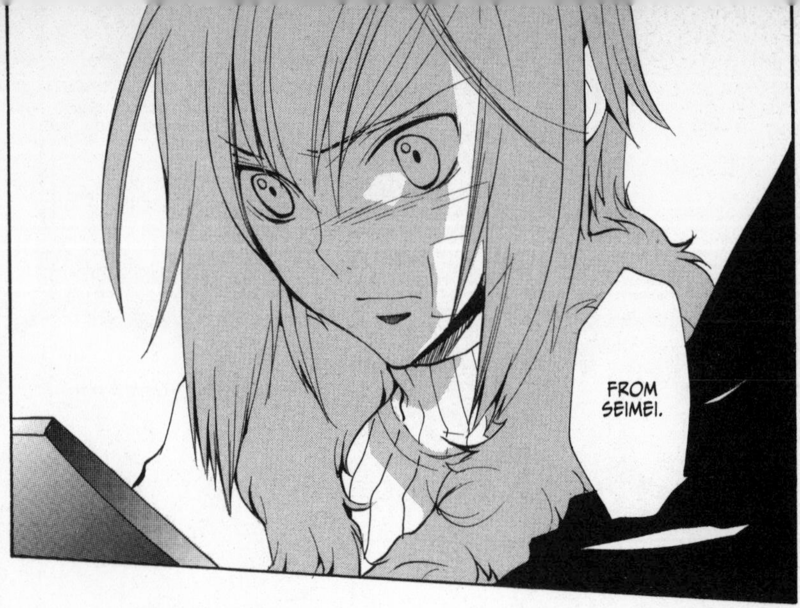
FROM SEIMEI.

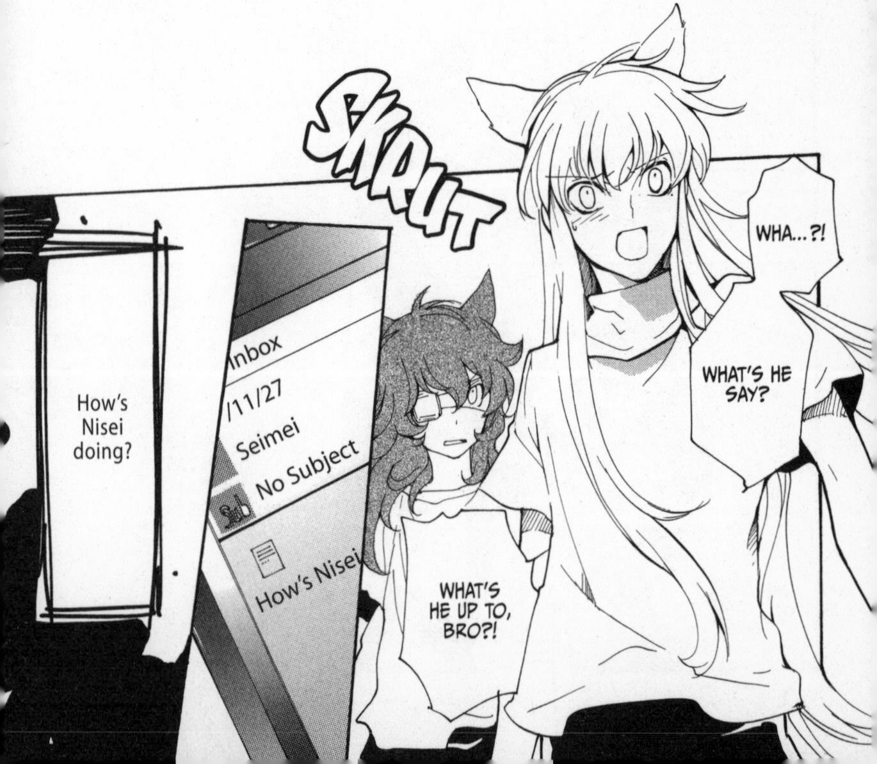
WHA...?!
WHAT'S HE SAY?
SKRUT
WHAT'S HE UP TO, BRO?!
Inbox
/11/27
Seimei
No Subject
How's Nisei
How's Nisei doing?

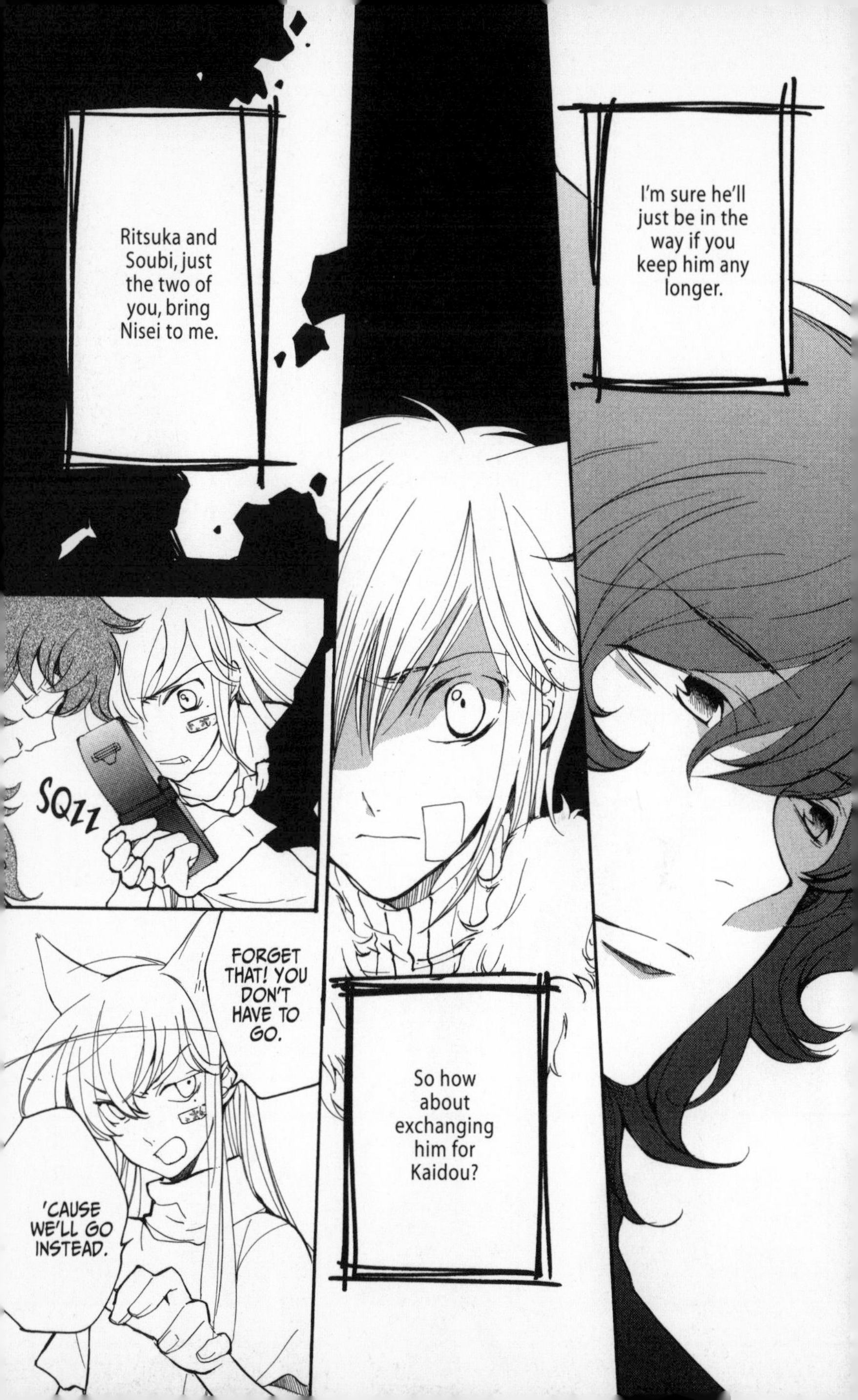

I'm sure he'll just be in the way if you keep him any longer.
So how about exchanging him for Kaidou?
Ritsuka and Soubi, just the two of you, bring Nisei to me.
SQZZ
FORGET THAT! YOU DON'T HAVE TO GO.
'CAUSE WE'LL GO INSTEAD.

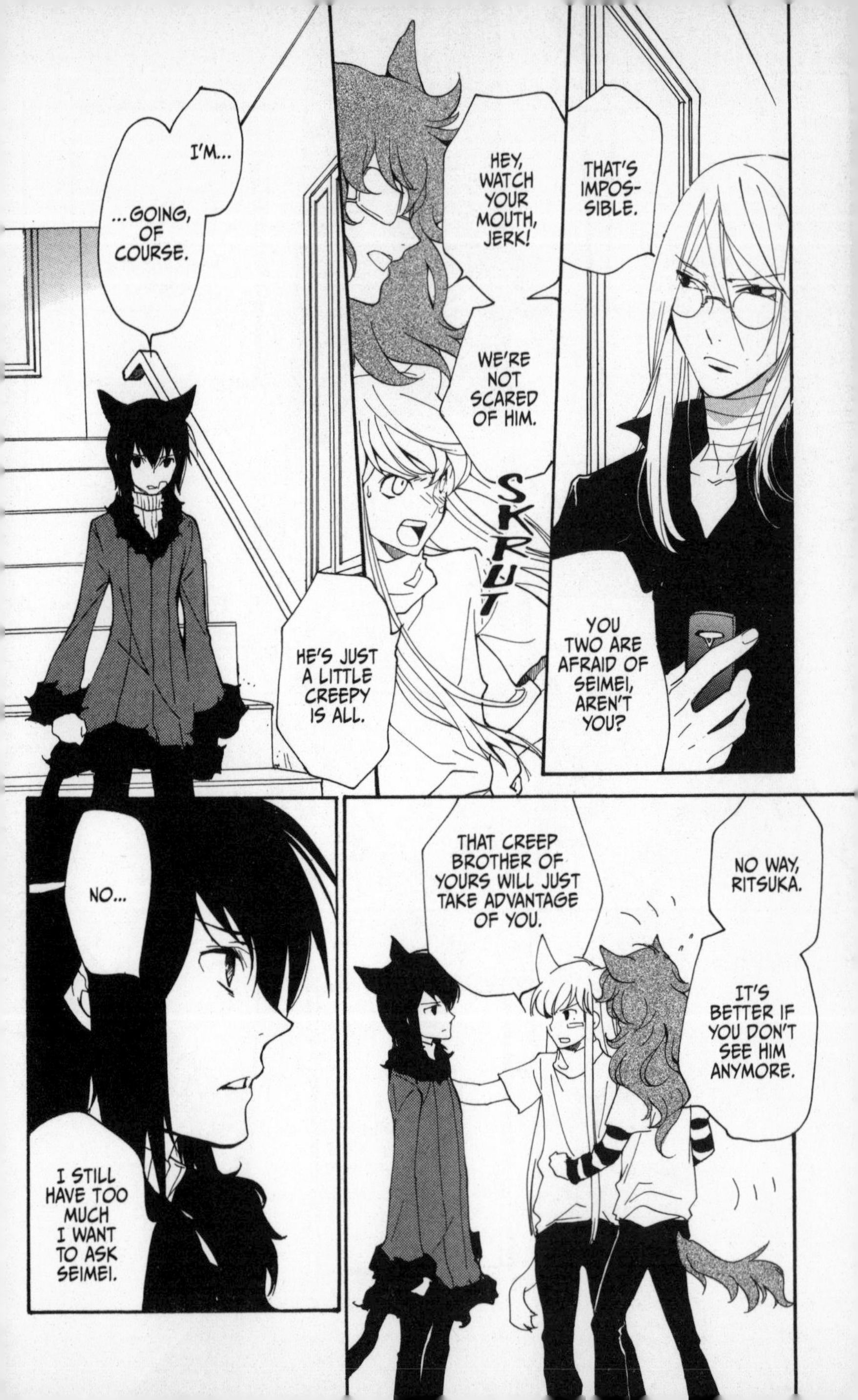
THAT'S IMPOSSIBLE.
YOU TWO ARE AFRAID OF SEIMEI, AREN'T YOU?
HEY, WATCH YOUR MOUTH, JERK!
WE'RE NOT SCARED OF HIM.
SKRUT
HE'S JUST A LITTLE CREEPY IS ALL.
I'M...
...GOING, OF COURSE.
NO WAY, RITSUKA.
IT'S BETTER IF YOU DON'T SEE HIM ANYMORE.
THAT CREEP BROTHER OF YOURS WILL JUST TAKE ADVANTAGE OF YOU.
NO...
I STILL HAVE TOO MUCH I WANT TO ASK SEIMEI.

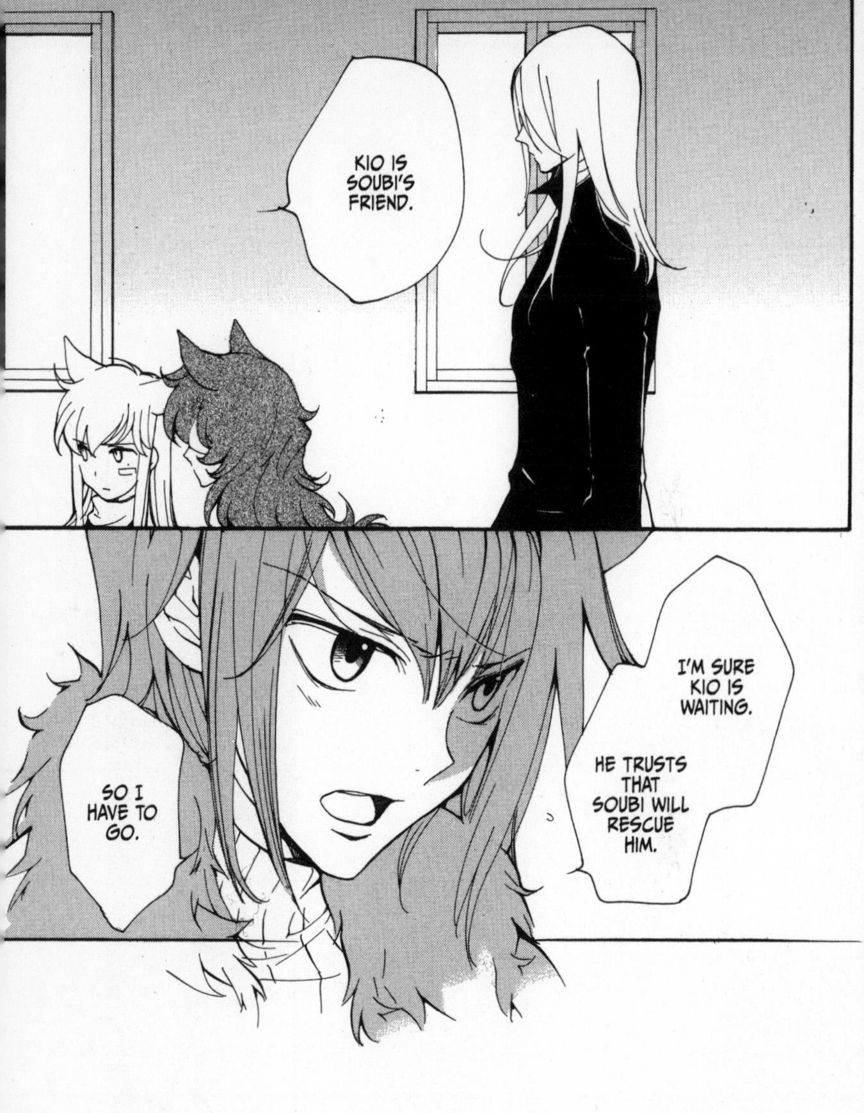
KIO IS SOUBI'S FRIEND.
I'M SURE KIO IS WAITING.
HE TRUSTS THAT SOUBI WILL RESCUE HIM.
SO I HAVE TO GO.

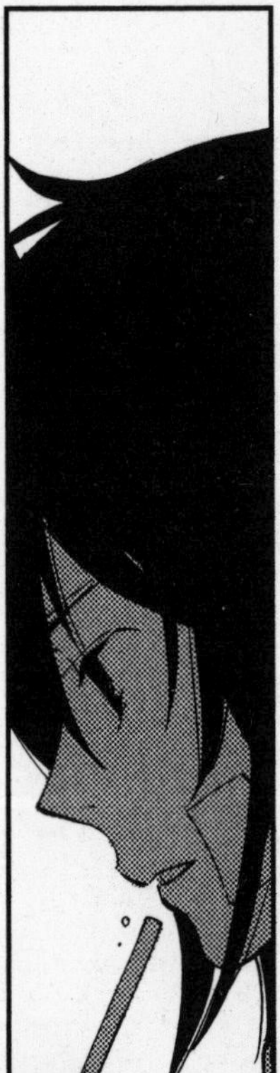
MILK

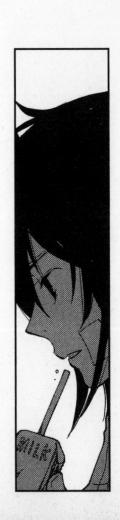

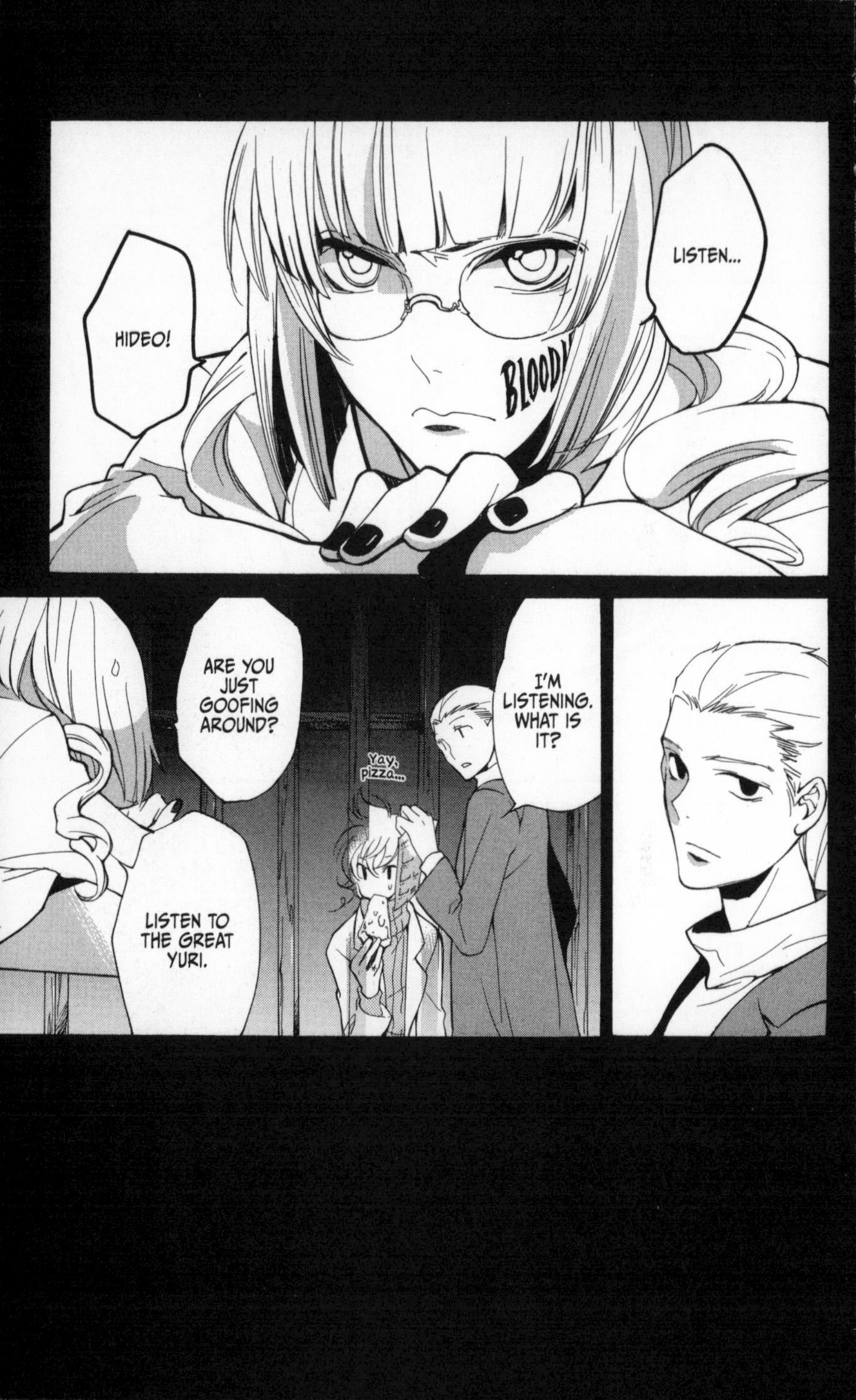
LISTEN...
HIDEO!
BLOOD
I'M LISTENING. WHAT IS IT?
ARE YOU JUST GOOFING AROUND?
Yay, pizza...
LISTEN TO THE GREAT YURI.

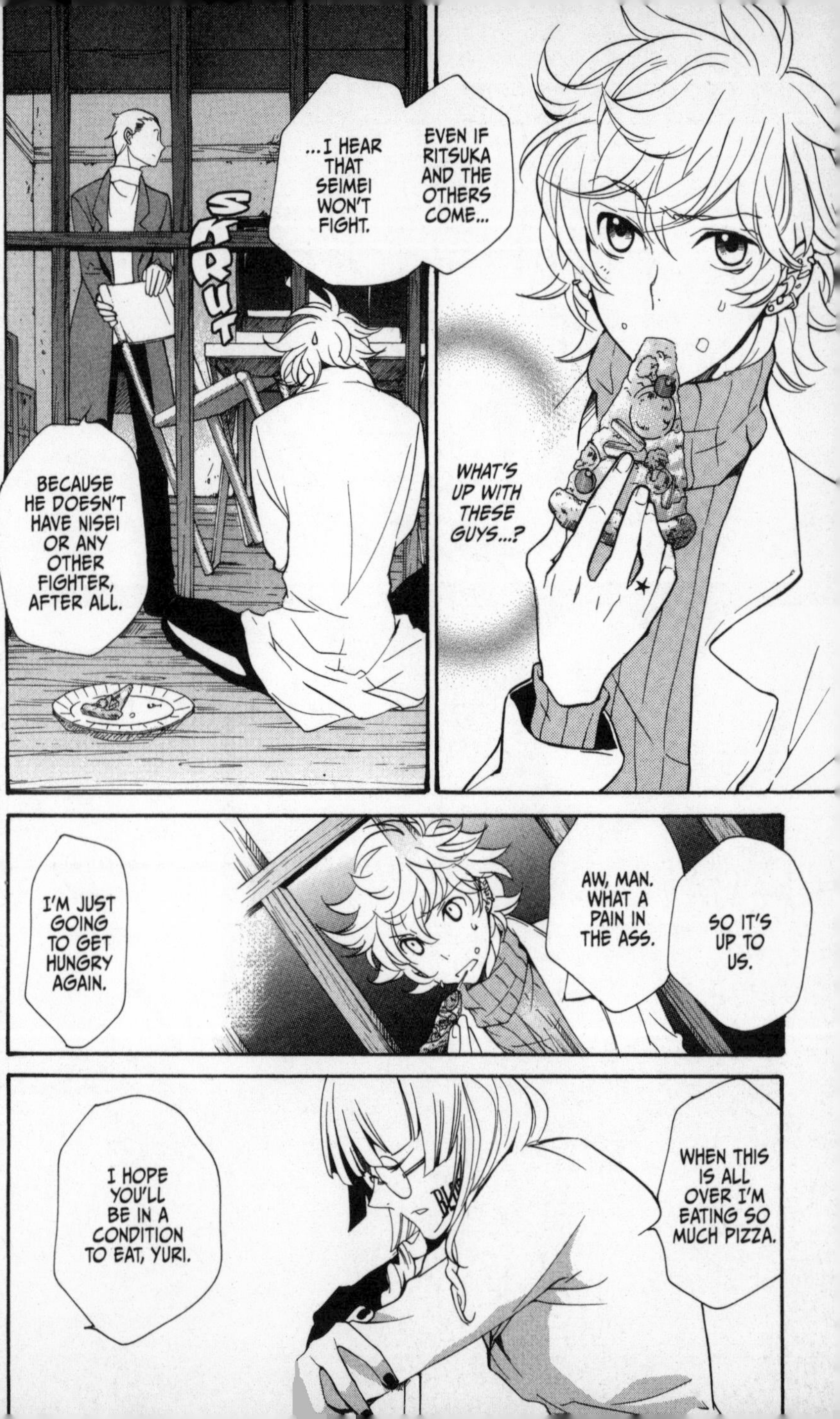
EVEN IF RITSUKA AND THE OTHERS COME...
...I HEAR THAT SEIMEI WON'T FIGHT.
SKRUT
WHAT'S UP WITH THESE GUYS...?
BECAUSE HE DOESN'T HAVE NISEI OR ANY OTHER FIGHTER, AFTER ALL.
SO IT'S UP TO US.
AW, MAN. WHAT A PAIN IN THE ASS.
I'M JUST GOING TO GET HUNGRY AGAIN.
WHEN THIS IS ALL OVER I'M EATING SO MUCH PIZZA.
I HOPE YOU'LL BE IN A CONDITION TO EAT, YURI.

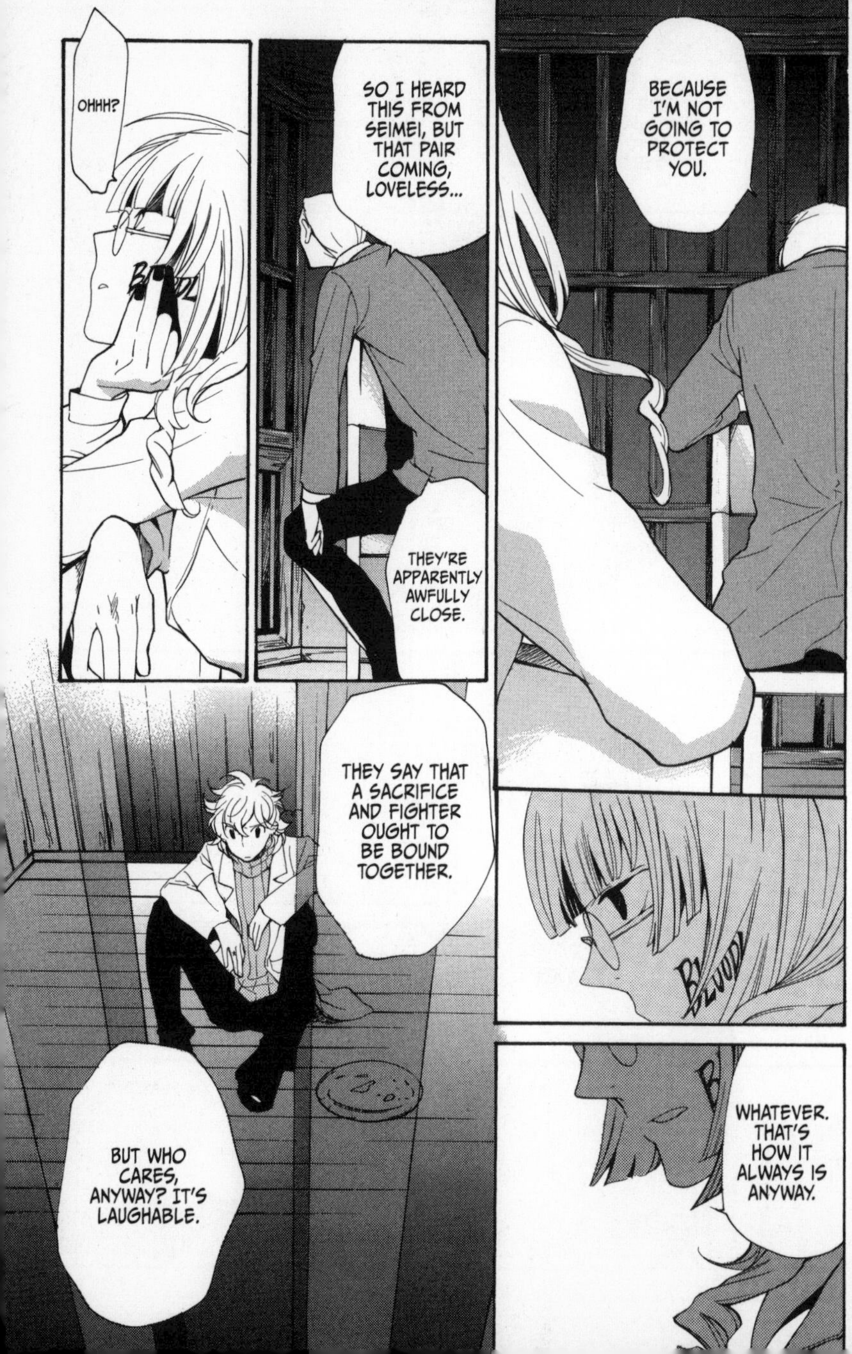
SO I HEARD THIS FROM SEIMEI, BUT THAT PAIR COMING, LOVELESS...
THEY'RE APPARENTLY AWFULLY CLOSE.
OHHH?
THEY SAY THAT A SACRIFICE AND FIGHTER OUGHT TO BE BOUND TOGETHER.
BUT WHO CARES, ANYWAY? IT'S LAUGHABLE.
BECAUSE I'M NOT GOING TO PROTECT YOU.
WHATEVER. THAT'S HOW IT ALWAYS IS ANYWAY.

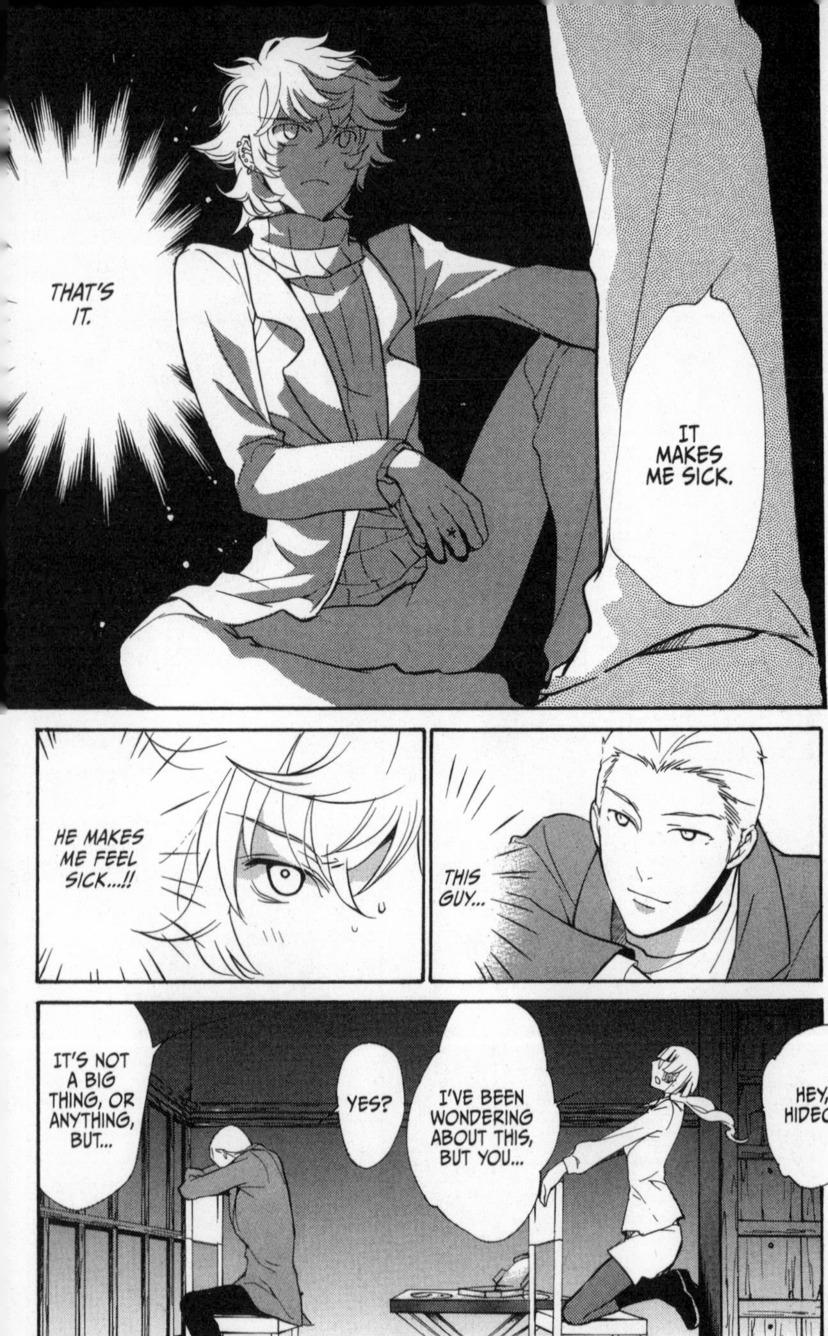
IT MAKES ME SICK.
THAT'S IT.
THIS GUY...
HE MAKES ME FEEL SICK...!!
HEY, HIDEO.
I'VE BEEN WONDERING ABOUT THIS, BUT YOU...
YES?
IT'S NOT A BIG THING, OR ANYTHING, BUT...

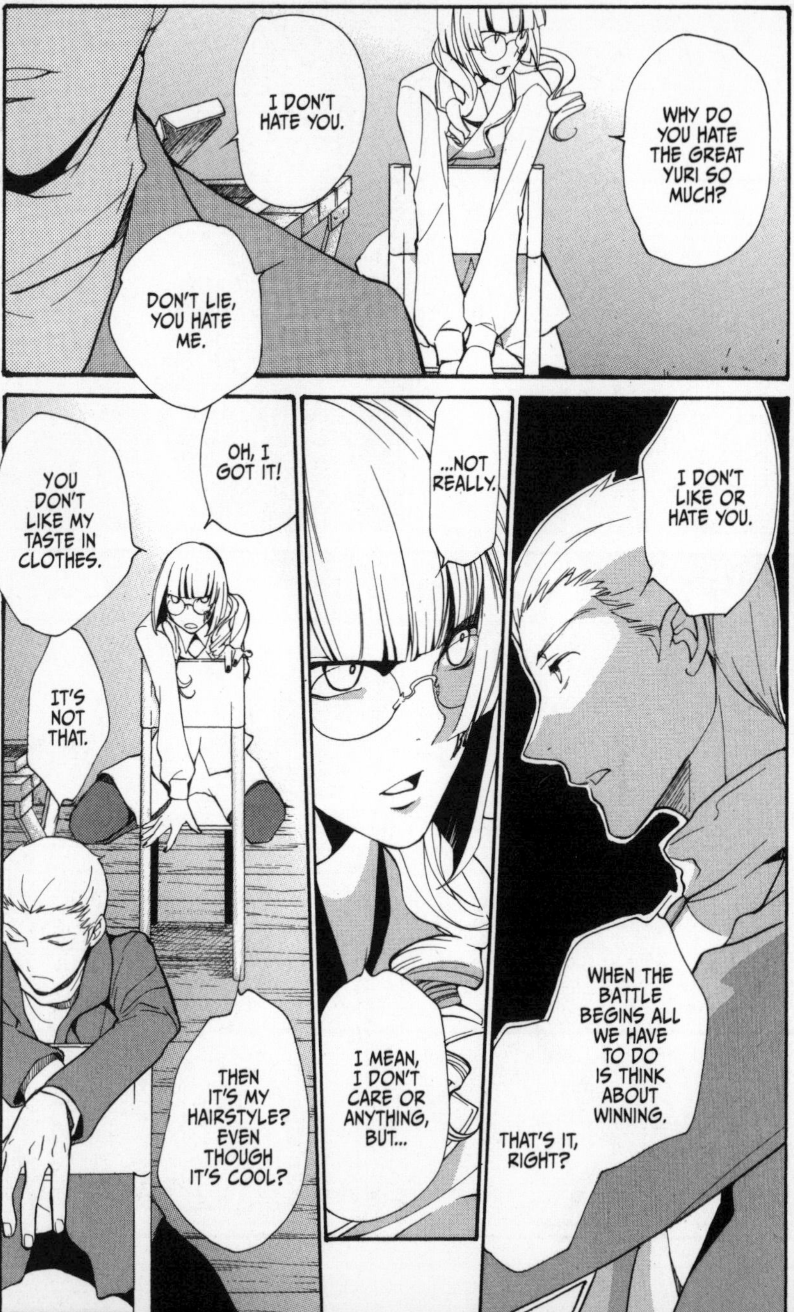
WHY DO YOU HATE THE GREAT YURI SO MUCH?
I DON'T HATE YOU.
DON'T LIE, YOU HATE ME.
I DON'T LIKE OR HATE YOU.
WHEN THE BATTLE BEGINS ALL WE HAVE TO DO IS THINK ABOUT WINNING.
THAT'S IT, RIGHT?
...NOT REALLY.
I MEAN, I DON'T CARE OR ANYTHING, BUT...
OH, I GOT IT!
YOU DON'T LIKE MY TASTE IN CLOTHES.
IT'S NOT THAT.
THEN IT'S MY HAIRSTYLE? EVEN THOUGH IT'S COOL?

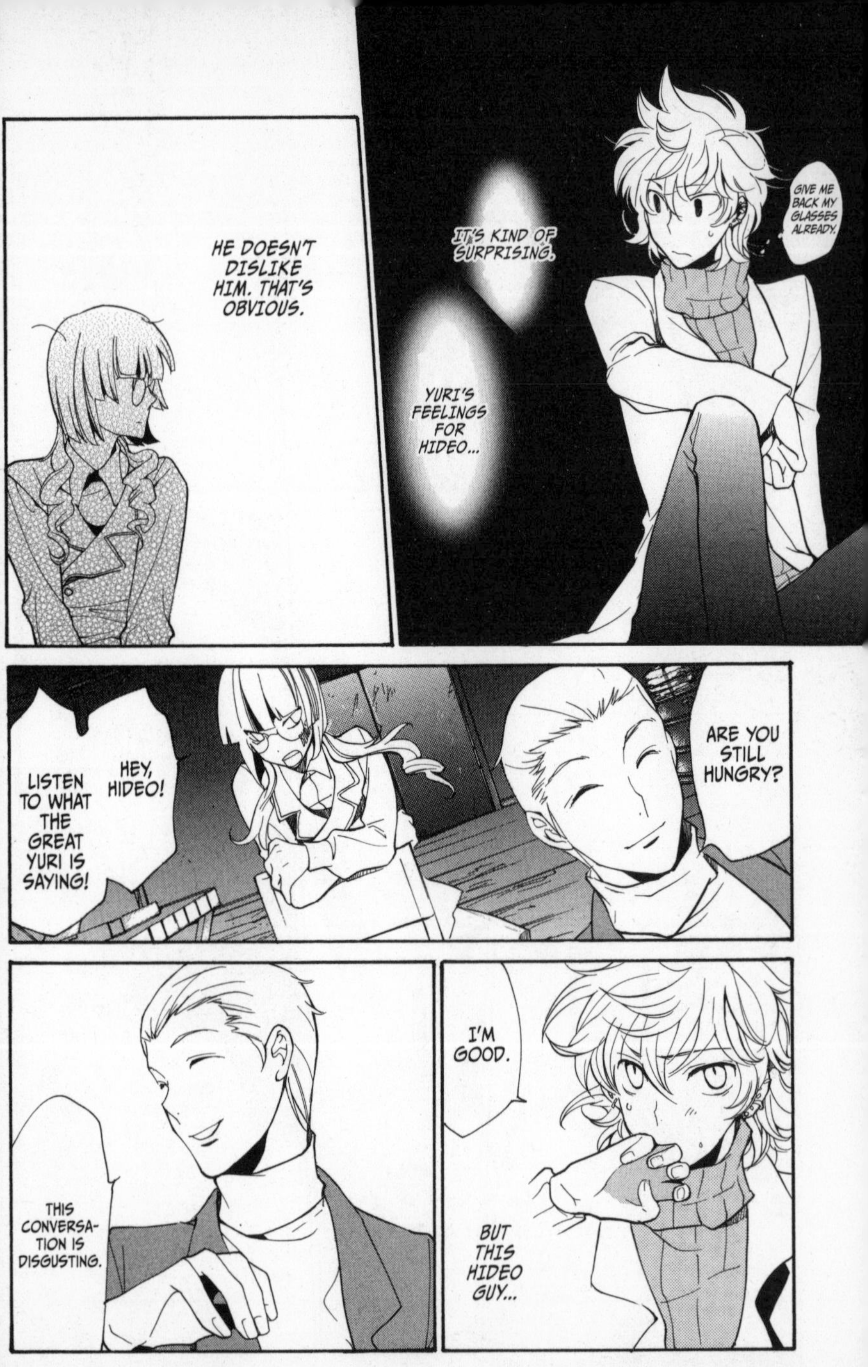
GIVE ME BACK MY GLASSES ALREADY.
IT'S KIND OF SURPRISING.
YURI'S FEELINGS FOR HIDEO...
HE DOESN'T DISLIKE HIM. THAT'S OBVIOUS.
ARE YOU STILL HUNGRY?
HEY, HIDEO!
LISTEN TO WHAT THE GREAT YURI IS SAYING!
I'M GOOD.
BUT THIS HIDEO GUY...
THIS CONVERSA-TION IS DISGUSTING.

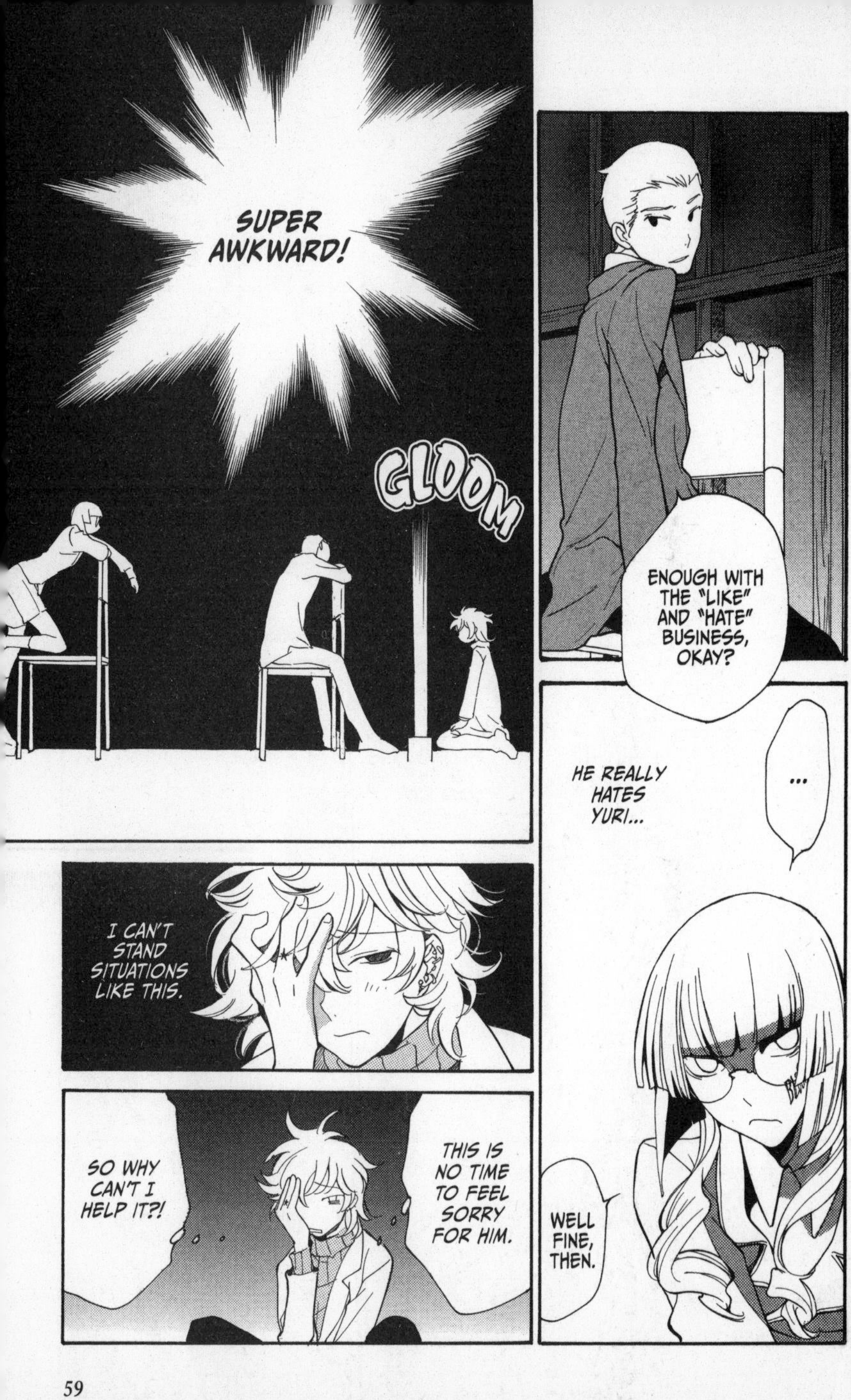
ENOUGH WITH THE "LIKE" AND "HATE" BUSINESS, OKAY?
...
HE REALLY HATES YURI...
WELL FINE, THEN.
SUPER AWKWARD!
GLOOM
I CAN'T STAND SITUATIONS LIKE THIS.
THIS IS NO TIME TO FEEL SORRY FOR HIM.
SO WHY CAN'T I HELP IT?!

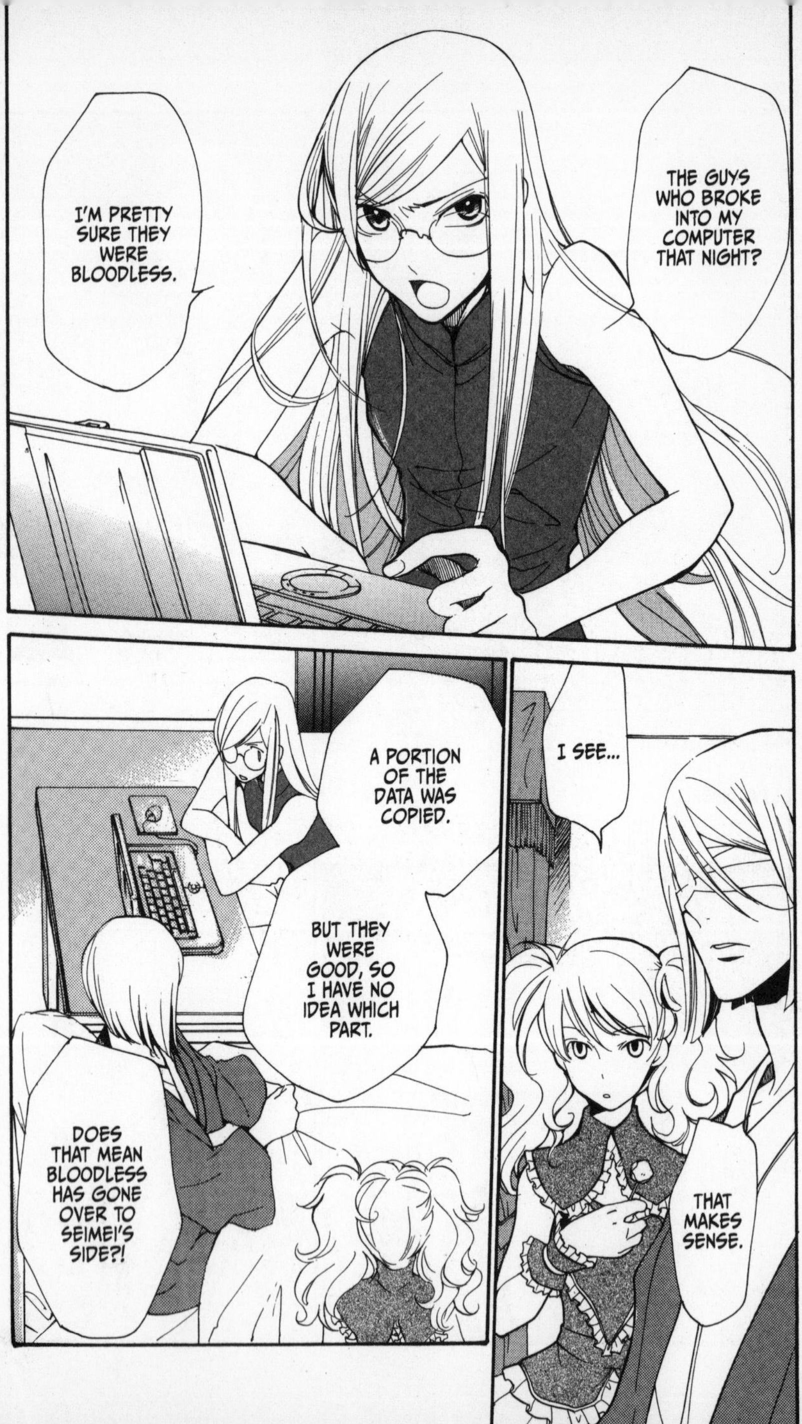
THE GUYS WHO BROKE INTO MY COMPUTER THAT NIGHT?
I'M PRETTY SURE THEY WERE BLOODLESS.
I SEE...
THAT MAKES SENSE.
A PORTION OF THE DATA WAS COPIED.
BUT THEY WERE GOOD, SO I HAVE NO IDEA WHICH PART.
DOES THAT MEAN BLOODLESS HAS GONE OVER TO SEIMEI'S SIDE?!

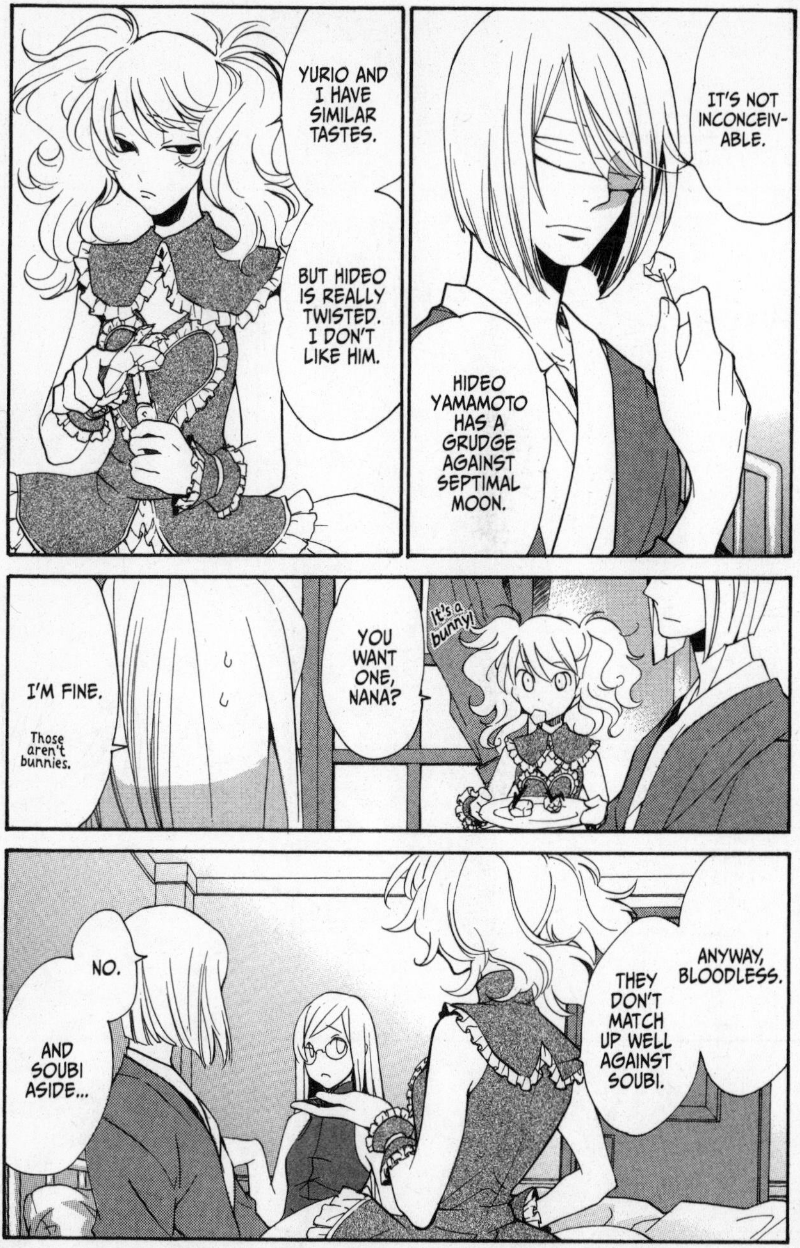
IT'S NOT INCONCEIV-ABLE.
HIDEO YAMAMOTO HAS A GRUDGE AGAINST SEPTIMAL MOON.
YURIO AND I HAVE SIMILAR TASTES.
BUT HIDEO IS REALLY TWISTED. I DON'T LIKE HIM.
It's a bunny!
YOU WANT ONE, NANA?
I'M FINE.
Those aren't bunnies.
ANYWAY, BLOODLESS.
THEY DON'T MATCH UP WELL AGAINST SOUBI.
NO.
AND SOUBI ASIDE...

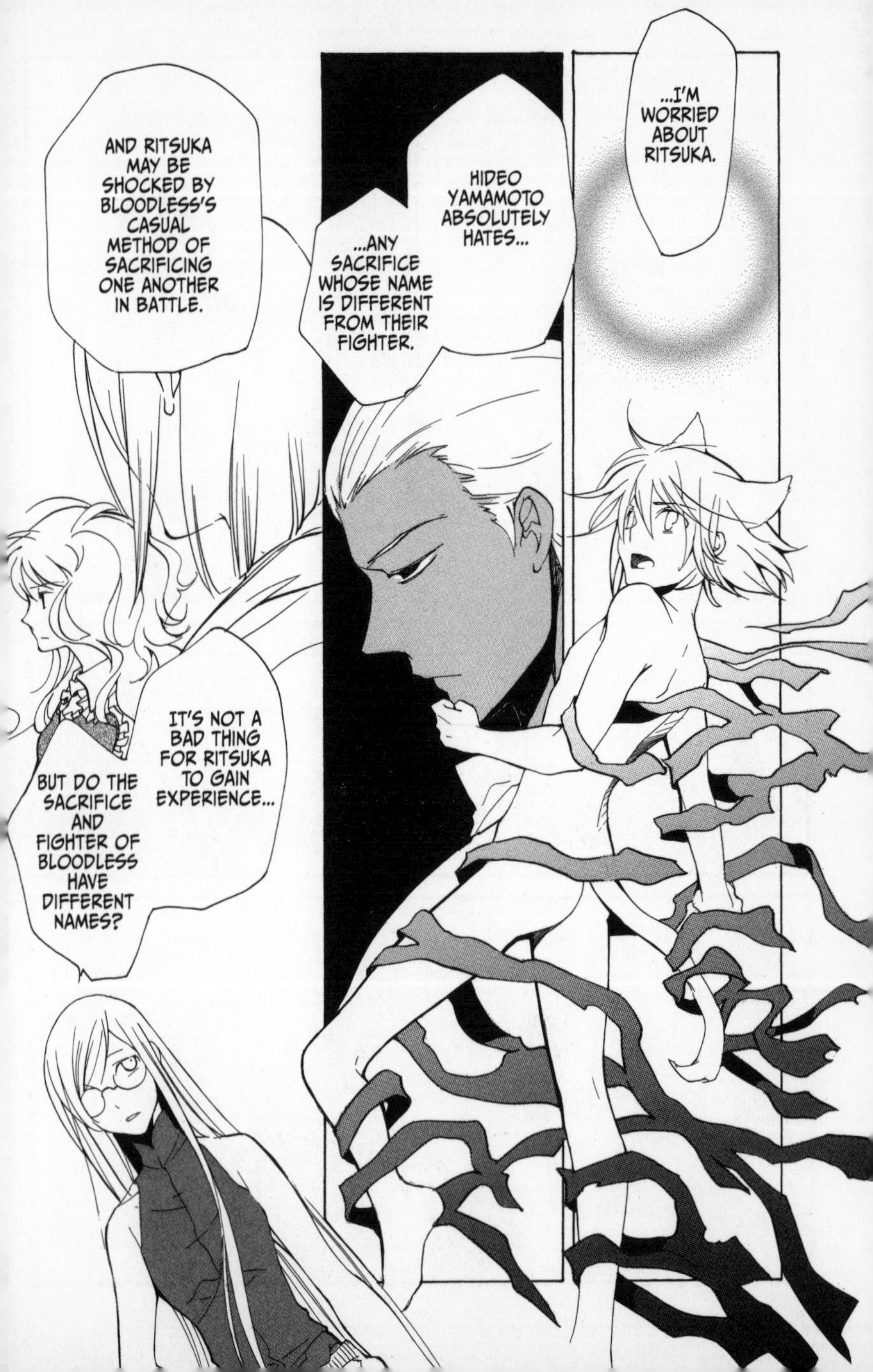
...I'M WORRIED ABOUT RITSUKA.
HIDEO YAMAMOTO ABSOLUTELY HATES...
...ANY SACRIFICE WHOSE NAME IS DIFFERENT FROM THEIR FIGHTER.
AND RITSUKA MAY BE SHOCKED BY BLOODLESS'S CASUAL METHOD OF SACRIFICING ONE ANOTHER IN BATTLE.
IT'S NOT A BAD THING FOR RITSUKA TO GAIN EXPERIENCE...
BUT DO THE SACRIFICE AND FIGHTER OF BLOODLESS HAVE DIFFERENT NAMES?

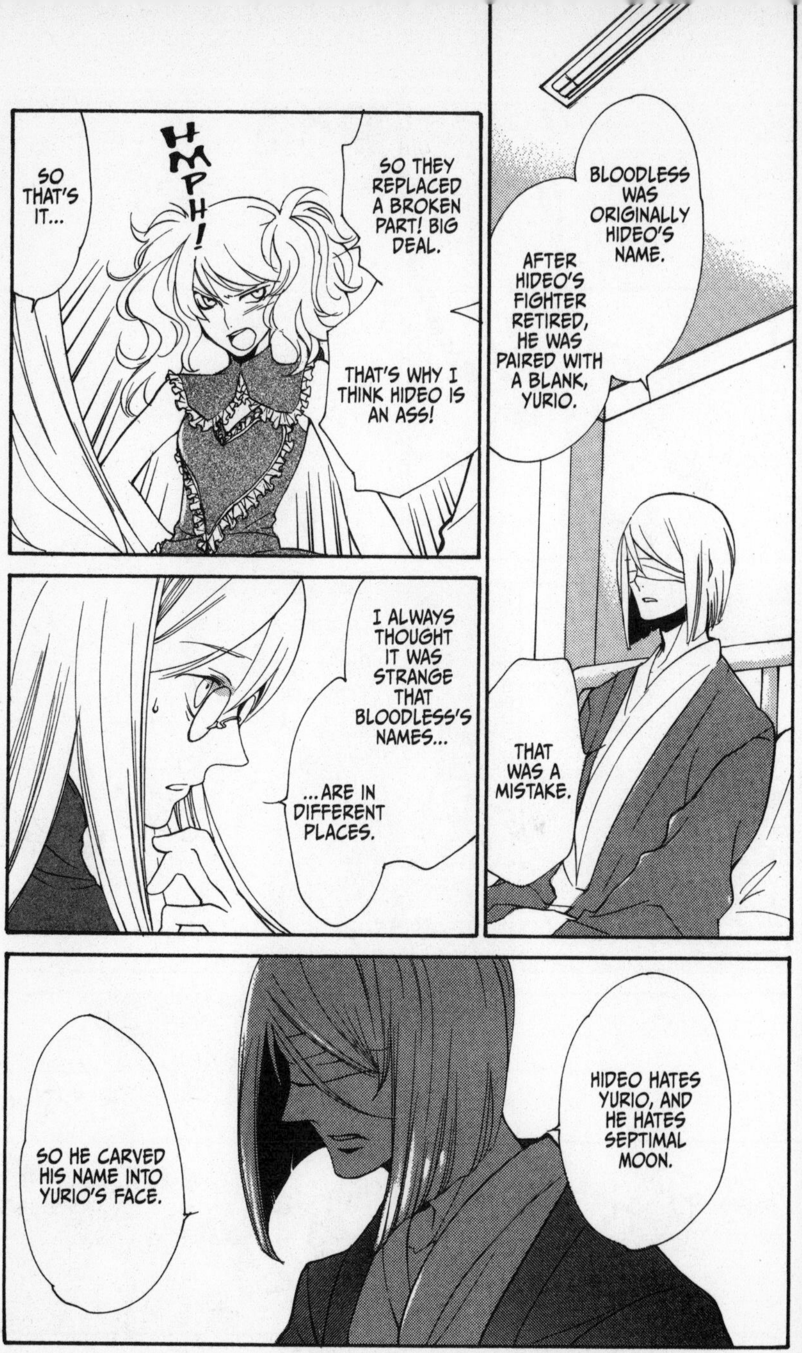
BLOODLESS WAS ORIGINALLY HIDEO'S NAME.
AFTER HIDEO'S FIGHTER RETIRED, HE WAS PAIRED WITH A BLANK, YURIO.
THAT WAS A MISTAKE.
HMPH!
SO THEY REPLACED A BROKEN PART! BIG DEAL.
THAT'S WHY I THINK HIDEO IS AN ASS!
SO THAT'S IT...
I ALWAYS THOUGHT IT WAS STRANGE THAT BLOODLESS'S NAMES...
...ARE IN DIFFERENT PLACES.
HIDEO HATES YURIO, AND HE HATES SEPTIMAL MOON.
SO HE CARVED HIS NAME INTO YURIO'S FACE.

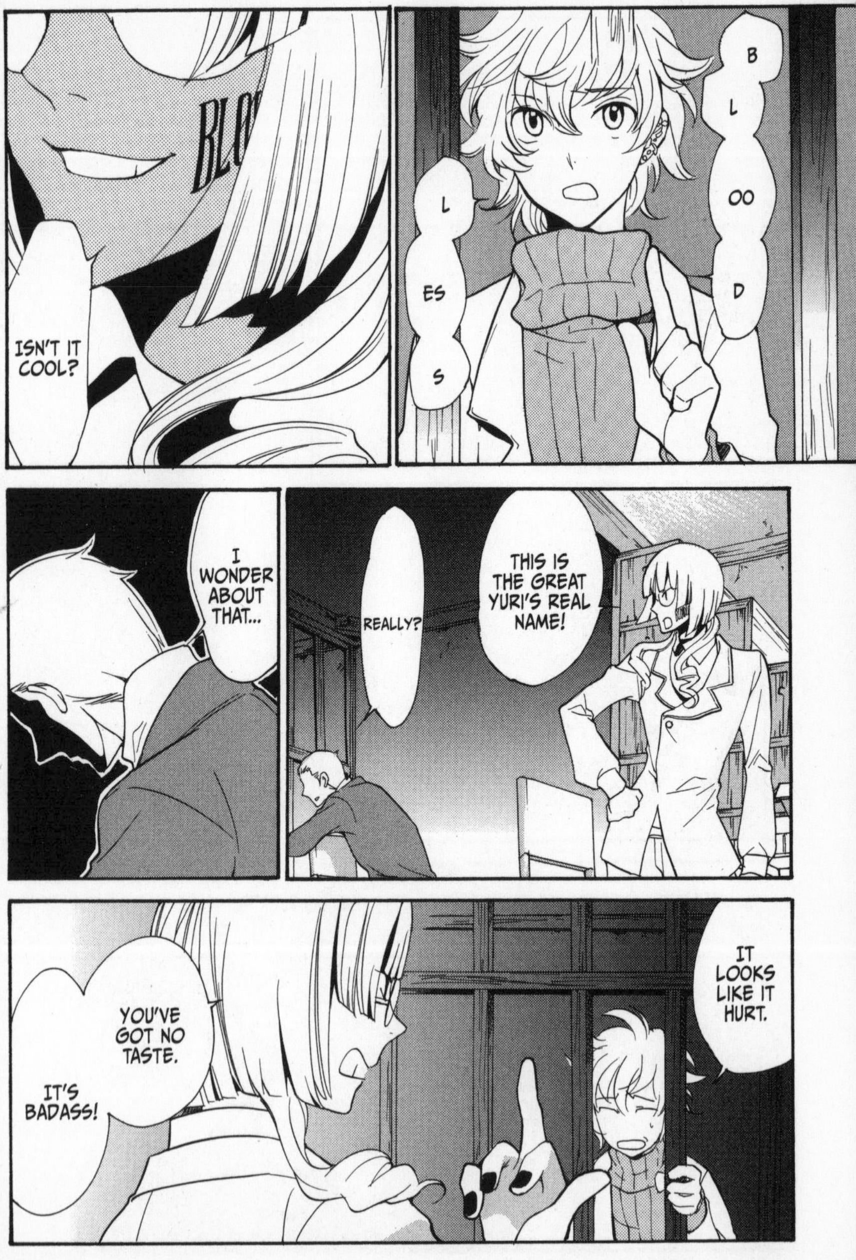
BLOOD
LESS
ISN'T IT COOL?
THIS IS THE GREAT YURI'S REAL NAME!
REALLY?
I WONDER ABOUT THAT...
IT LOOKS LIKE IT HURT.
YOU'VE GOT NO TASTE.
IT'S BADASS!

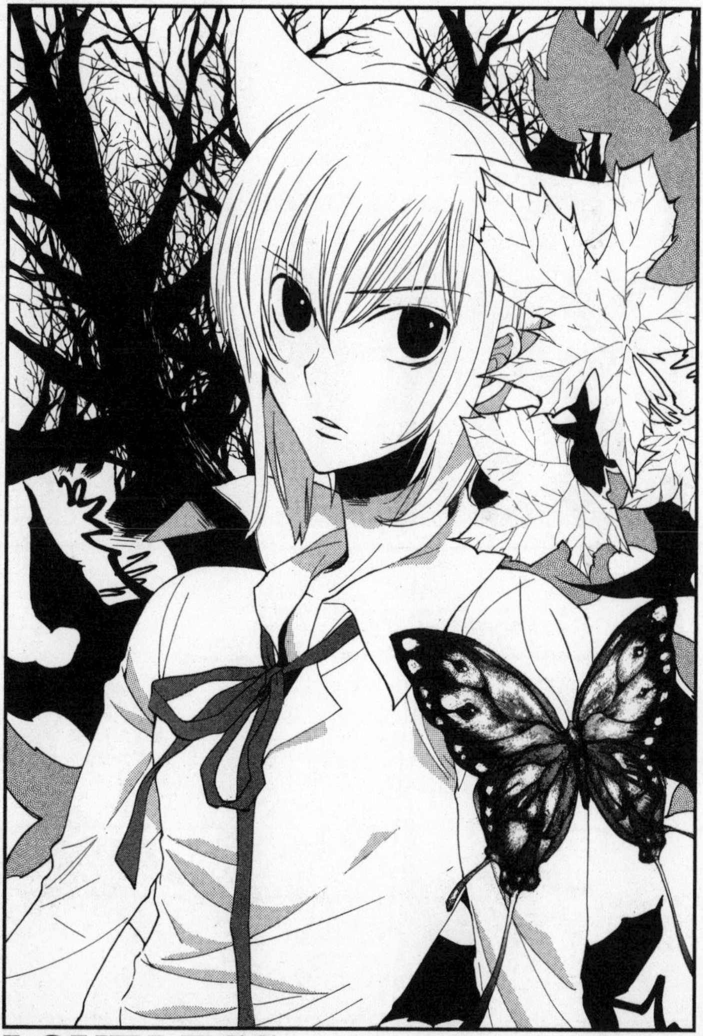

LOVELESS

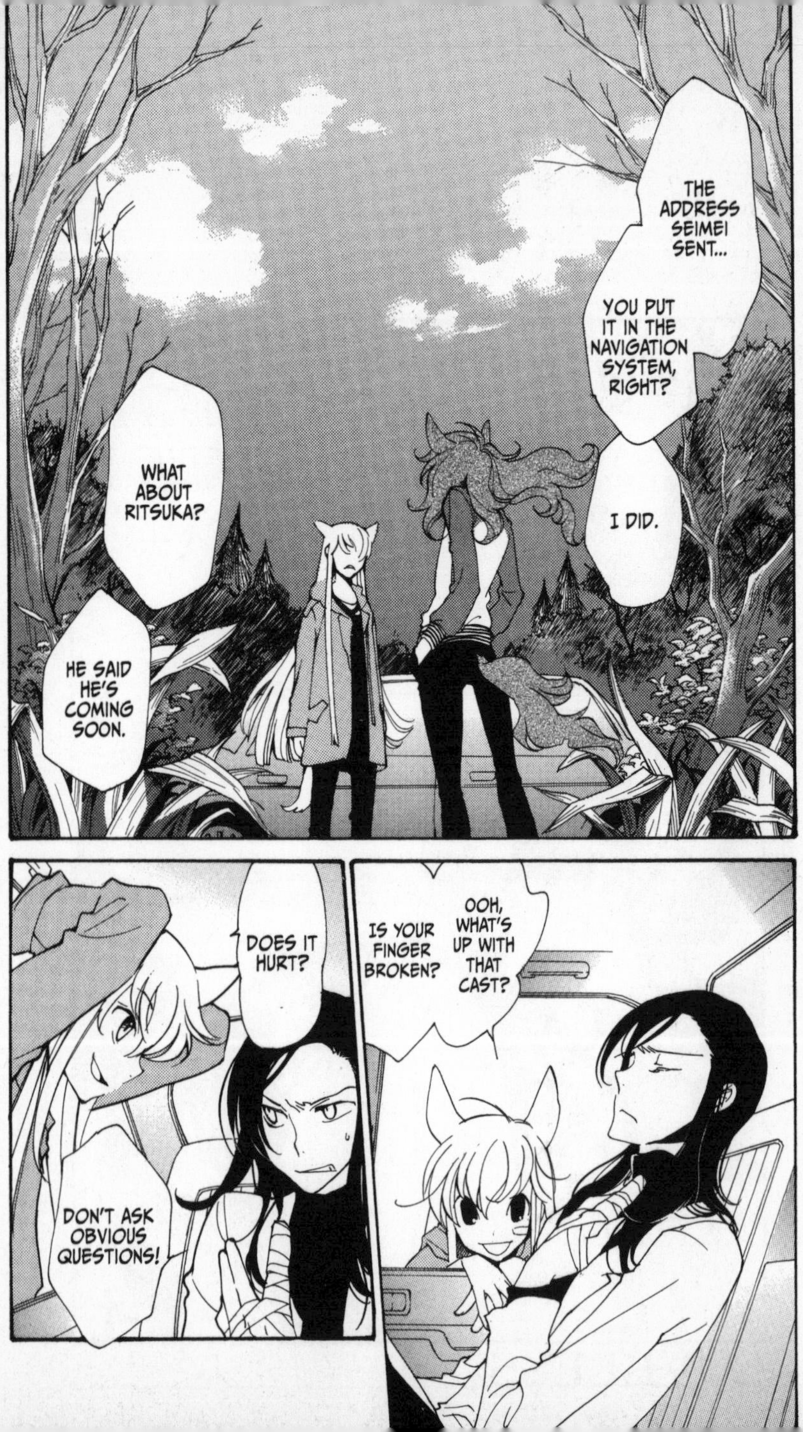
THE ADDRESS SEIMEI SENT...
YOU PUT IT IN THE NAVIGATION SYSTEM, RIGHT?
I DID.
WHAT ABOUT RITSUKA?
HE SAID HE'S COMING SOON.
OOH, WHAT'S UP WITH THAT CAST?
IS YOUR FINGER BROKEN?
DOES IT HURT?
DON'T ASK OBVIOUS QUESTIONS!

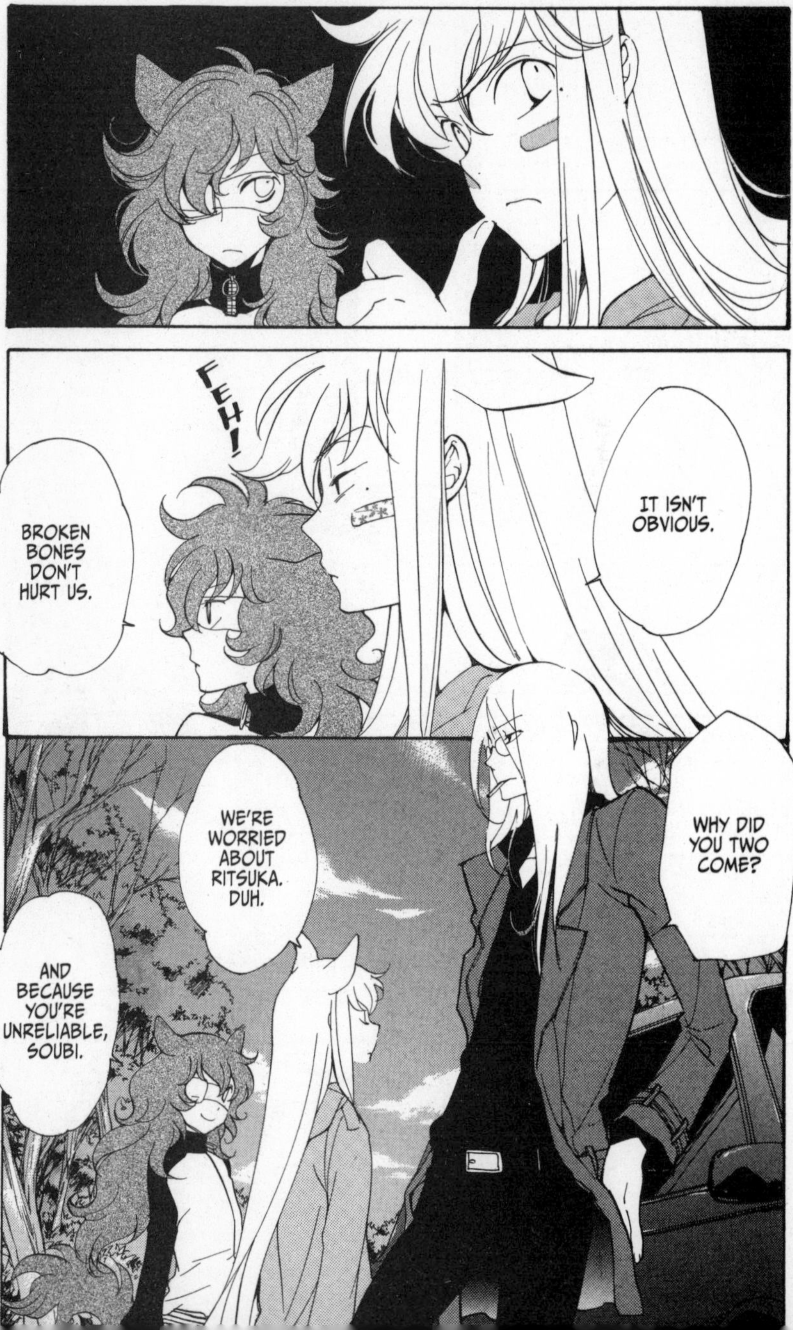
IT ISN'T OBVIOUS.
FEH!
BROKEN BONES DON'T HURT US.
WHY DID YOU TWO COME?
WE'RE WORRIED ABOUT RITSUKA. DUH.
AND BECAUSE YOU'RE UNRELIABLE, SOUBI.

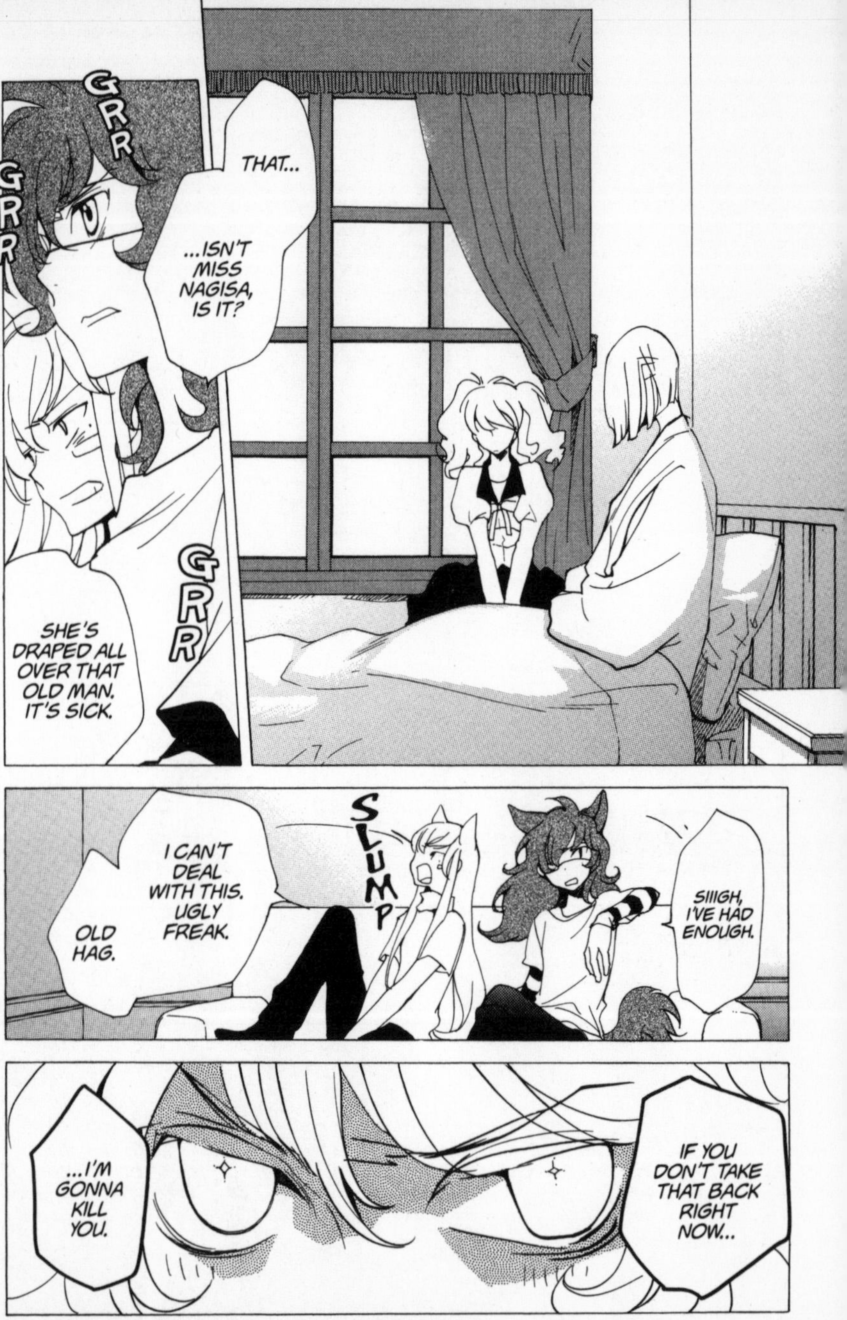
THAT...
...ISN'T MISS NAGISA, IS IT?
GRR
GRR
GRR
SHE'S DRAPED ALL OVER THAT OLD MAN. IT'S SICK.
SIIIGH, I'VE HAD ENOUGH.
SLUMP
I CAN'T DEAL WITH THIS. UGLY FREAK.
OLD HAG.
IF YOU DON'T TAKE THAT BACK RIGHT NOW...
...I'M GONNA KILL YOU.

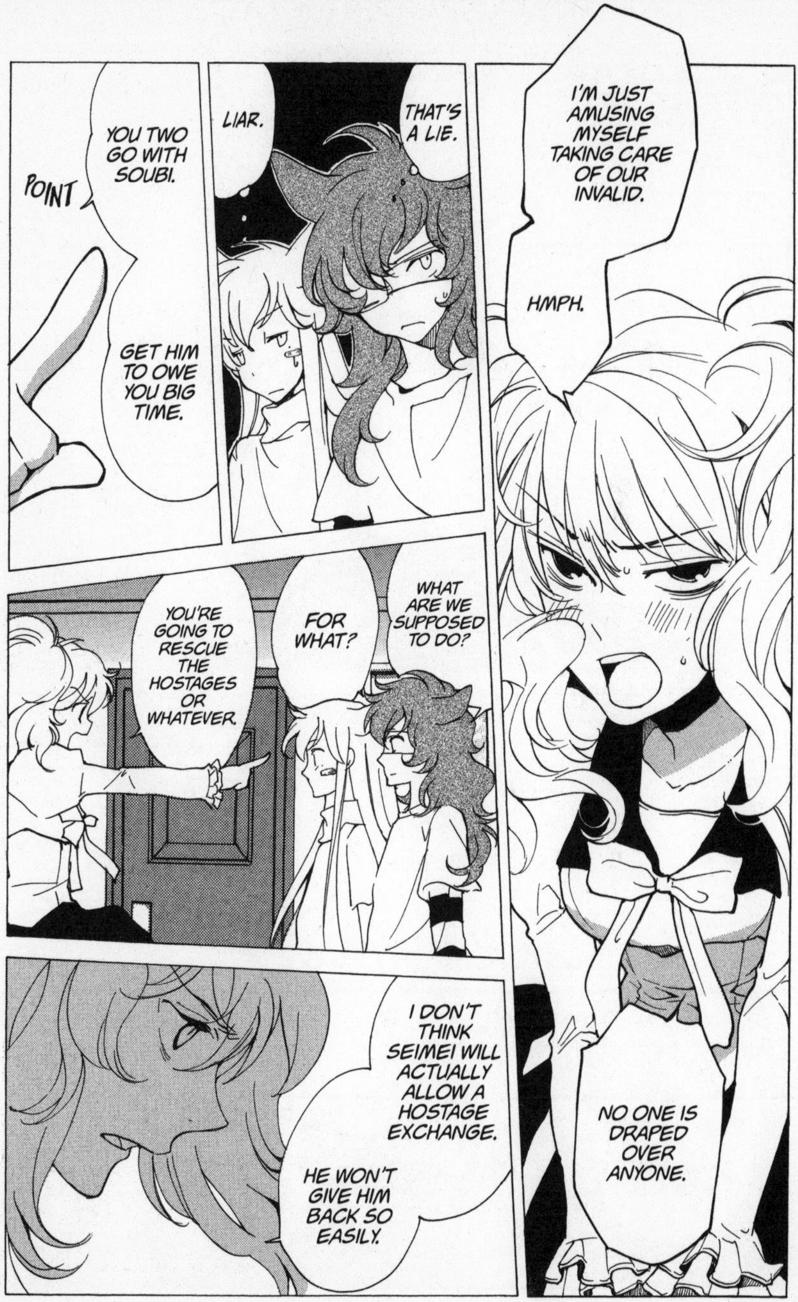
I'M JUST AMUSING MYSELF TAKING CARE OF OUR INVALID.
HMPH.
NO ONE IS DRAPED OVER ANYONE.
THAT'S A LIE.
LIAR.
YOU TWO GO WITH SOUBI.
POINT
GET HIM TO OWE YOU BIG TIME.
WHAT ARE WE SUPPOSED TO DO?
FOR WHAT?
YOU'RE GOING TO RESCUE THE HOSTAGES OR WHATEVER.
I DON'T THINK SEIMEI WILL ACTUALLY ALLOW A HOSTAGE EXCHANGE.
HE WON'T GIVE HIM BACK SO EASILY.

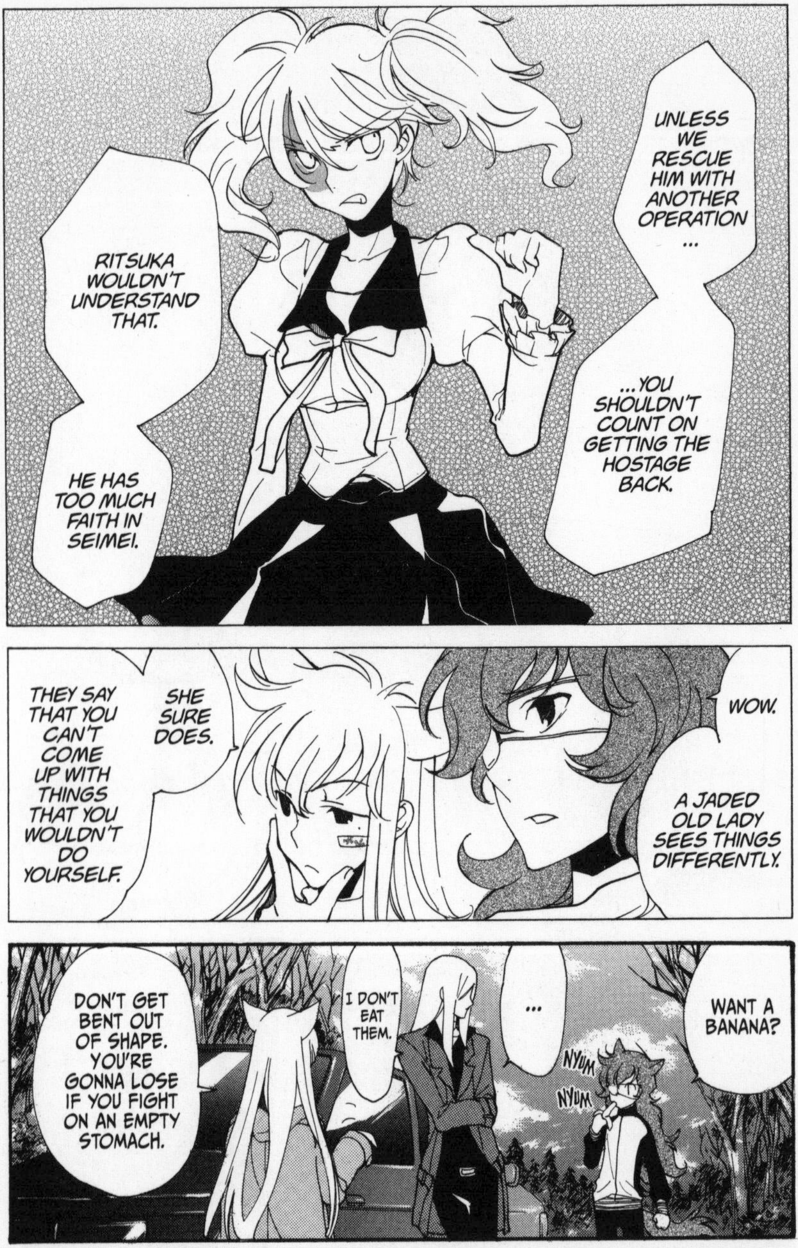
UNLESS WE RESCUE HIM WITH ANOTHER OPERATION ...
...YOU SHOULDN'T COUNT ON GETTING THE HOSTAGE BACK.
RITSUKA WOULDN'T UNDERSTAND THAT.
HE HAS TOO MUCH FAITH IN SEIMEI.
WOW.
A JADED OLD LADY SEES THINGS DIFFERENTLY.
SHE SURE DOES.
THEY SAY THAT YOU CAN'T COME UP WITH THINGS THAT YOU WOULDN'T DO YOURSELF.
WANT A BANANA?
NYUM
NYUM
...
I DON'T EAT THEM.
DON'T GET BENT OUT OF SHAPE. YOU'RE GONNA LOSE IF YOU FIGHT ON AN EMPTY STOMACH.

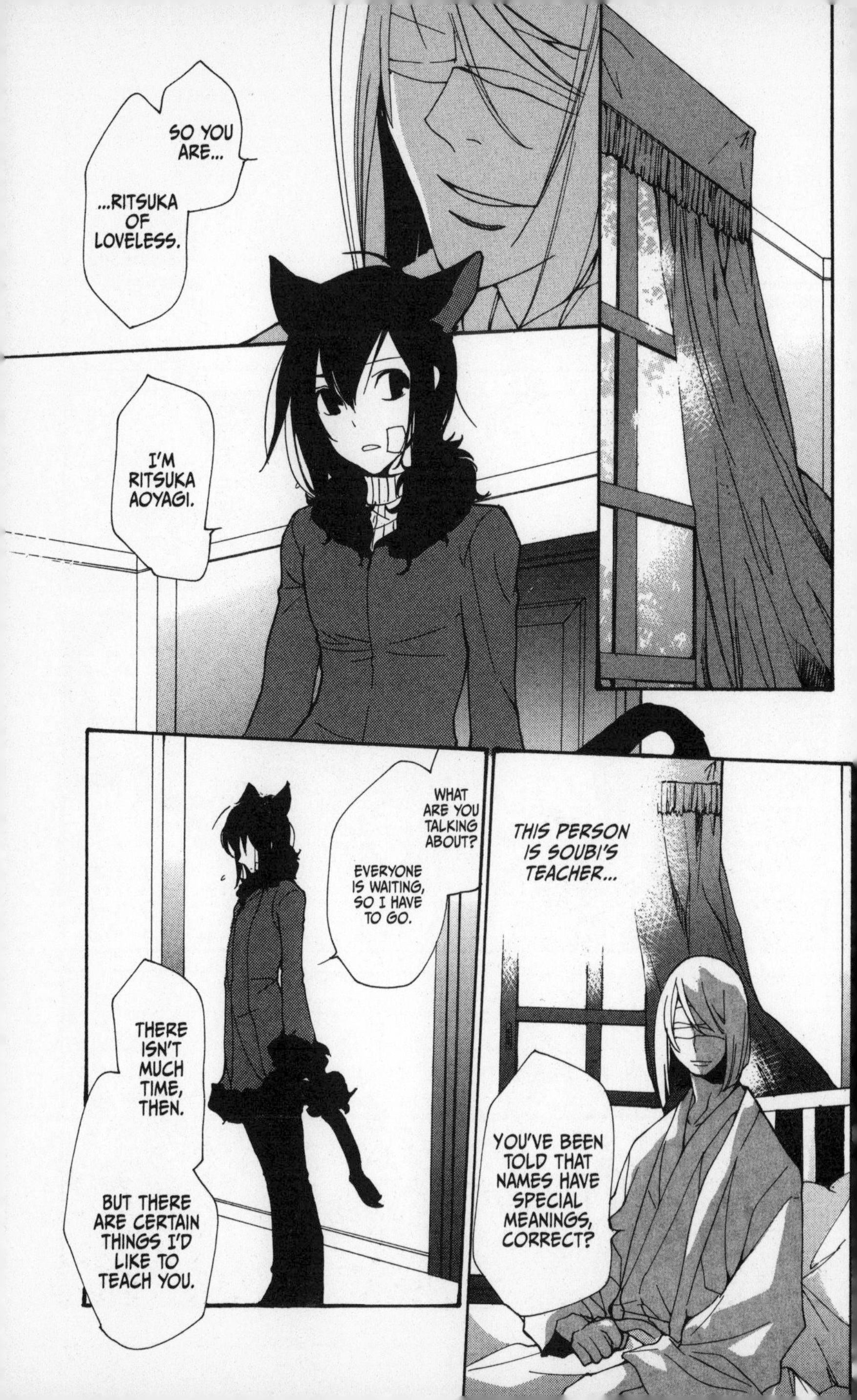
SO YOU ARE...
...RITSUKA OF LOVELESS.
I'M RITSUKA AOYAGI.
THIS PERSON IS SOUBI'S TEACHER...
YOU'VE BEEN TOLD THAT NAMES HAVE SPECIAL MEANINGS, CORRECT?
WHAT ARE YOU TALKING ABOUT?
EVERYONE IS WAITING, SO I HAVE TO GO.
THERE ISN'T MUCH TIME, THEN.
BUT THERE ARE CERTAIN THINGS I'D LIKE TO TEACH YOU.

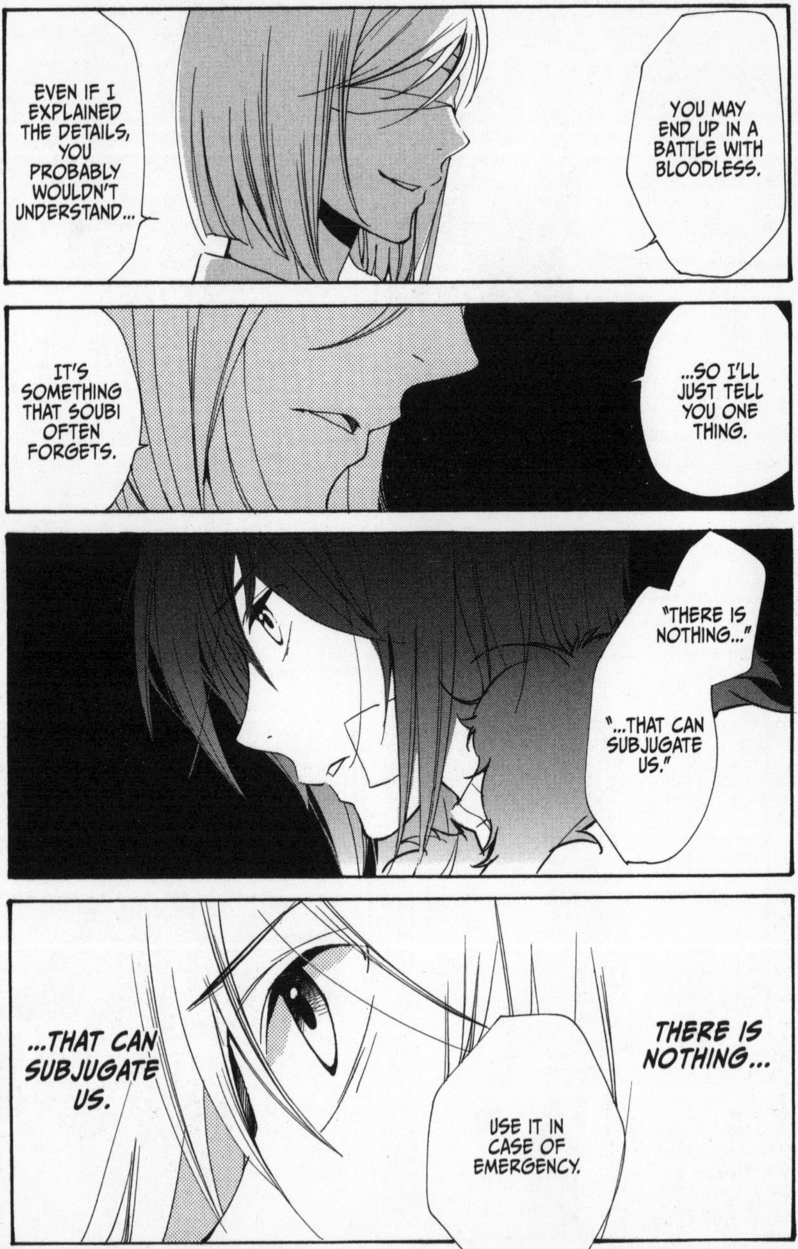

YOU MAY END UP IN A BATTLE WITH BLOODLESS.
EVEN IF I EXPLAINED THE DETAILS, YOU PROBABLY WOULDN'T UNDERSTAND...
...SO I'LL JUST TELL YOU ONE THING.
IT'S SOMETHING THAT SOUBI OFTEN FORGETS.
"THERE IS NOTHING..."
"...THAT CAN SUBJUGATE US."
THERE IS NOTHING...
...THAT CAN SUBJUGATE US.
USE IT IN CASE OF EMERGENCY.

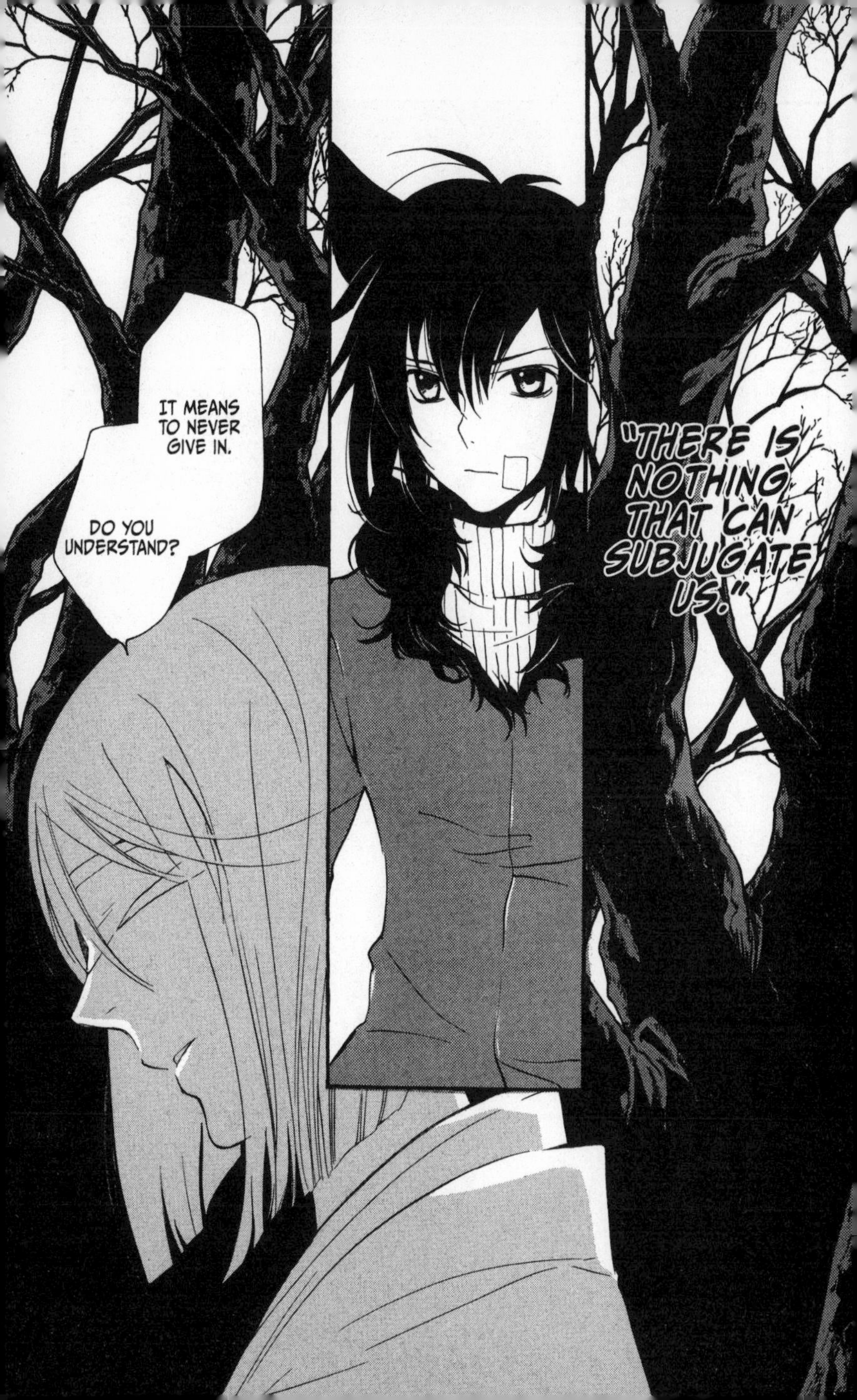
"THERE IS NOTHING THAT CAN SUBJUGATE US."
IT MEANS TO NEVER GIVE IN.
DO YOU UNDERSTAND?

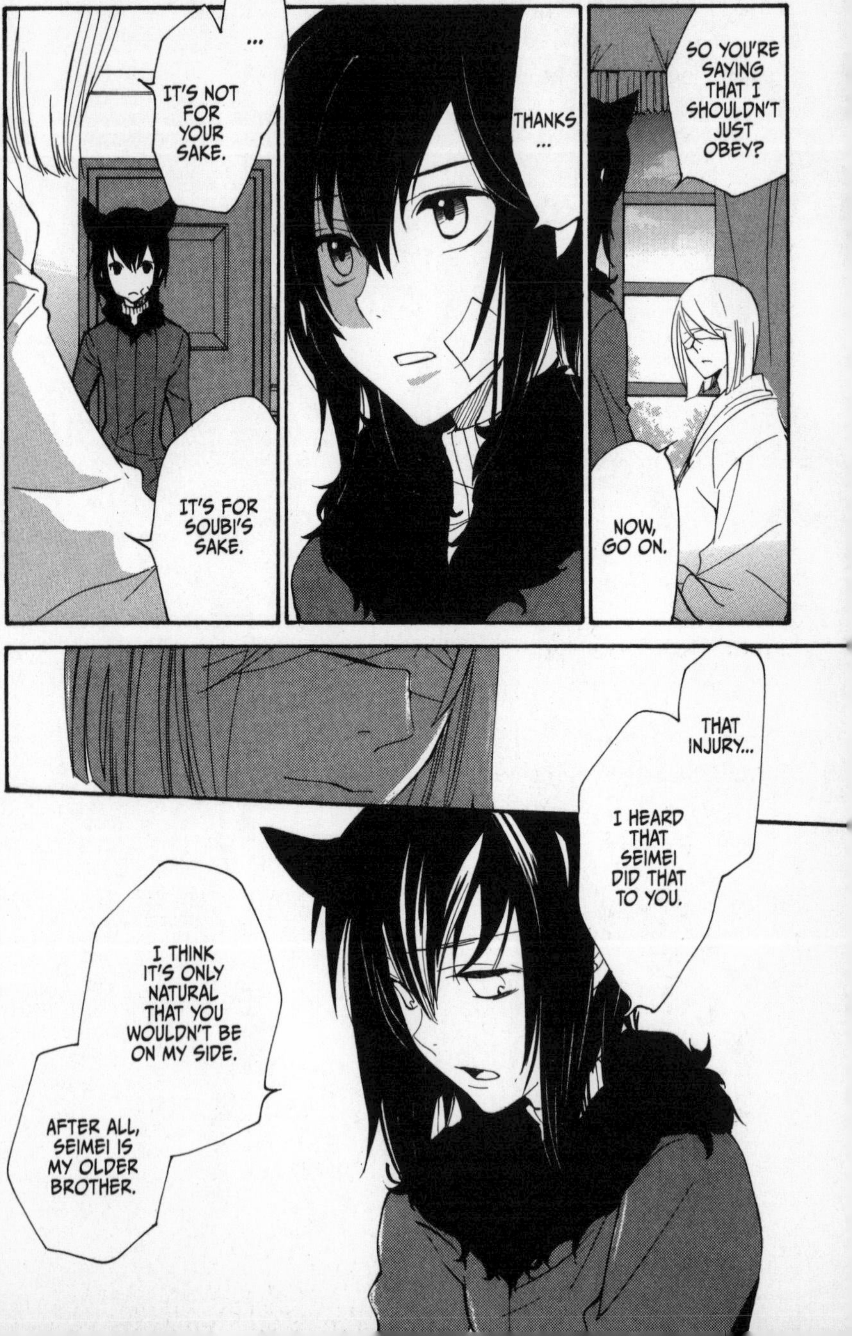
SO YOU'RE SAYING THAT I SHOULDN'T JUST OBEY?
NOW, GO ON.
THANKS...
...
IT'S NOT FOR YOUR SAKE.
IT'S FOR SOUBI'S SAKE.
THAT INJURY...
I HEARD THAT SEIMEI DID THAT TO YOU.
I THINK IT'S ONLY NATURAL THAT YOU WOULDN'T BE ON MY SIDE.
AFTER ALL, SEIMEI IS MY OLDER BROTHER.

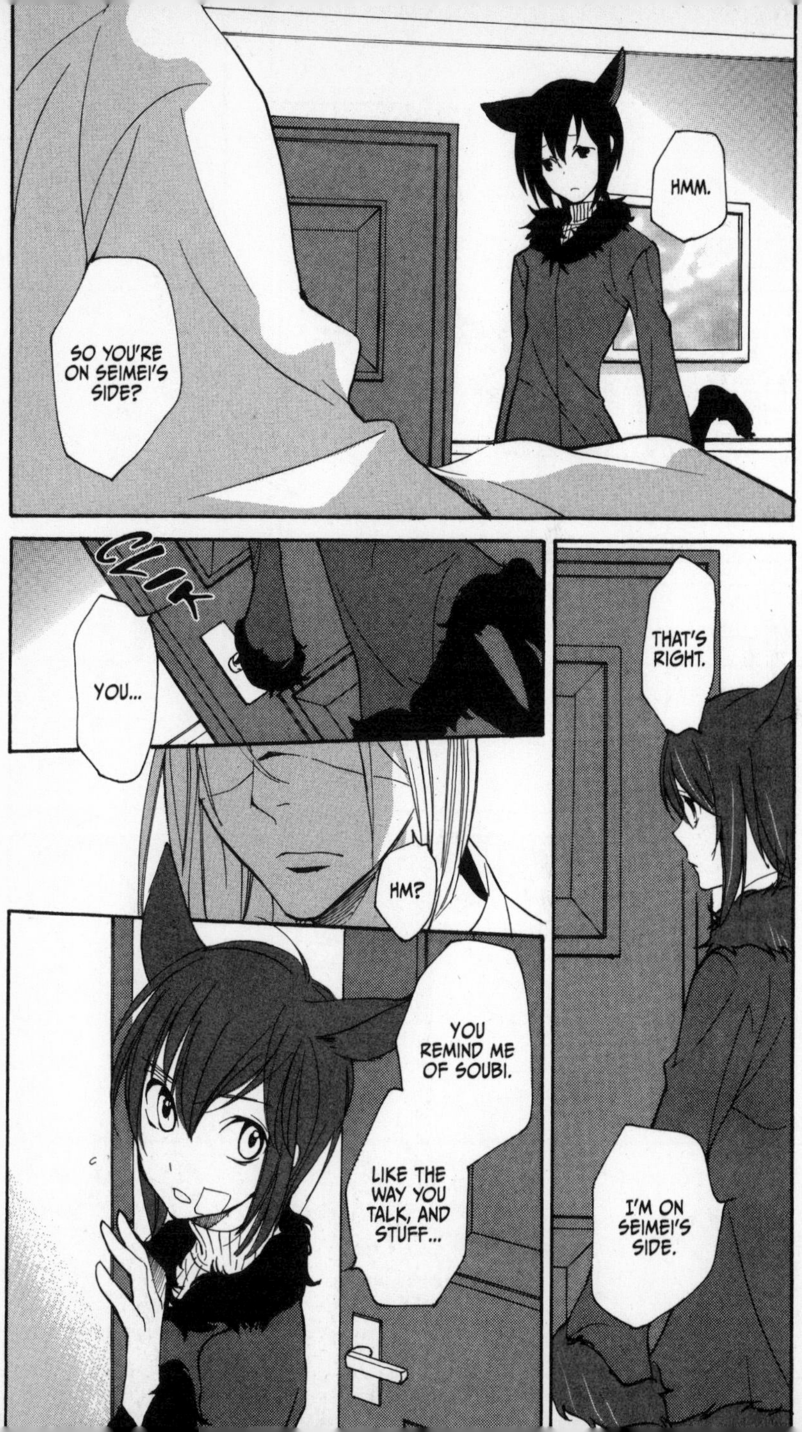
HMM.
SO YOU'RE ON SEIMEI'S SIDE?
THAT'S RIGHT.
I'M ON SEIMEI'S SIDE.
CLIK
YOU...
HM?
YOU REMIND ME OF SOUBI.
LIKE THE WAY YOU TALK, AND STUFF...

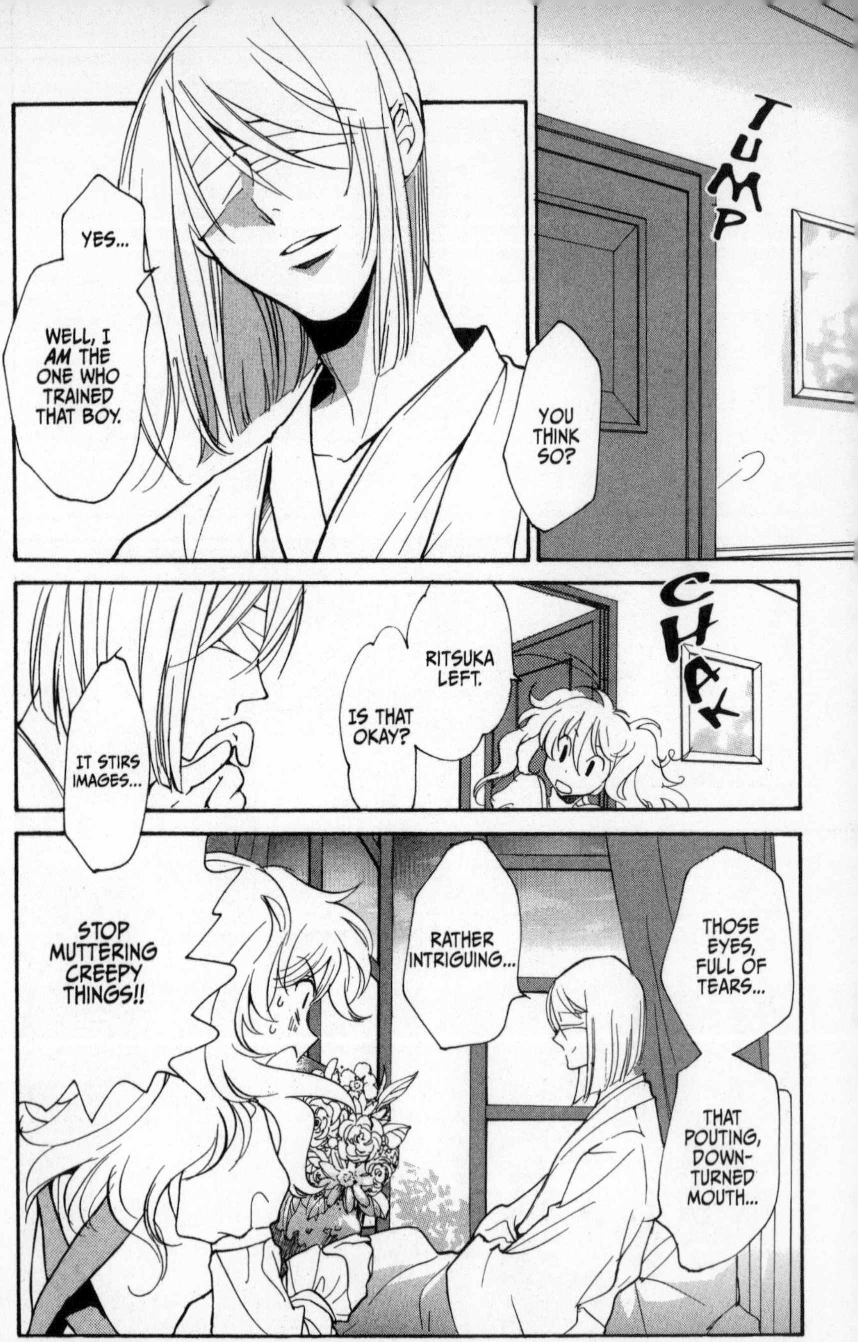
TUMP
YOU THINK SO?
YES...
WELL, I *AM* THE ONE WHO TRAINED THAT BOY.
CHAK
RITSUKA LEFT.
IS THAT OKAY?
IT STIRS IMAGES...
THOSE EYES, FULL OF TEARS...
THAT POUTING, DOWN-TURNED MOUTH...
RATHER INTRIGUING...
STOP MUTTERING CREEPY THINGS!!

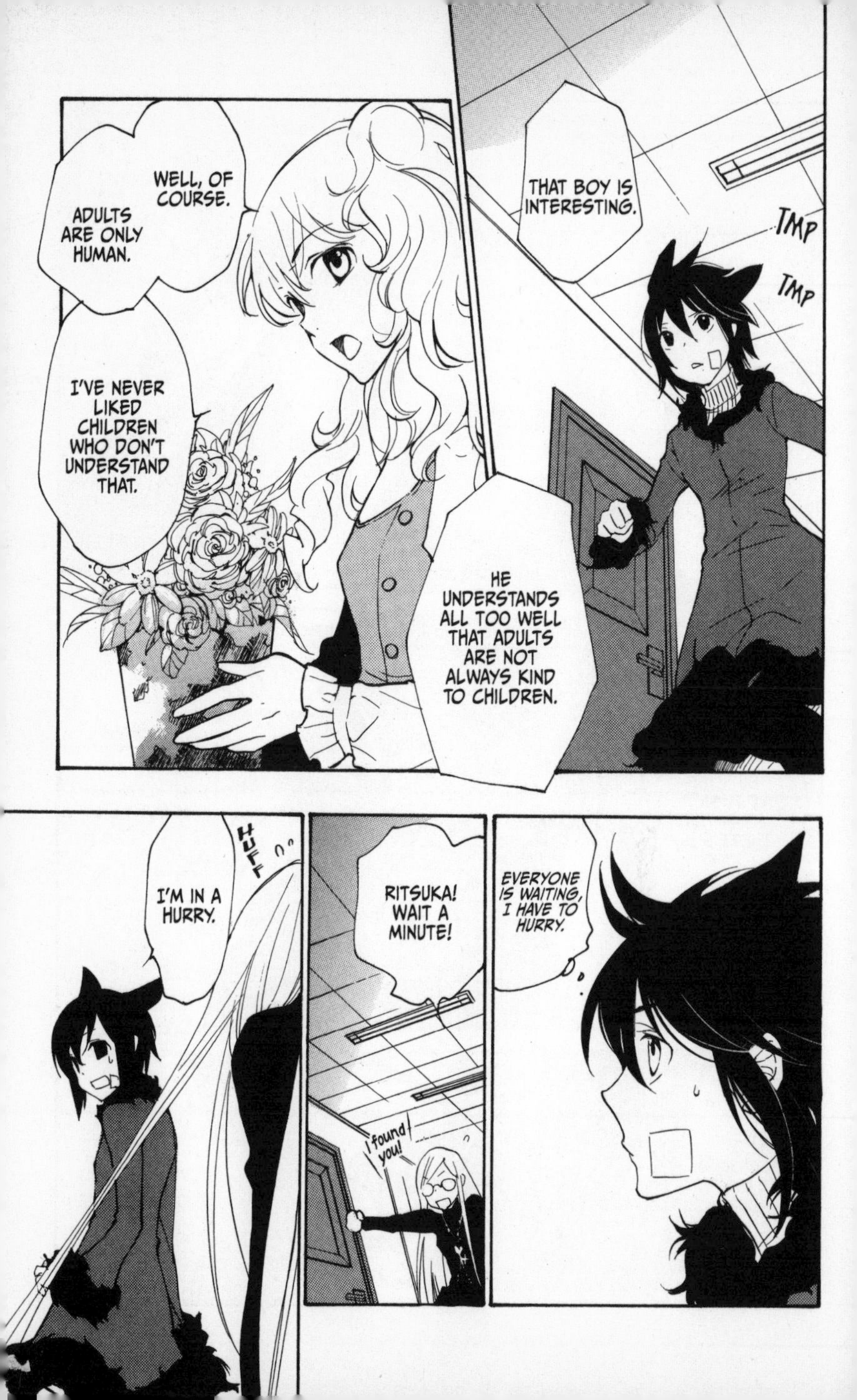
THAT BOY IS INTERESTING.
TMP
TMP
HE UNDERSTANDS ALL TOO WELL THAT ADULTS ARE NOT ALWAYS KIND TO CHILDREN.
WELL, OF COURSE.
ADULTS ARE ONLY HUMAN.
I'VE NEVER LIKED CHILDREN WHO DON'T UNDERSTAND THAT.
EVERYONE IS WAITING, I HAVE TO HURRY.
RITSUKA! WAIT A MINUTE!
I found you!
I'M IN A HURRY.
HUFF

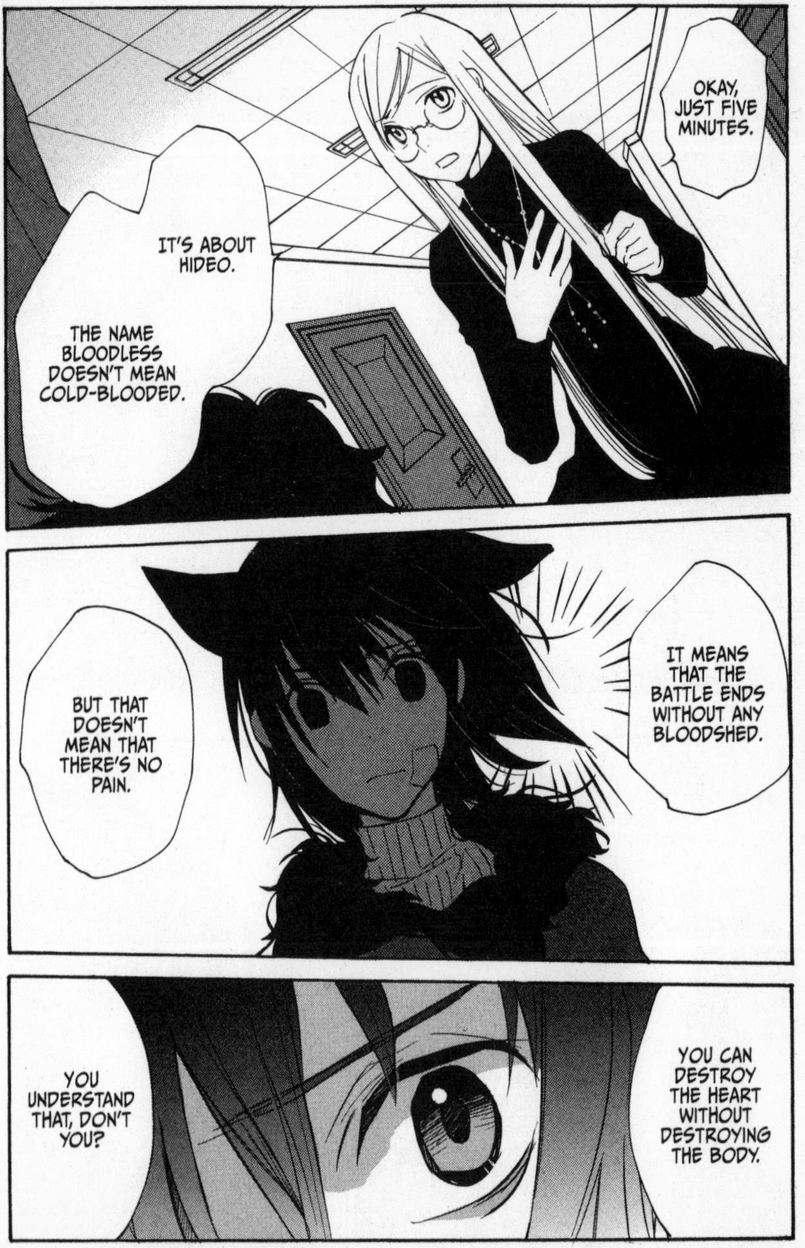
OKAY, JUST FIVE MINUTES.
IT'S ABOUT HIDEO.
THE NAME BLOODLESS DOESN'T MEAN COLD-BLOODED.
IT MEANS THAT THE BATTLE ENDS WITHOUT ANY BLOODSHED.
BUT THAT DOESN'T MEAN THAT THERE'S NO PAIN.
YOU CAN DESTROY THE HEART WITHOUT DESTROYING THE BODY.
YOU UNDERSTAND THAT, DON'T YOU?

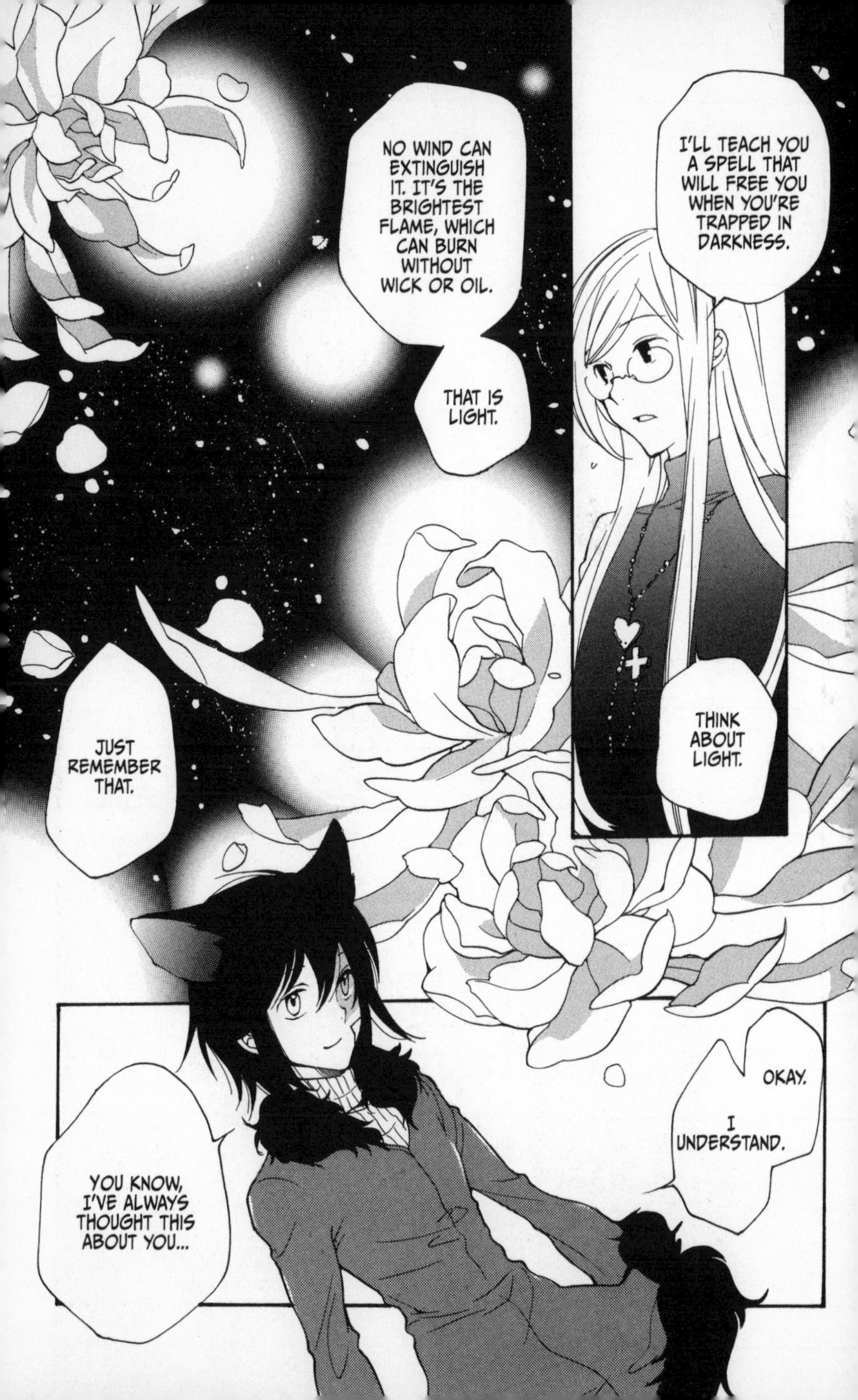
I'LL TEACH YOU A SPELL THAT WILL FREE YOU WHEN YOU'RE TRAPPED IN DARKNESS.
NO WIND CAN EXTINGUISH IT. IT'S THE BRIGHTEST FLAME, WHICH CAN BURN WITHOUT WICK OR OIL.
THAT IS LIGHT.
THINK ABOUT LIGHT.
JUST REMEMBER THAT.
OKAY.
I UNDERSTAND.
YOU KNOW, I'VE ALWAYS THOUGHT THIS ABOUT YOU...

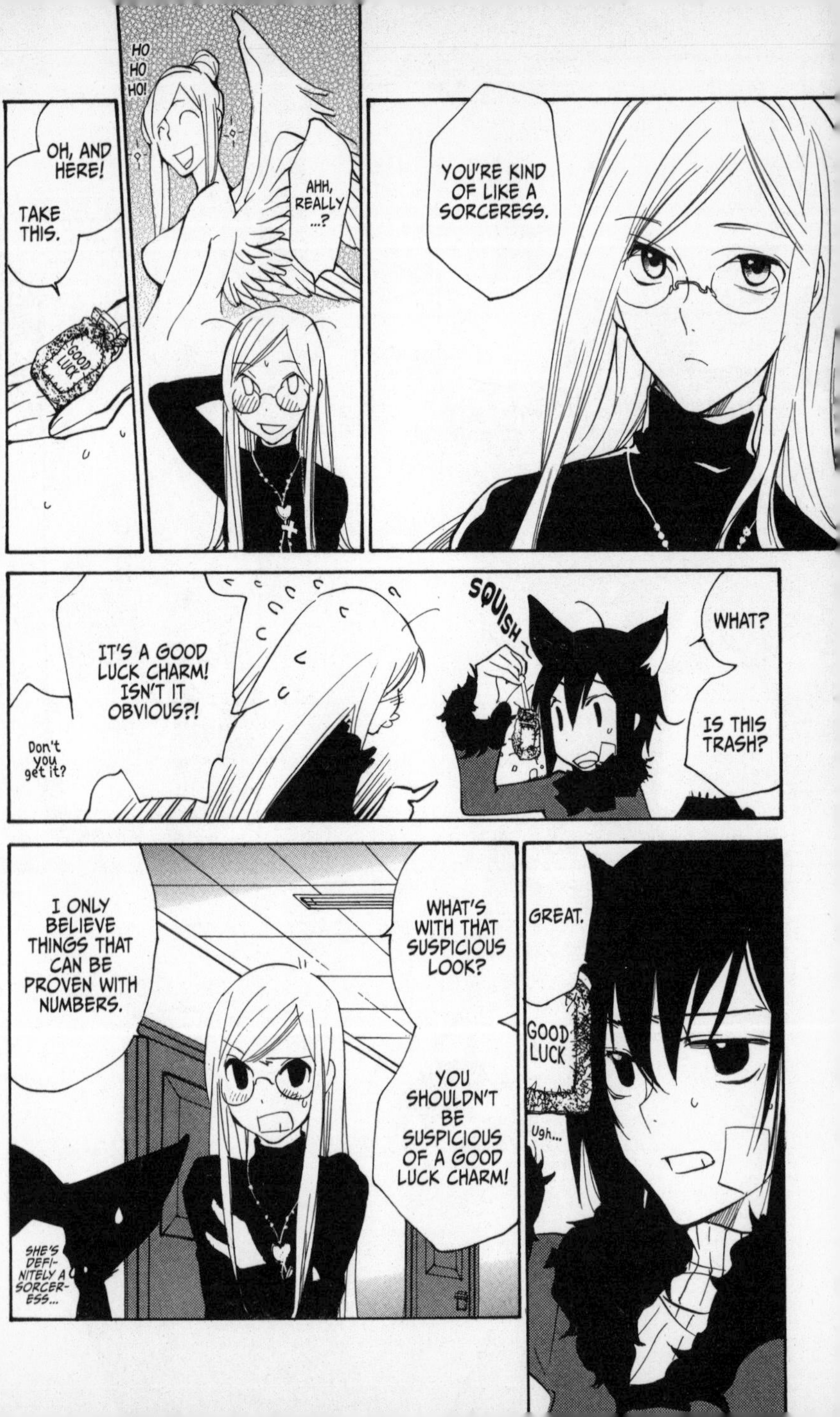
YOU'RE KIND OF LIKE A SORCERESS.
HO HO HO!
AHH, REALLY ...?
OH, AND HERE!
TAKE THIS.
GOOD LUCK
WHAT?
IS THIS TRASH?
SQUISH
IT'S A GOOD LUCK CHARM! ISN'T IT OBVIOUS?!
Don't you get it?
GREAT.
GOOD LUCK
Ugh...
WHAT'S WITH THAT SUSPICIOUS LOOK?
YOU SHOULDN'T BE SUSPICIOUS OF A GOOD LUCK CHARM!
I ONLY BELIEVE THINGS THAT CAN BE PROVEN WITH NUMBERS.
SHE'S DEFI-NITELY A SORCER-ESS...

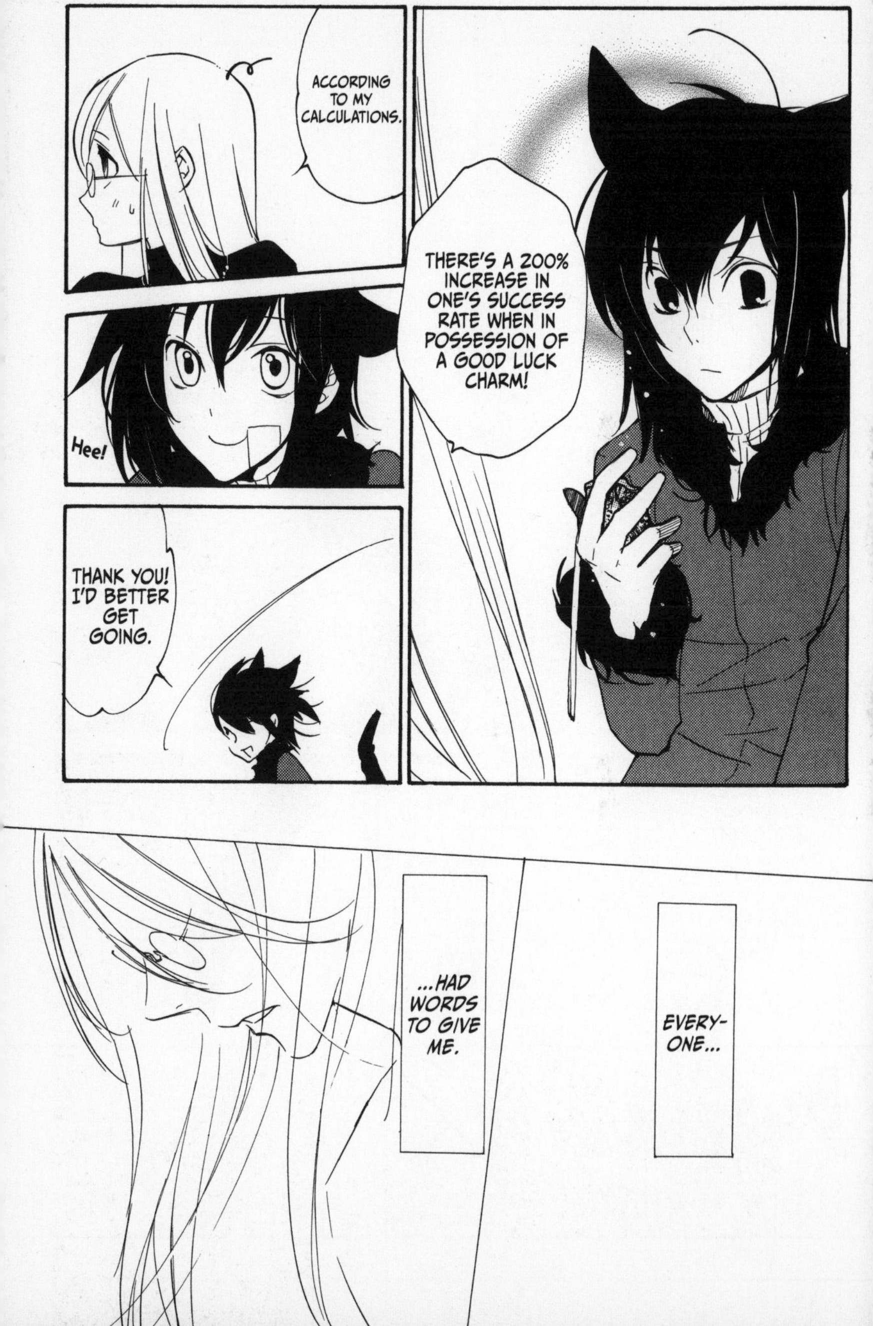
THERE'S A 200% INCREASE IN ONE'S SUCCESS RATE WHEN IN POSSESSION OF A GOOD LUCK CHARM!
ACCORDING TO MY CALCULATIONS.
Hee!
THANK YOU! I'D BETTER GET GOING.
EVERY-ONE...
...HAD WORDS TO GIVE ME.

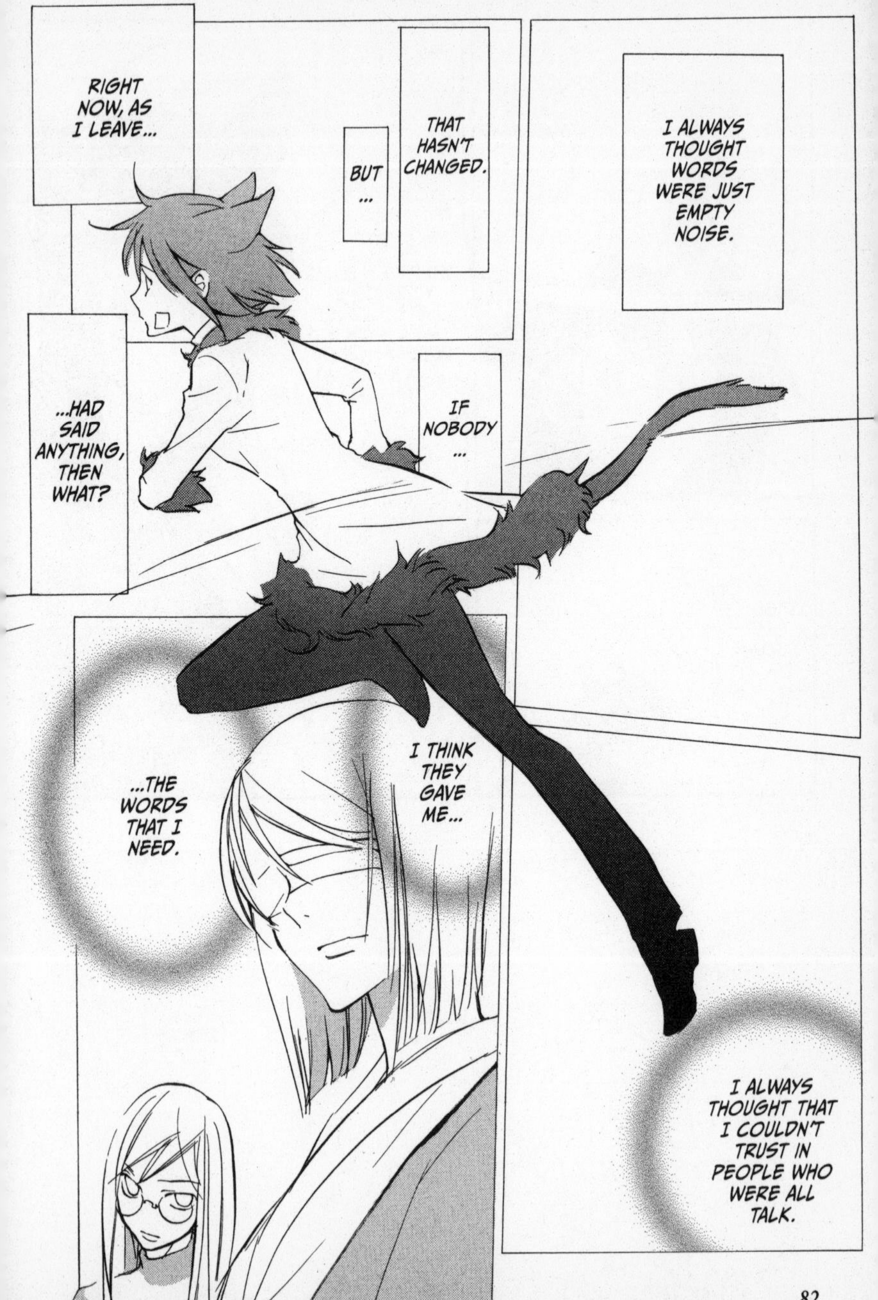
I ALWAYS THOUGHT WORDS WERE JUST EMPTY NOISE.
THAT HASN'T CHANGED.
BUT ...
RIGHT NOW, AS I LEAVE...
IF NOBODY ...
...HAD SAID ANYTHING, THEN WHAT?
I ALWAYS THOUGHT THAT I COULDN'T TRUST IN PEOPLE WHO WERE ALL TALK.
I THINK THEY GAVE ME...
...THE WORDS THAT I NEED.

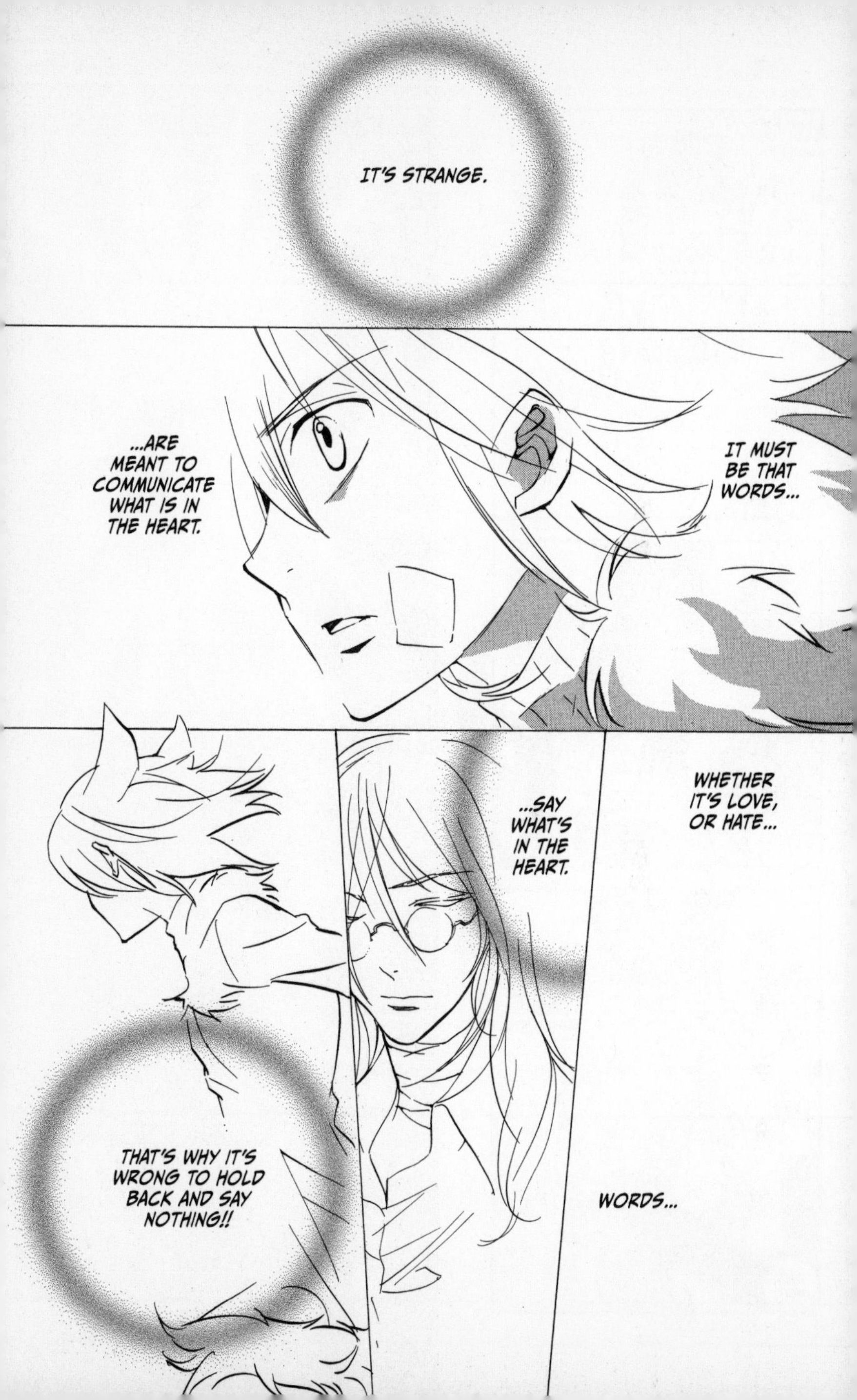
IT'S STRANGE.
IT MUST BE THAT WORDS...
...ARE MEANT TO COMMUNICATE WHAT IS IN THE HEART.
WHETHER IT'S LOVE, OR HATE...
WORDS...
...SAY WHAT'S IN THE HEART.
THAT'S WHY IT'S WRONG TO HOLD BACK AND SAY NOTHING!!

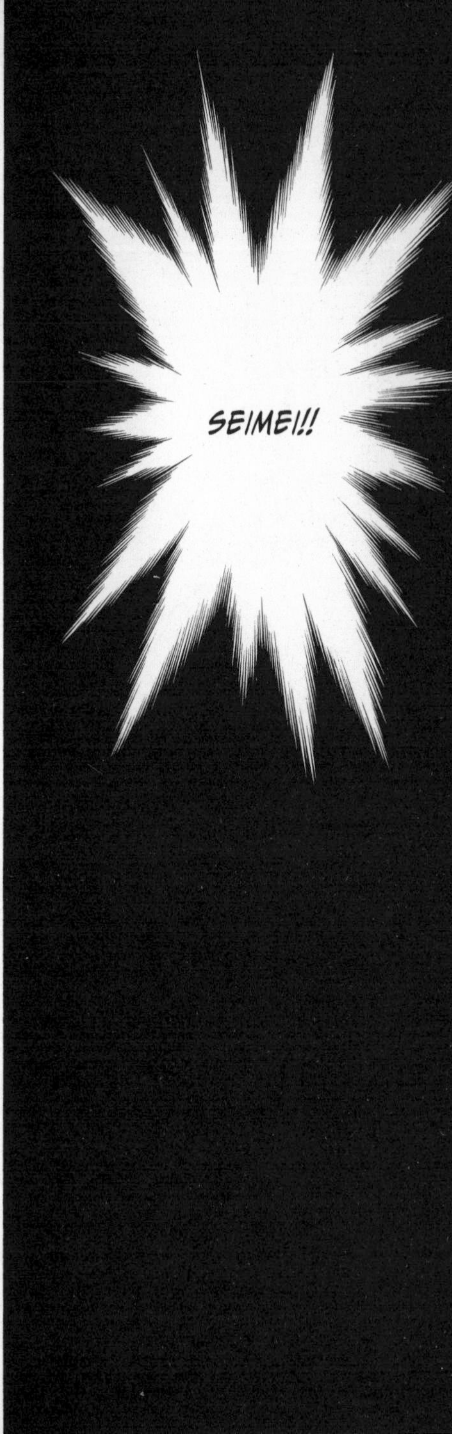
SEIMEI!!

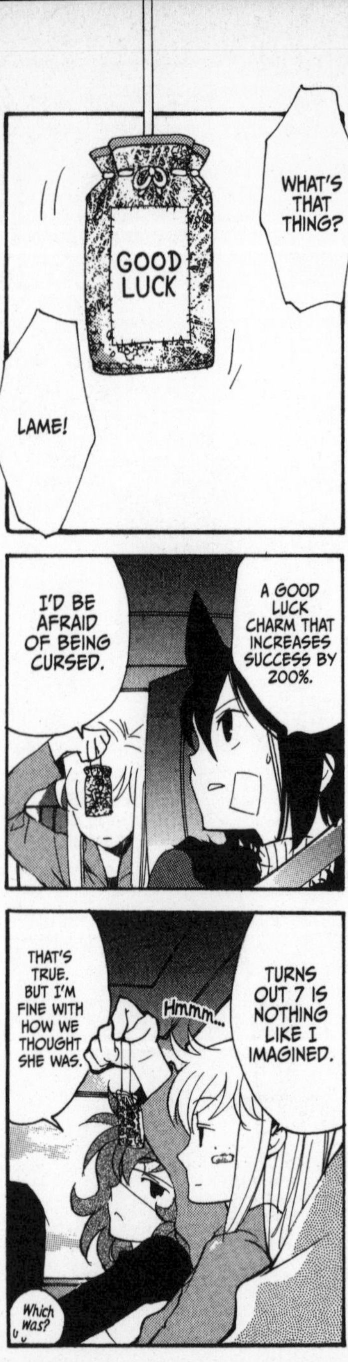
WHAT'S THAT THING?
GOOD LUCK
LAME!
A GOOD LUCK CHARM THAT INCREASES SUCCESS BY 200%.
I'D BE AFRAID OF BEING CURSED.
TURNS OUT 7 IS NOTHING LIKE I IMAGINED.
Hmmm...
THAT'S TRUE. BUT I'M FINE WITH HOW WE THOUGHT SHE WAS.
Which was?

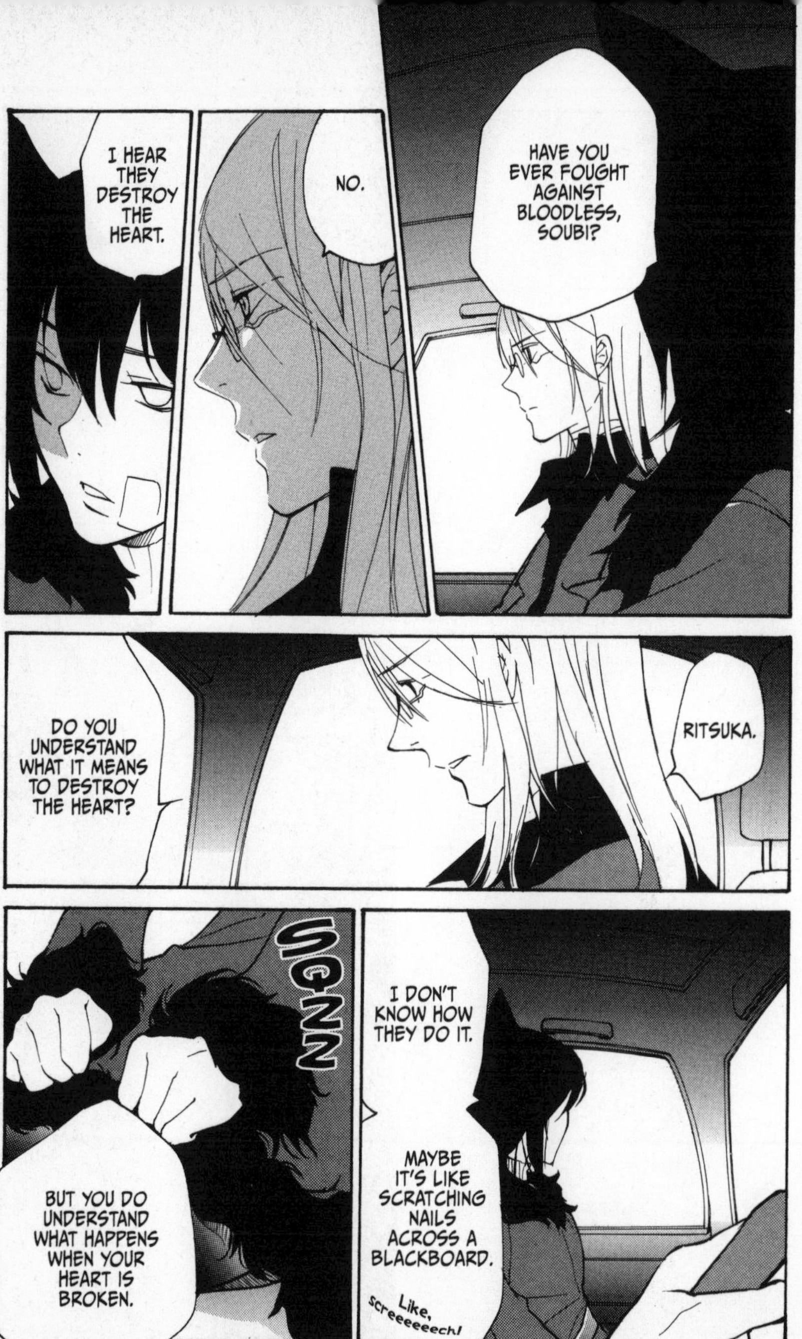
HAVE YOU EVER FOUGHT AGAINST BLOODLESS, SOUBI?
NO.
I HEAR THEY DESTROY THE HEART.
RITSUKA.
DO YOU UNDERSTAND WHAT IT MEANS TO DESTROY THE HEART?
I DON'T KNOW HOW THEY DO IT.
MAYBE IT'S LIKE SCRATCHING NAILS ACROSS A BLACKBOARD.
Like, Screeeeeeech!
SQZZ
BUT YOU DO UNDERSTAND WHAT HAPPENS WHEN YOUR HEART IS BROKEN.

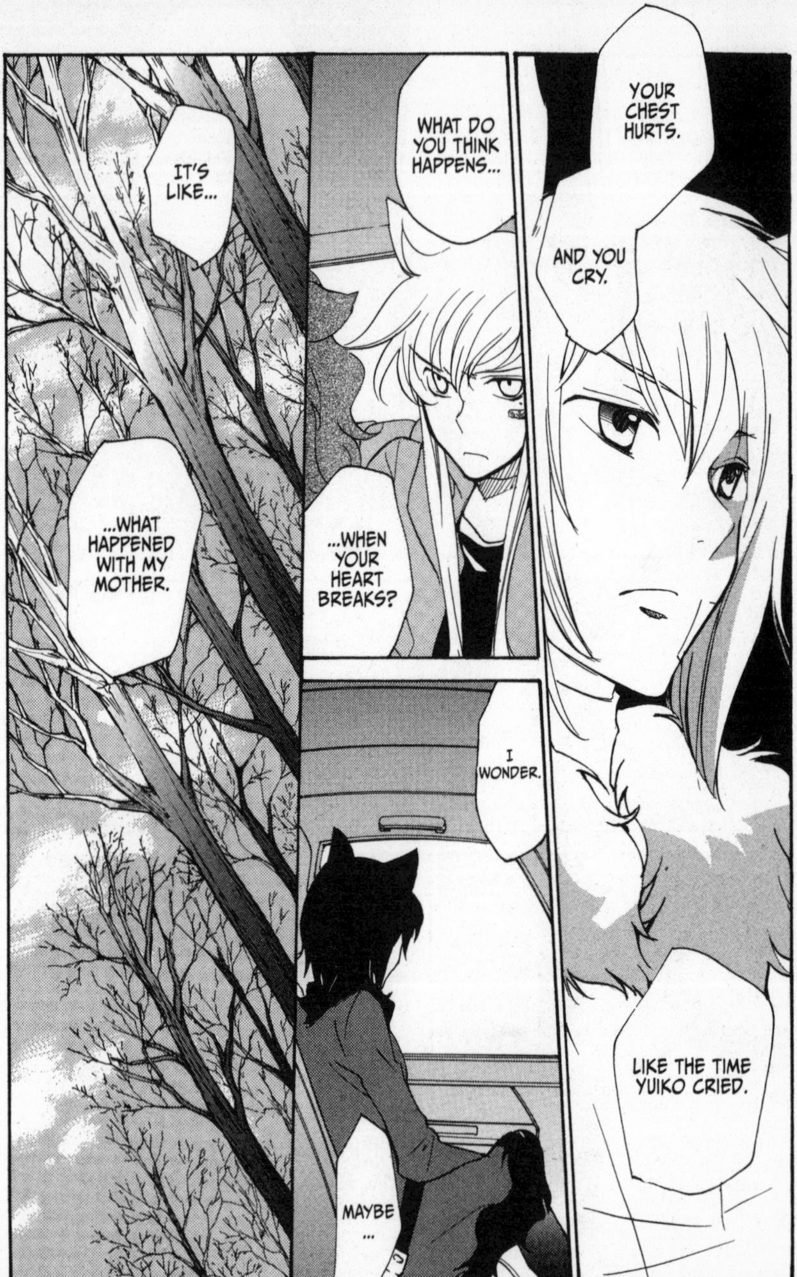
YOUR CHEST HURTS.
AND YOU CRY.
LIKE THE TIME YUIKO CRIED.
WHAT DO YOU THINK HAPPENS...
...WHEN YOUR HEART BREAKS?
I WONDER.
MAYBE ...
IT'S LIKE...
...WHAT HAPPENED WITH MY MOTHER.

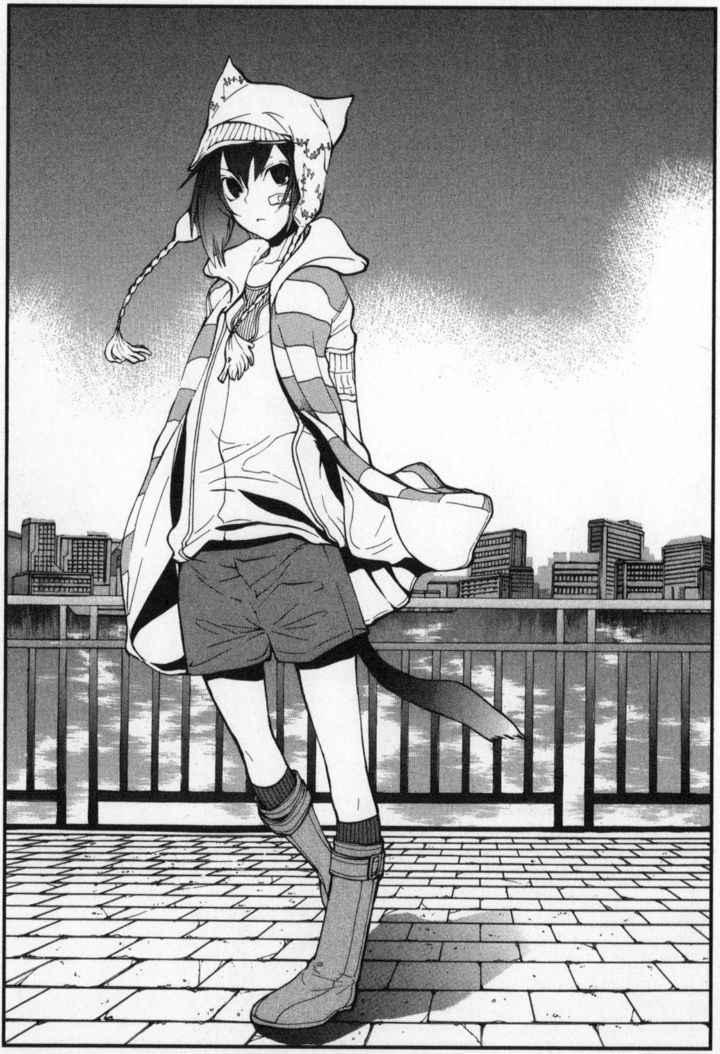

LOVELESS

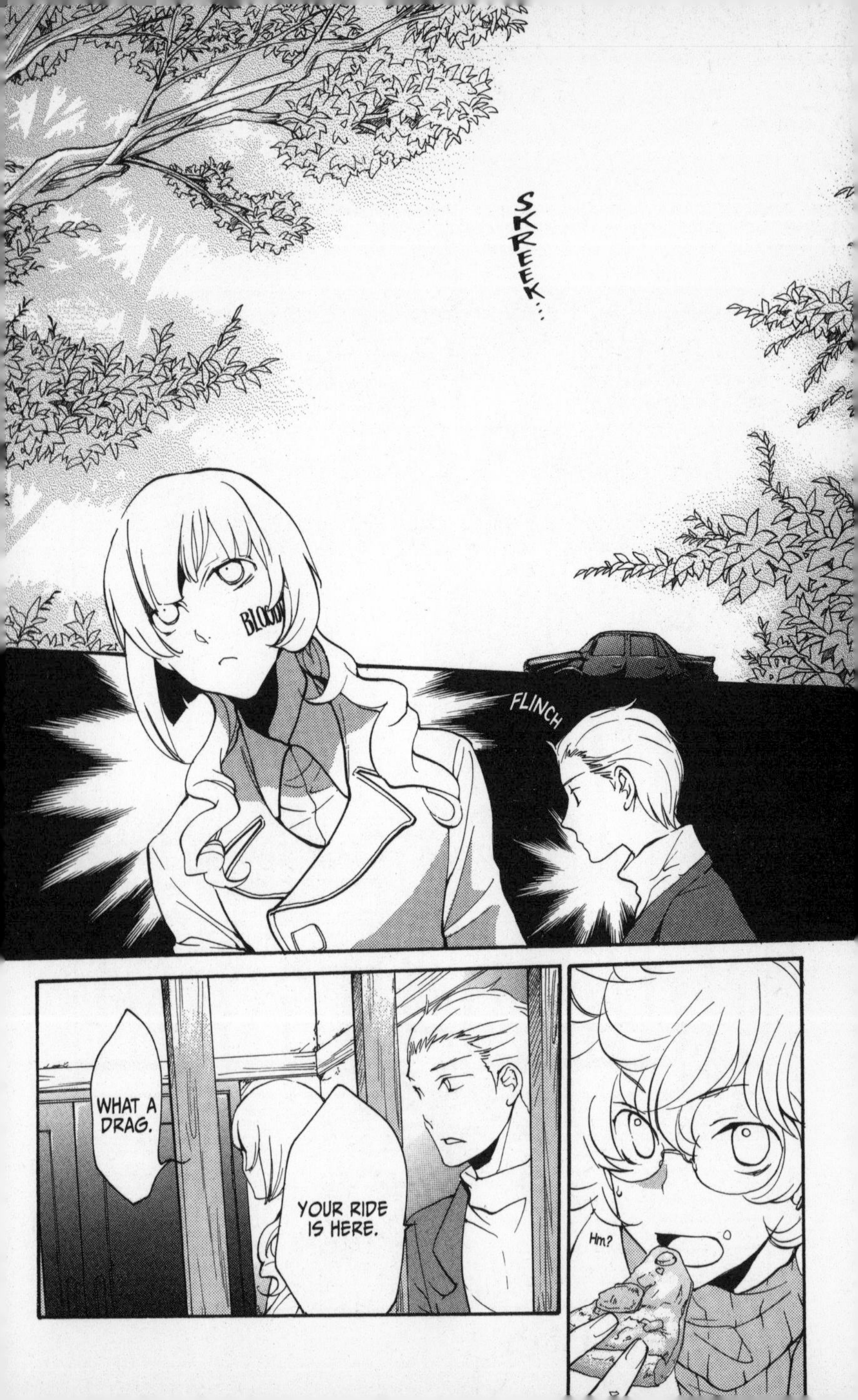
SKREEK...
BLOOD
FLINCH
Hm?
YOUR RIDE IS HERE.
WHAT A DRAG.

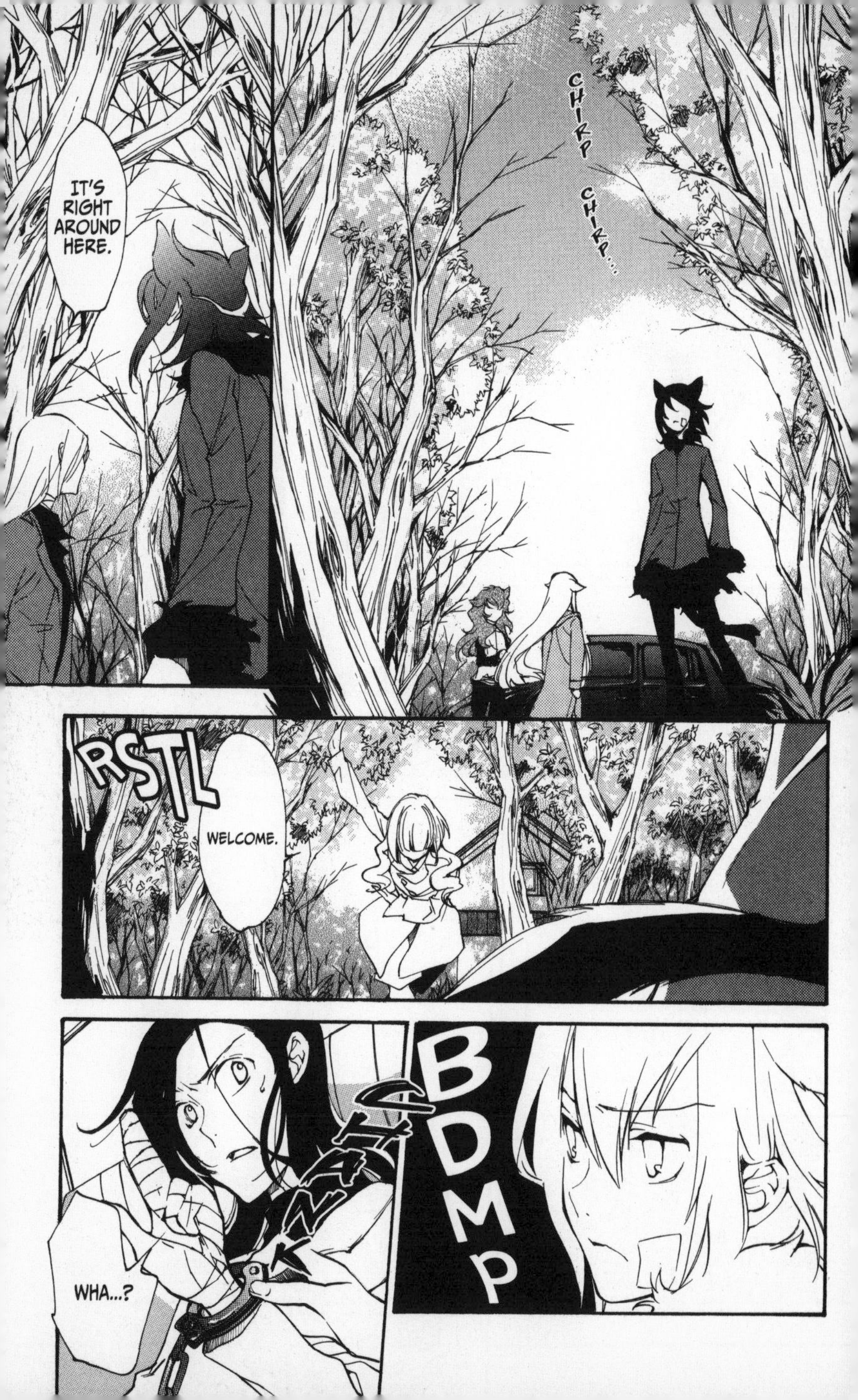
CHIRP CHIRP...
IT'S RIGHT AROUND HERE.
RSTL
WELCOME.
BDMP
CHANK
WHA...?

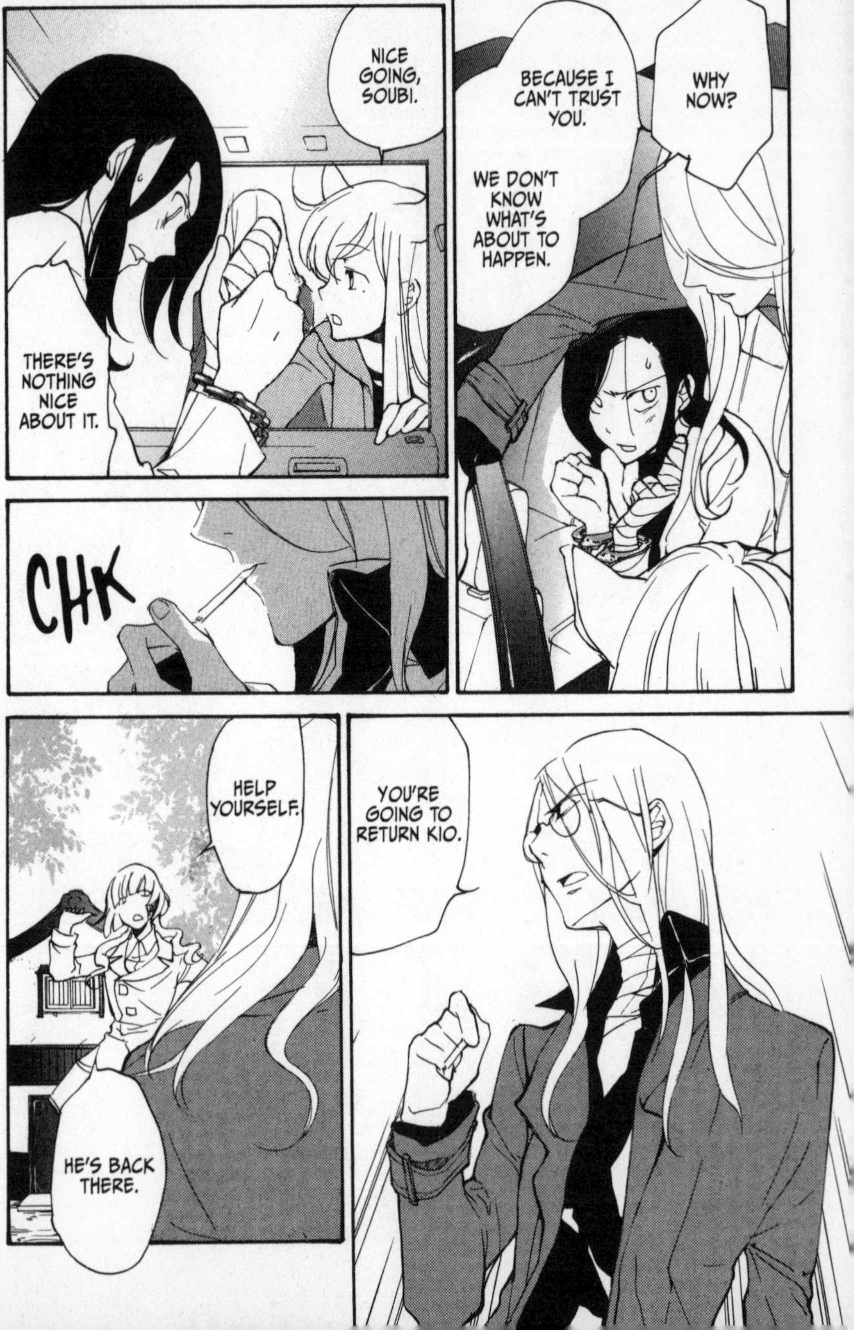
WHY NOW?
BECAUSE I CAN'T TRUST YOU.
WE DON'T KNOW WHAT'S ABOUT TO HAPPEN.
NICE GOING, SOUBI.
THERE'S NOTHING NICE ABOUT IT.
CHK
YOU'RE GOING TO RETURN KIO.
HELP YOURSELF.
HE'S BACK THERE.

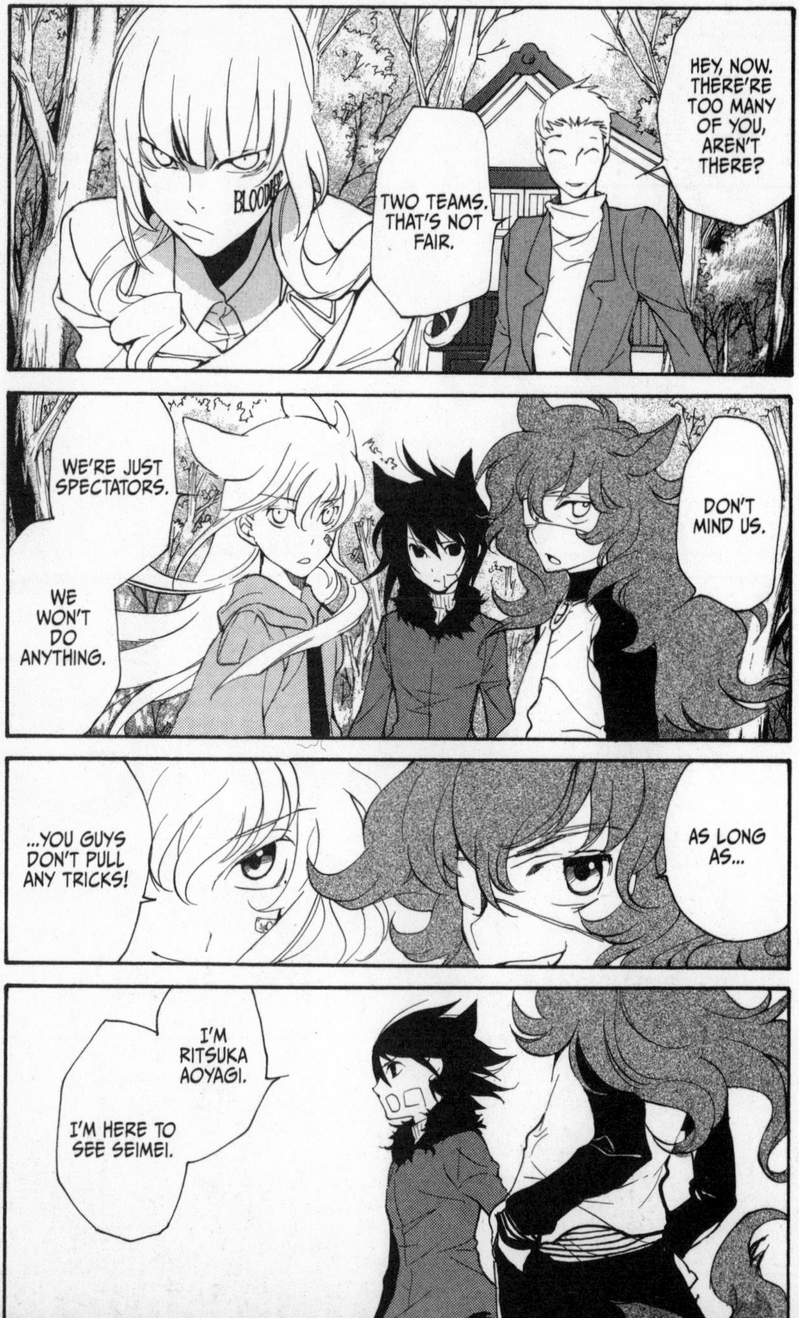
HEY, NOW. THERE'RE TOO MANY OF YOU, AREN'T THERE?
TWO TEAMS. THAT'S NOT FAIR.
DON'T MIND US.
WE'RE JUST SPECTATORS.
WE WON'T DO ANYTHING.
AS LONG AS...
...YOU GUYS DON'T PULL ANY TRICKS!
I'M RITSUKA AOYAGI.
I'M HERE TO SEE SEIMEI.

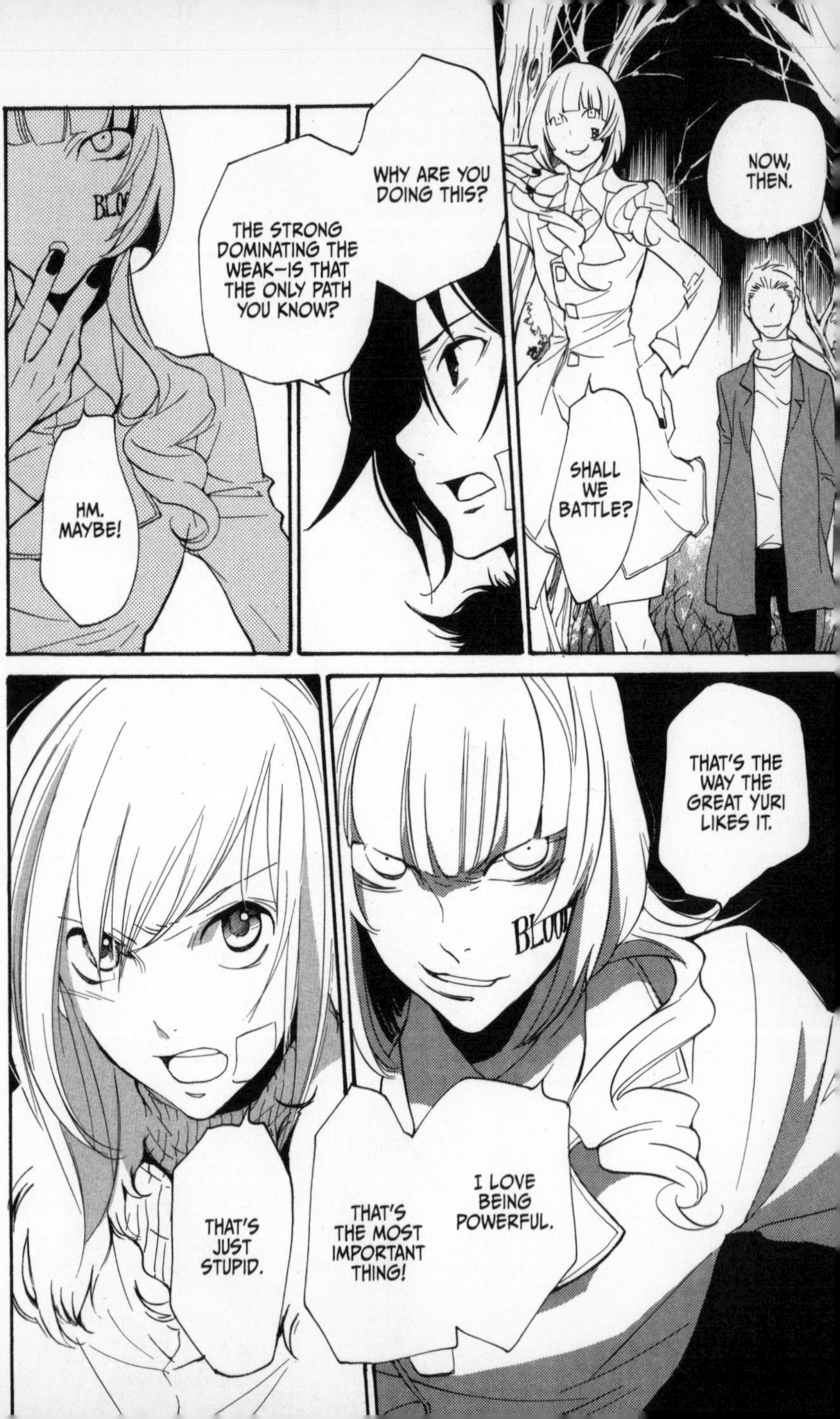
NOW, THEN.
SHALL WE BATTLE?
WHY ARE YOU DOING THIS?
THE STRONG DOMINATING THE WEAK—IS THAT THE ONLY PATH YOU KNOW?
HM. MAYBE!
THAT'S THE WAY THE GREAT YURI LIKES IT.
I LOVE BEING POWERFUL.
THAT'S THE MOST IMPORTANT THING!
THAT'S JUST STUPID.

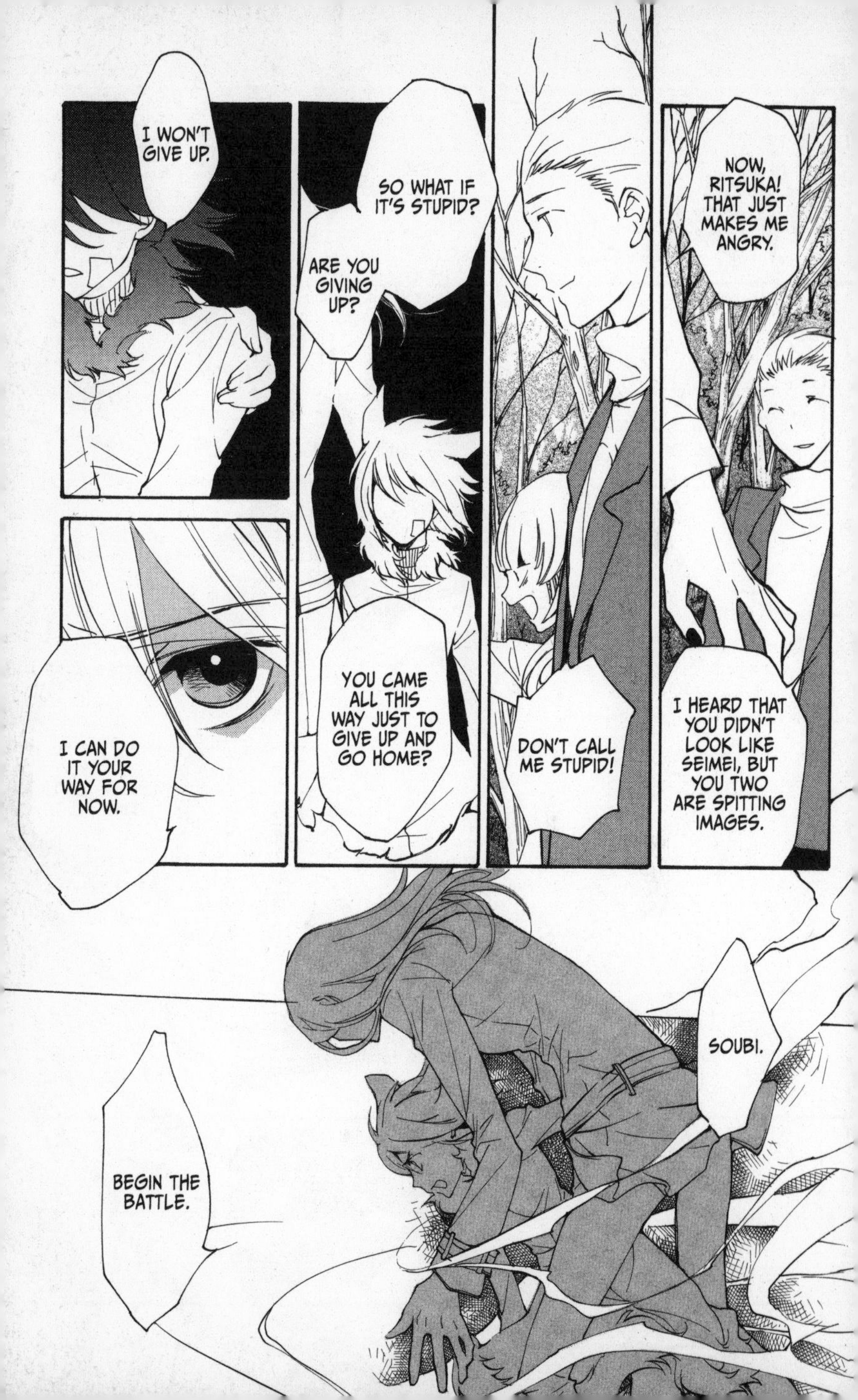
NOW, RITSUKA! THAT JUST MAKES ME ANGRY.
I HEARD THAT YOU DIDN'T LOOK LIKE SEIMEI, BUT YOU TWO ARE SPITTING IMAGES.
DON'T CALL ME STUPID!
SO WHAT IF IT'S STUPID?
ARE YOU GIVING UP?
YOU CAME ALL THIS WAY JUST TO GIVE UP AND GO HOME?
I WON'T GIVE UP.
I CAN DO IT YOUR WAY FOR NOW.
SOUBI.
BEGIN THE BATTLE.

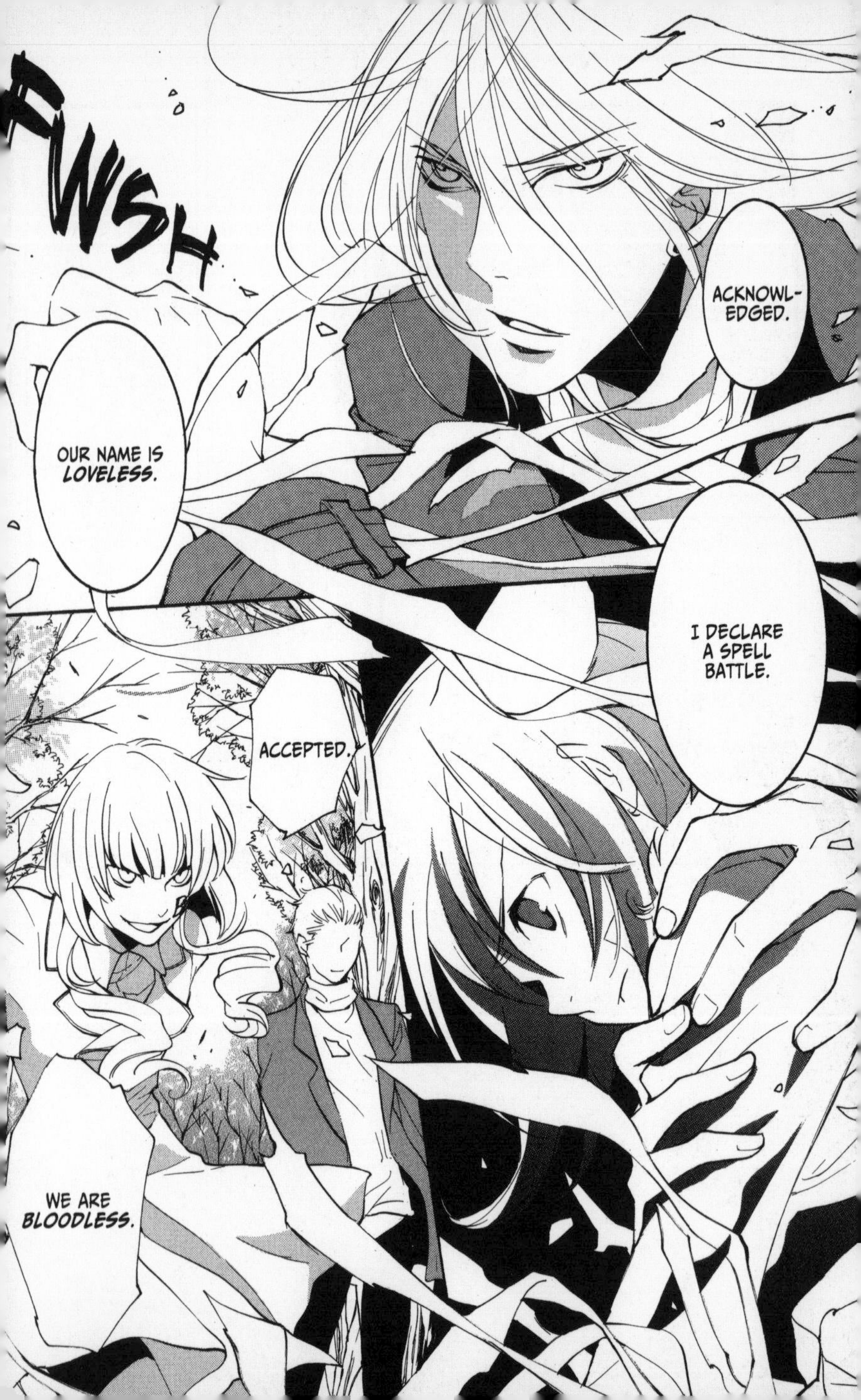
ACKNOWL-EDGED.
FWSH
OUR NAME IS *LOVELESS.*
I DECLARE A SPELL BATTLE.
ACCEPTED.
WE ARE *BLOODLESS.*

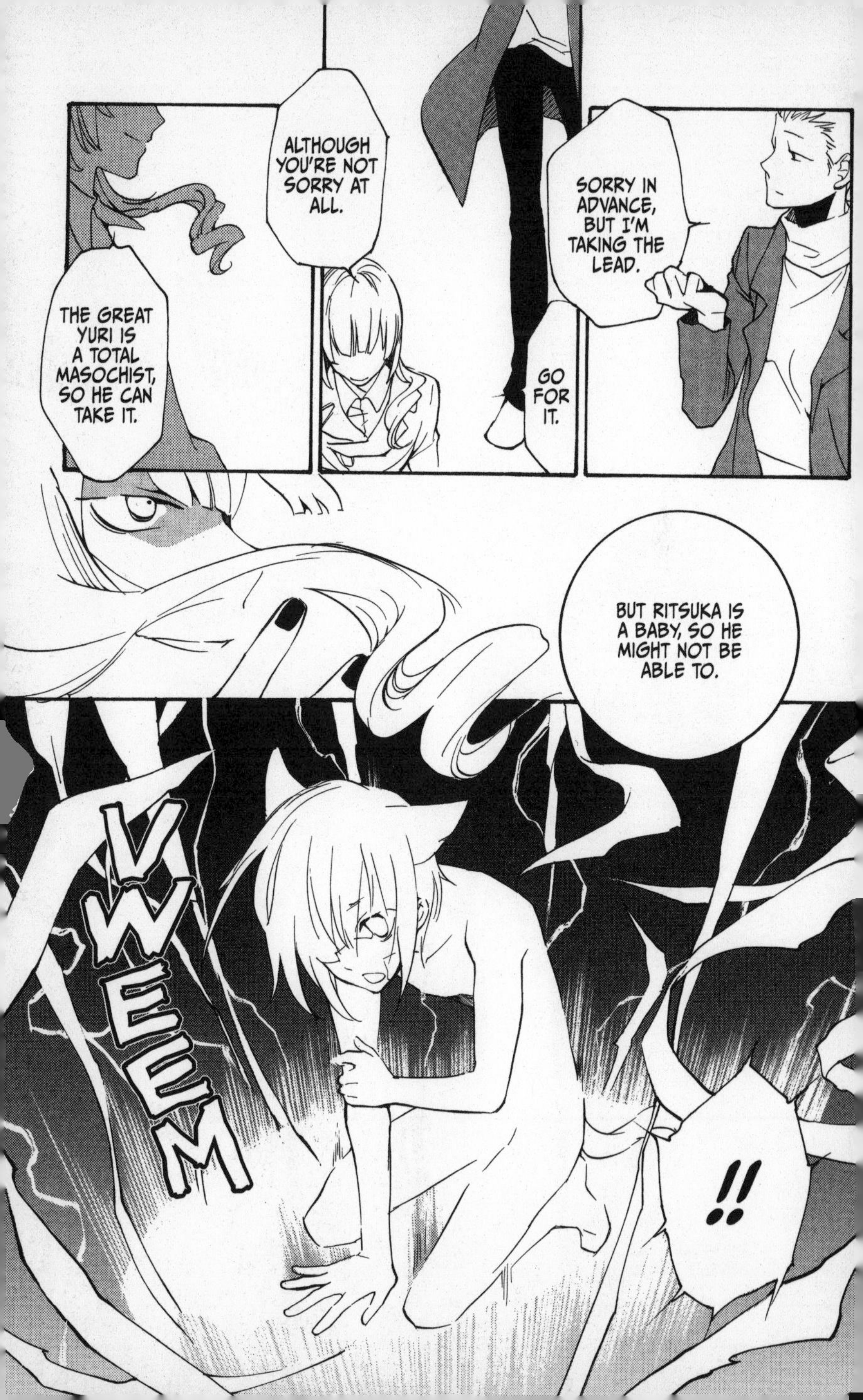
SORRY IN ADVANCE, BUT I'M TAKING THE LEAD.
ALTHOUGH YOU'RE NOT SORRY AT ALL.
GO FOR IT.
THE GREAT YURI IS A TOTAL MASOCHIST, SO HE CAN TAKE IT.
BUT RITSUKA IS A BABY, SO HE MIGHT NOT BE ABLE TO.
VWEEM
!!

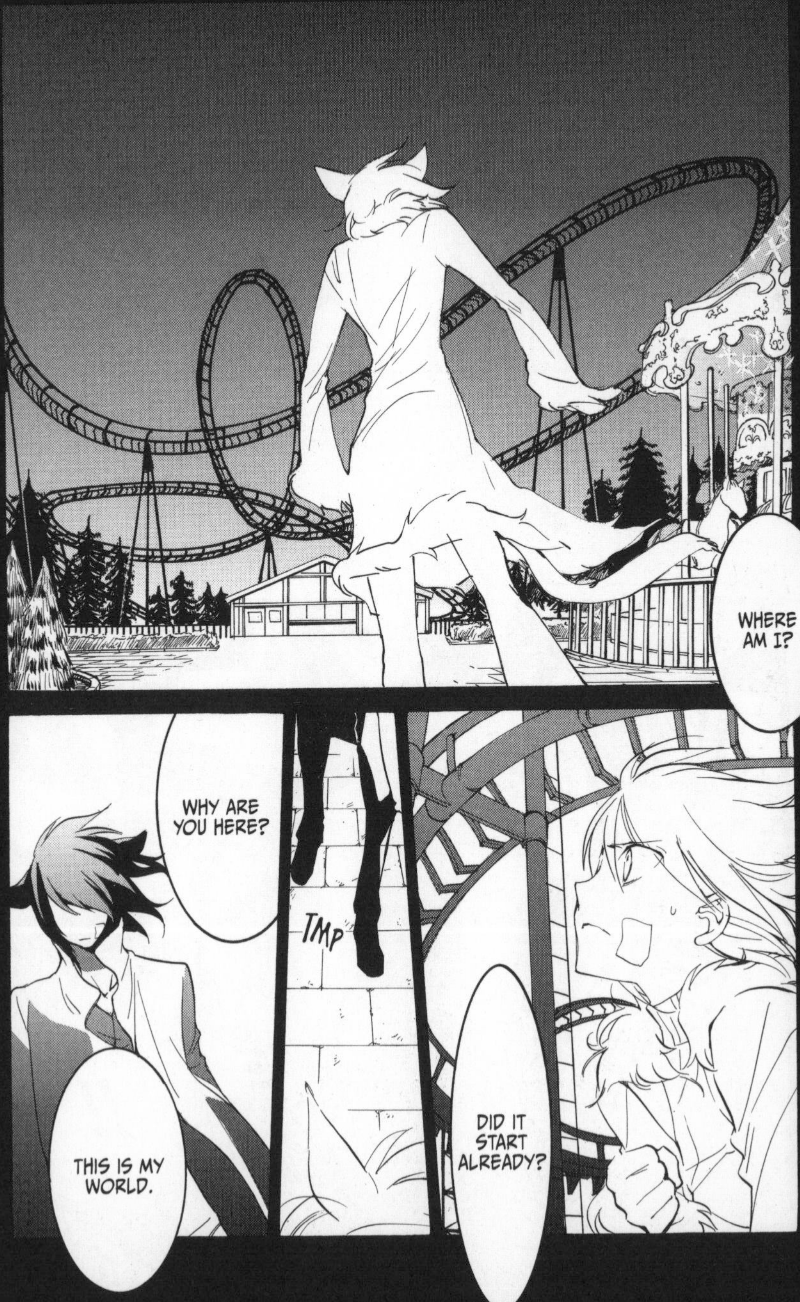
WHERE AM I?
DID IT START ALREADY?
TMP
WHY ARE YOU HERE?
THIS IS MY WORLD.

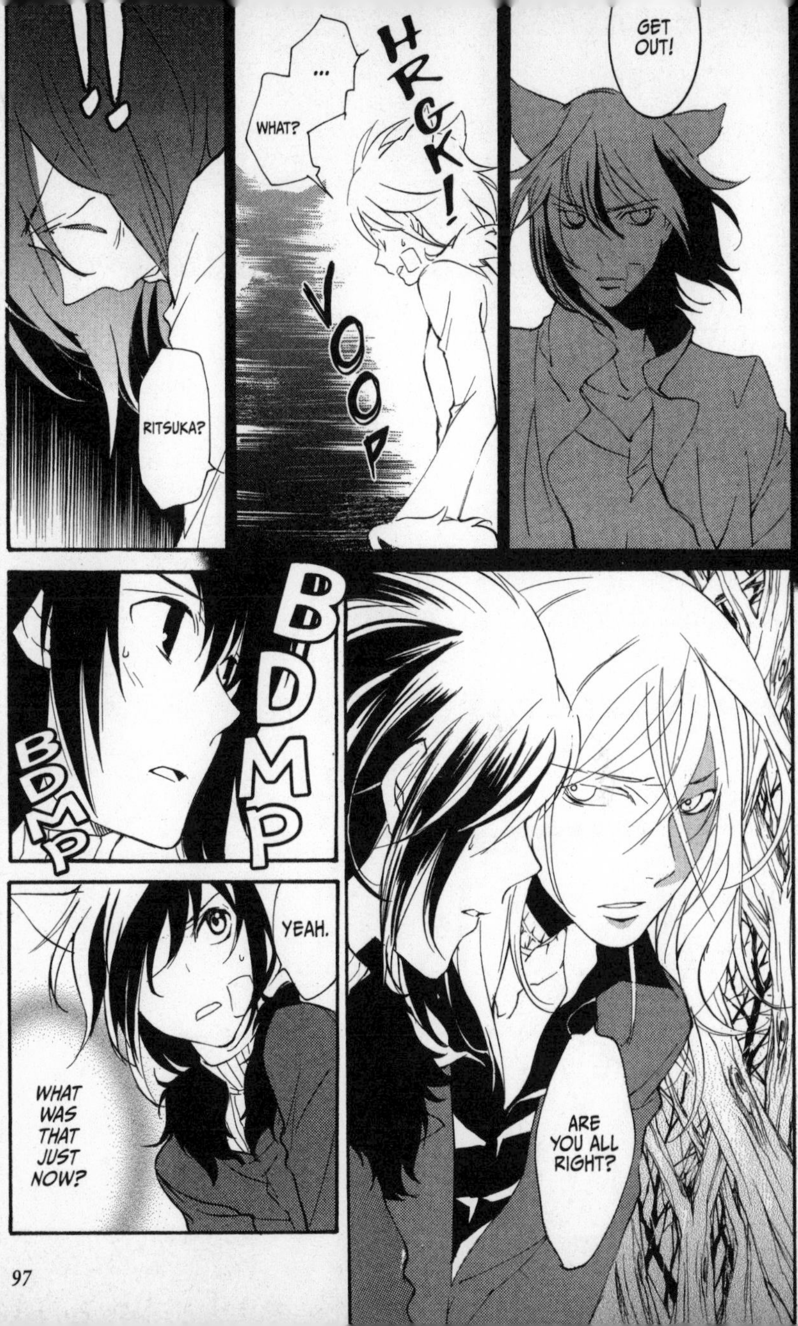
GET OUT!
HRGK!
...
WHAT?
VOOP
RITSUKA?
ARE YOU ALL RIGHT?
BDMP
BDMP
YEAH.
WHAT WAS THAT JUST NOW?

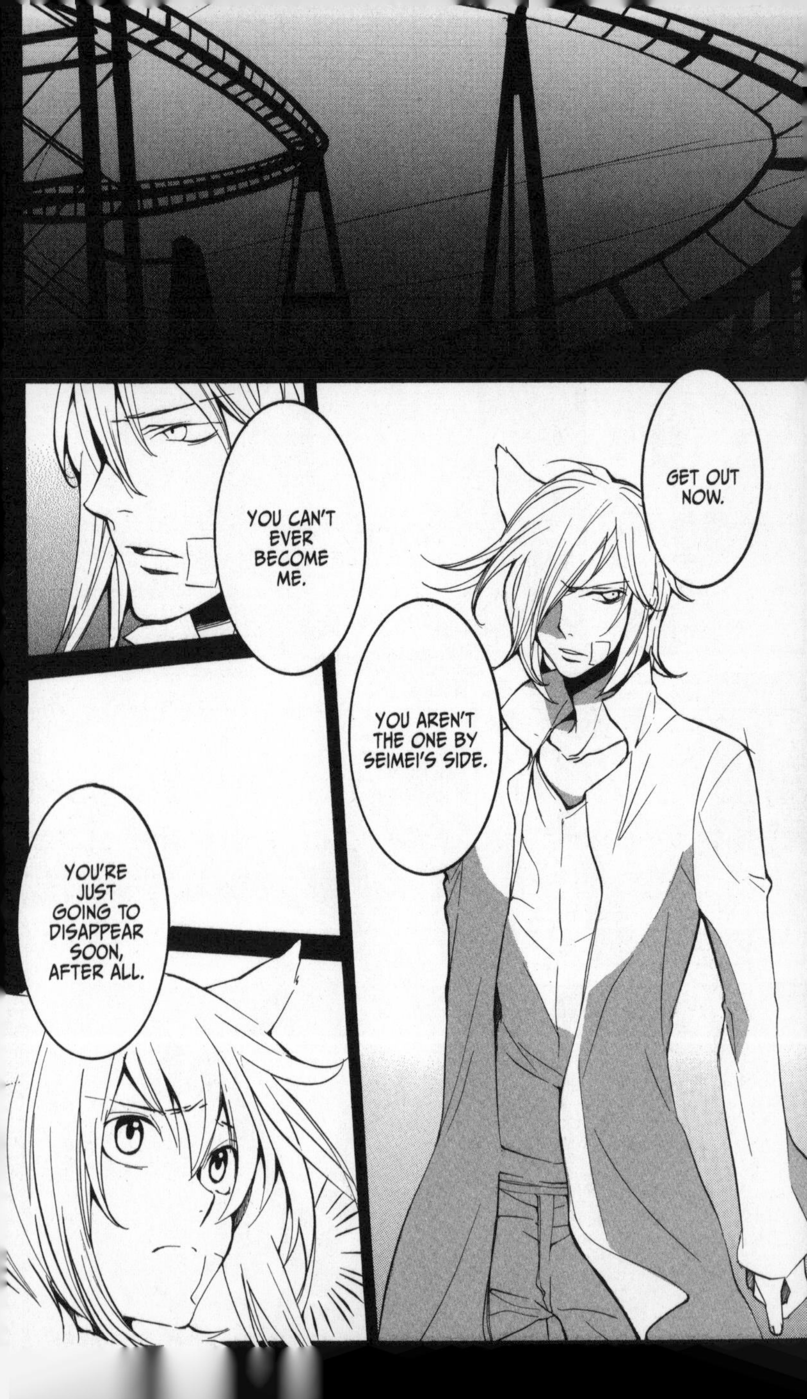
GET OUT NOW.
YOU AREN'T THE ONE BY SEIMEI'S SIDE.
YOU CAN'T EVER BECOME ME.
YOU'RE JUST GOING TO DISAPPEAR SOON, AFTER ALL.

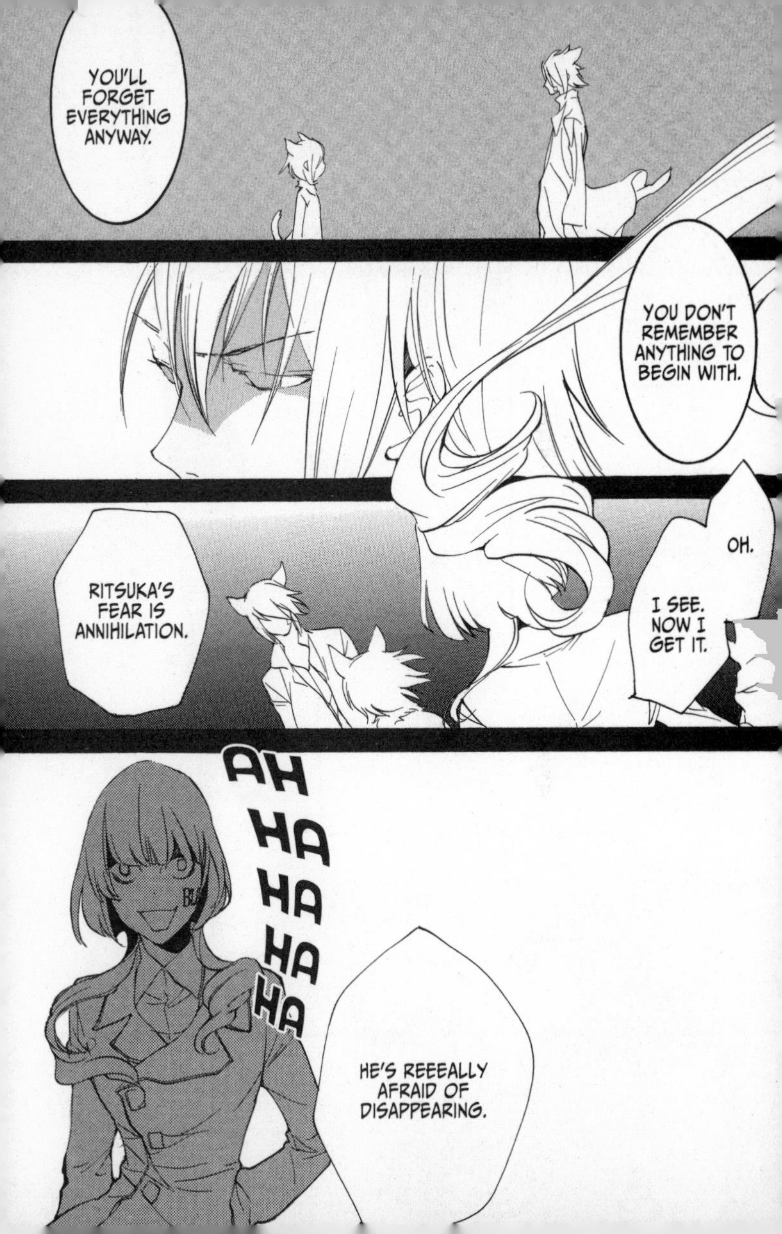
YOU'LL FORGET EVERYTHING ANYWAY.
YOU DON'T REMEMBER ANYTHING TO BEGIN WITH.
OH.
I SEE. NOW I GET IT.
RITSUKA'S FEAR IS ANNIHILATION.
AH HA HA HA HA
HE'S REEEALLY AFRAID OF DISAPPEARING.

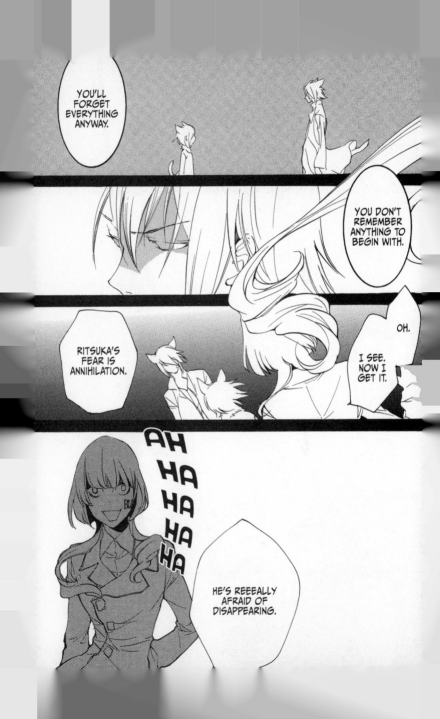

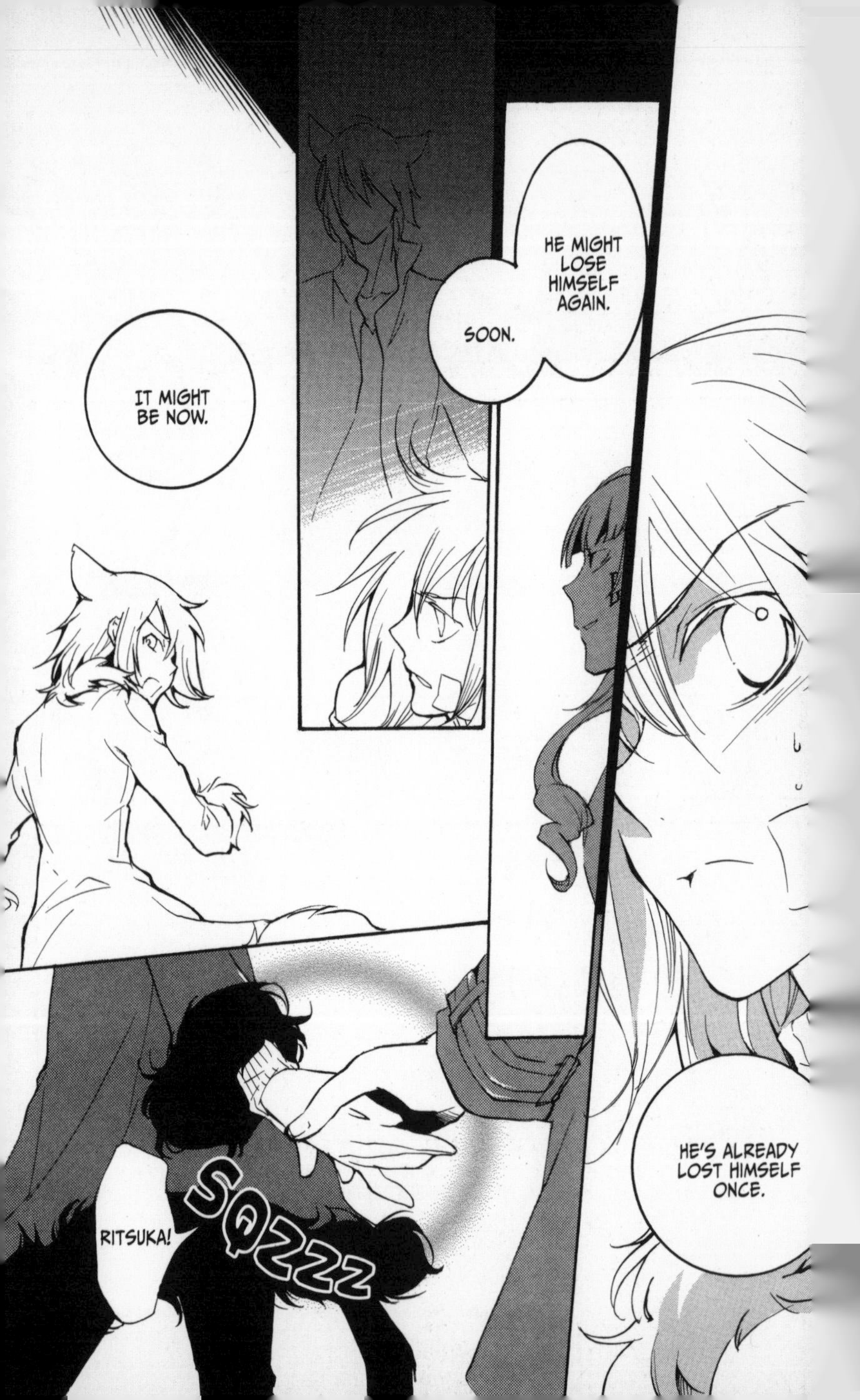
HE'S ALREADY LOST HIMSELF ONCE.
HE MIGHT LOSE HIMSELF AGAIN.
SOON.
IT MIGHT BE NOW.
SQZZZ
RITSUKA!

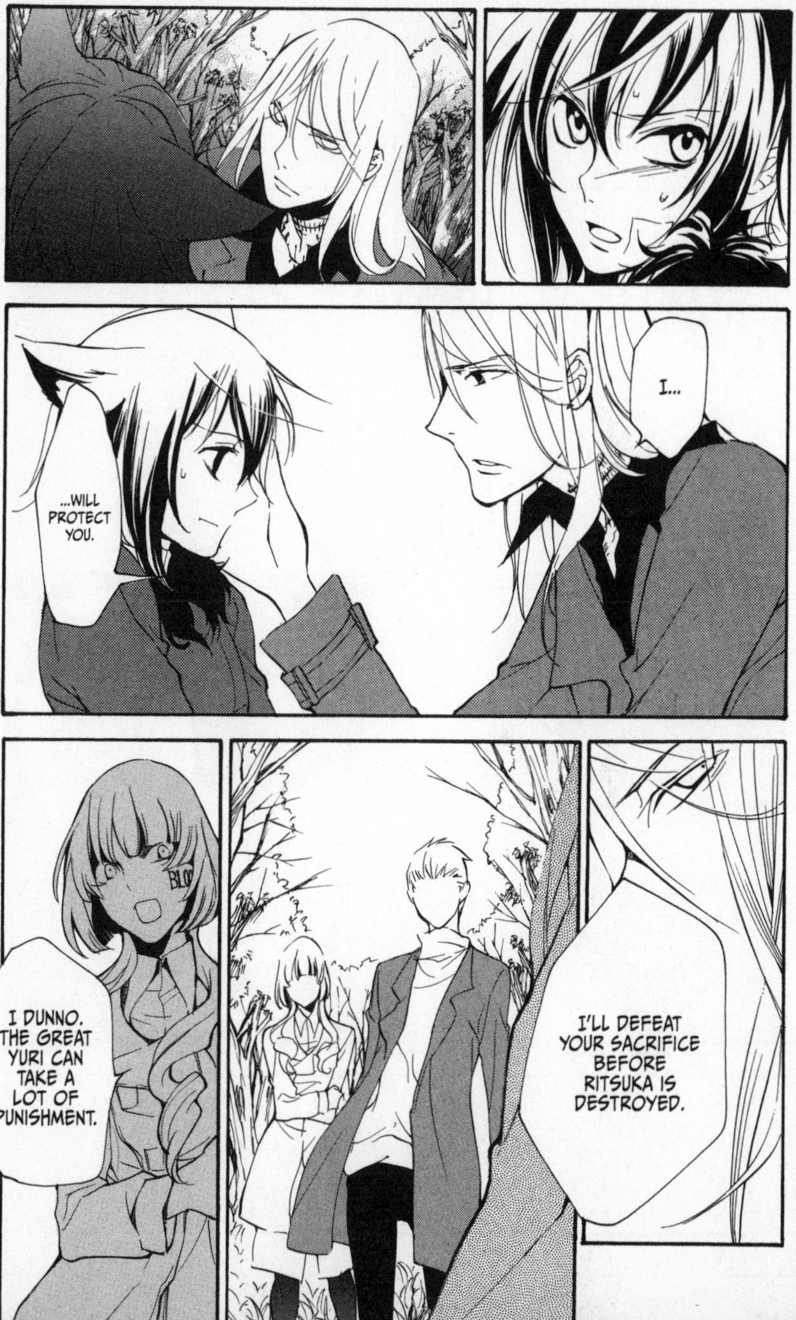
I...
...WILL PROTECT YOU.
I'LL DEFEAT YOUR SACRIFICE BEFORE RITSUKA IS DESTROYED.
I DUNNO. THE GREAT YURI CAN TAKE A LOT OF PUNISHMENT.

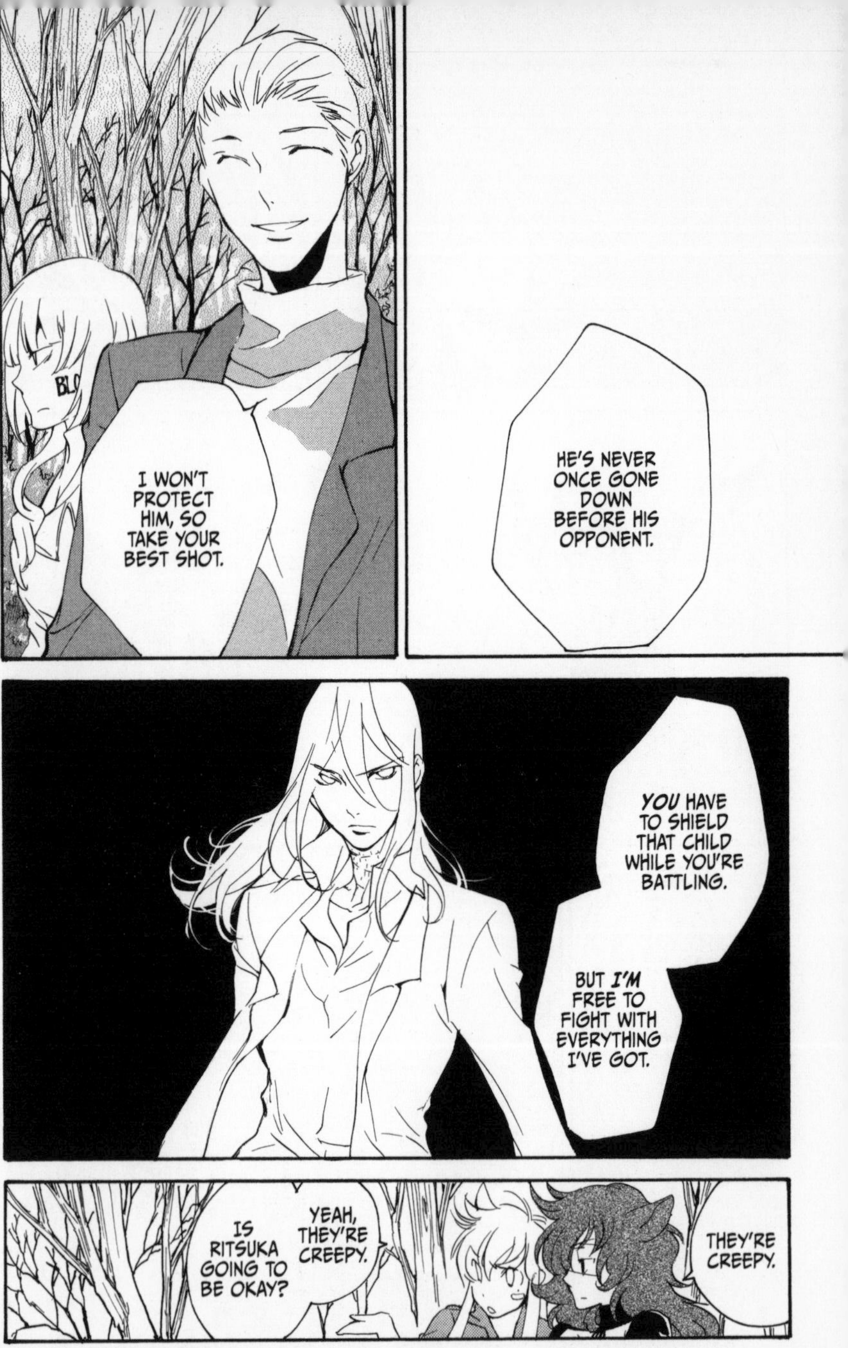
HE'S NEVER ONCE GONE DOWN BEFORE HIS OPPONENT.
I WON'T PROTECT HIM, SO TAKE YOUR BEST SHOT.
YOU HAVE TO SHIELD THAT CHILD WHILE YOU'RE BATTLING.
BUT *I'M* FREE TO FIGHT WITH EVERYTHING I'VE GOT.
THEY'RE CREEPY.
YEAH, THEY'RE CREEPY.
IS RITSUKA GOING TO BE OKAY?

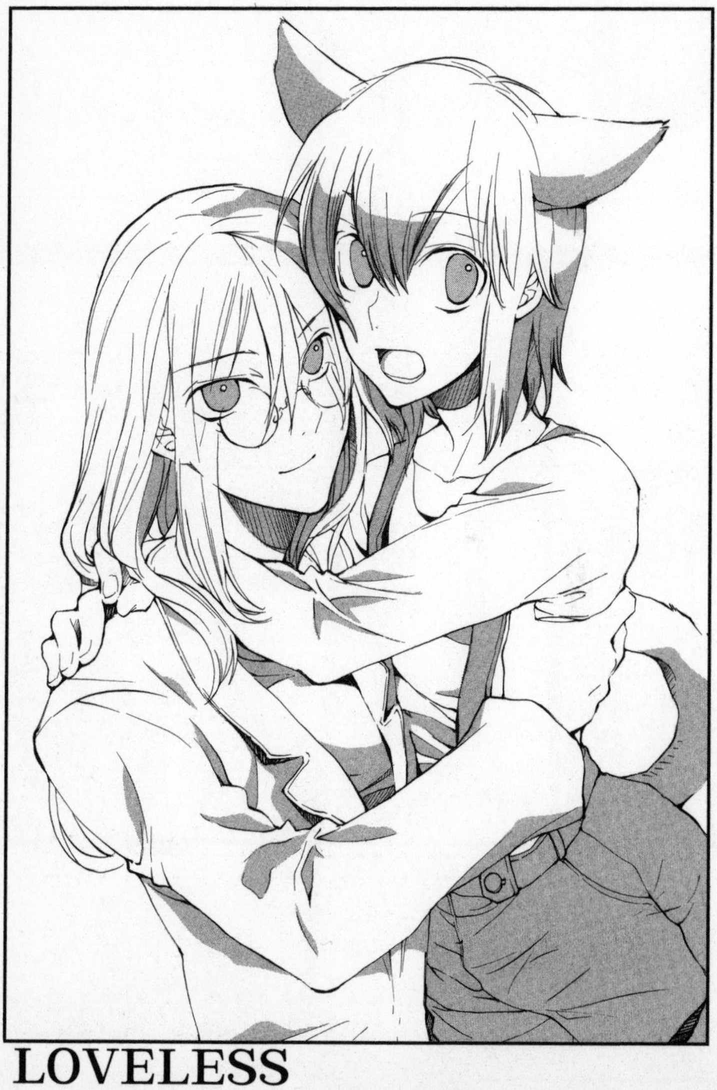

LOVELESS

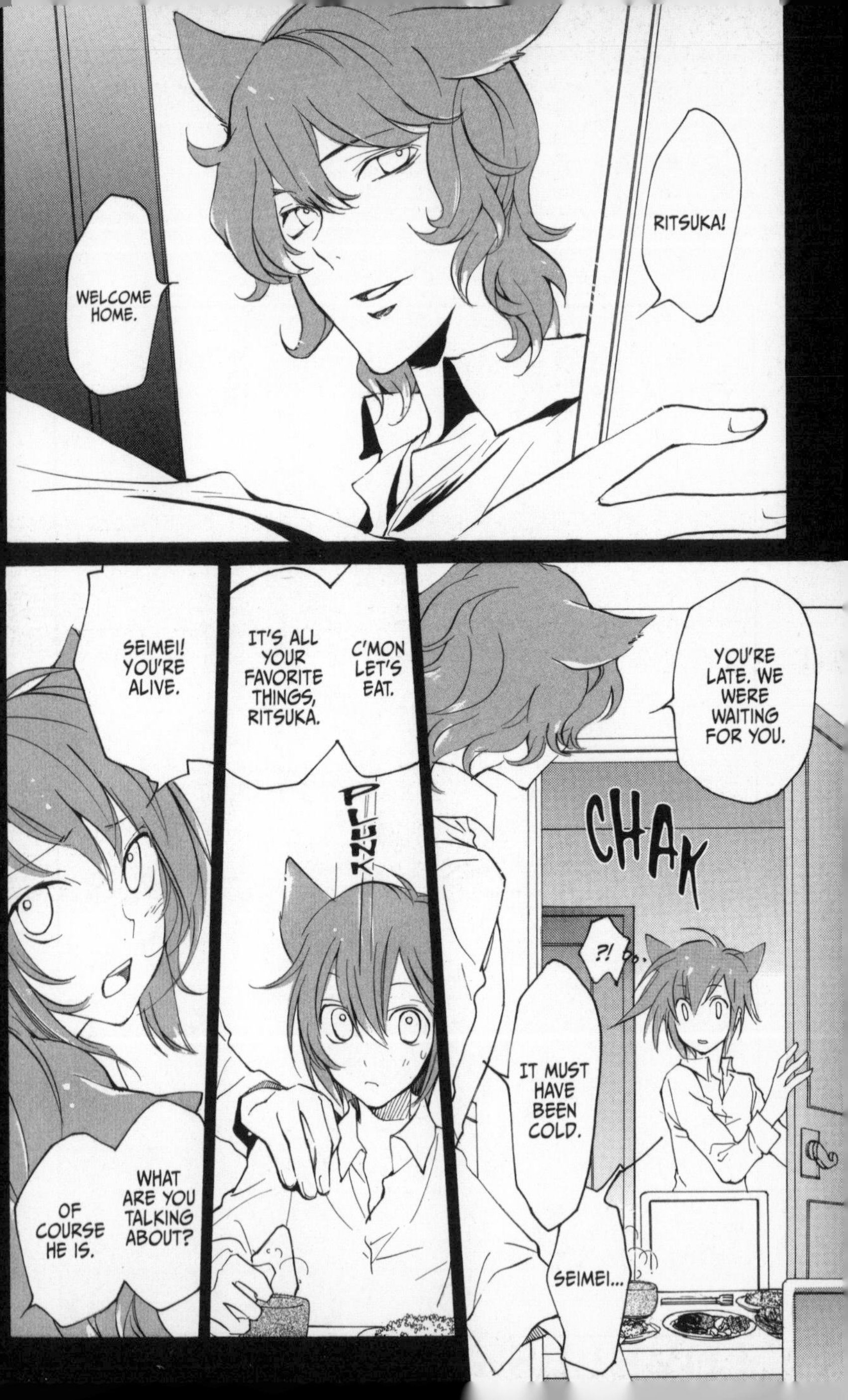
RITSUKA!
WELCOME HOME.
YOU'RE LATE. WE WERE WAITING FOR YOU.
CHAK
?!
IT MUST HAVE BEEN COLD.
SEIMEI...
C'MON LET'S EAT.
IT'S ALL YOUR FAVORITE THINGS, RITSUKA.
PLUNK
SEIMEI! YOU'RE ALIVE.
WHAT ARE YOU TALKING ABOUT?
OF COURSE HE IS.

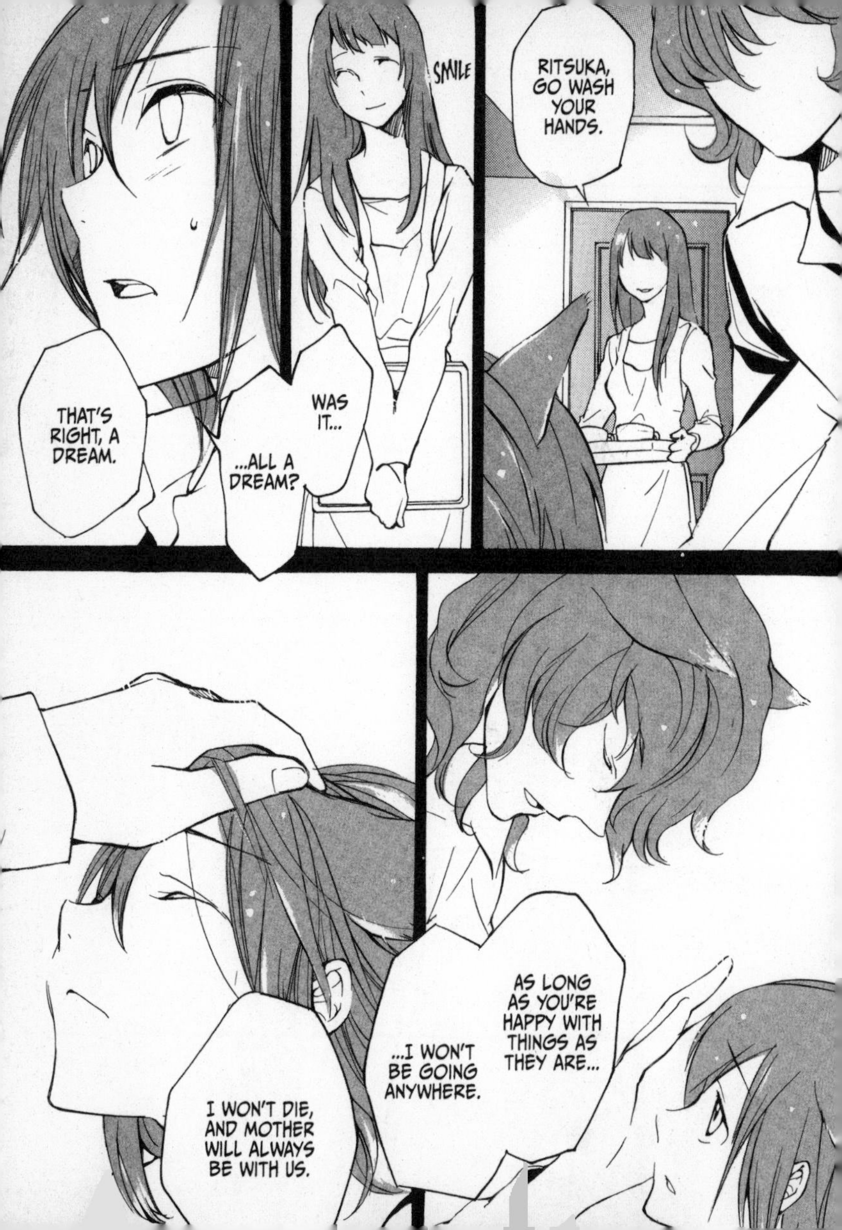
RITSUKA, GO WASH YOUR HANDS.
SMILE
WAS IT...
...ALL A DREAM?
THAT'S RIGHT, A DREAM.
AS LONG AS YOU'RE HAPPY WITH THINGS AS THEY ARE...
...I WON'T BE GOING ANYWHERE.
I WON'T DIE, AND MOTHER WILL ALWAYS BE WITH US.

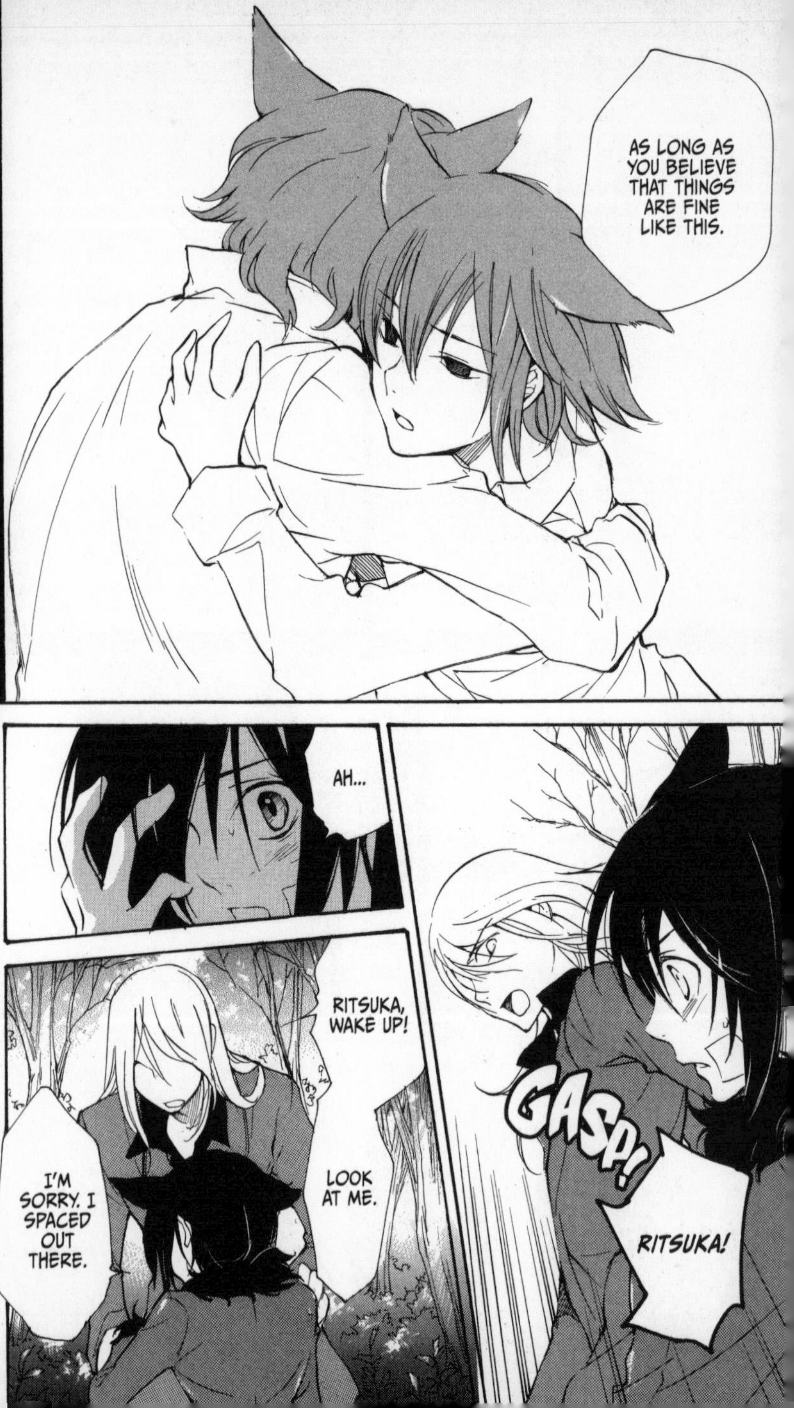
AS LONG AS YOU BELIEVE THAT THINGS ARE FINE LIKE THIS.
GASP!
RITSUKA!
AH...
RITSUKA, WAKE UP!
LOOK AT ME.
I'M SORRY. I SPACED OUT THERE.

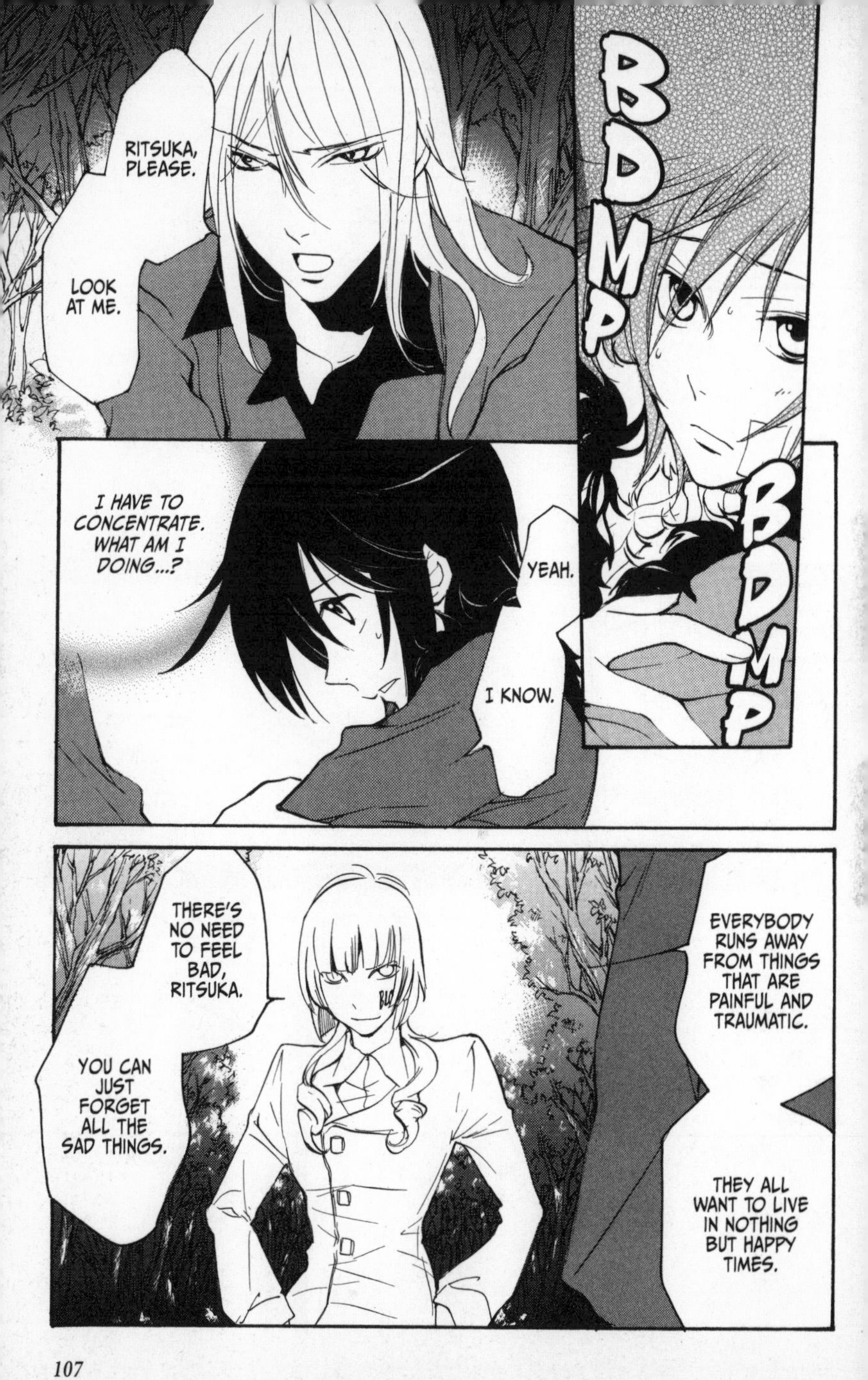
BDMP
BDMP
RITSUKA, PLEASE.
LOOK AT ME.
YEAH.
I KNOW.
I HAVE TO CONCENTRATE. WHAT AM I DOING...?
EVERYBODY RUNS AWAY FROM THINGS THAT ARE PAINFUL AND TRAUMATIC.
THEY ALL WANT TO LIVE IN NOTHING BUT HAPPY TIMES.
THERE'S NO NEED TO FEEL BAD, RITSUKA.
YOU CAN JUST FORGET ALL THE SAD THINGS.

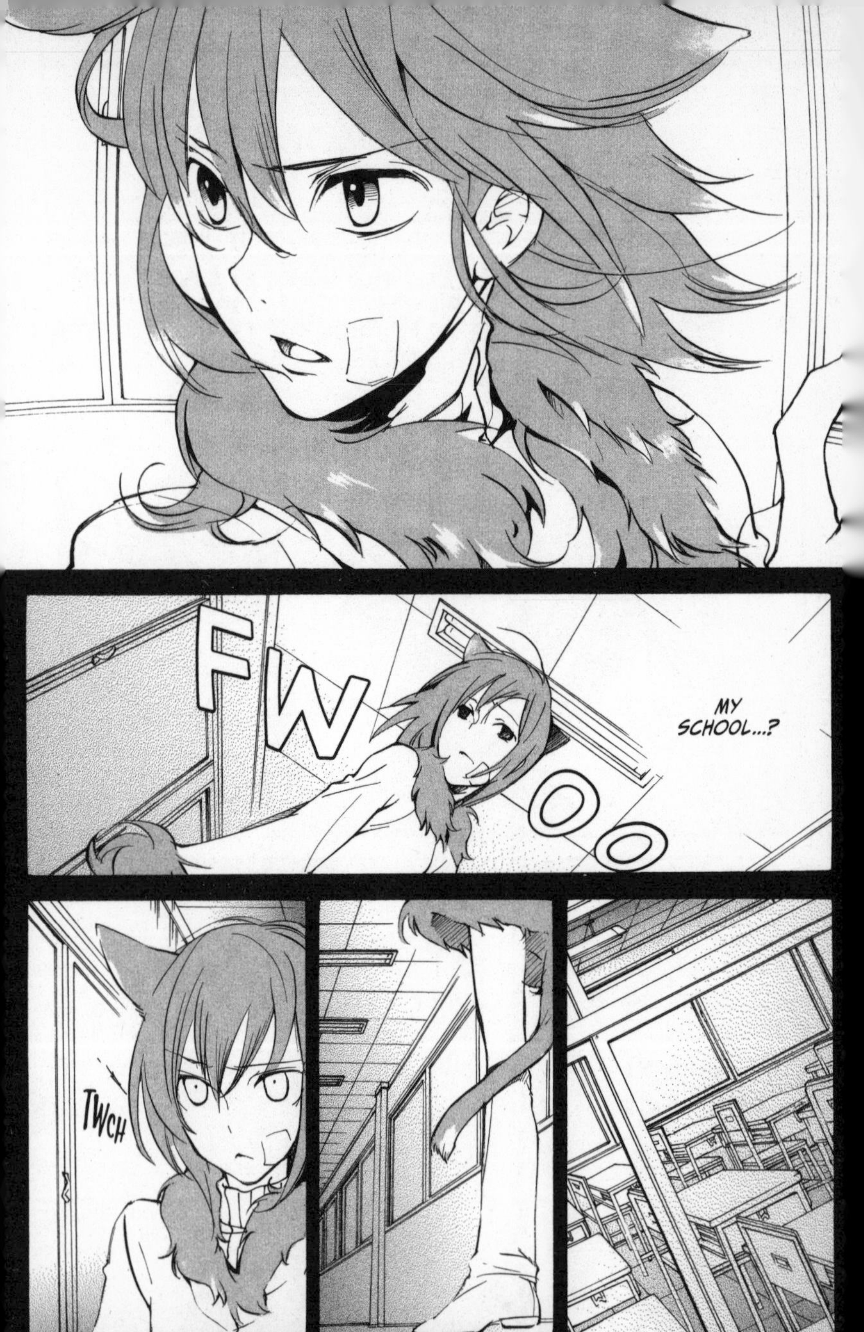
FWOO
MY SCHOOL...?
TWCH

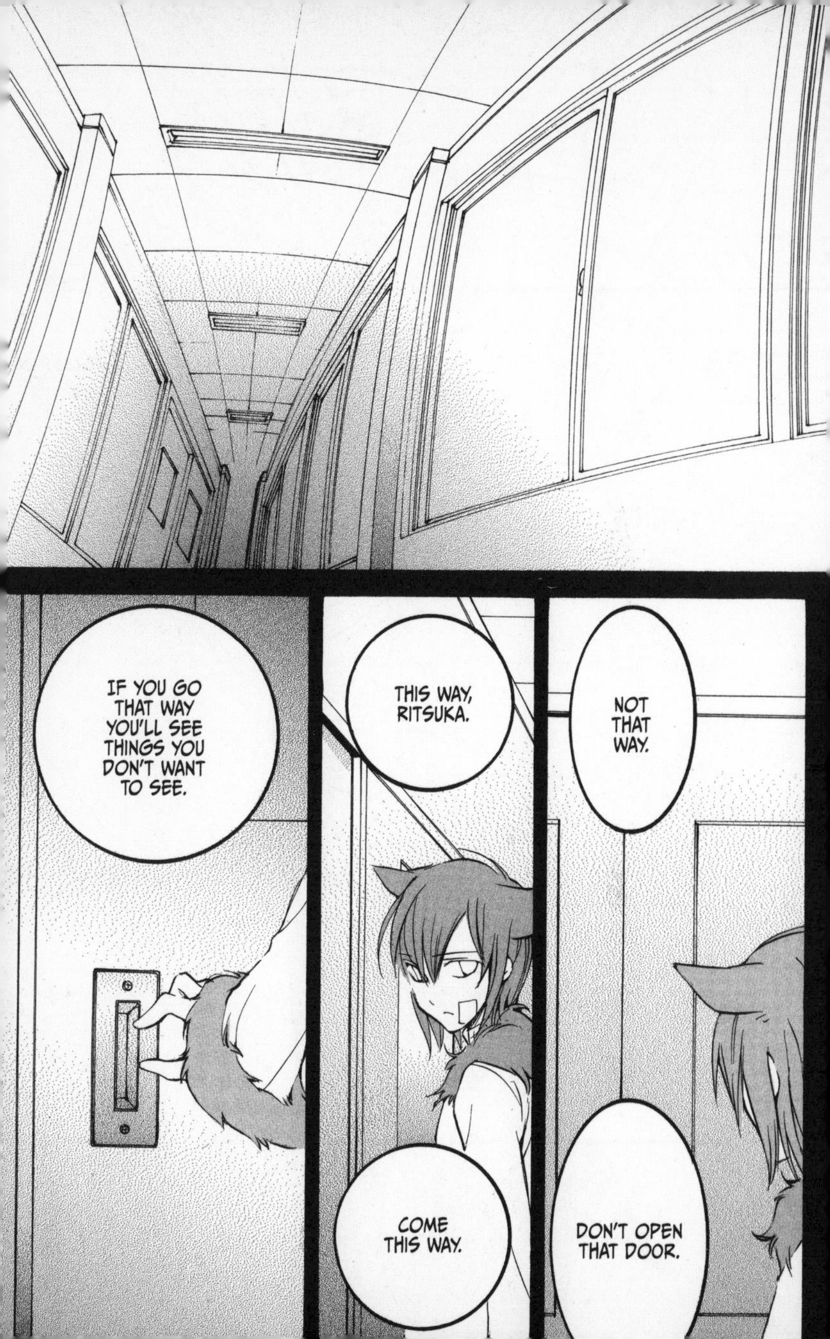
NOT THAT WAY.
DON'T OPEN THAT DOOR.
THIS WAY, RITSUKA.
COME THIS WAY.
IF YOU GO THAT WAY YOU'LL SEE THINGS YOU DON'T WANT TO SEE.

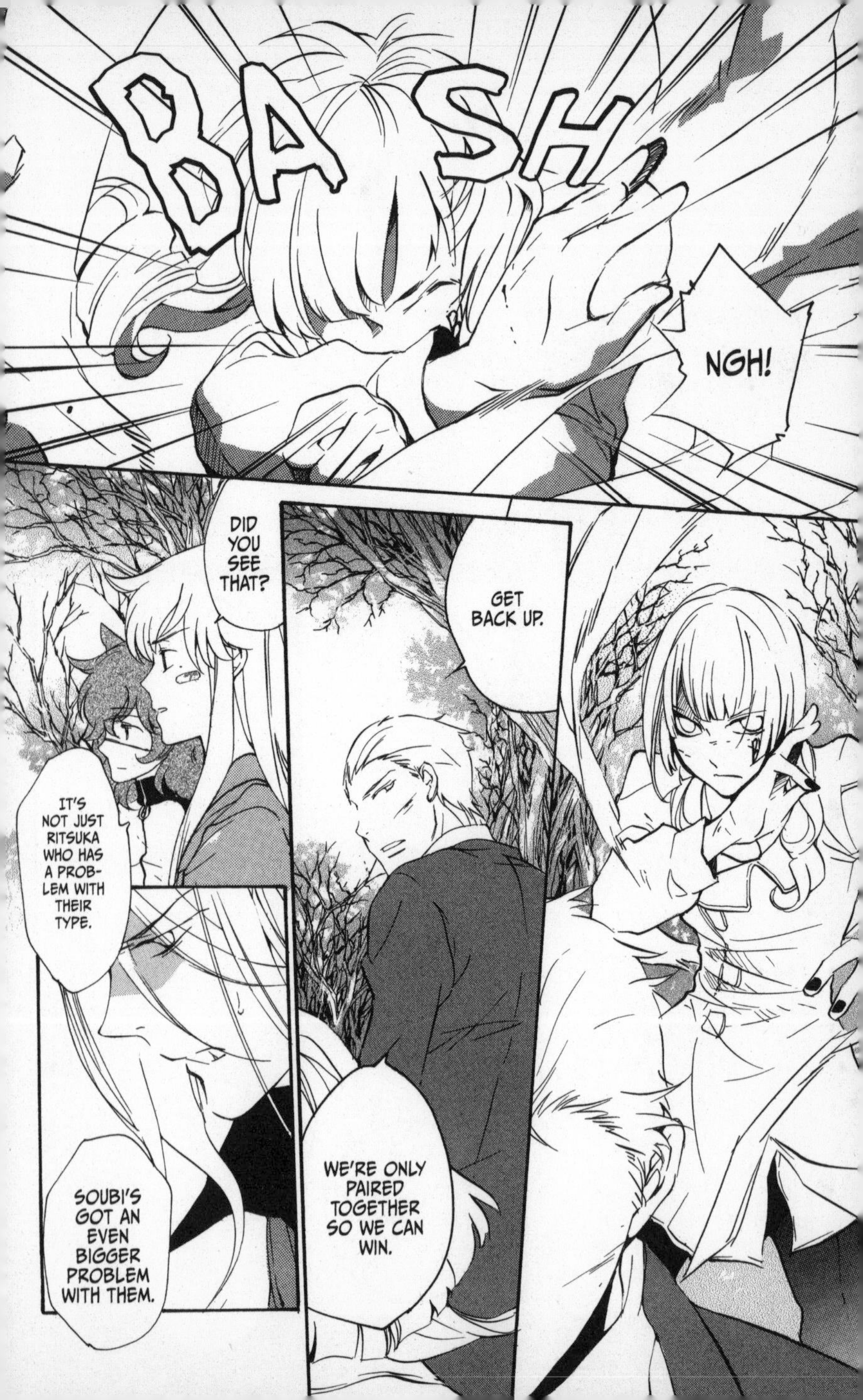
BASH
NGH!
GET BACK UP.
WE'RE ONLY PAIRED TOGETHER SO WE CAN WIN.
DID YOU SEE THAT?
IT'S NOT JUST RITSUKA WHO HAS A PROB-LEM WITH THEIR TYPE.
SOUBI'S GOT AN EVEN BIGGER PROBLEM WITH THEM.

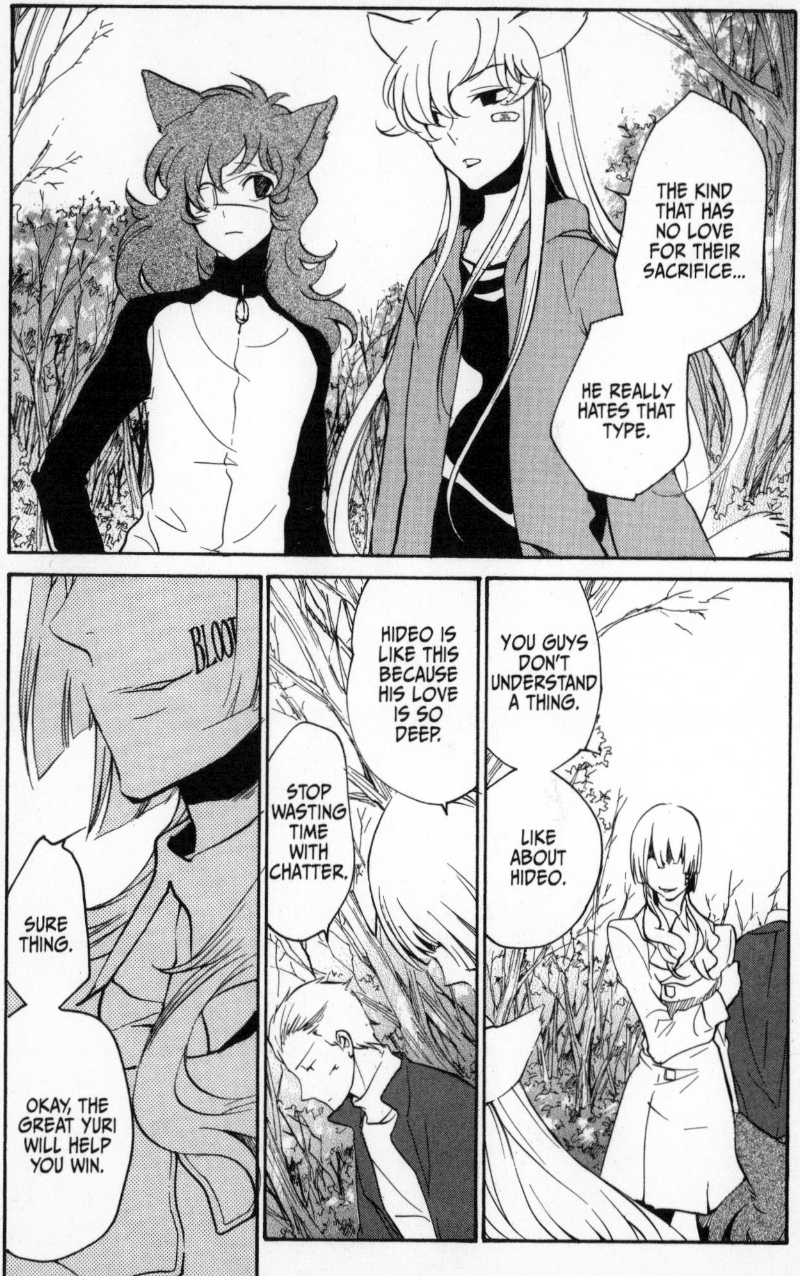
THE KIND THAT HAS NO LOVE FOR THEIR SACRIFICE...
HE REALLY HATES THAT TYPE.
YOU GUYS DON'T UNDERSTAND A THING.
LIKE ABOUT HIDEO.
HIDEO IS LIKE THIS BECAUSE HIS LOVE IS SO DEEP.
STOP WASTING TIME WITH CHATTER.
SURE THING.
OKAY, THE GREAT YURI WILL HELP YOU WIN.

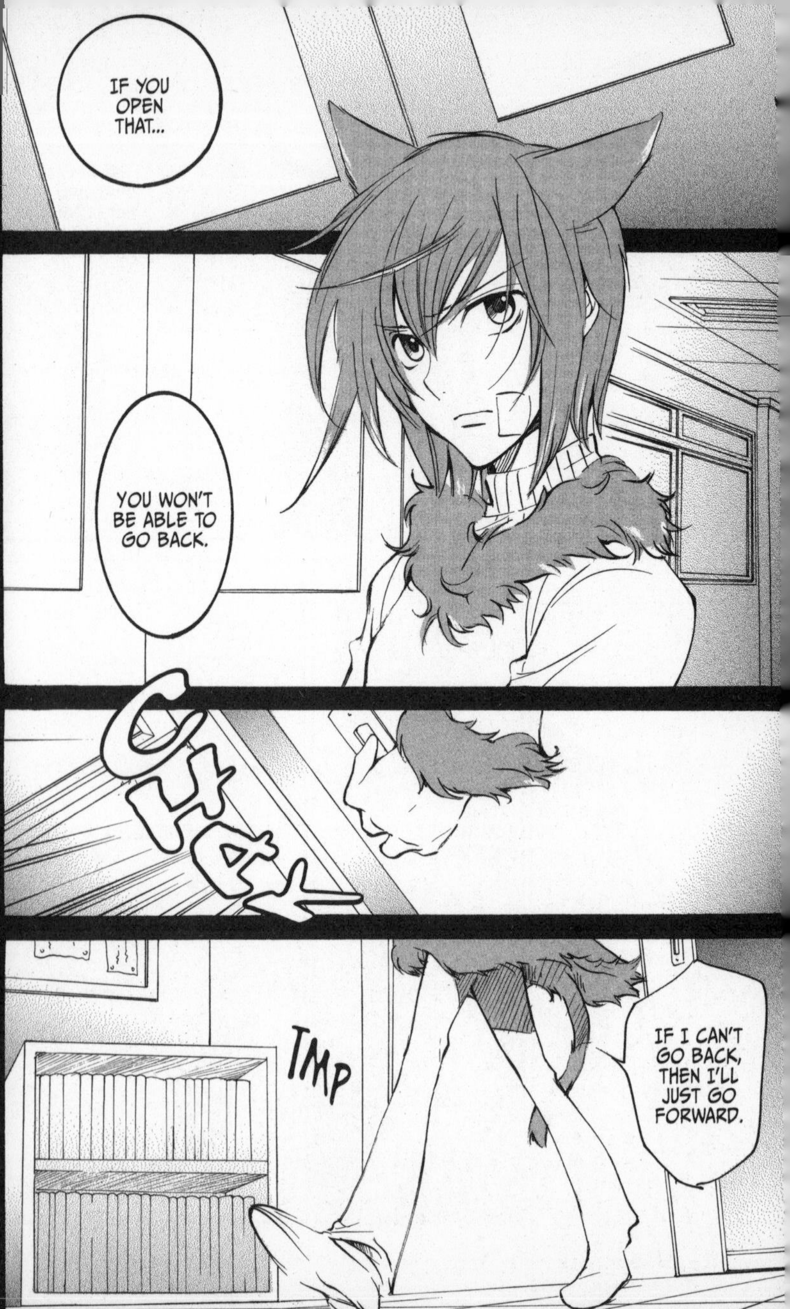
IF YOU OPEN THAT...
YOU WON'T BE ABLE TO GO BACK.
CLATTER
IF I CAN'T GO BACK, THEN I'LL JUST GO FORWARD.
TMP

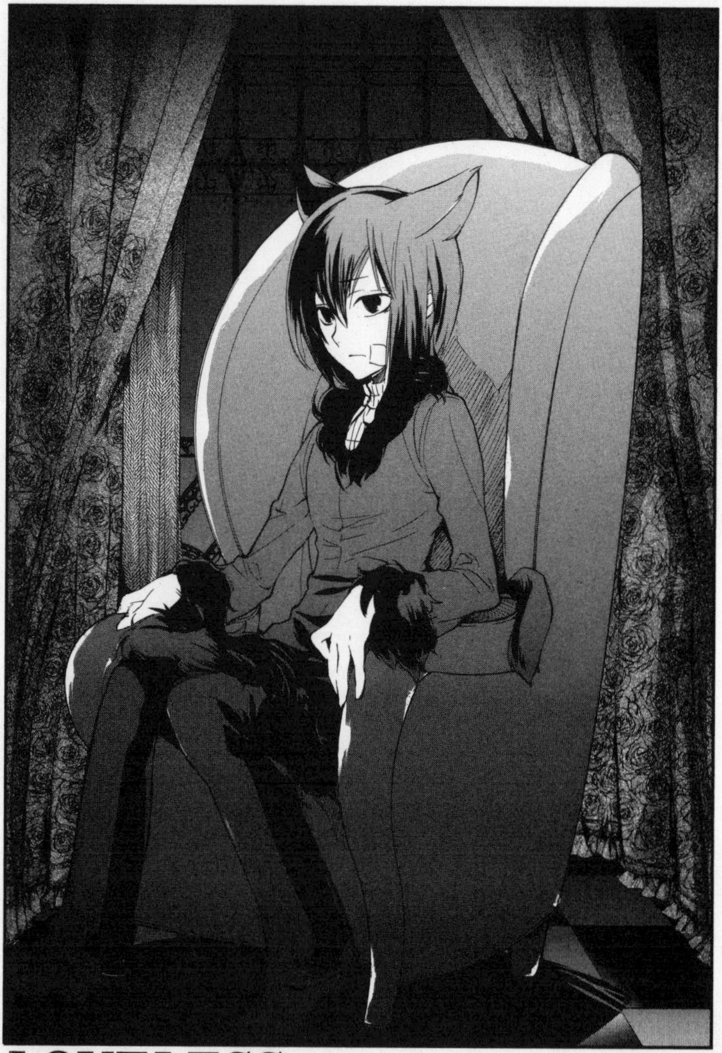

LOVELESS

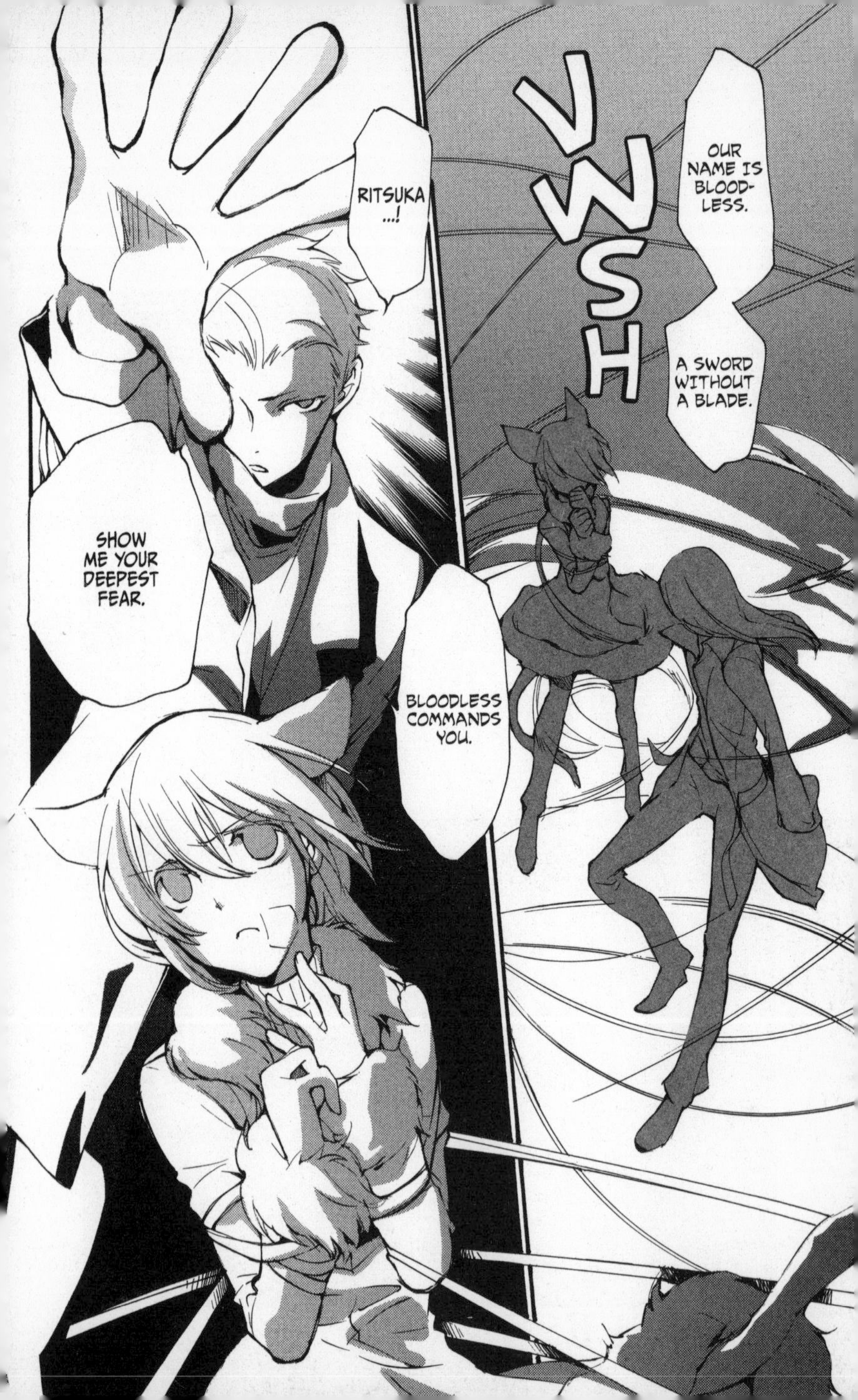
OUR NAME IS BLOOD-LESS.
VWSH
A SWORD WITHOUT A BLADE.
RITSUKA ...!
SHOW ME YOUR DEEPEST FEAR.
BLOODLESS COMMANDS YOU.

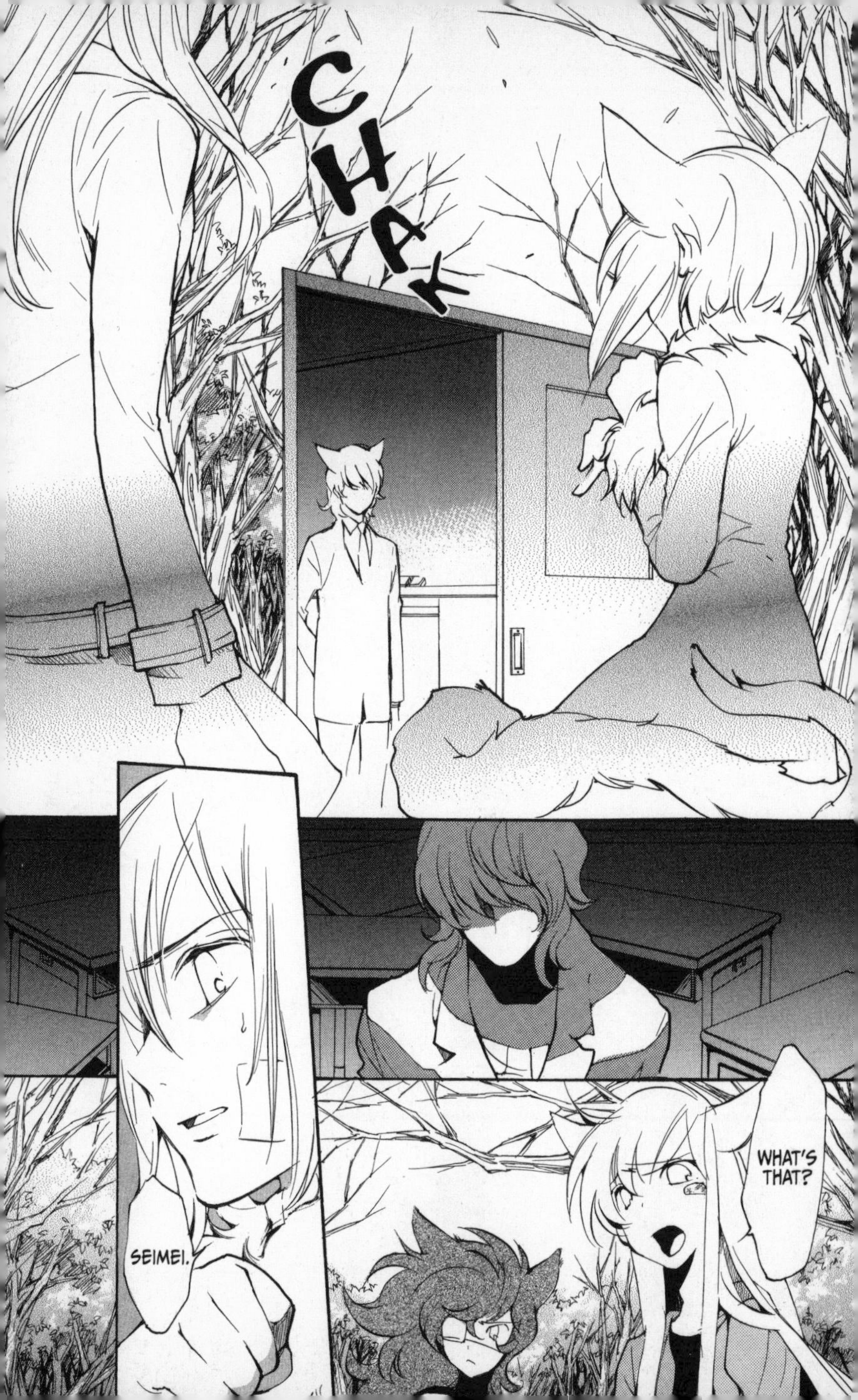
CHAK
WHAT'S THAT?
SEIMEI.

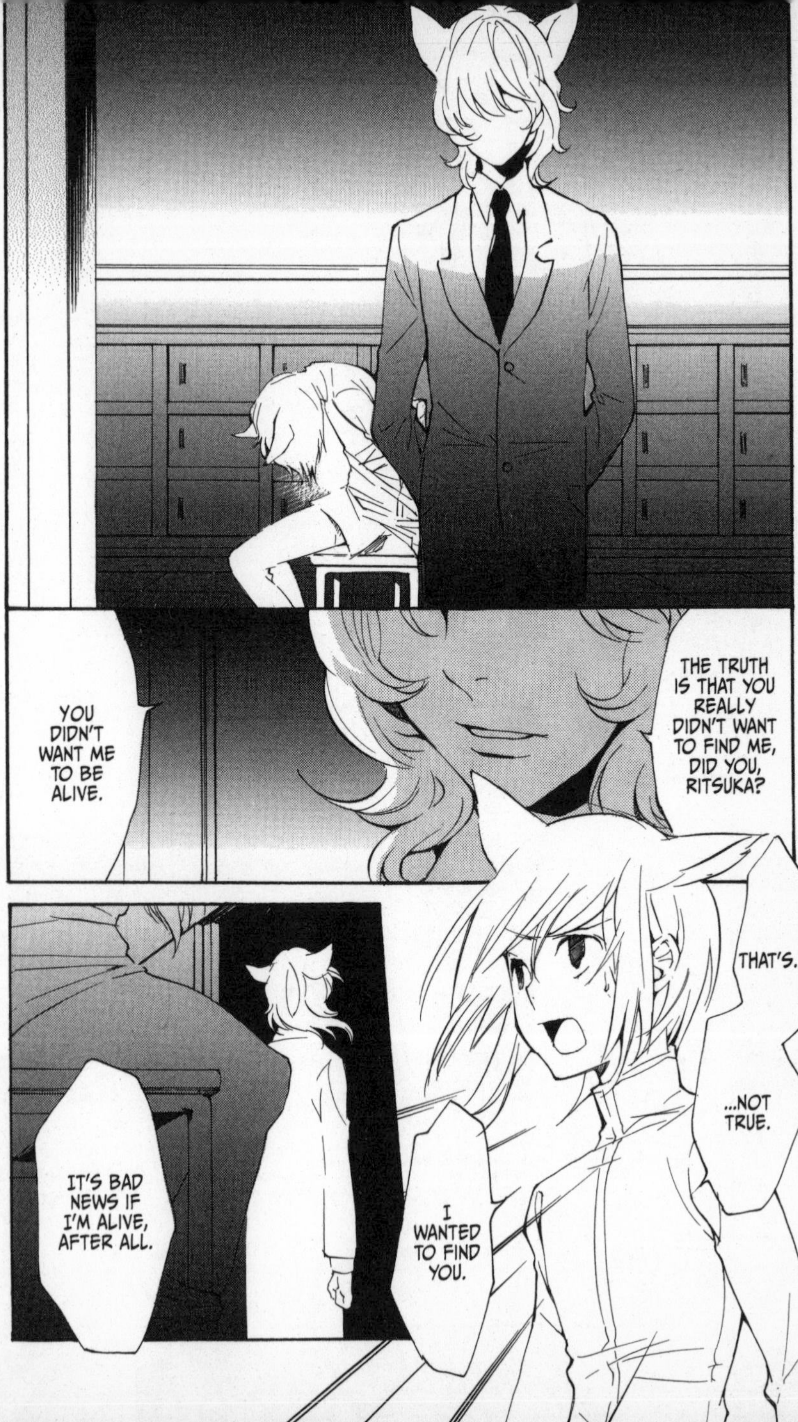
THE TRUTH IS THAT YOU REALLY DIDN'T WANT TO FIND ME, DID YOU, RITSUKA?
YOU DIDN'T WANT ME TO BE ALIVE.
THAT'S...
...NOT TRUE.
I WANTED TO FIND YOU.
IT'S BAD NEWS IF I'M ALIVE, AFTER ALL.

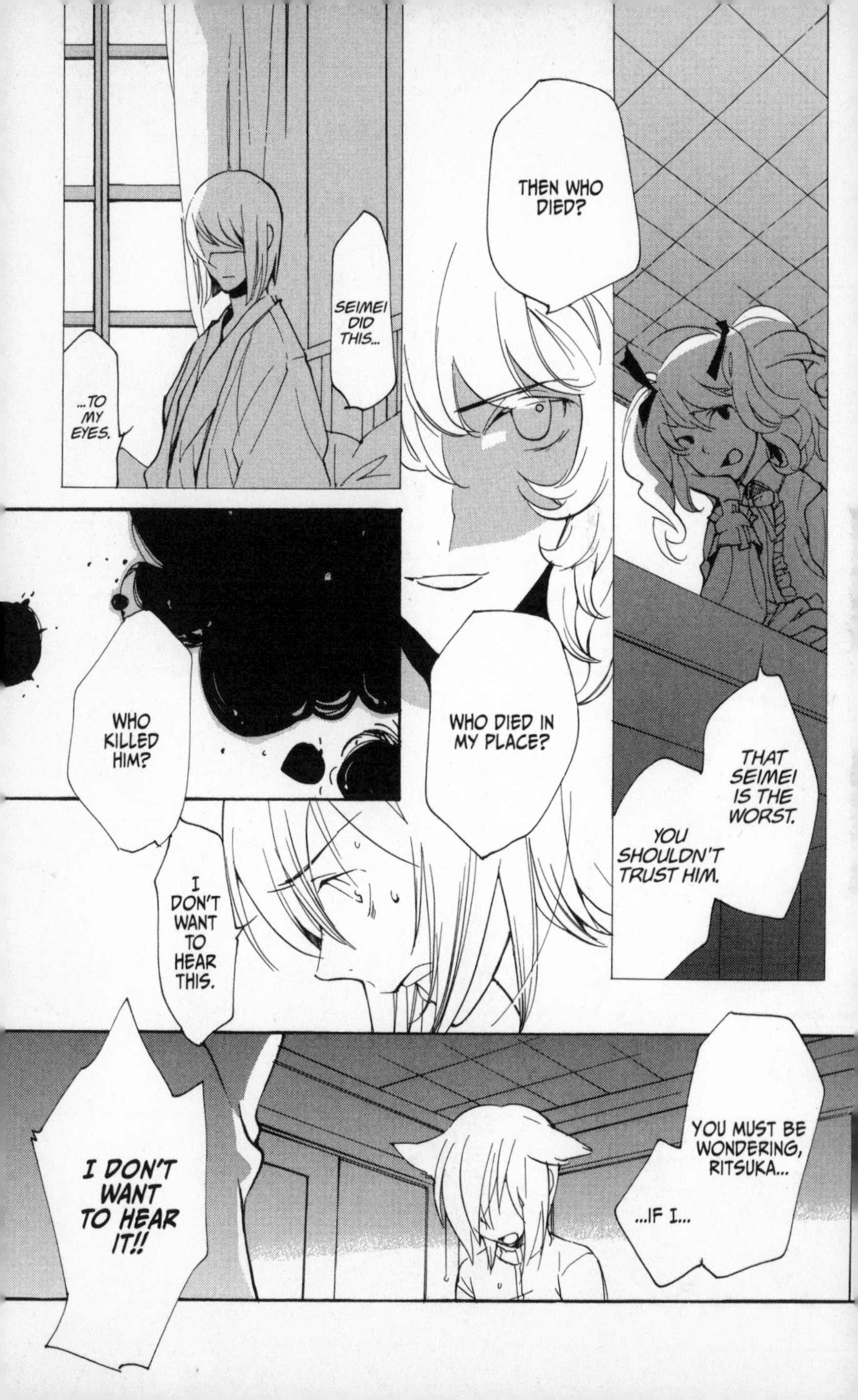
THAT SEIMEI IS THE WORST.
YOU SHOULDN'T TRUST HIM.
SEIMEI DID THIS...
...TO MY EYES.
THEN WHO DIED?
WHO DIED IN MY PLACE?
WHO KILLED HIM?
I DON'T WANT TO HEAR THIS.
YOU MUST BE WONDERING, RITSUKA...
...IF I...
I DON'T WANT TO HEAR IT!!

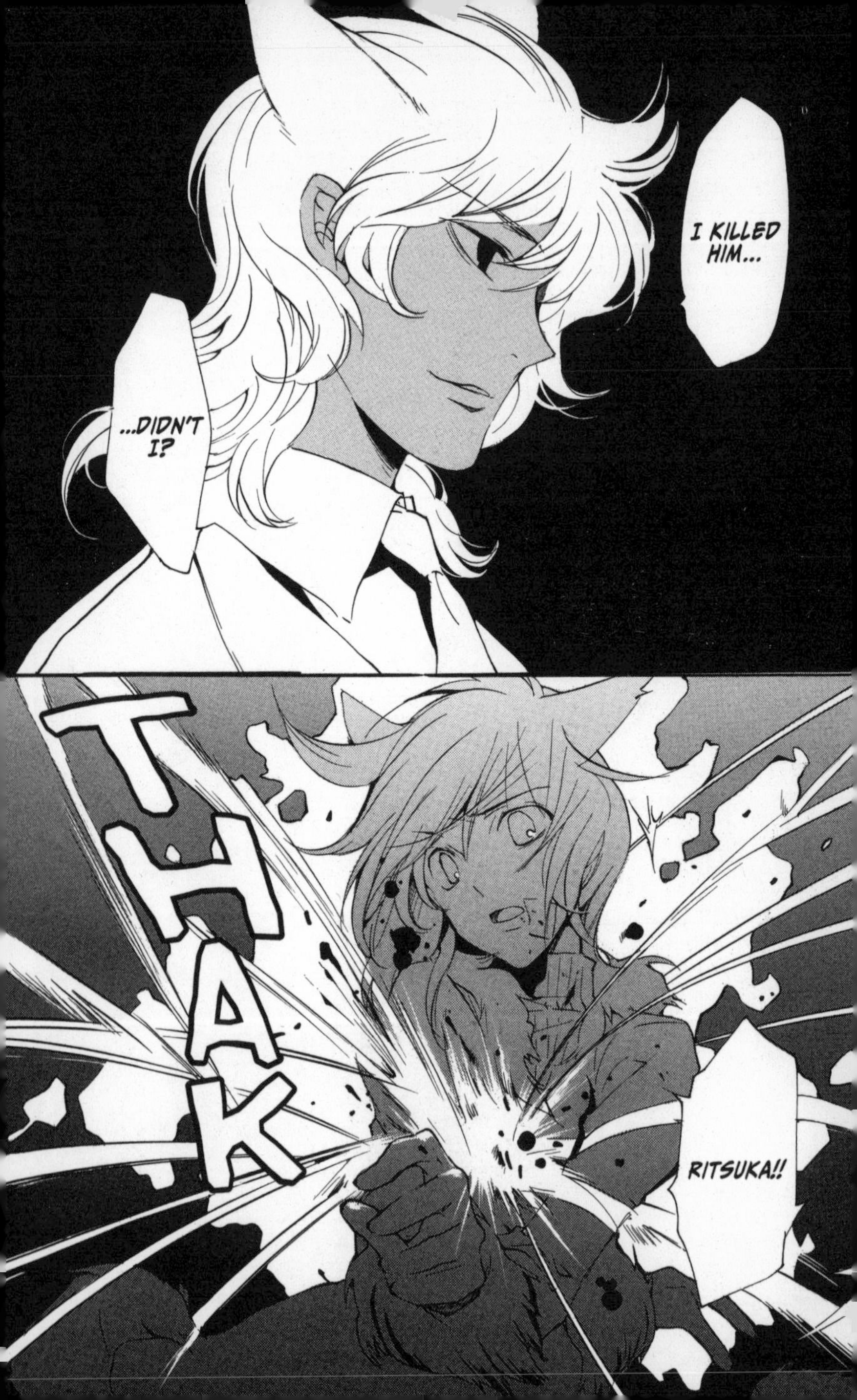
I KILLED HIM...
...DIDN'T I?
THAK
RITSUKA!!

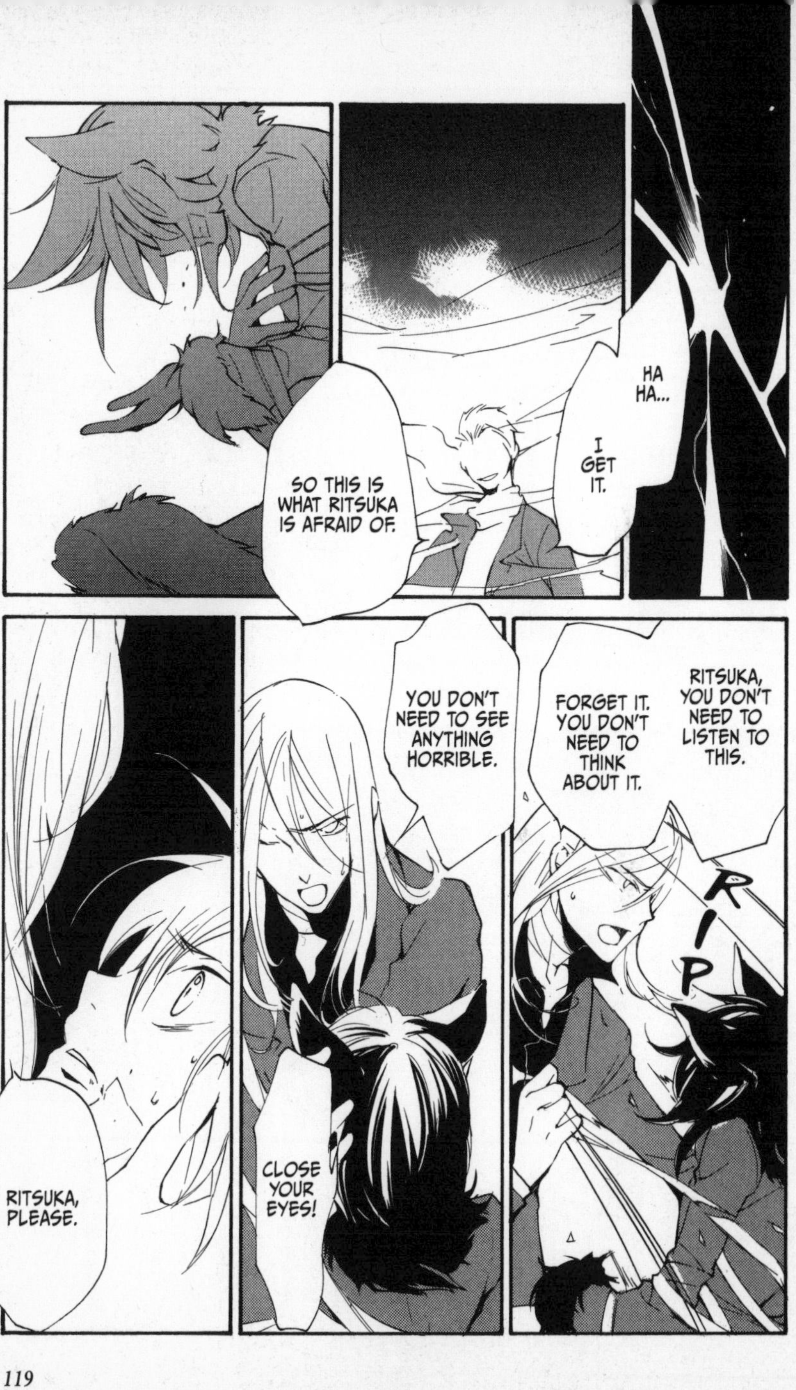
HA HA...
I GET IT.
SO THIS IS WHAT RITSUKA IS AFRAID OF.
RITSUKA, YOU DON'T NEED TO LISTEN TO THIS.
FORGET IT. YOU DON'T NEED TO THINK ABOUT IT.
RIP
YOU DON'T NEED TO SEE ANYTHING HORRIBLE.
CLOSE YOUR EYES!
RITSUKA, PLEASE.

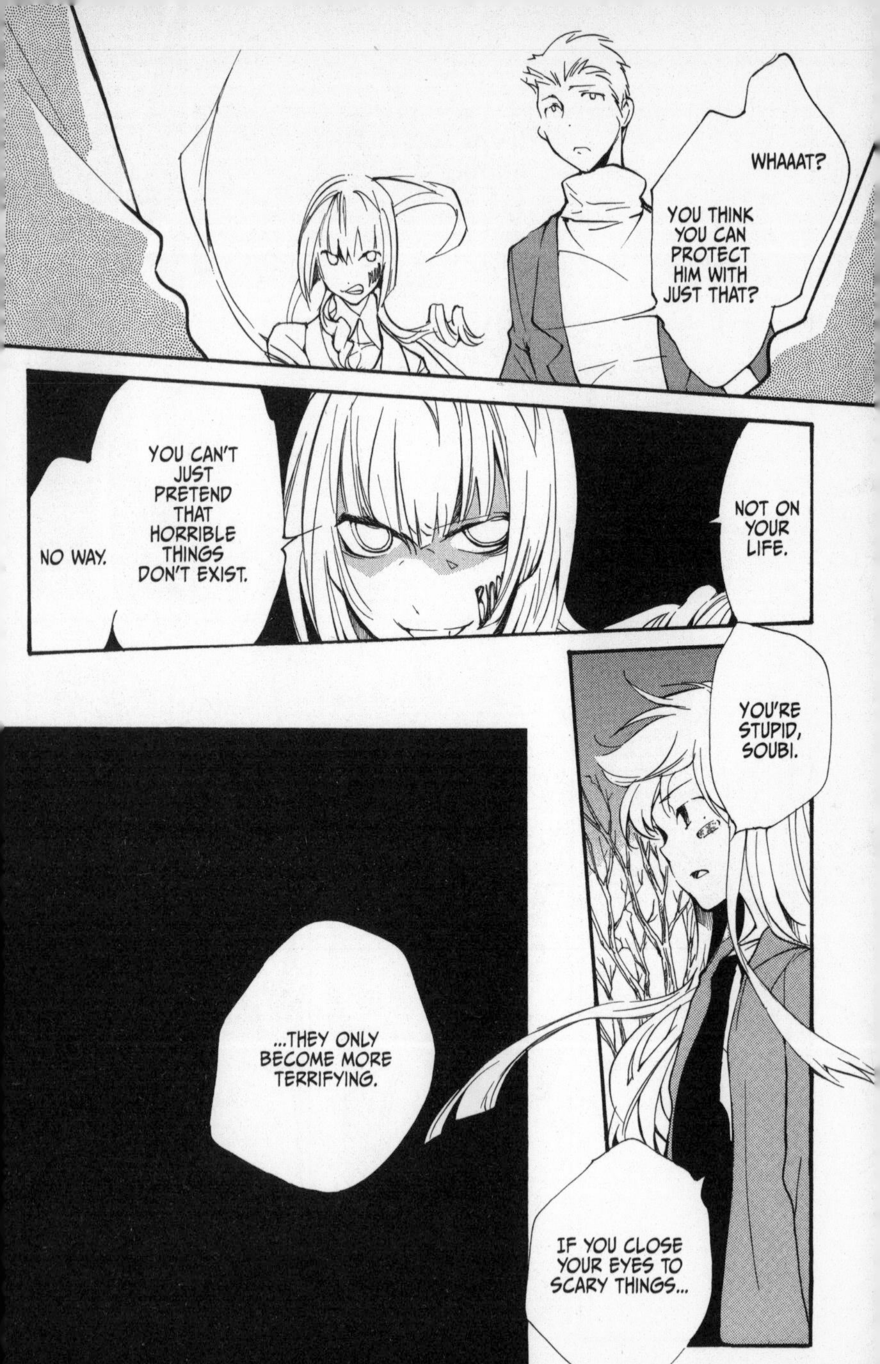
WHAAAT?
YOU THINK YOU CAN PROTECT HIM WITH JUST THAT?
NOT ON YOUR LIFE.
YOU CAN'T JUST PRETEND THAT HORRIBLE THINGS DON'T EXIST.
NO WAY.
YOU'RE STUPID, SOUBI.
IF YOU CLOSE YOUR EYES TO SCARY THINGS...
...THEY ONLY BECOME MORE TERRIFYING.

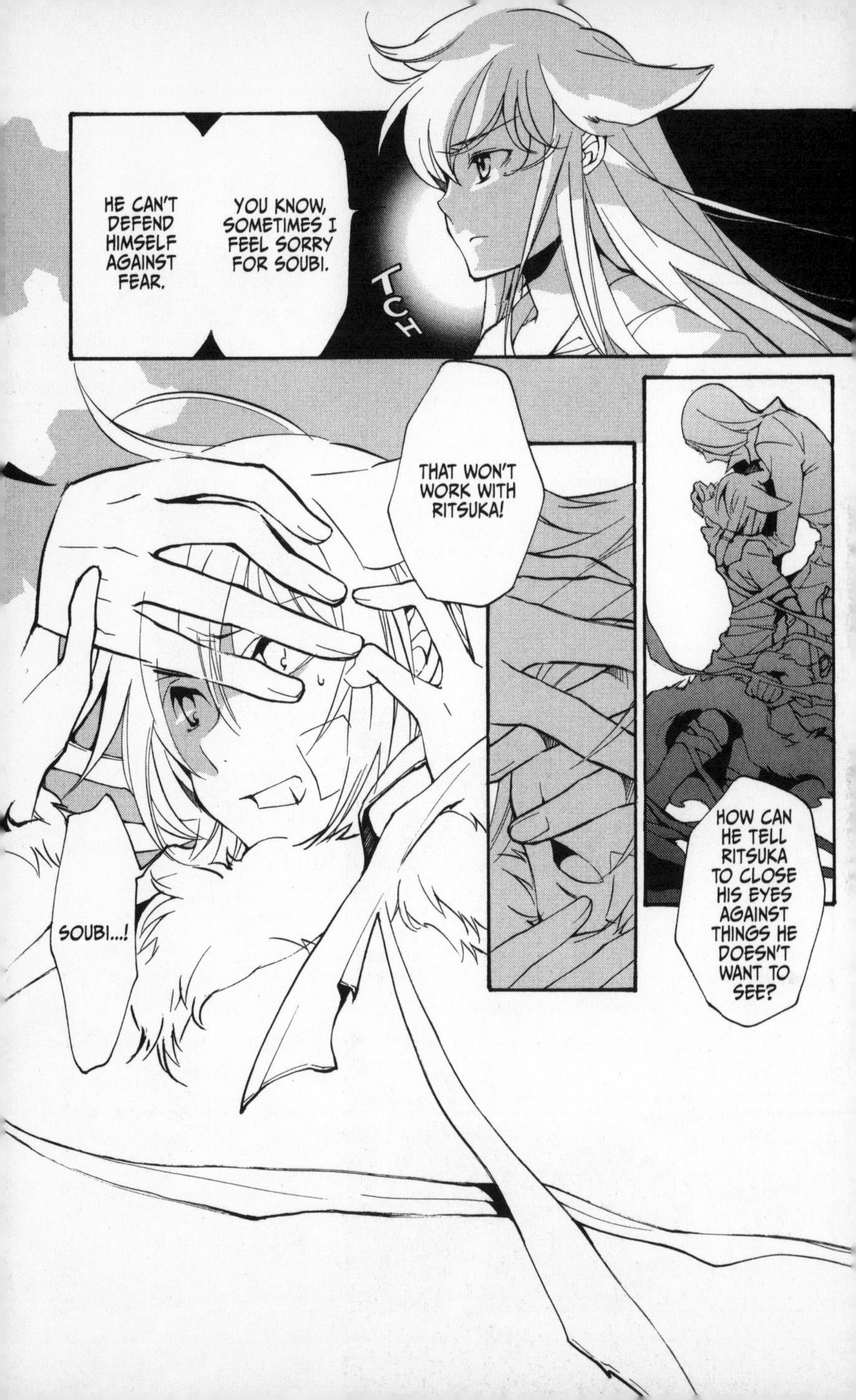
YOU KNOW, SOMETIMES I FEEL SORRY FOR SOUBI.
HE CAN'T DEFEND HIMSELF AGAINST FEAR.
TCH
HOW CAN HE TELL RITSUKA TO CLOSE HIS EYES AGAINST THINGS HE DOESN'T WANT TO SEE?
THAT WON'T WORK WITH RITSUKA!
SOUBI...!

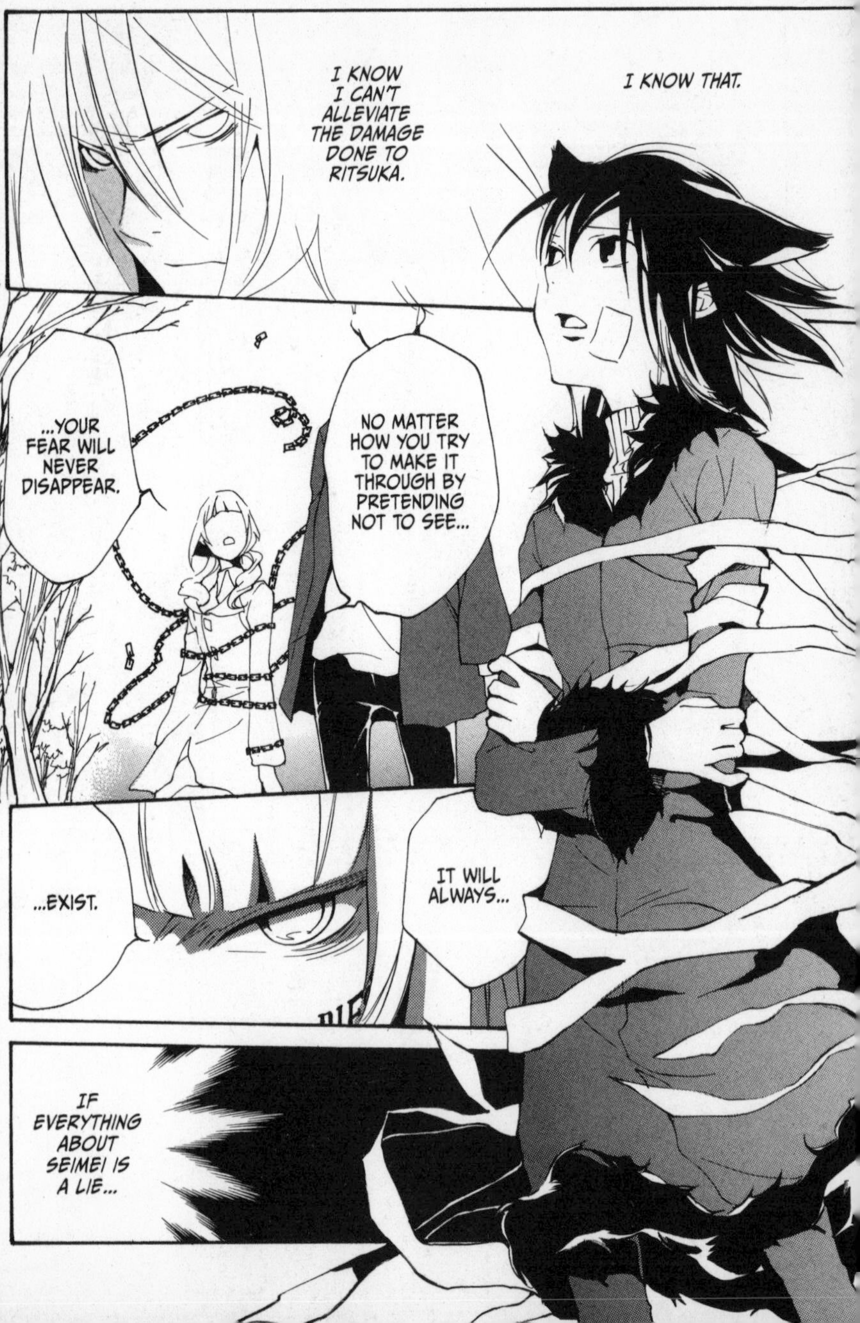
I KNOW THAT.
I KNOW I CAN'T ALLEVIATE THE DAMAGE DONE TO RITSUKA.
NO MATTER HOW YOU TRY TO MAKE IT THROUGH BY PRETENDING NOT TO SEE...
...YOUR FEAR WILL NEVER DISAPPEAR.
IT WILL ALWAYS...
...EXIST.
IF EVERYTHING ABOUT SEIMEI IS A LIE...

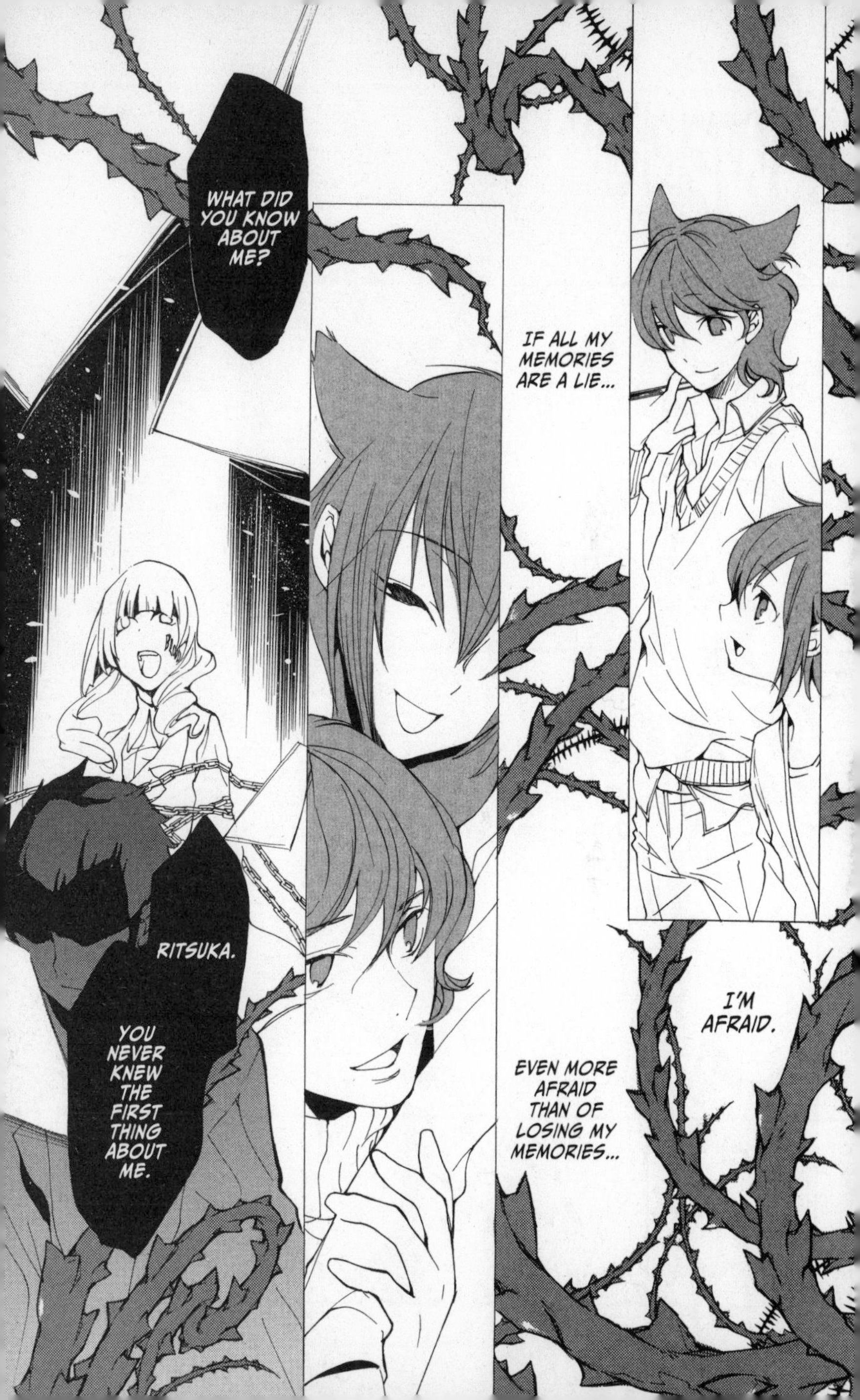
IF ALL MY MEMORIES ARE A LIE...
I'M AFRAID.
EVEN MORE AFRAID THAN OF LOSING MY MEMORIES...
WHAT DID YOU KNOW ABOUT ME?
RITSUKA.
YOU NEVER KNEW THE FIRST THING ABOUT ME.

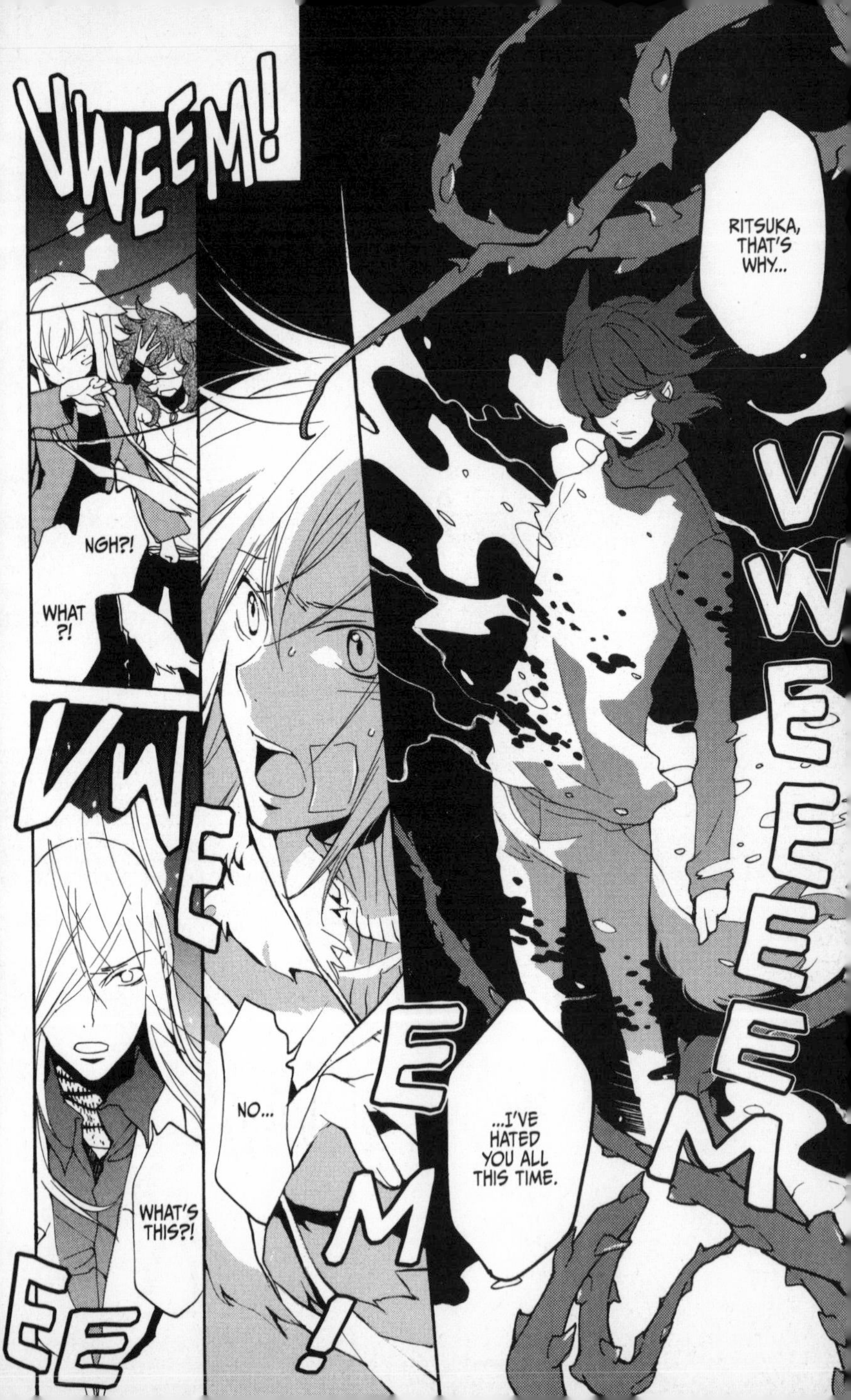
RITSUKA, THAT'S WHY...
VWEEEEM
...I'VE HATED YOU ALL THIS TIME.
NO...
VWEEM!
NGH?!
WHAT ?!
VWEEEEM!
WHAT'S THIS?!

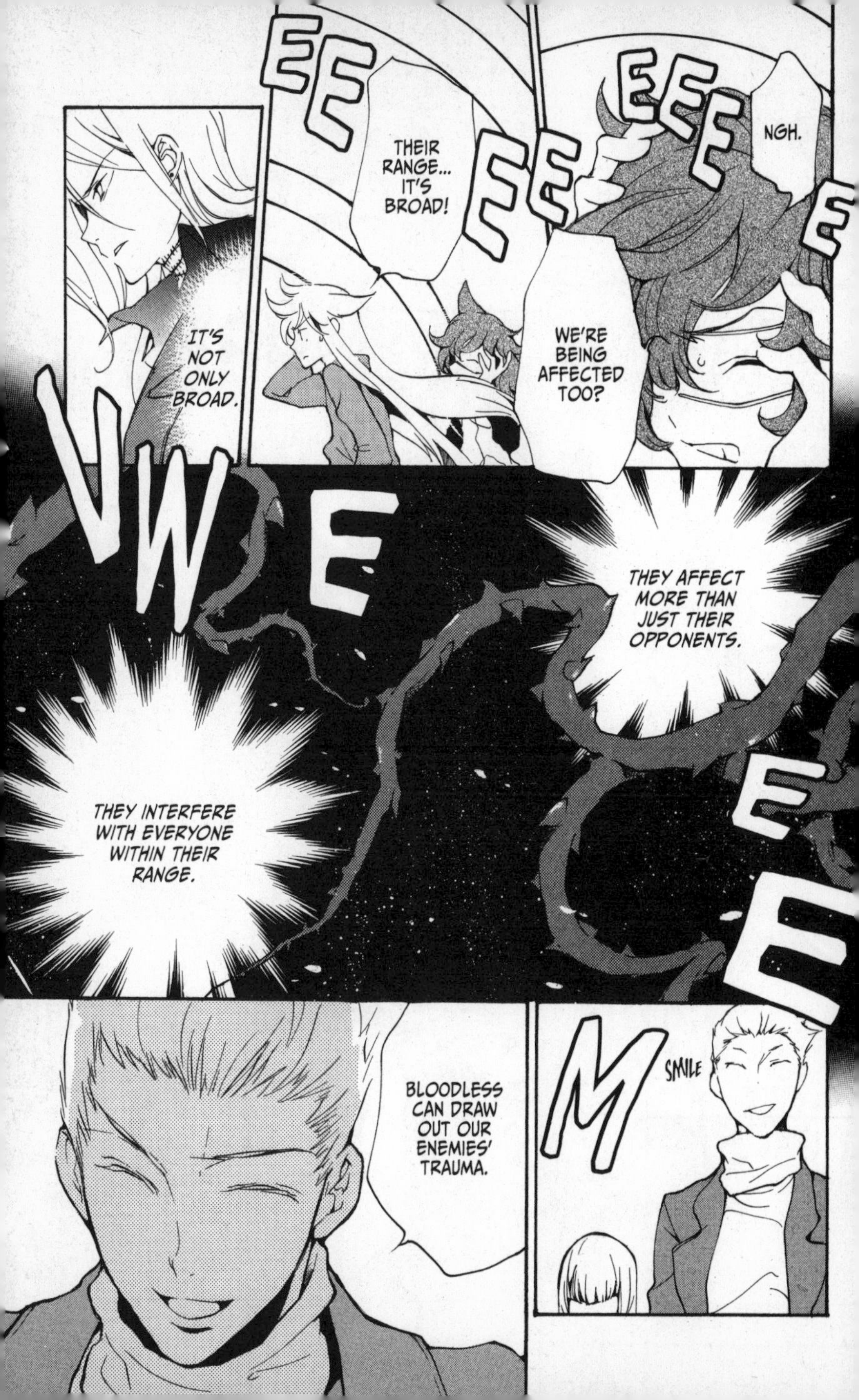
EEEEE
NGH.
WE'RE BEING AFFECTED TOO?
EE
EE
THEIR RANGE... IT'S BROAD!
IT'S NOT ONLY BROAD.
THEY AFFECT MORE THAN JUST THEIR OPPONENTS.
VWE
THEY INTERFERE WITH EVERYONE WITHIN THEIR RANGE.
EE
M
SMILE
BLOODLESS CAN DRAW OUT OUR ENEMIES' TRAUMA.

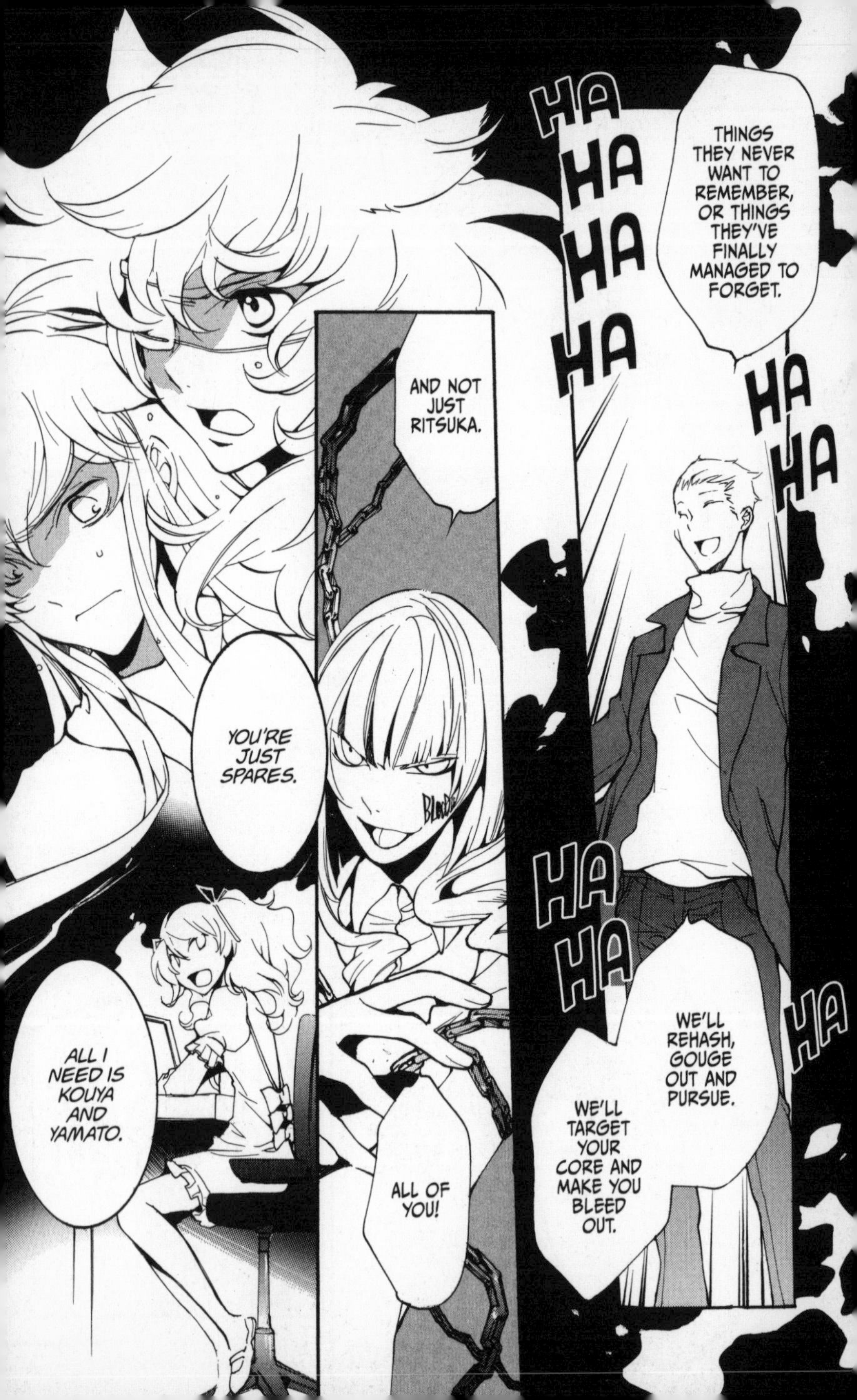
THINGS THEY NEVER WANT TO REMEMBER, OR THINGS THEY'VE FINALLY MANAGED TO FORGET.
HA HA HA HA
HA HA
HA HA
HA
WE'LL REHASH, GOUGE OUT AND PURSUE.
WE'LL TARGET YOUR CORE AND MAKE YOU BLEED OUT.
AND NOT JUST RITSUKA.
ALL OF YOU!
YOU'RE JUST SPARES.
ALL I NEED IS KOUYA AND YAMATO.

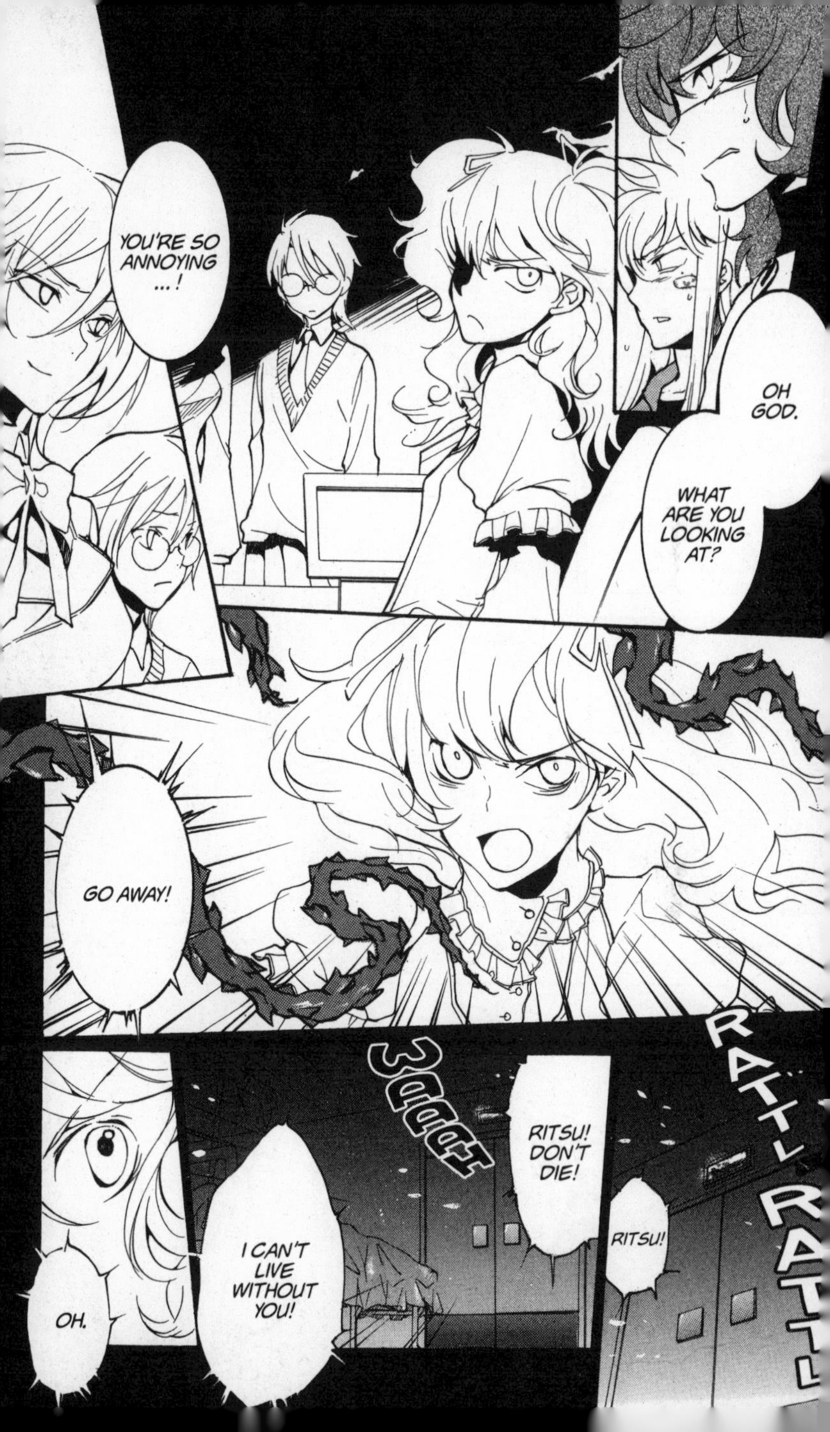
OH GOD.
WHAT ARE YOU LOOKING AT?
YOU'RE SO ANNOYING ...!
GO AWAY!
RATTL RATTL
RITSU! DON'T DIE!
RITSU!
I CAN'T LIVE WITHOUT YOU!
OH.

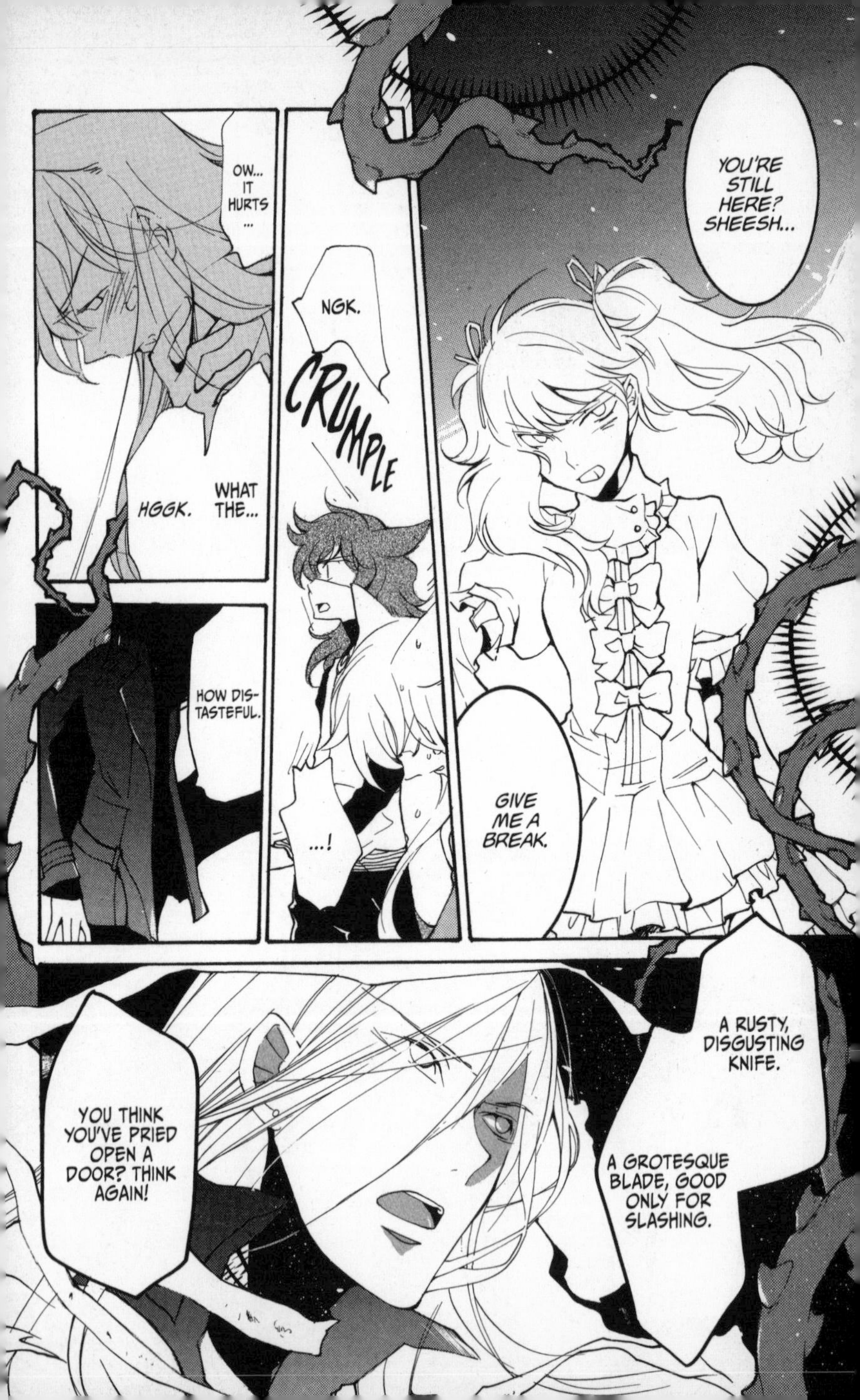
YOU'RE STILL HERE? SHEESH...
GIVE ME A BREAK.
NGK.
CRUMPLE
...!
OW... IT HURTS ...
WHAT THE...
HGGK.
HOW DIS-TASTEFUL.
A RUSTY, DISGUSTING KNIFE.
A GROTESQUE BLADE, GOOD ONLY FOR SLASHING.
YOU THINK YOU'VE PRIED OPEN A DOOR? THINK AGAIN!

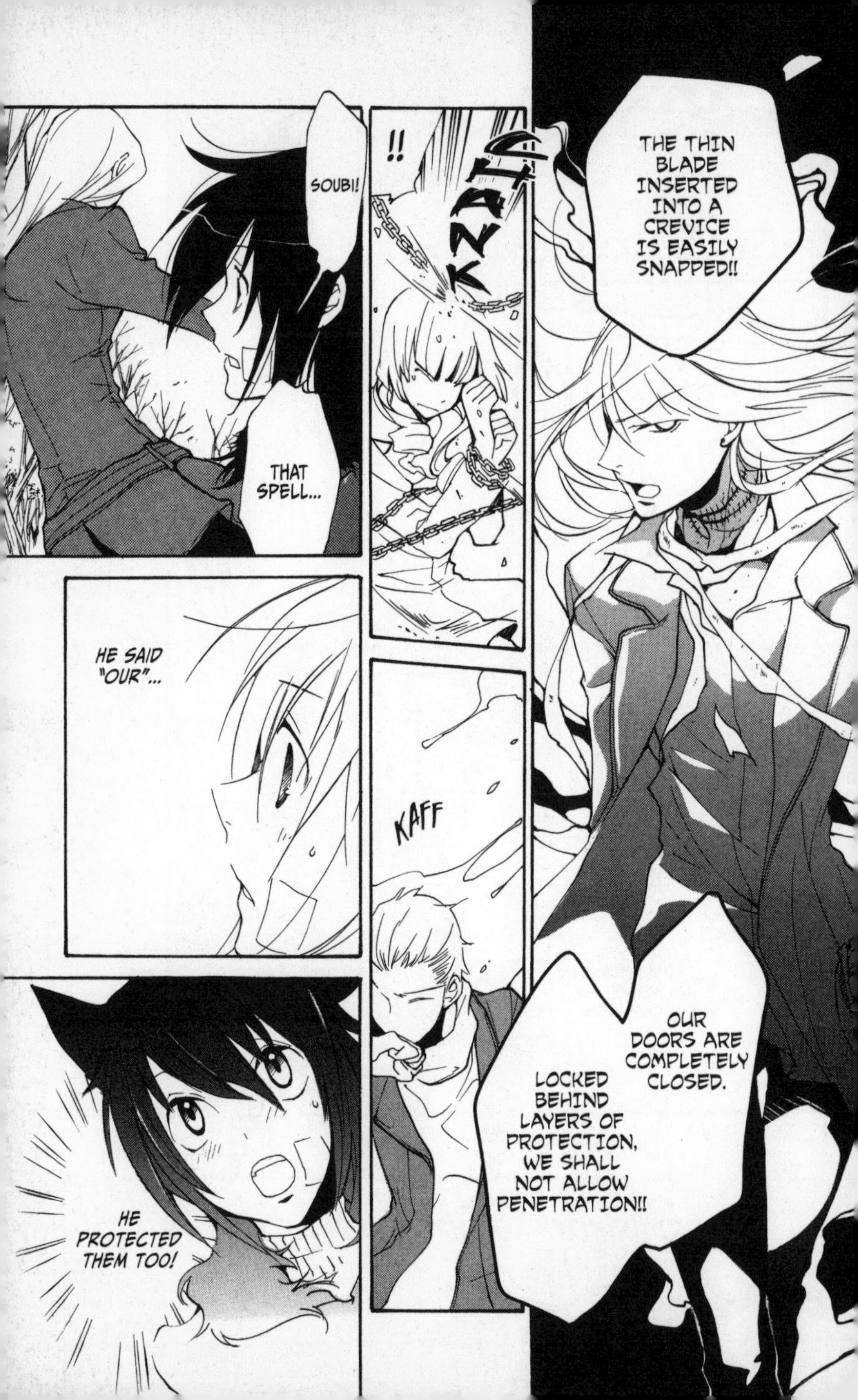
THE THIN BLADE INSERTED INTO A CREVICE IS EASILY SNAPPED!!
OUR DOORS ARE COMPLETELY CLOSED.
LOCKED BEHIND LAYERS OF PROTECTION, WE SHALL NOT ALLOW PENETRATION!!
!!
CHANK
SOUBI!
THAT SPELL...
KAFF
HE SAID "OUR"...
HE PROTECTED THEM TOO!

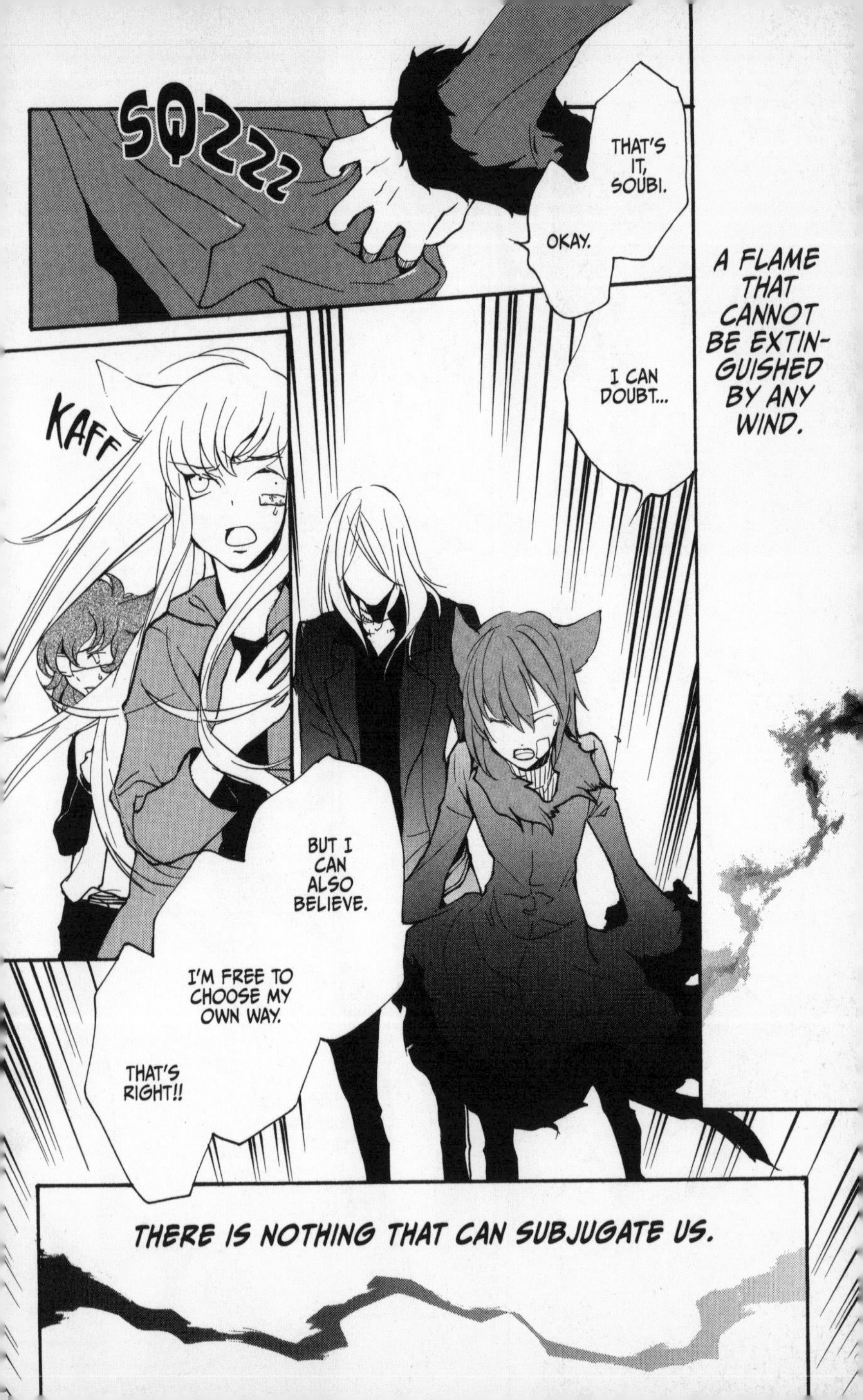
SQZZZ
THAT'S IT, SOUBI.
OKAY.
A FLAME THAT CANNOT BE EXTIN-GUISHED BY ANY WIND.
I CAN DOUBT...
KAFF
BUT I CAN ALSO BELIEVE.
I'M FREE TO CHOOSE MY OWN WAY.
THAT'S RIGHT!!
THERE IS NOTHING THAT CAN SUBJUGATE US.

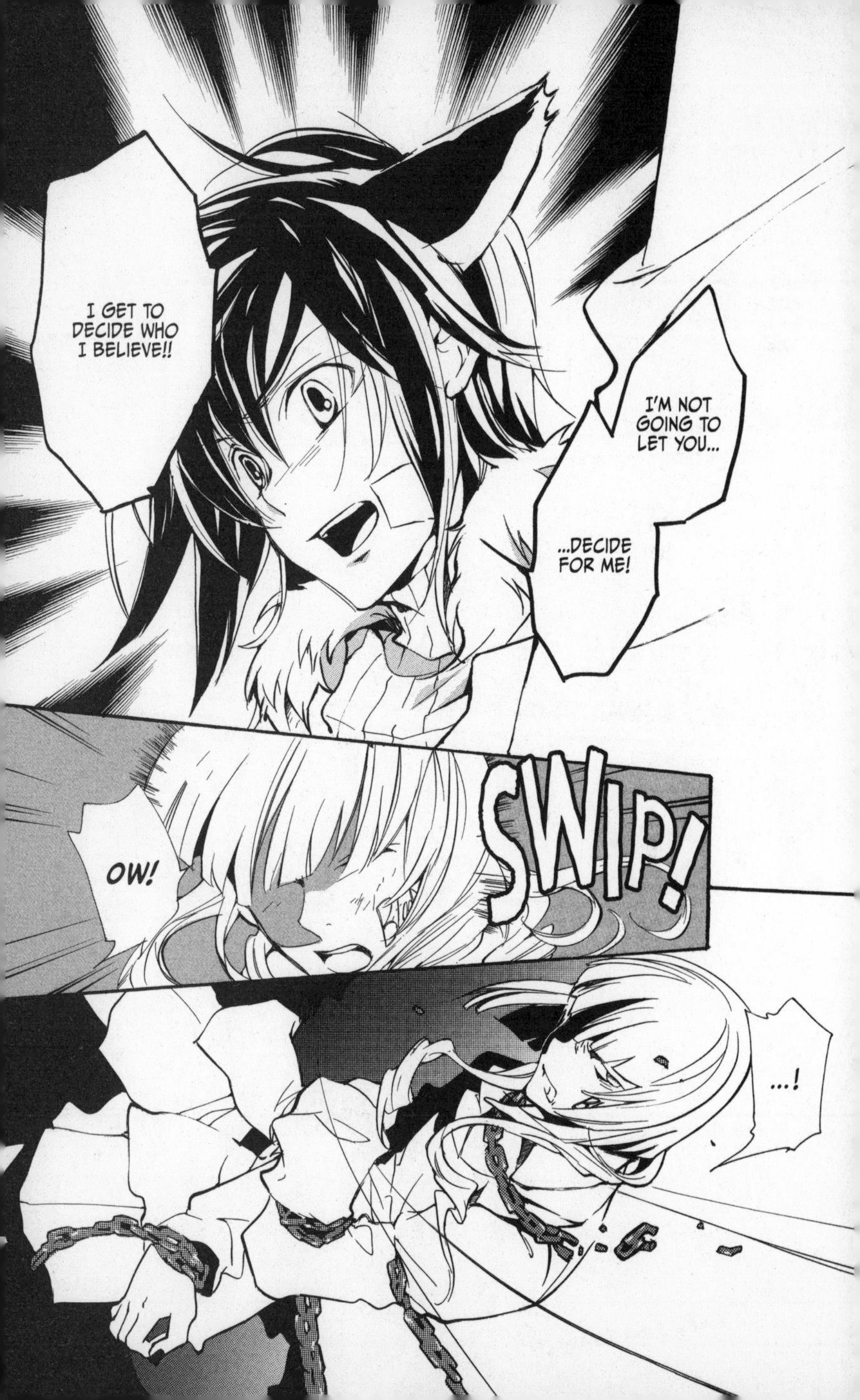
I GET TO DECIDE WHO I BELIEVE!!
I'M NOT GOING TO LET YOU...
...DECIDE FOR ME!
SWIP!
OW!
...!

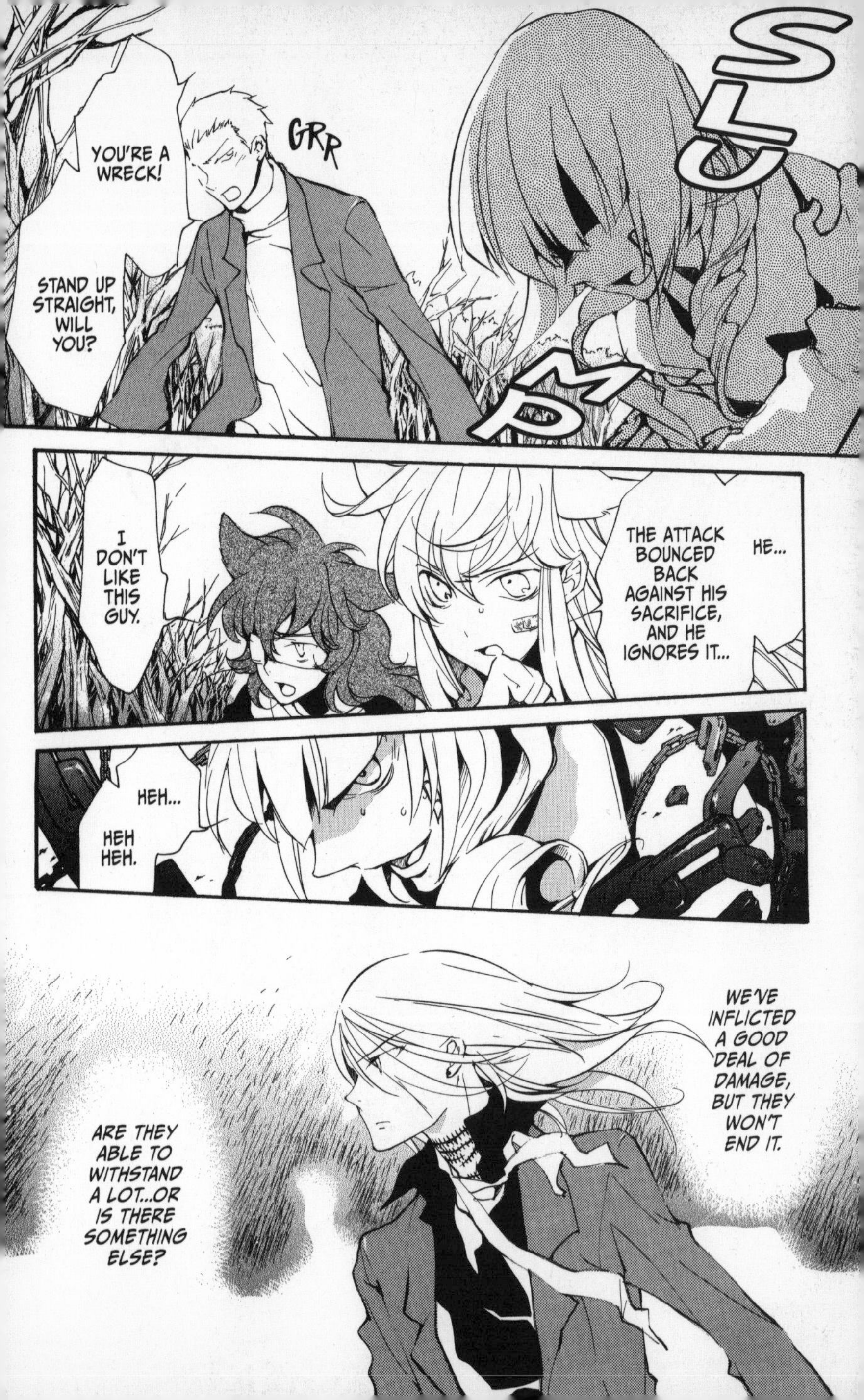
SLUMP
GRR
YOU'RE A WRECK!
STAND UP STRAIGHT, WILL YOU?
HE...
THE ATTACK BOUNCED BACK AGAINST HIS SACRIFICE, AND HE IGNORES IT...
I DON'T LIKE THIS GUY.
HEH...
HEH HEH.
WE'VE INFLICTED A GOOD DEAL OF DAMAGE, BUT THEY WON'T END IT.
ARE THEY ABLE TO WITHSTAND A LOT...OR IS THERE SOMETHING ELSE?

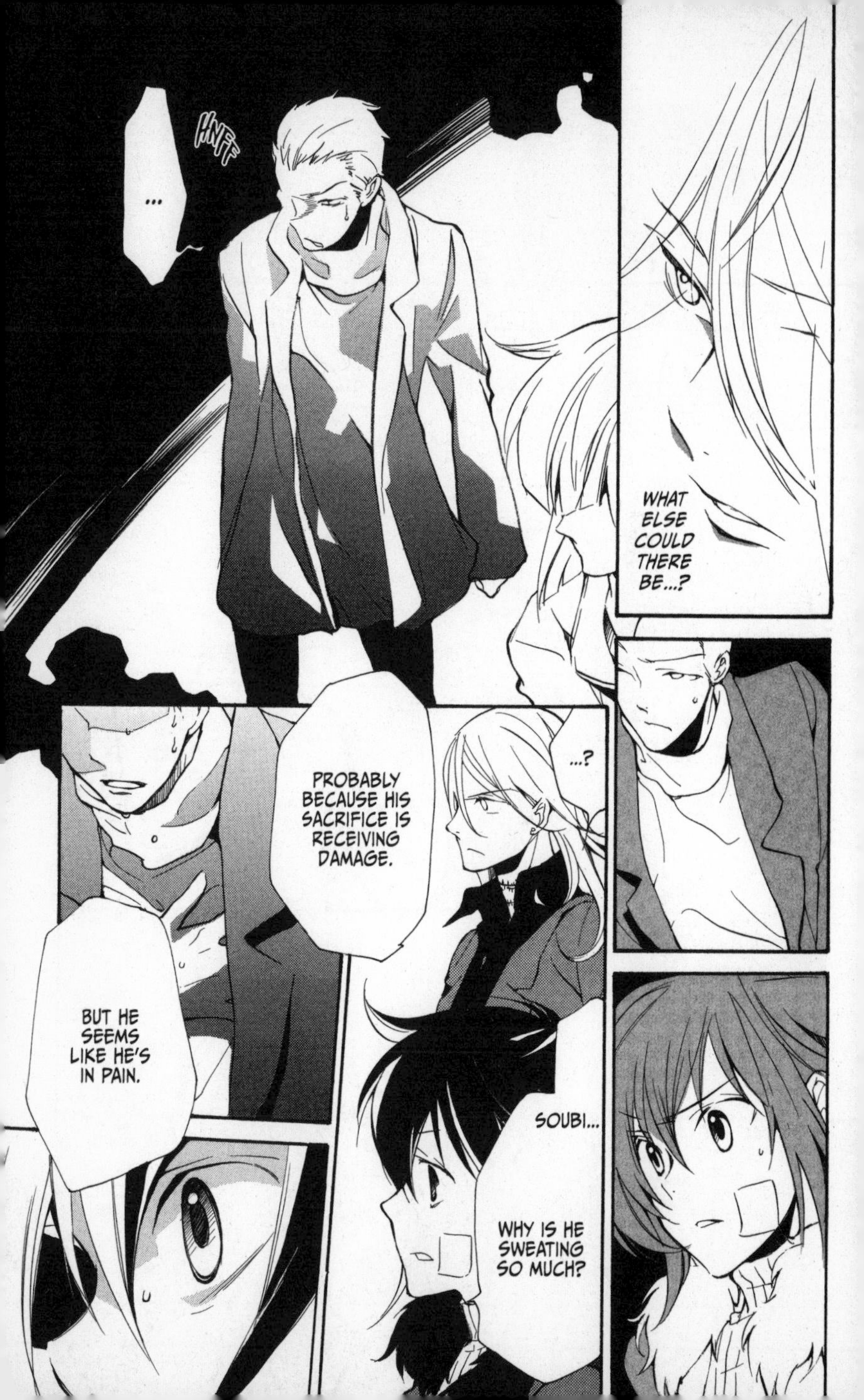
WHAT ELSE COULD THERE BE...?
HNFF
...
...?
PROBABLY BECAUSE HIS SACRIFICE IS RECEIVING DAMAGE.
BUT HE SEEMS LIKE HE'S IN PAIN.
SOUBI...
WHY IS HE SWEATING SO MUCH?

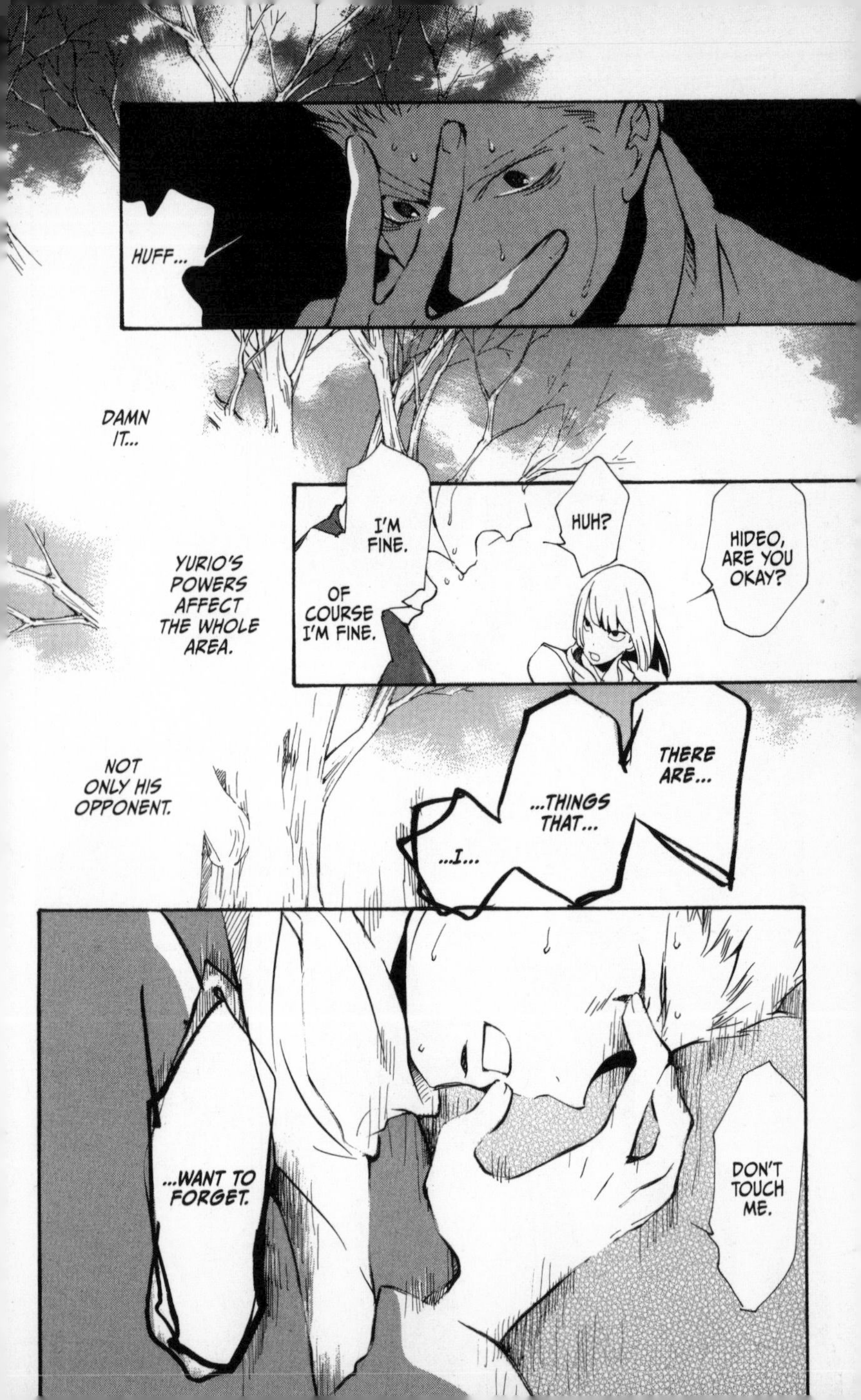
HUFF...
DAMN IT...
HIDEO, ARE YOU OKAY?
HUH?
I'M FINE.
OF COURSE I'M FINE.
YURIO'S POWERS AFFECT THE WHOLE AREA.
NOT ONLY HIS OPPONENT.
THERE ARE...
...THINGS THAT...
...I...
DON'T TOUCH ME.
...WANT TO FORGET.

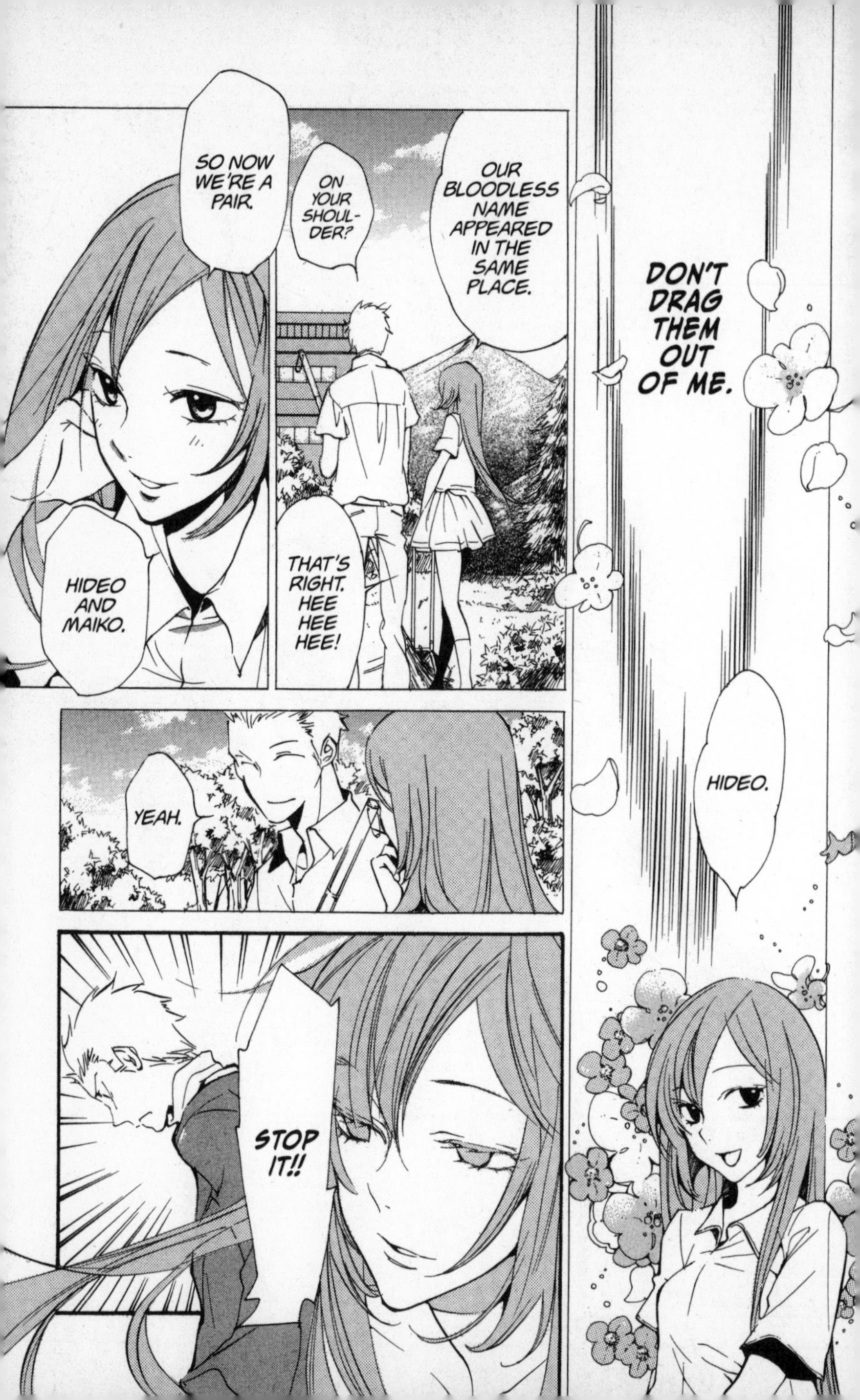
DON'T DRAG THEM OUT OF ME.
HIDEO.
OUR BLOODLESS NAME APPEARED IN THE SAME PLACE.
ON YOUR SHOULDER?
THAT'S RIGHT. HEE HEE HEE!
SO NOW WE'RE A PAIR.
HIDEO AND MAIKO.
YEAH.
STOP IT!!

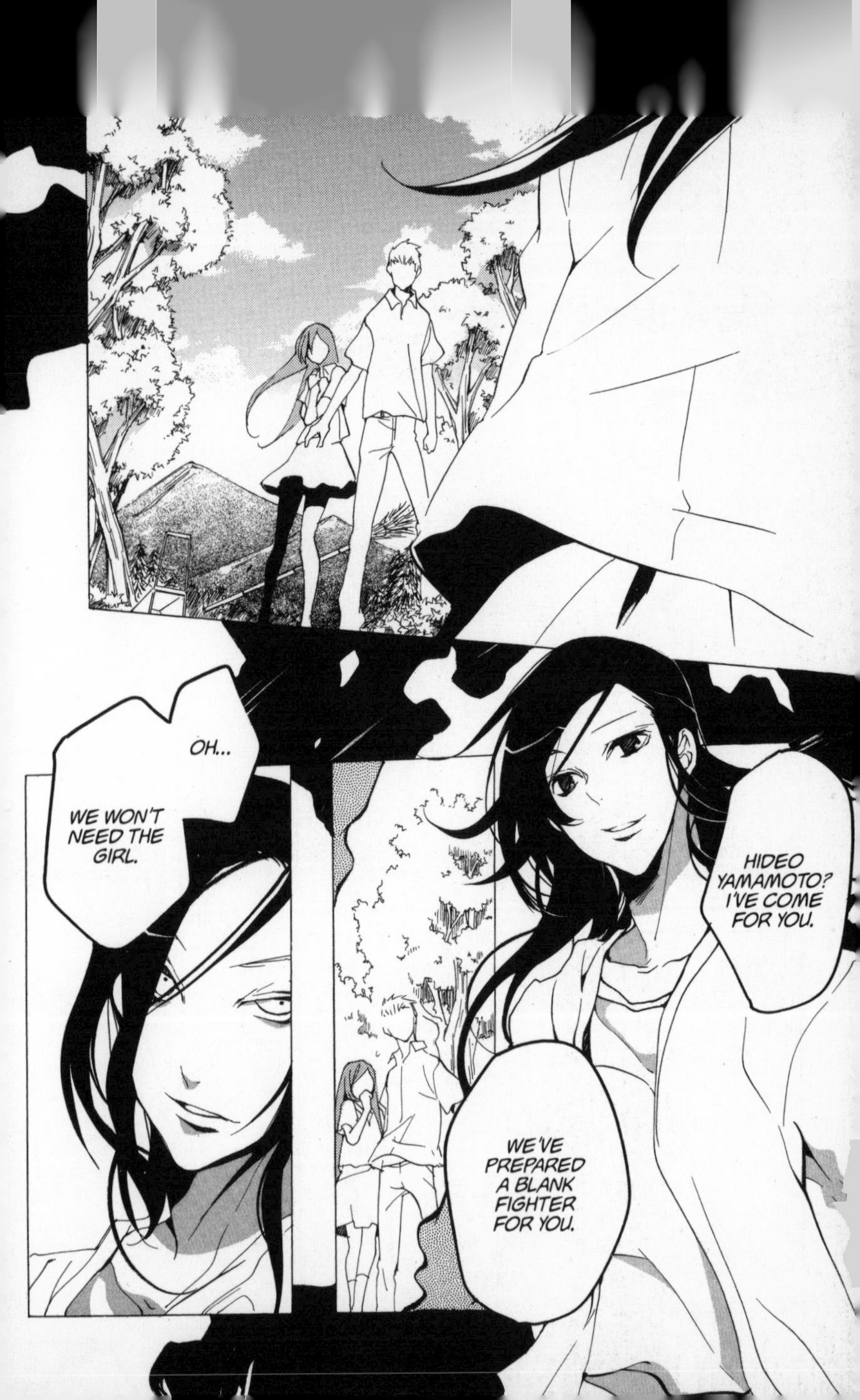
HIDEO YAMAMOTO? I'VE COME FOR YOU.
WE'VE PREPARED A BLANK FIGHTER FOR YOU.
OH...
WE WON'T NEED THE GIRL.

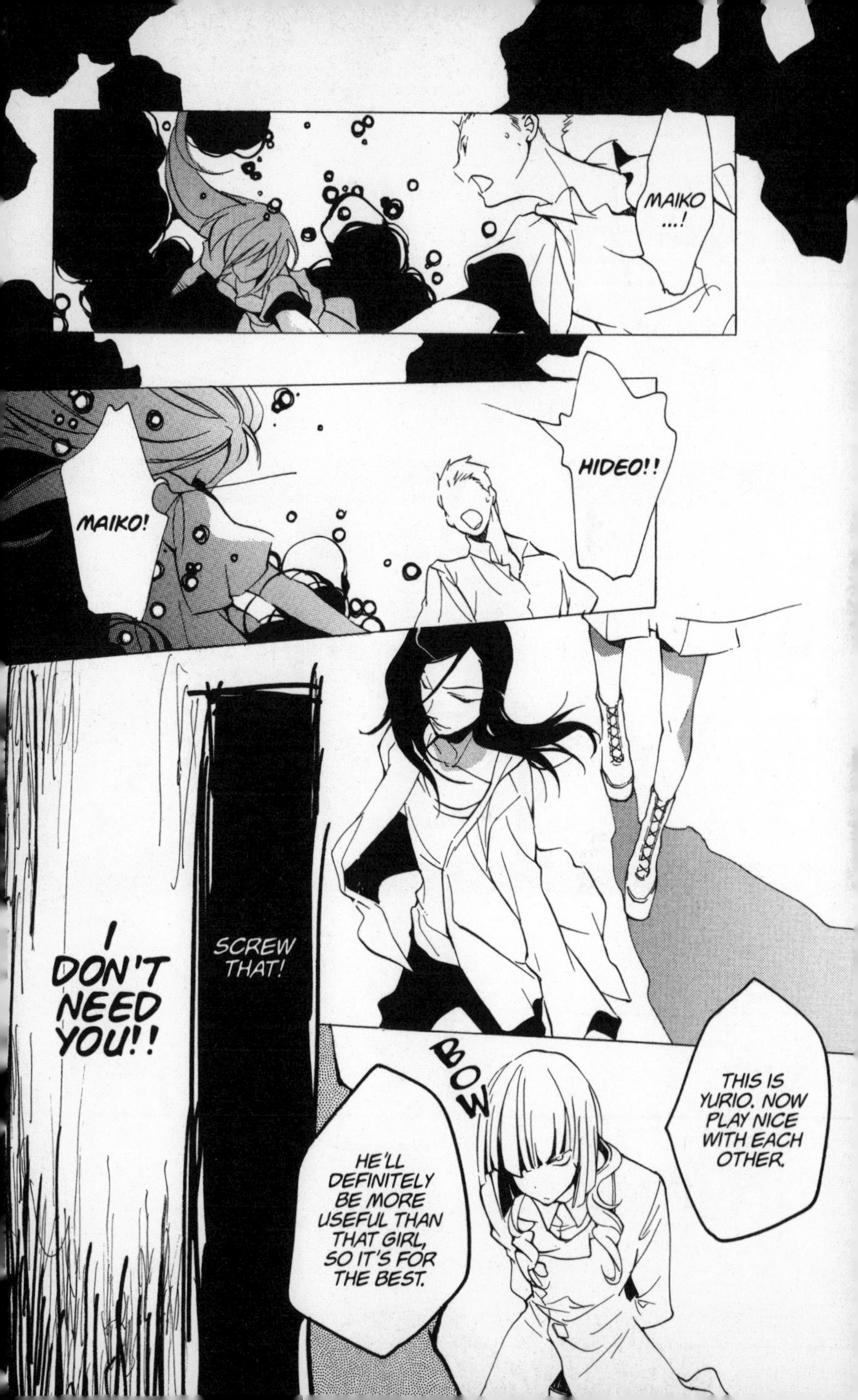
MAIKO ...!
HIDEO!!
MAIKO!
BOW
THIS IS YURIO. NOW PLAY NICE WITH EACH OTHER.
HE'LL DEFINITELY BE MORE USEFUL THAN THAT GIRL, SO IT'S FOR THE BEST.
SCREW THAT!
I DON'T NEED YOU!!

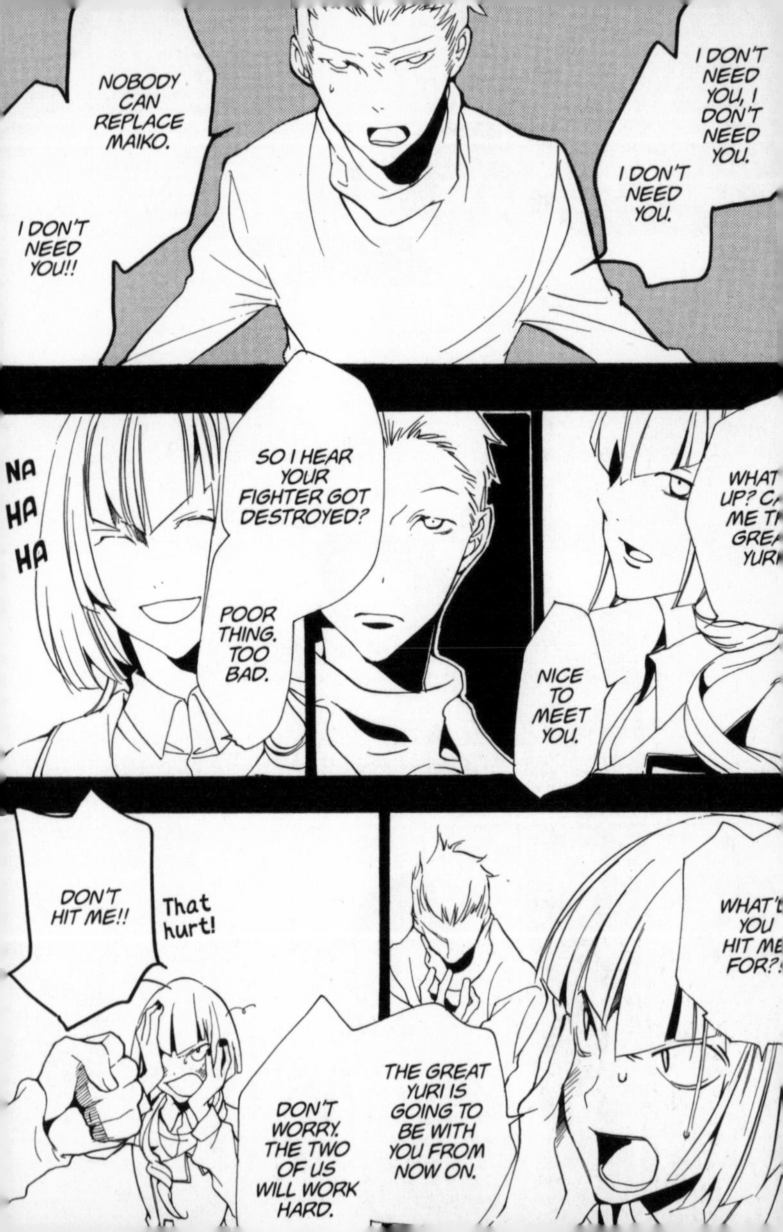
I DON'T NEED YOU, I DON'T NEED YOU.
I DON'T NEED YOU.
NOBODY CAN REPLACE MAIKO.
I DON'T NEED YOU!!
WHAT UP? CA ME TH GREA YUR
NICE TO MEET YOU.
SO I HEAR YOUR FIGHTER GOT DESTROYED?
POOR THING. TOO BAD.
NA HA HA
WHAT' YOU HIT ME FOR?!
THE GREAT YURI IS GOING TO BE WITH YOU FROM NOW ON.
DON'T WORRY. THE TWO OF US WILL WORK HARD.
DON'T HIT ME!!
That hurt!

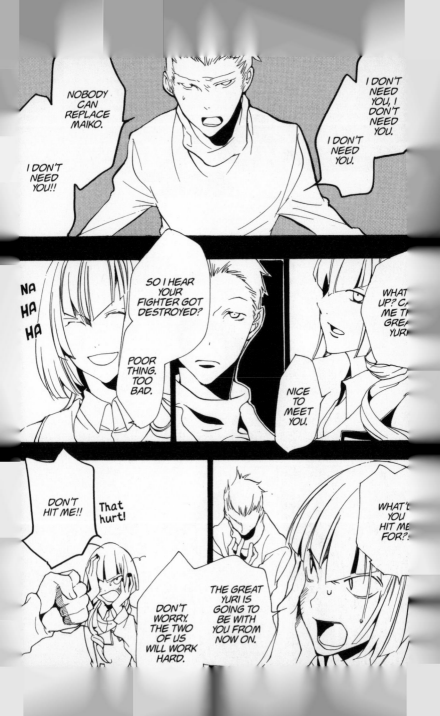

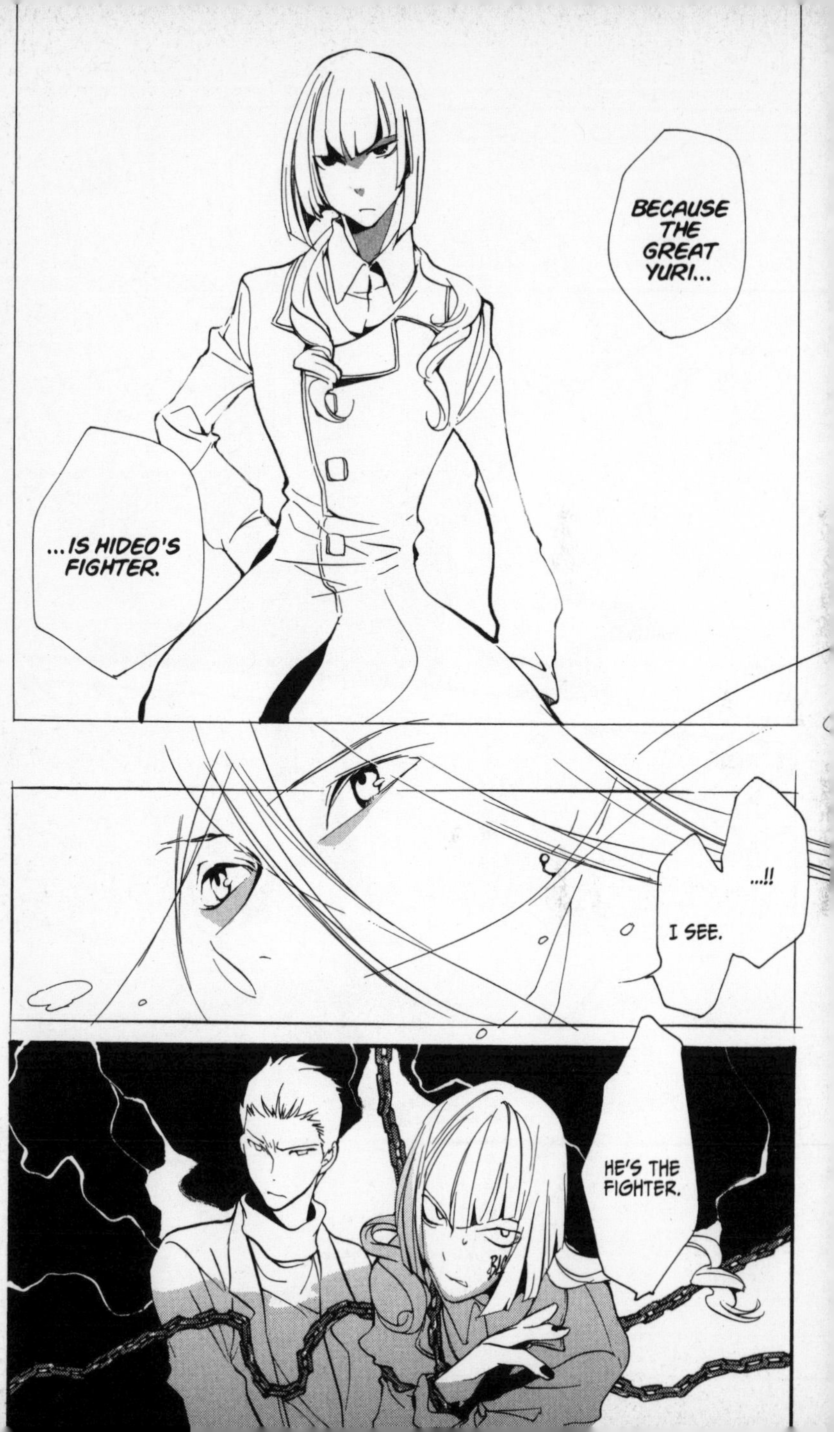
BECAUSE THE GREAT YURI...
...IS HIDEO'S FIGHTER.
...!!
I SEE.
HE'S THE FIGHTER.

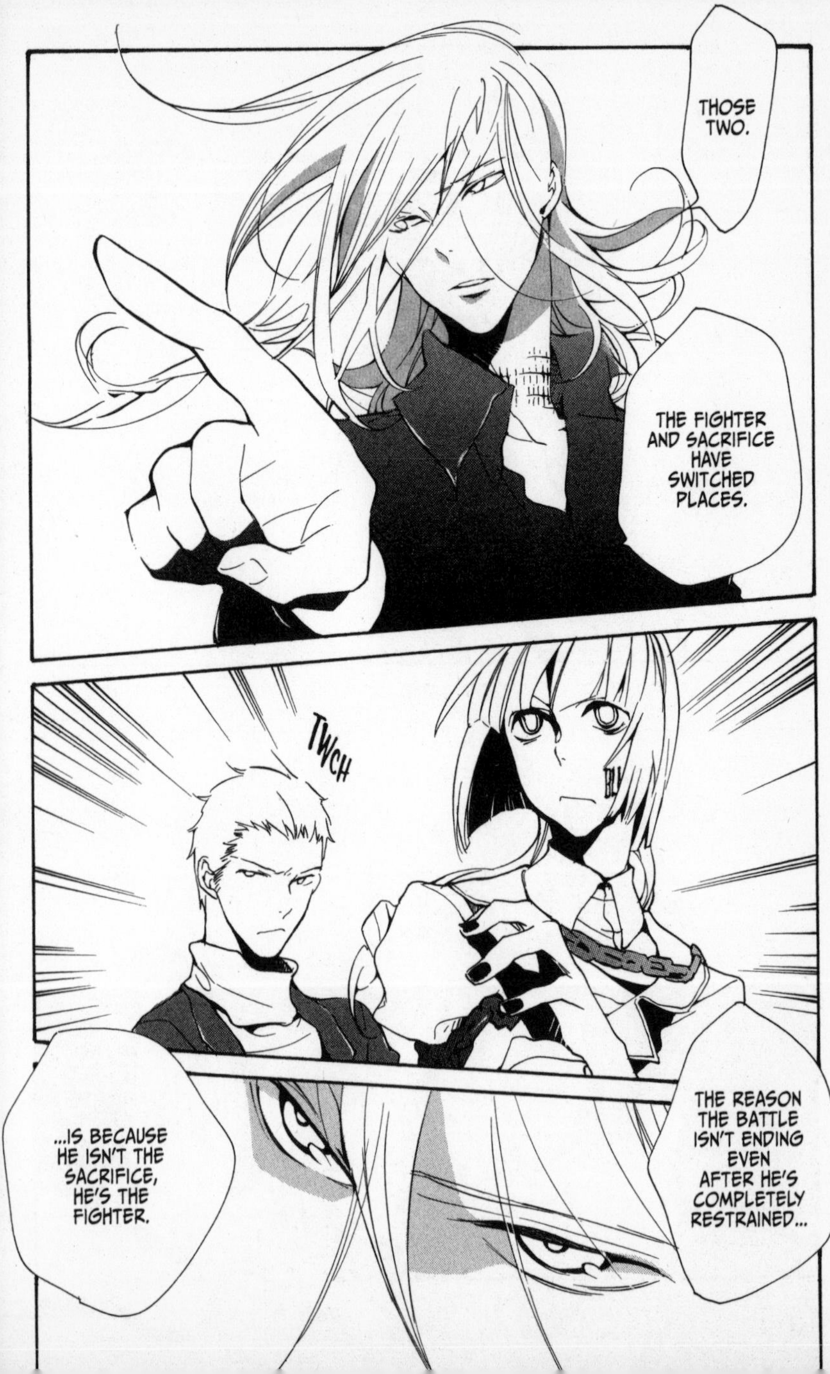
THOSE TWO.
THE FIGHTER AND SACRIFICE HAVE SWITCHED PLACES.
TWCH
THE REASON THE BATTLE ISN'T ENDING EVEN AFTER HE'S COMPLETELY RESTRAINED...
...IS BECAUSE HE ISN'T THE SACRIFICE, HE'S THE FIGHTER.

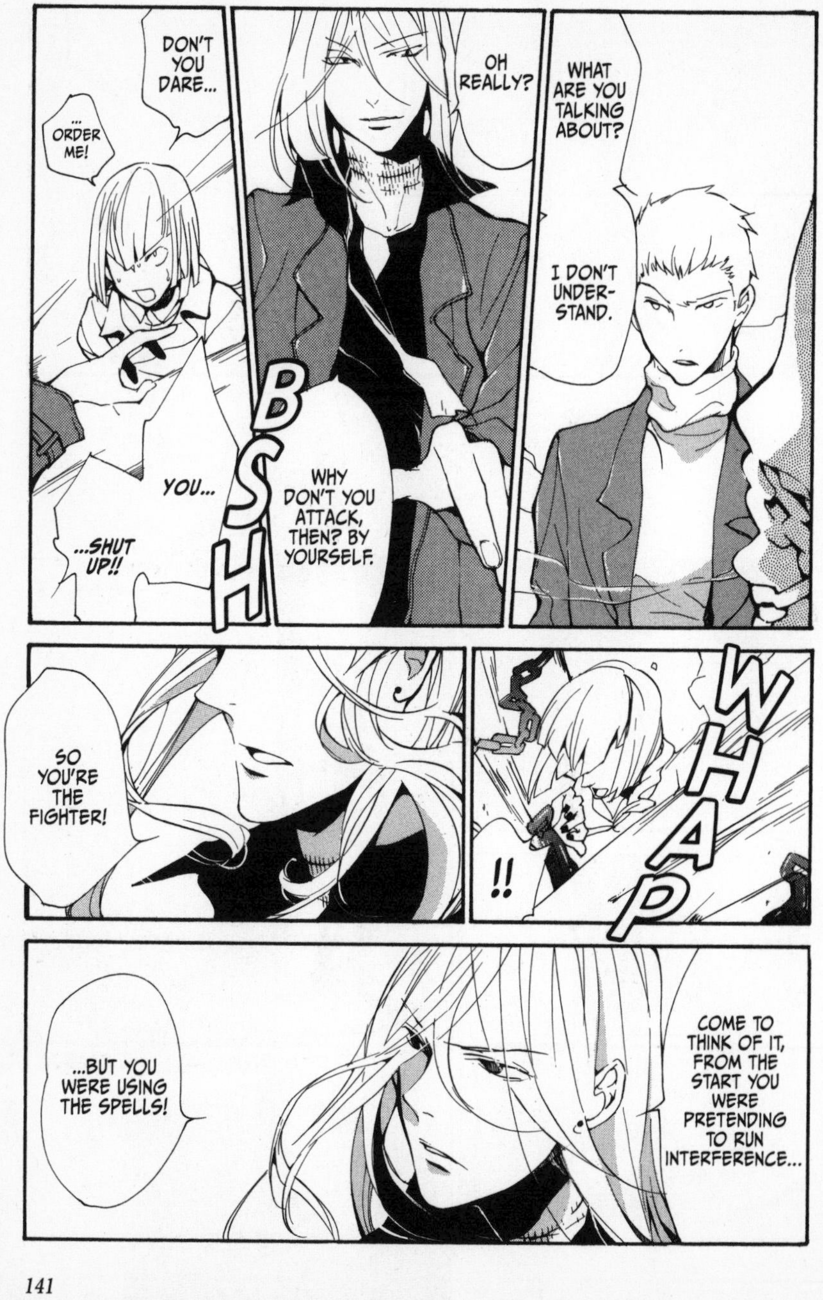
WHAT ARE YOU TALKING ABOUT?
I DON'T UNDER-STAND.
OH REALLY?
WHY DON'T YOU ATTACK, THEN? BY YOURSELF.
BSH
DON'T YOU DARE...
...ORDER ME!
YOU...
...SHUT UP!!
WHAP
!!
SO YOU'RE THE FIGHTER!
COME TO THINK OF IT, FROM THE START YOU WERE PRETENDING TO RUN INTERFERENCE...
...BUT YOU WERE USING THE SPELLS!

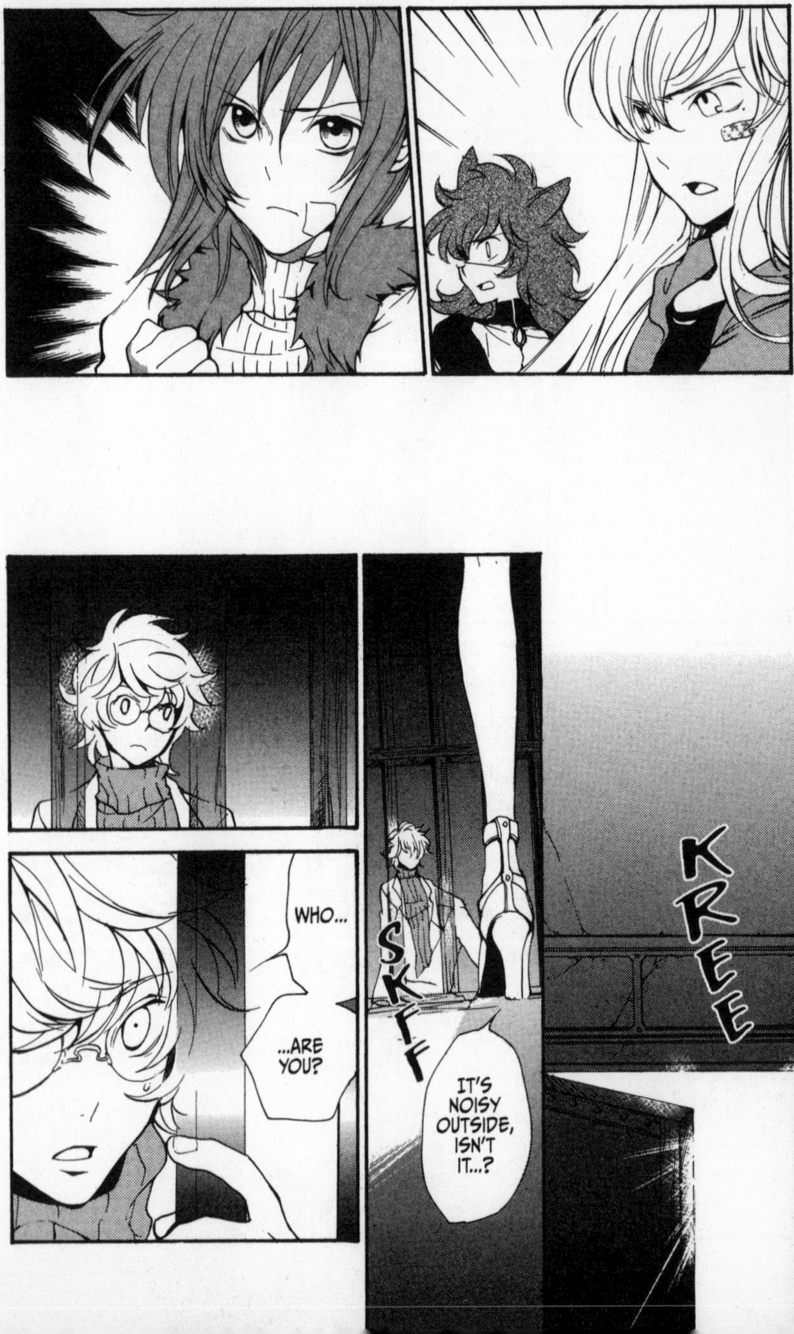
KREE
SKFF
IT'S NOISY OUTSIDE, ISN'T IT...?
WHO...
...ARE YOU?

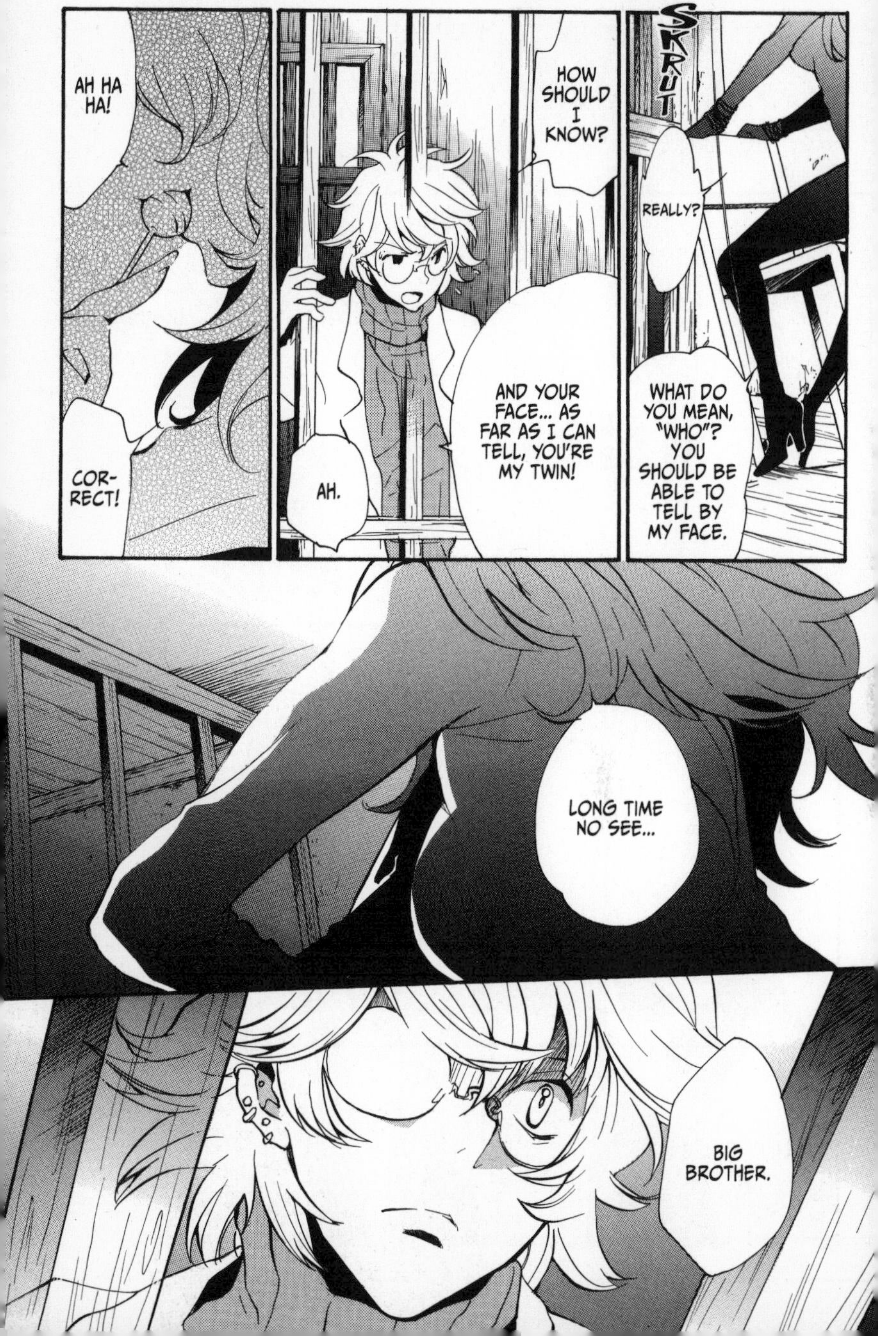
SKRUT
REALLY?
WHAT DO YOU MEAN, "WHO"? YOU SHOULD BE ABLE TO TELL BY MY FACE.
HOW SHOULD I KNOW?
AND YOUR FACE... AS FAR AS I CAN TELL, YOU'RE MY TWIN!
AH.
AH HA HA!
COR-RECT!
LONG TIME NO SEE...
BIG BROTHER.

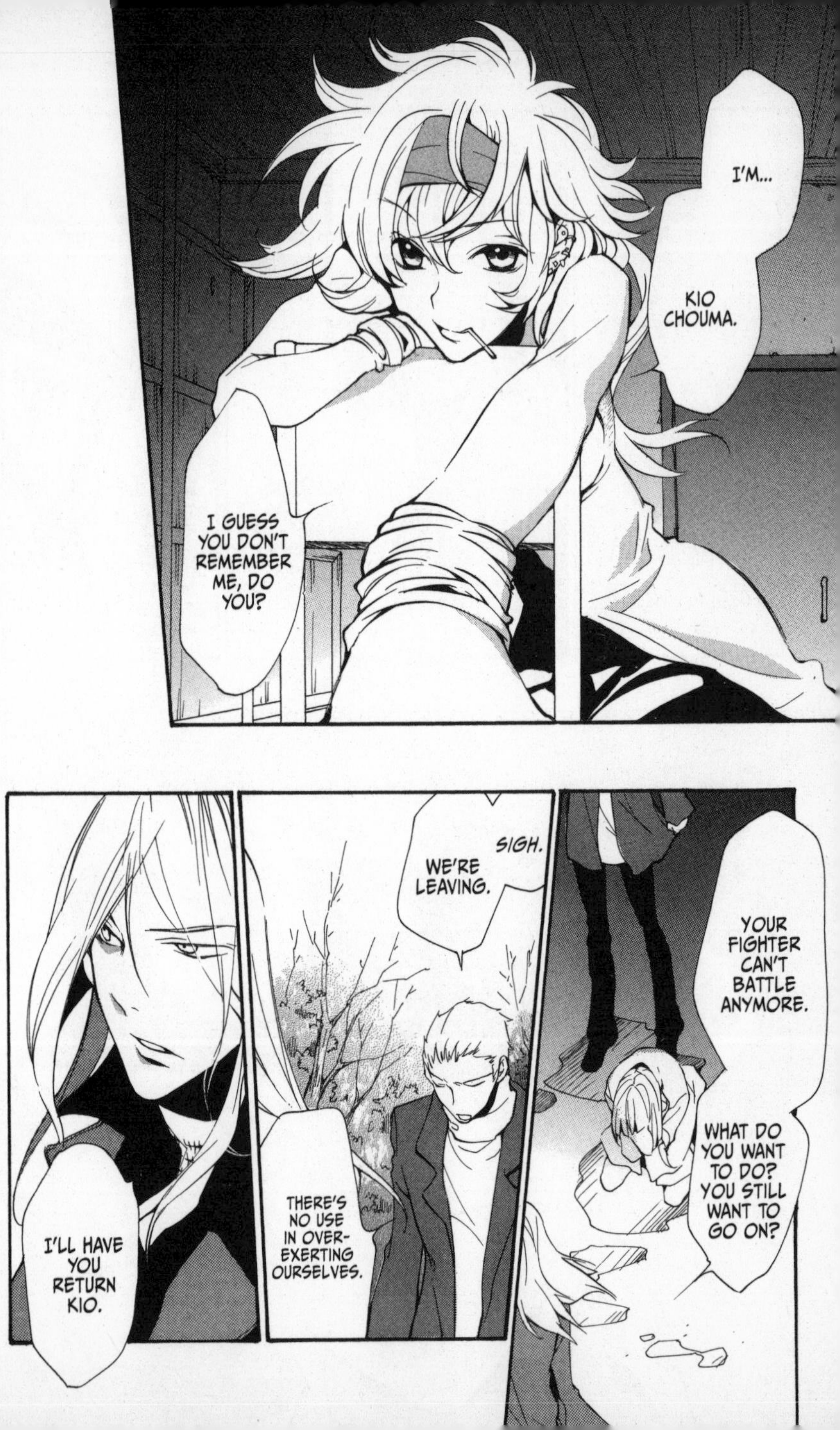

I'M...
KIO CHOUMA.
I GUESS YOU DON'T REMEMBER ME, DO YOU?
YOUR FIGHTER CAN'T BATTLE ANYMORE.
WHAT DO YOU WANT TO DO? YOU STILL WANT TO GO ON?
SIGH.
WE'RE LEAVING.
THERE'S NO USE IN OVER-EXERTING OURSELVES.
I'LL HAVE YOU RETURN KIO.

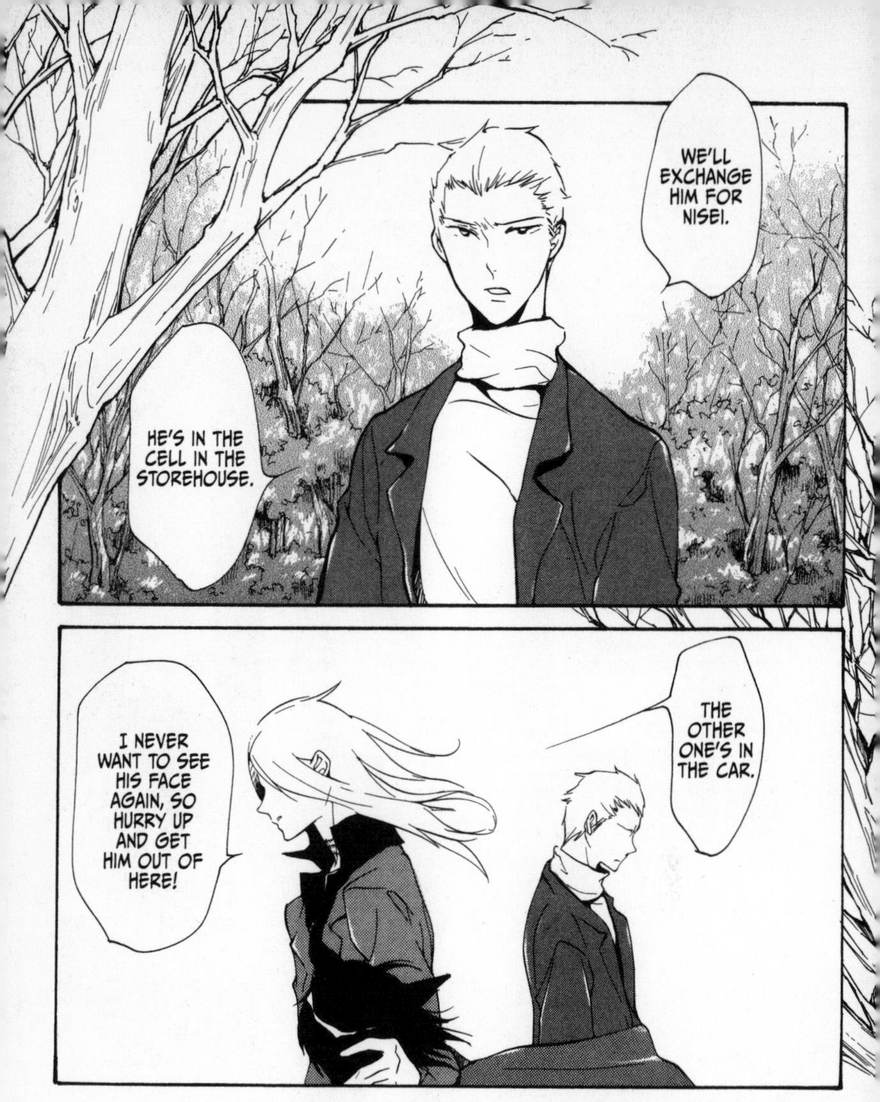
WE'LL EXCHANGE HIM FOR NISEI.
HE'S IN THE CELL IN THE STOREHOUSE.
THE OTHER ONE'S IN THE CAR.
I NEVER WANT TO SEE HIS FACE AGAIN, SO HURRY UP AND GET HIM OUT OF HERE!

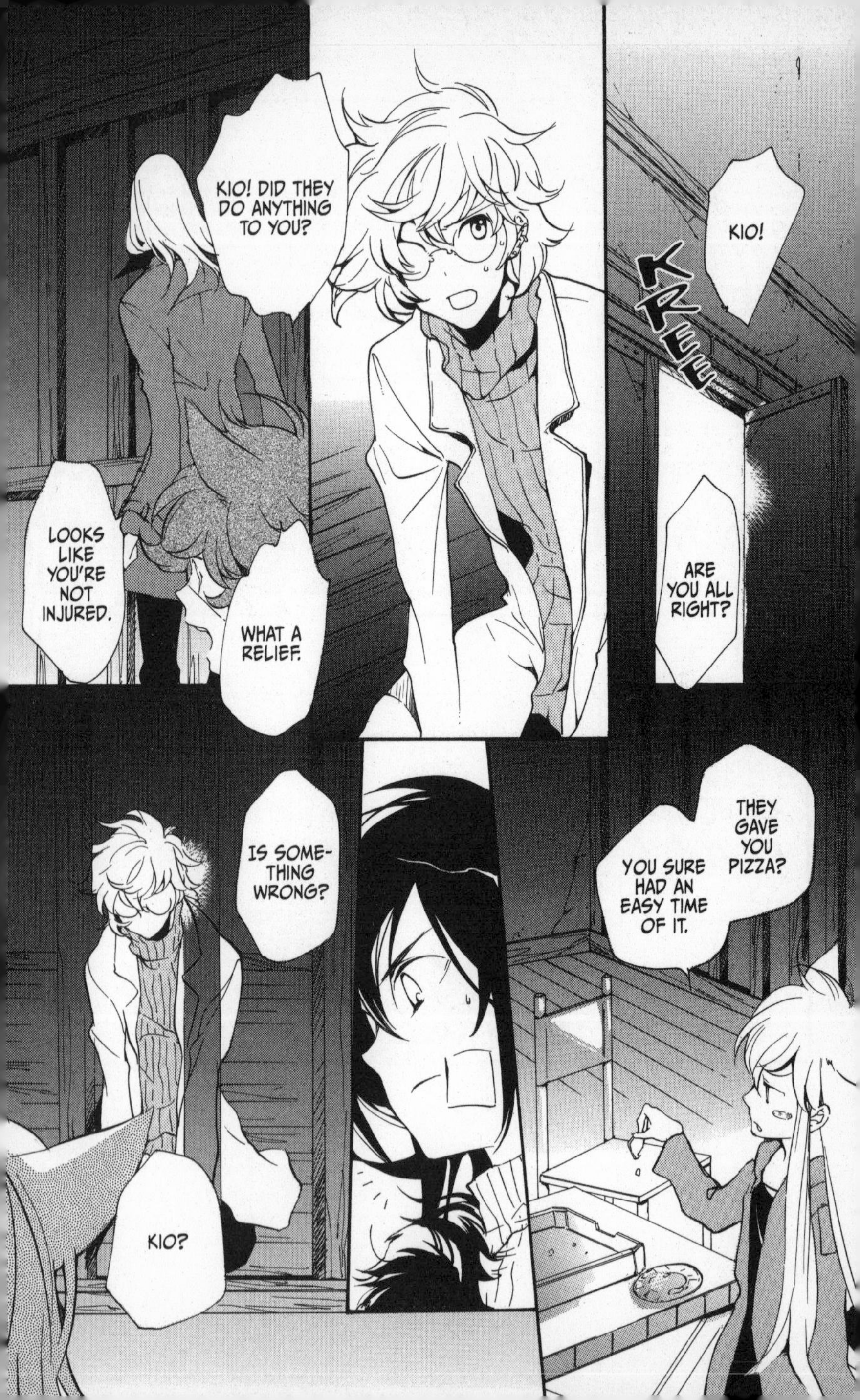
KIO!
KREEE
ARE YOU ALL RIGHT?
KIO! DID THEY DO ANYTHING TO YOU?
LOOKS LIKE YOU'RE NOT INJURED.
WHAT A RELIEF.
THEY GAVE YOU PIZZA?
YOU SURE HAD AN EASY TIME OF IT.
IS SOME-THING WRONG?
KIO?

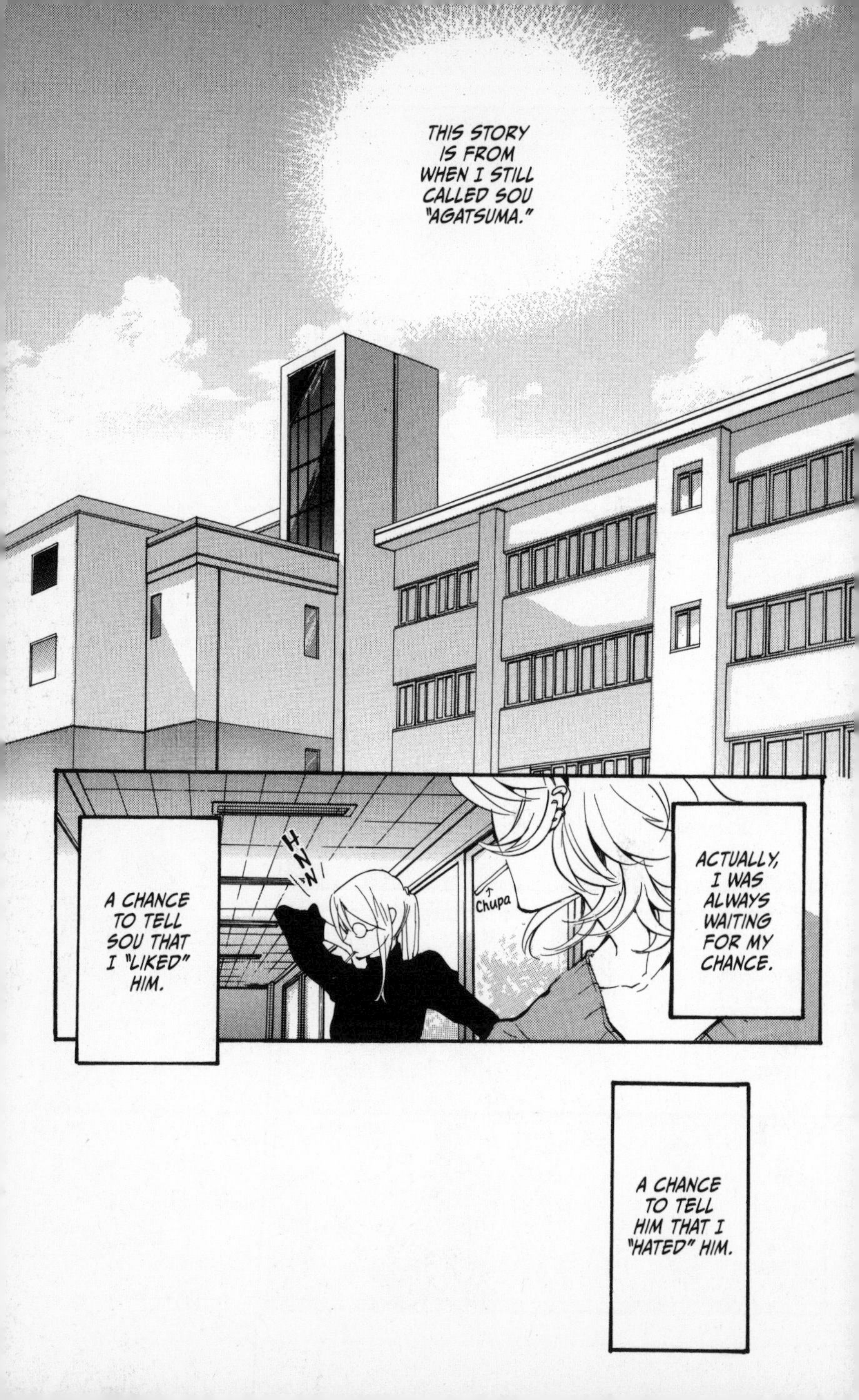
THIS STORY IS FROM WHEN I STILL CALLED SOU "AGATSUMA."
ACTUALLY, I WAS ALWAYS WAITING FOR MY CHANCE.
Chupa
HNN
A CHANCE TO TELL SOU THAT I "LIKED" HIM.
A CHANCE TO TELL HIM THAT I "HATED" HIM.

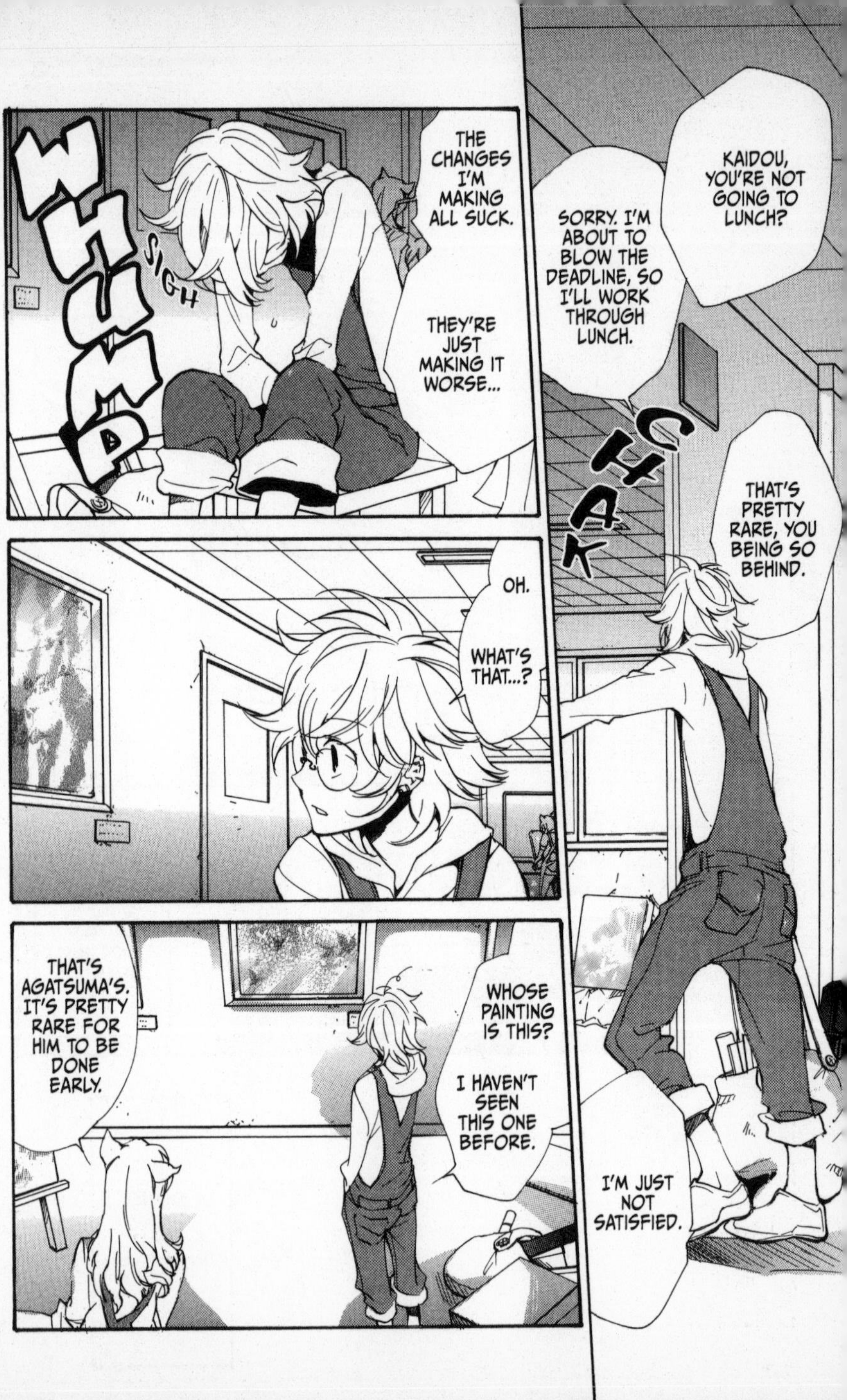
KAIDOU, YOU'RE NOT GOING TO LUNCH?
SORRY. I'M ABOUT TO BLOW THE DEADLINE, SO I'LL WORK THROUGH LUNCH.
CHAK
THAT'S PRETTY RARE, YOU BEING SO BEHIND.
I'M JUST NOT SATISFIED.
THE CHANGES I'M MAKING ALL SUCK.
THEY'RE JUST MAKING IT WORSE...
SIGH
WHUMP
OH.
WHAT'S THAT...?
WHOSE PAINTING IS THIS?
I HAVEN'T SEEN THIS ONE BEFORE.
THAT'S AGATSUMA'S. IT'S PRETTY RARE FOR HIM TO BE DONE EARLY.

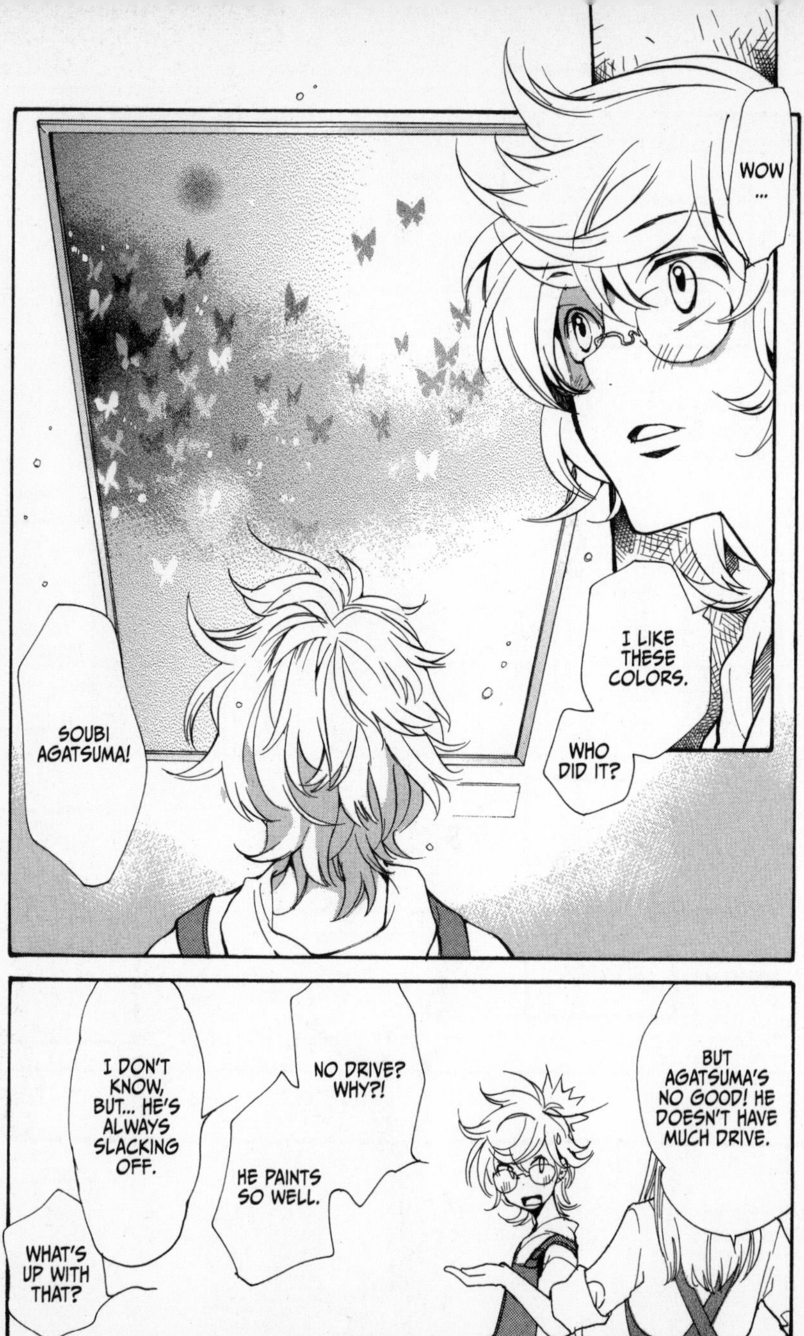
WOW...
I LIKE THESE COLORS.
WHO DID IT?
SOUBI AGATSUMA!
BUT AGATSUMA'S NO GOOD! HE DOESN'T HAVE MUCH DRIVE.
NO DRIVE? WHY?!
HE PAINTS SO WELL.
I DON'T KNOW, BUT... HE'S ALWAYS SLACKING OFF.
WHAT'S UP WITH THAT?

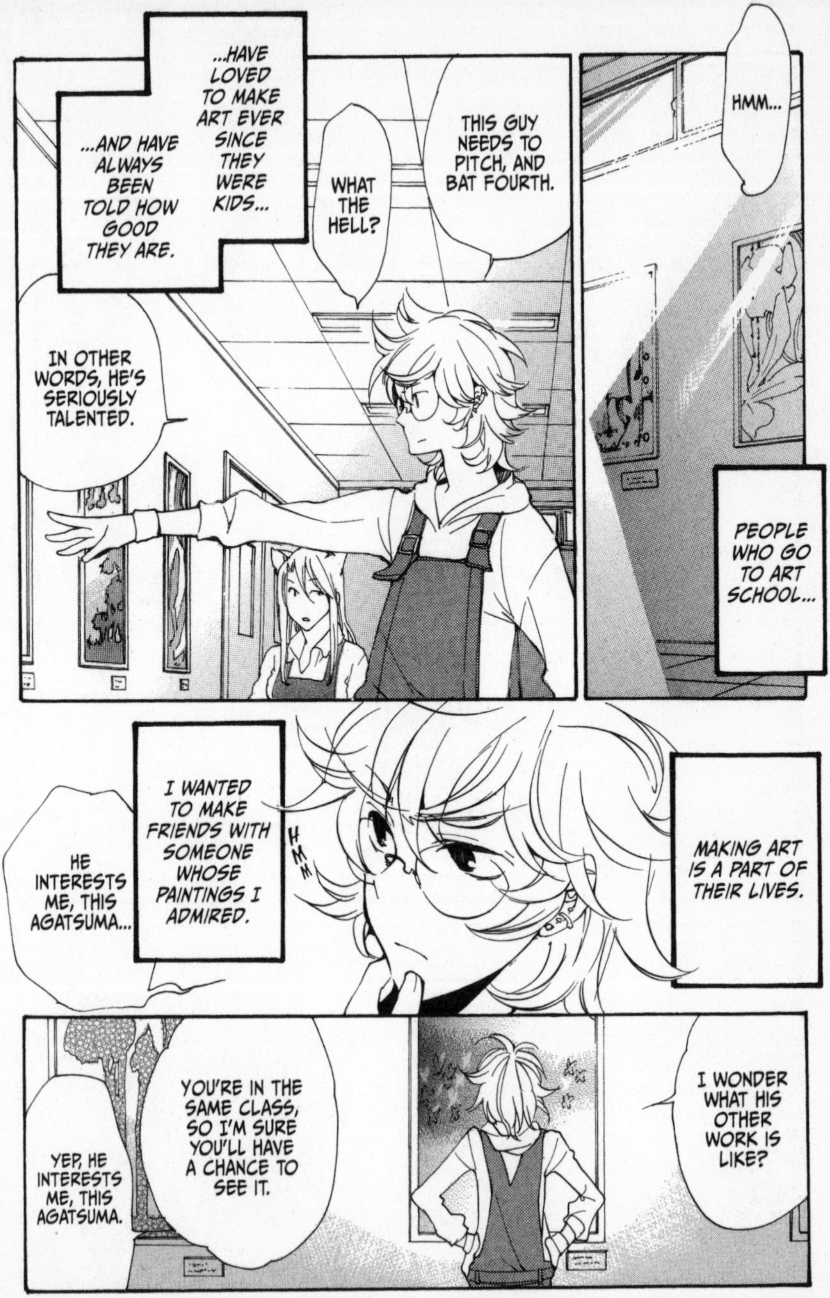
HMM...
PEOPLE WHO GO TO ART SCHOOL...
THIS GUY NEEDS TO PITCH, AND BAT FOURTH.
WHAT THE HELL?
...HAVE LOVED TO MAKE ART EVER SINCE THEY WERE KIDS...
...AND HAVE ALWAYS BEEN TOLD HOW GOOD THEY ARE.
IN OTHER WORDS, HE'S SERIOUSLY TALENTED.
MAKING ART IS A PART OF THEIR LIVES.
HMM
I WANTED TO MAKE FRIENDS WITH SOMEONE WHOSE PAINTINGS I ADMIRED.
HE INTERESTS ME, THIS AGATSUMA...
I WONDER WHAT HIS OTHER WORK IS LIKE?
YOU'RE IN THE SAME CLASS, SO I'M SURE YOU'LL HAVE A CHANCE TO SEE IT.
YEP, HE INTERESTS ME, THIS AGATSUMA.

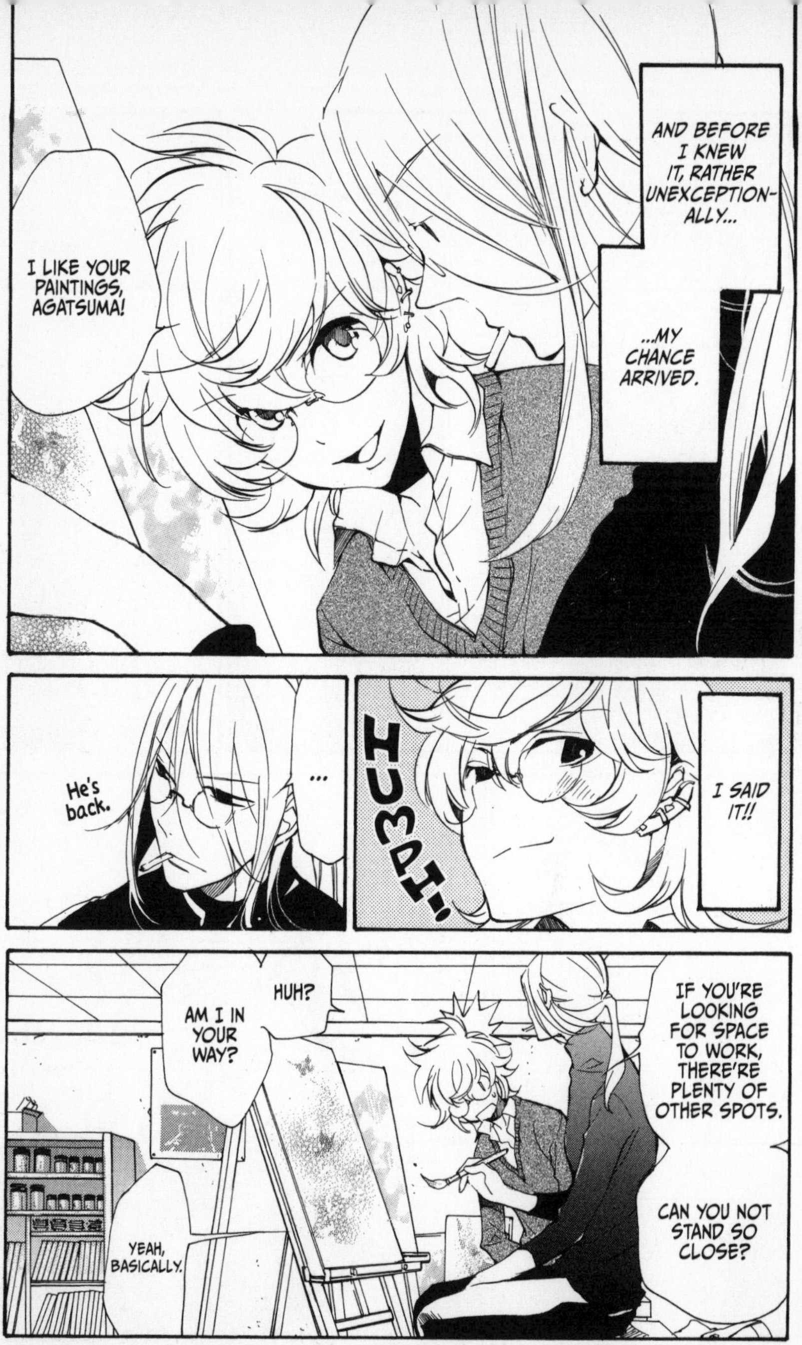
AND BEFORE I KNEW IT, RATHER UNEXCEPTION-ALLY...
...MY CHANCE ARRIVED.
I LIKE YOUR PAINTINGS, AGATSUMA!
I SAID IT!!
HUMPH!
...
He's back.
IF YOU'RE LOOKING FOR SPACE TO WORK, THERE'RE PLENTY OF OTHER SPOTS.
CAN YOU NOT STAND SO CLOSE?
HUH?
AM I IN YOUR WAY?
YEAH, BASICALLY.

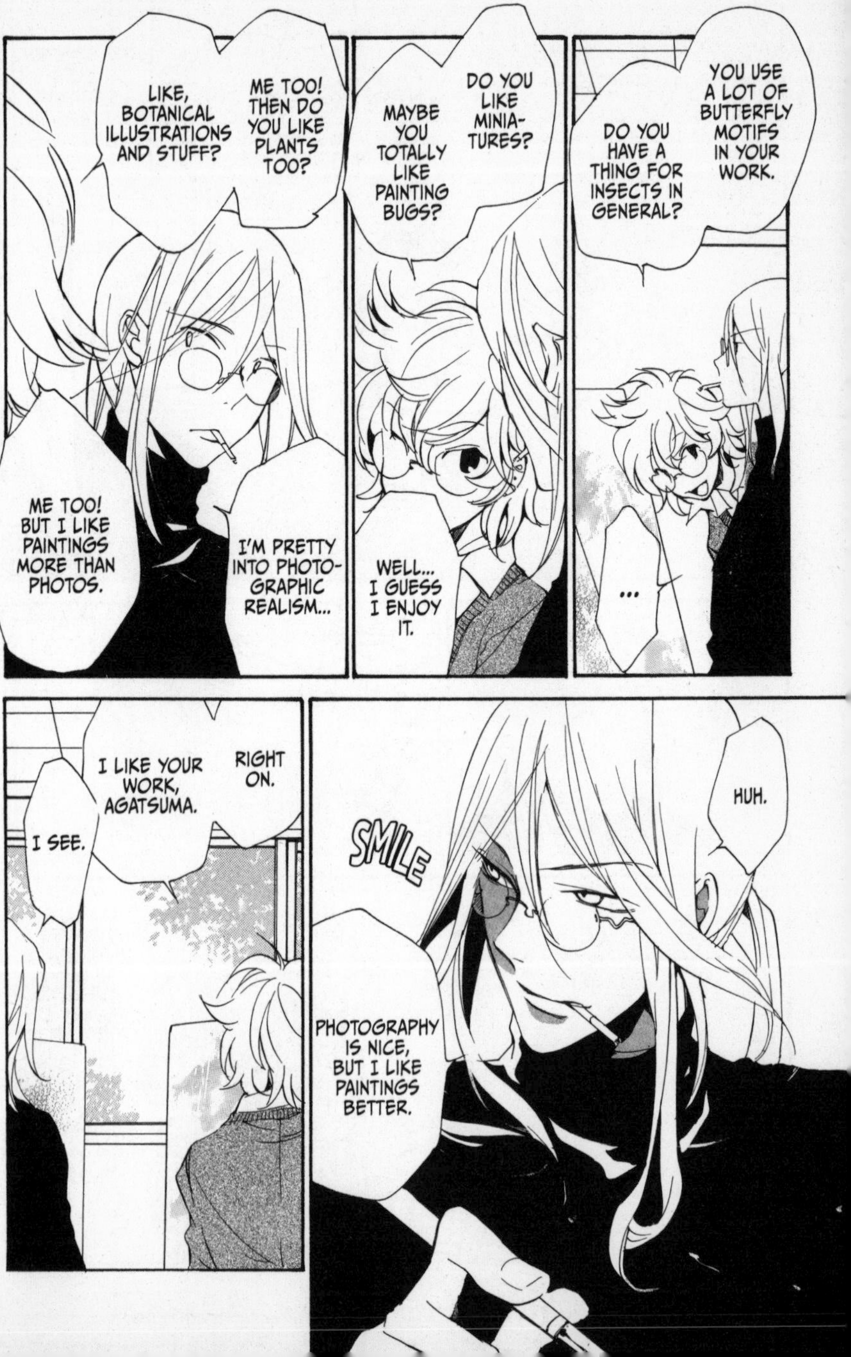
YOU USE A LOT OF BUTTERFLY MOTIFS IN YOUR WORK.
DO YOU HAVE A THING FOR INSECTS IN GENERAL?
...
DO YOU LIKE MINIA-TURES?
MAYBE YOU TOTALLY LIKE PAINTING BUGS?
WELL... I GUESS I ENJOY IT.
ME TOO! THEN DO YOU LIKE PLANTS TOO?
LIKE, BOTANICAL ILLUSTRATIONS AND STUFF?
I'M PRETTY INTO PHOTO-GRAPHIC REALISM...
ME TOO! BUT I LIKE PAINTINGS MORE THAN PHOTOS.
HUH.
SMILE
PHOTOGRAPHY IS NICE, BUT I LIKE PAINTINGS BETTER.
RIGHT ON.
I LIKE YOUR WORK, AGATSUMA.
I SEE.

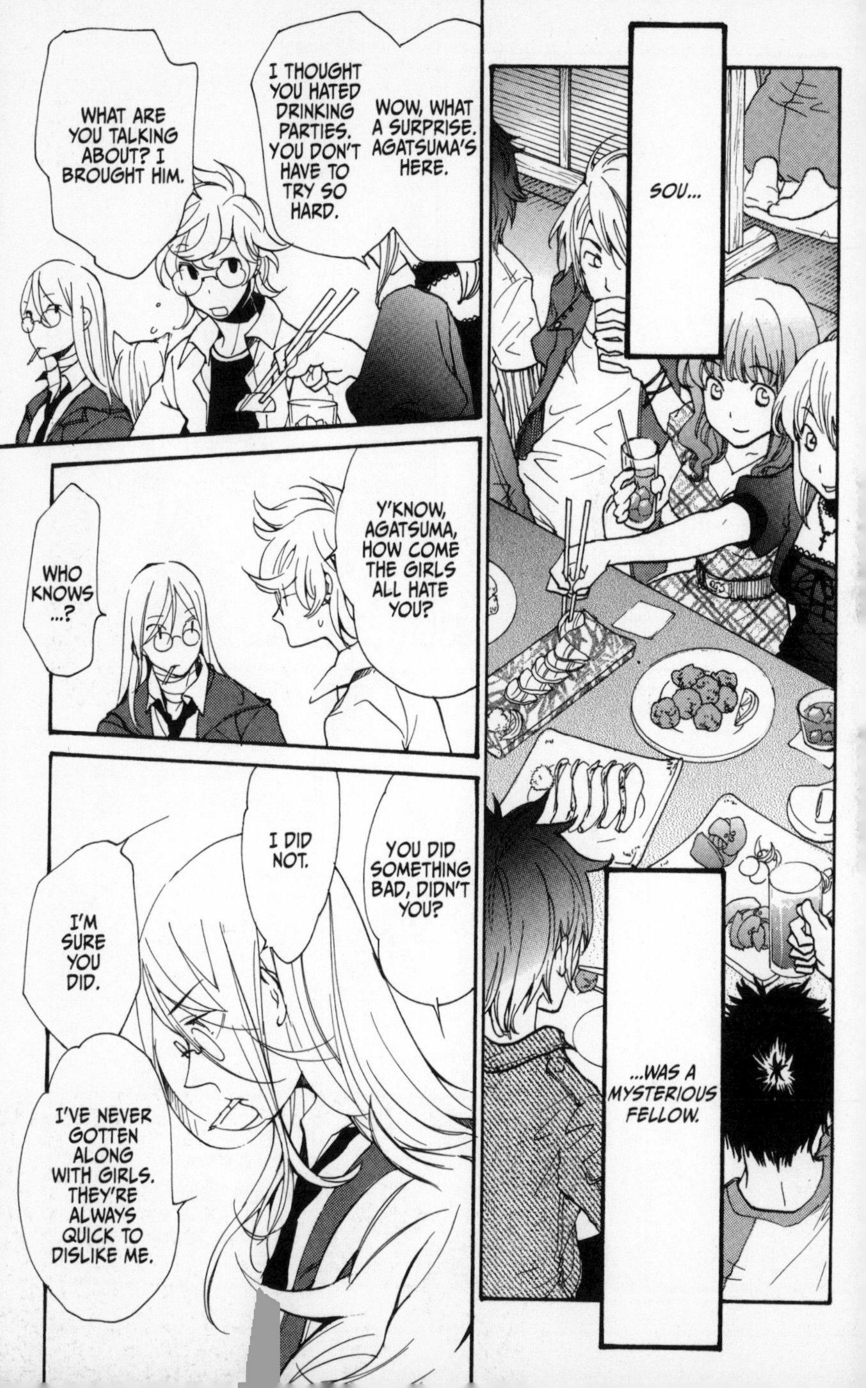
SOU...
...WAS A MYSTERIOUS FELLOW.
WOW, WHAT A SURPRISE. AGATSUMA'S HERE.
I THOUGHT YOU HATED DRINKING PARTIES. YOU DON'T HAVE TO TRY SO HARD.
WHAT ARE YOU TALKING ABOUT? I BROUGHT HIM.
Y'KNOW, AGATSUMA, HOW COME THE GIRLS ALL HATE YOU?
WHO KNOWS ...?
YOU DID SOMETHING BAD, DIDN'T YOU?
I DID NOT.
I'M SURE YOU DID.
I'VE NEVER GOTTEN ALONG WITH GIRLS. THEY'RE ALWAYS QUICK TO DISLIKE ME.

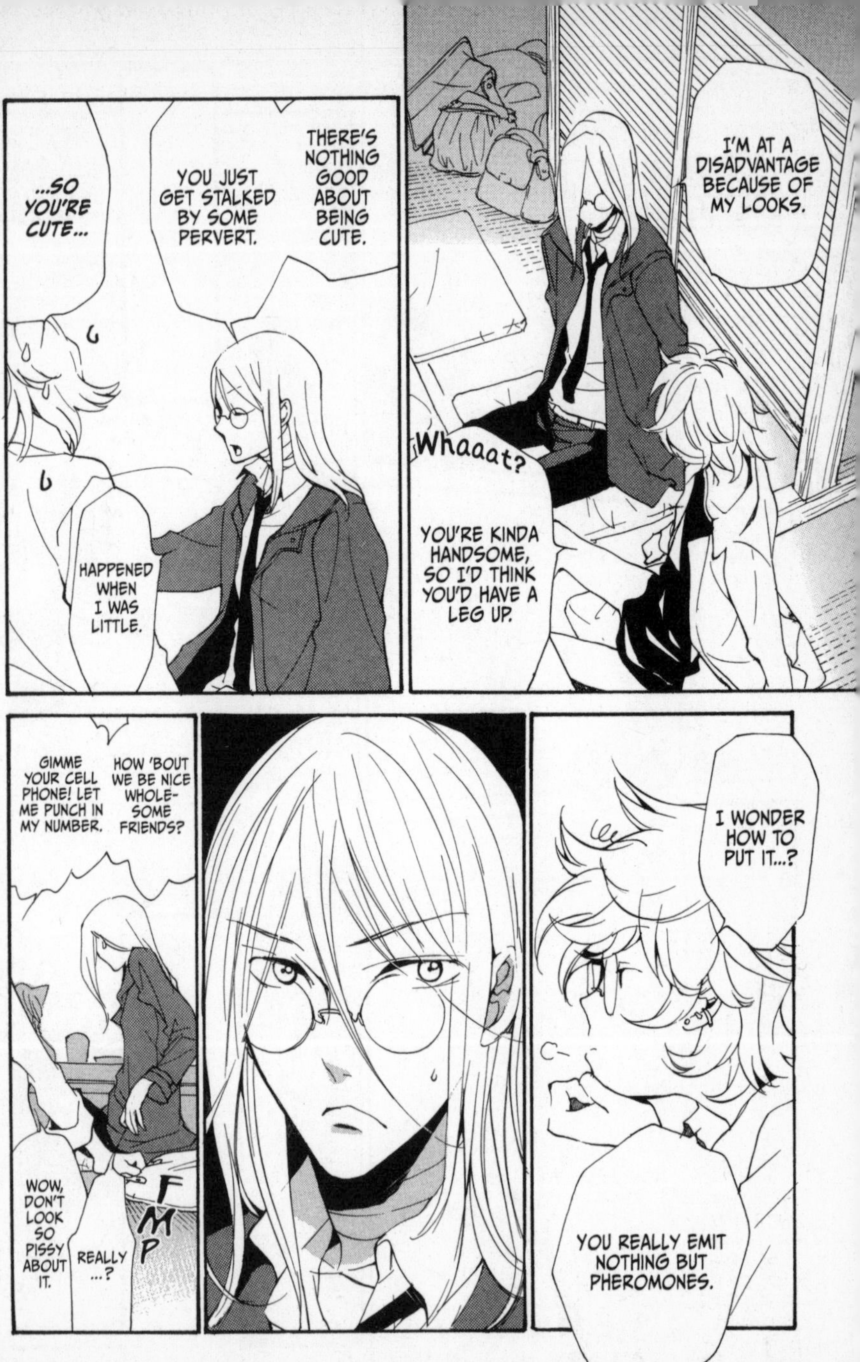
I'M AT A DISADVANTAGE BECAUSE OF MY LOOKS.
Whaaat?
YOU'RE KINDA HANDSOME, SO I'D THINK YOU'D HAVE A LEG UP.
THERE'S NOTHING GOOD ABOUT BEING CUTE.
YOU JUST GET STALKED BY SOME PERVERT.
...SO YOU'RE CUTE...
HAPPENED WHEN I WAS LITTLE.
I WONDER HOW TO PUT IT...?
YOU REALLY EMIT NOTHING BUT PHEROMONES.
HOW 'BOUT WE BE NICE WHOLE-SOME FRIENDS?
GIMME YOUR CELL PHONE! LET ME PUNCH IN MY NUMBER.
FMP
REALLY ...?
WOW, DON'T LOOK SO PISSY ABOUT IT.

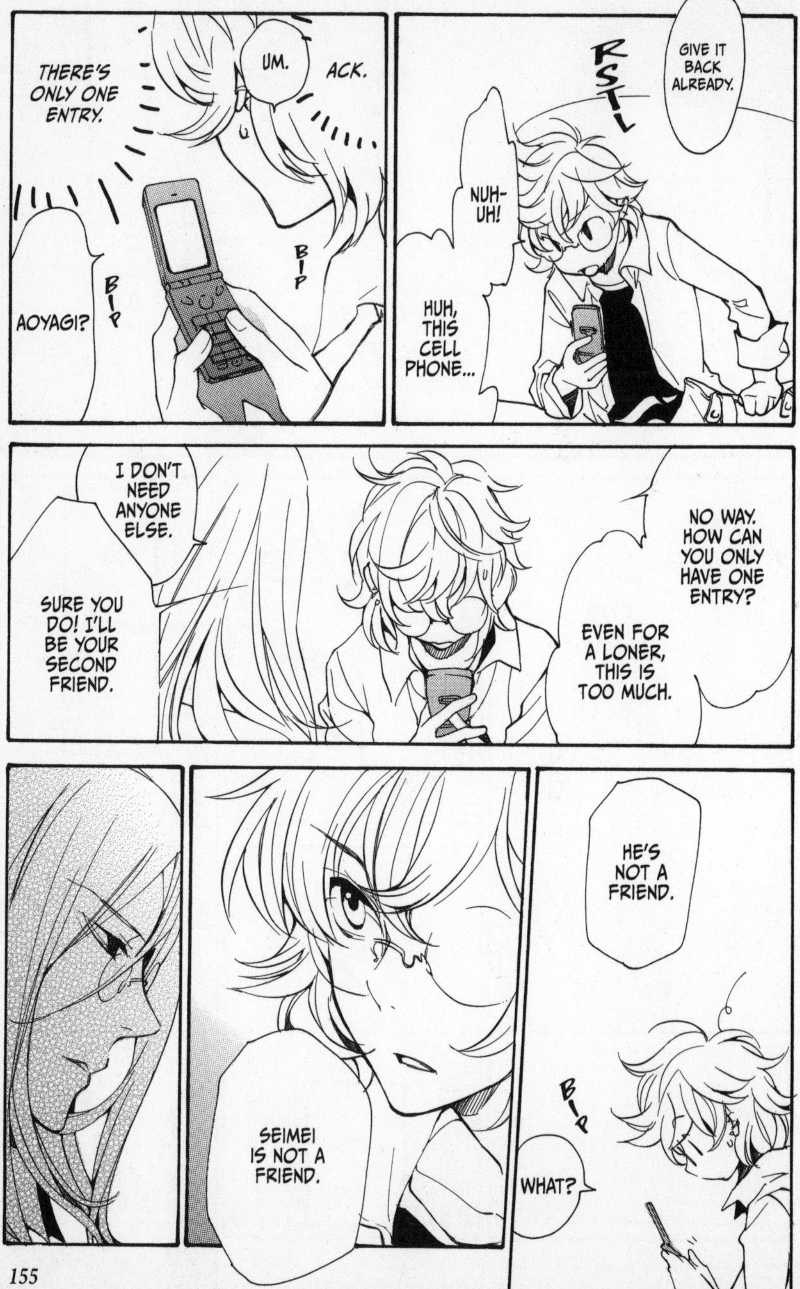
GIVE IT BACK ALREADY.
RSTL
NUH-UH!
HUH, THIS CELL PHONE...
UM.
ACK.
THERE'S ONLY ONE ENTRY.
BIP
BIP
AOYAGI?
NO WAY. HOW CAN YOU ONLY HAVE ONE ENTRY?
EVEN FOR A LONER, THIS IS TOO MUCH.
I DON'T NEED ANYONE ELSE.
SURE YOU DO! I'LL BE YOUR SECOND FRIEND.
HE'S NOT A FRIEND.
BIP
WHAT?
SEIMEI IS NOT A FRIEND.

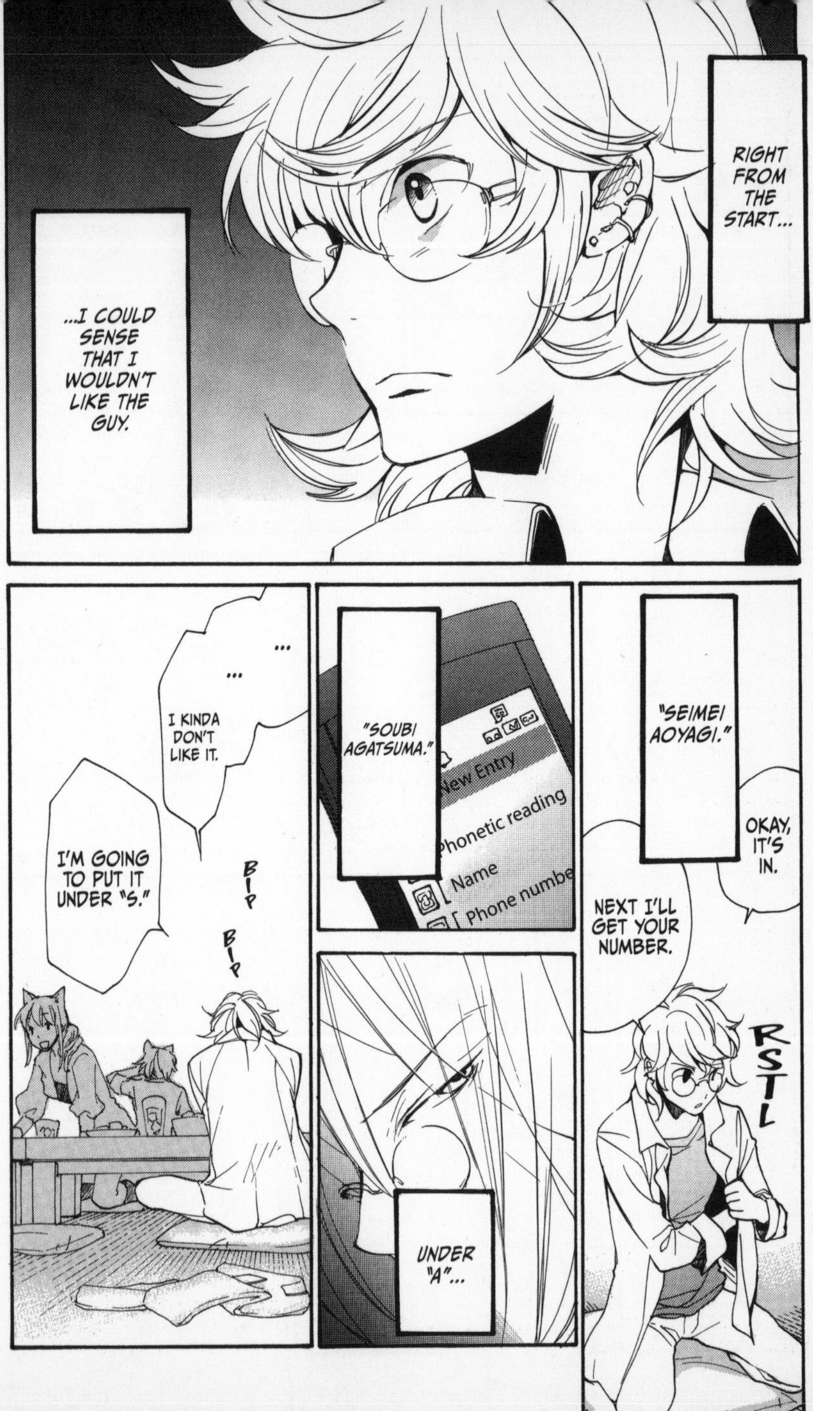
RIGHT FROM THE START...
...I COULD SENSE THAT I WOULDN'T LIKE THE GUY.
"SEIMEI AOYAGI."
OKAY, IT'S IN.
NEXT I'LL GET YOUR NUMBER.
RSTL
"SOUBI AGATSUMA."
New Entry
Phonetic reading
Name
Phone numbe
UNDER "A"...
...
...
I KINDA DON'T LIKE IT.
I'M GOING TO PUT IT UNDER "S."
BIP
BIP

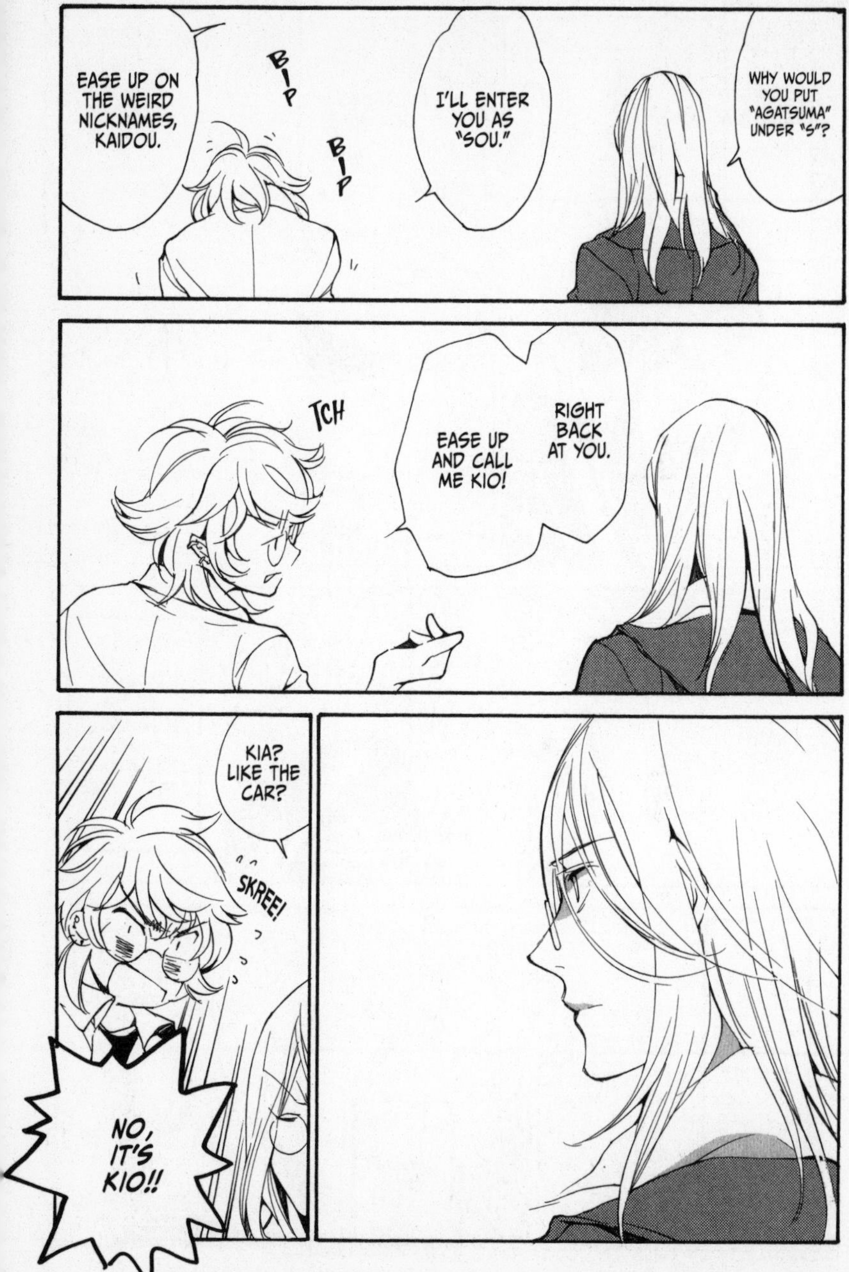
WHY WOULD YOU PUT "AGATSUMA" UNDER "S"?
I'LL ENTER YOU AS "SOU."
BIP
BIP
EASE UP ON THE WEIRD NICKNAMES, KAIDOU.
RIGHT BACK AT YOU.
EASE UP AND CALL ME KIO!
TCH
KIA? LIKE THE CAR?
SKREE!
NO, IT'S KIO!!

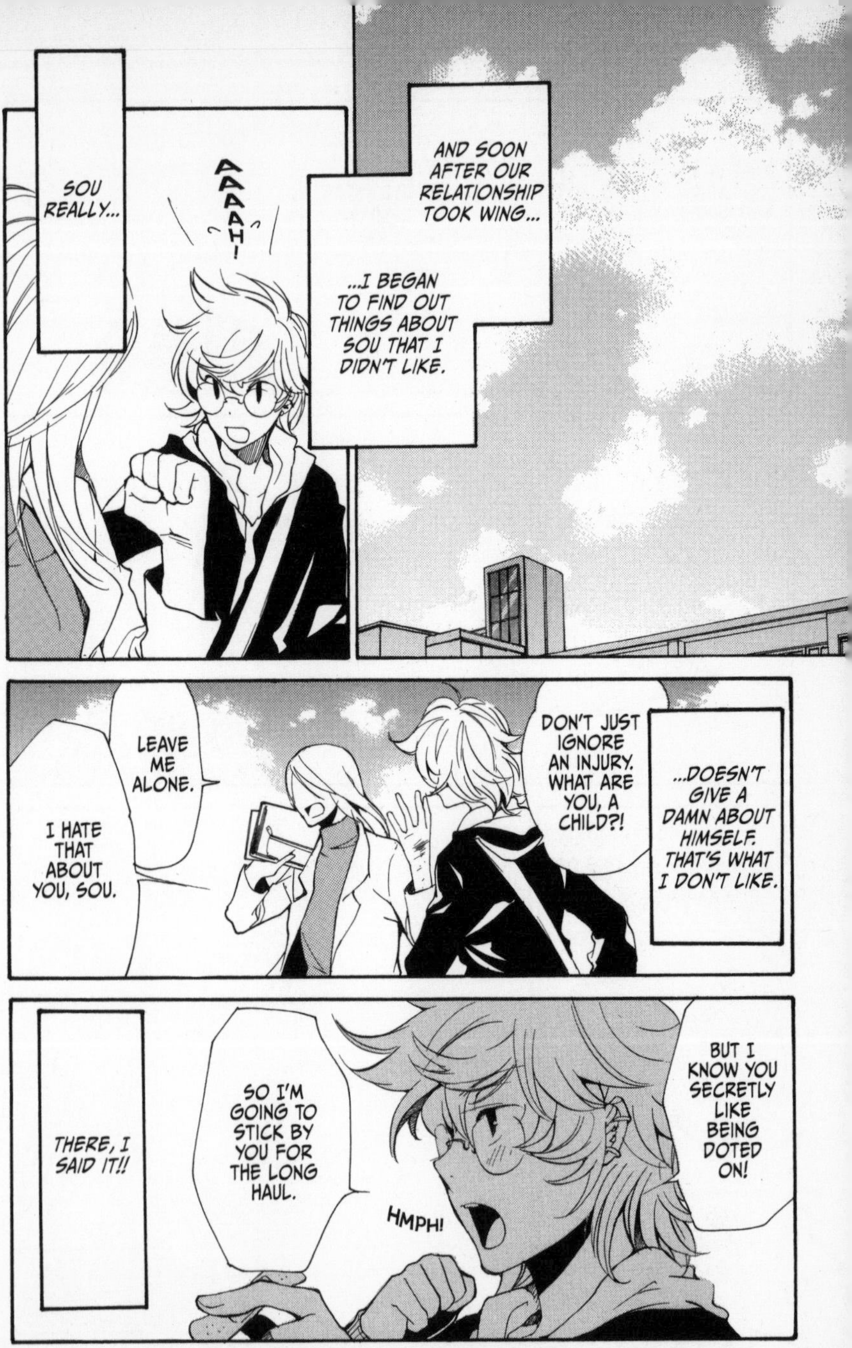
AND SOON AFTER OUR RELATIONSHIP TOOK WING...
...I BEGAN TO FIND OUT THINGS ABOUT SOU THAT I DIDN'T LIKE.
AAAAH!
SOU REALLY...
...DOESN'T GIVE A DAMN ABOUT HIMSELF. THAT'S WHAT I DON'T LIKE.
DON'T JUST IGNORE AN INJURY. WHAT ARE YOU, A CHILD?!
LEAVE ME ALONE.
I HATE THAT ABOUT YOU, SOU.
BUT I KNOW YOU SECRETLY LIKE BEING DOTED ON!
HMPH!
SO I'M GOING TO STICK BY YOU FOR THE LONG HAUL.
THERE, I SAID IT!!

LOVELESS 9 / END

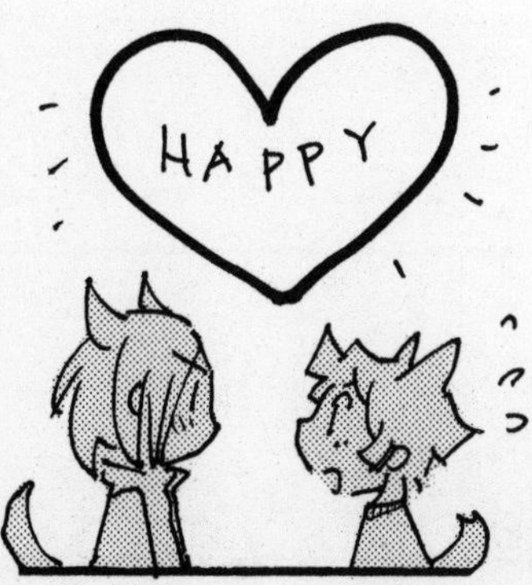
HAPPY

LOVELESS

loveless -Mimuro and Mei-

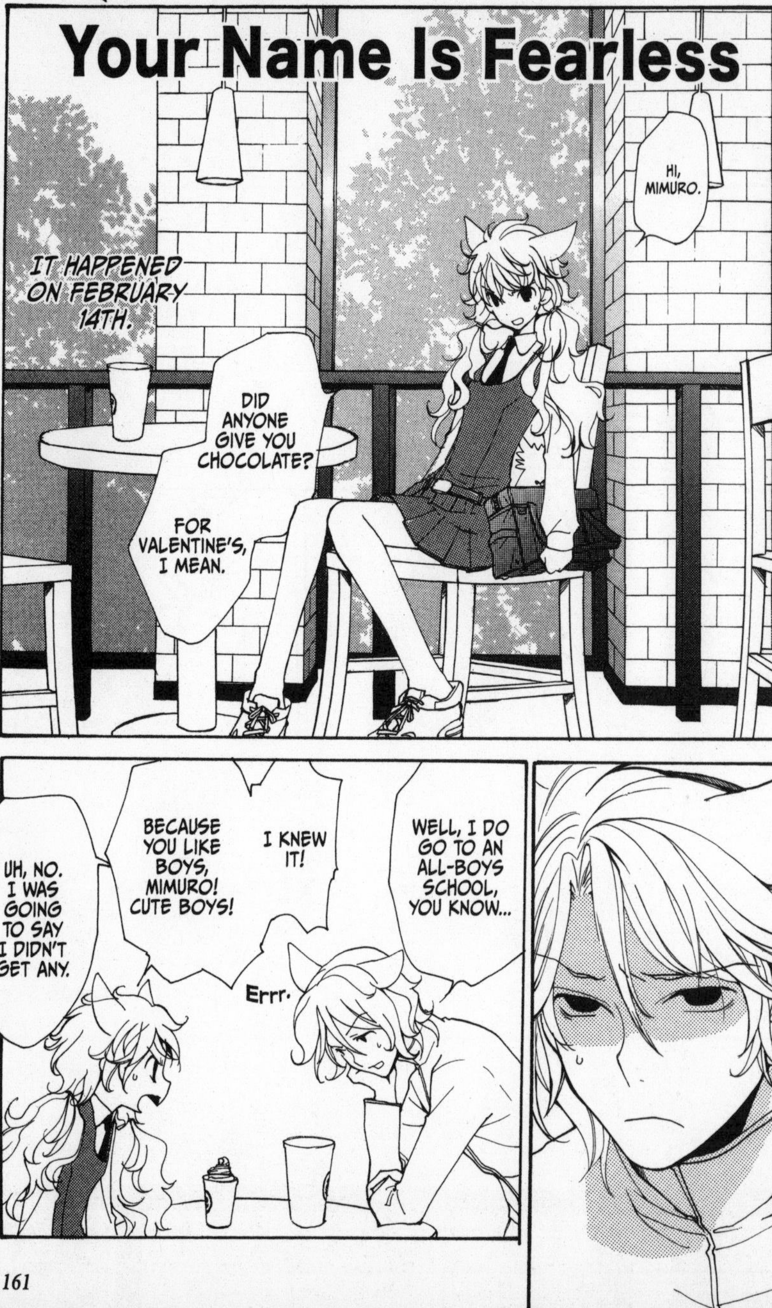
Your Name Is Fearless
HI, MIMURO.
IT HAPPENED ON FEBRUARY 14TH.
DID ANYONE GIVE YOU CHOCOLATE?
FOR VALENTINE'S, I MEAN.
WELL, I DO GO TO AN ALL-BOYS SCHOOL, YOU KNOW...
I KNEW IT!
BECAUSE YOU LIKE BOYS, MIMURO! CUTE BOYS!
Errr.
UH, NO. I WAS GOING TO SAY I DIDN'T GET ANY.

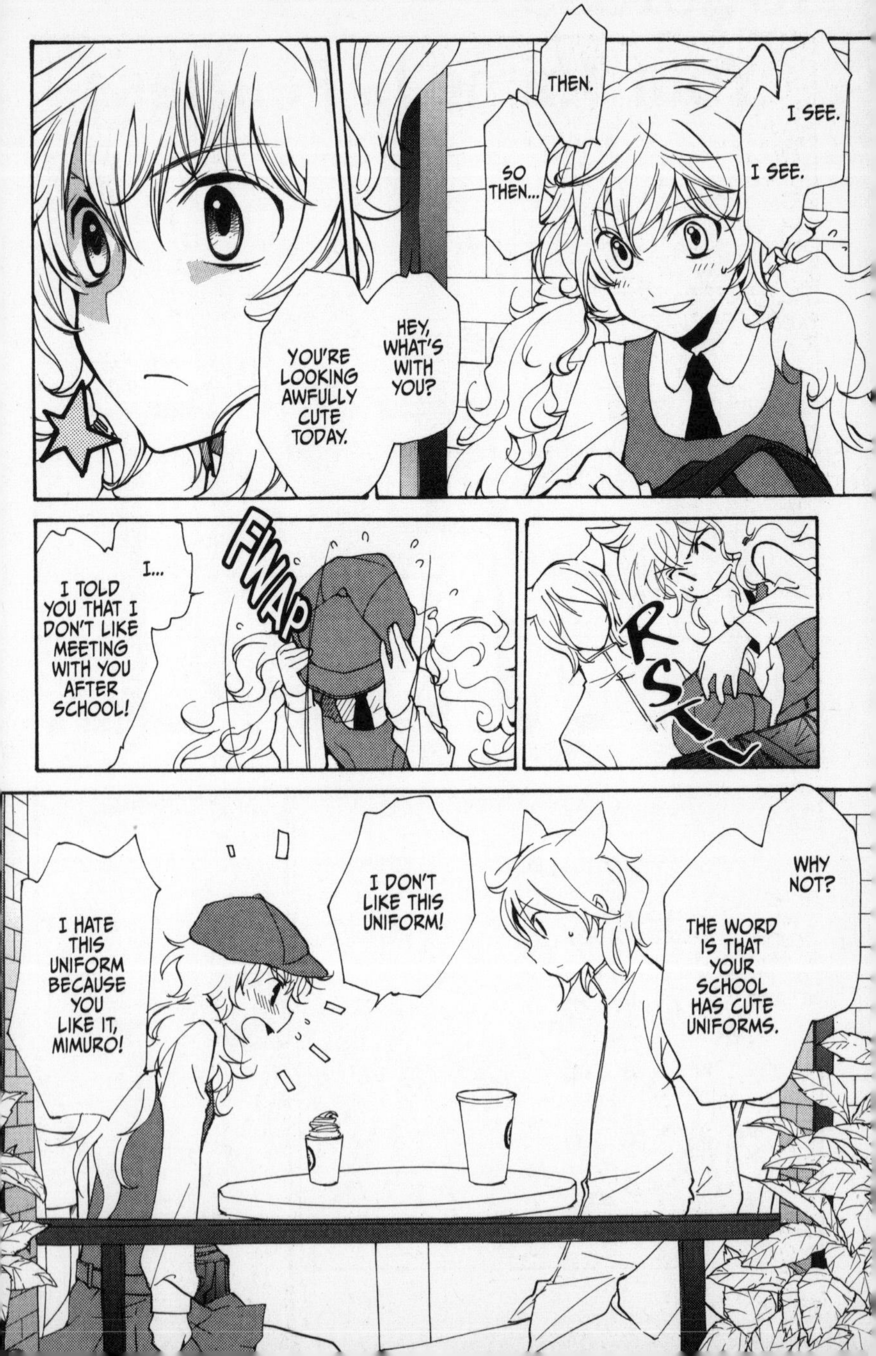
I SEE. I SEE.
THEN.
SO THEN...
HEY, WHAT'S WITH YOU? YOU'RE LOOKING AWFULLY CUTE TODAY.
RSTL
FWAP
I... I TOLD YOU THAT I DON'T LIKE MEETING WITH YOU AFTER SCHOOL!
WHY NOT? THE WORD IS THAT YOUR SCHOOL HAS CUTE UNIFORMS.
I DON'T LIKE THIS UNIFORM!
I HATE THIS UNIFORM BECAUSE YOU LIKE IT, MIMURO!

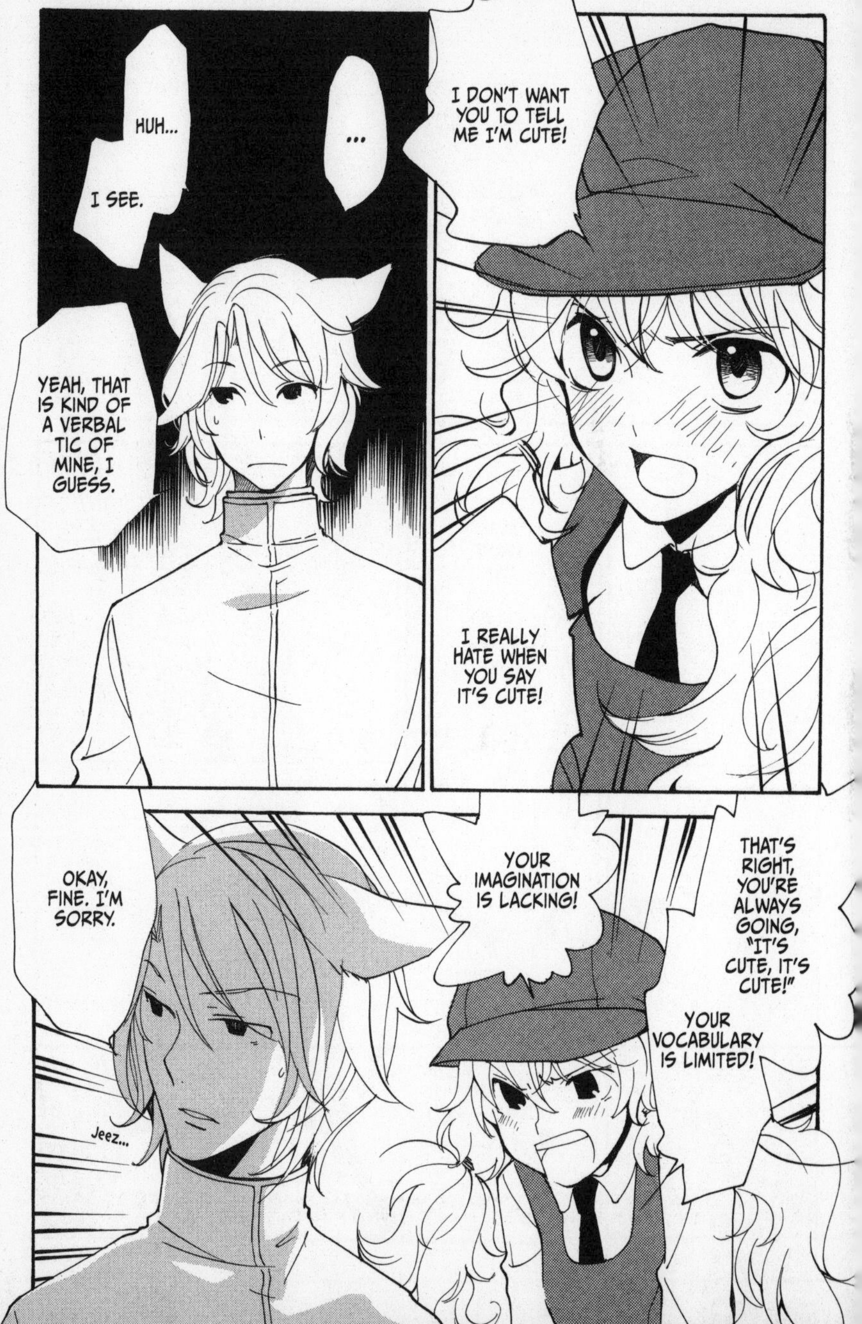
I DON'T WANT YOU TO TELL ME I'M CUTE!
I REALLY HATE WHEN YOU SAY IT'S CUTE!
...
HUH...
I SEE.
YEAH, THAT IS KIND OF A VERBAL TIC OF MINE, I GUESS.
THAT'S RIGHT, YOU'RE ALWAYS GOING, "IT'S CUTE, IT'S CUTE!"
YOUR VOCABULARY IS LIMITED!
YOUR IMAGINATION IS LACKING!
OKAY, FINE. I'M SORRY.
Jeez...

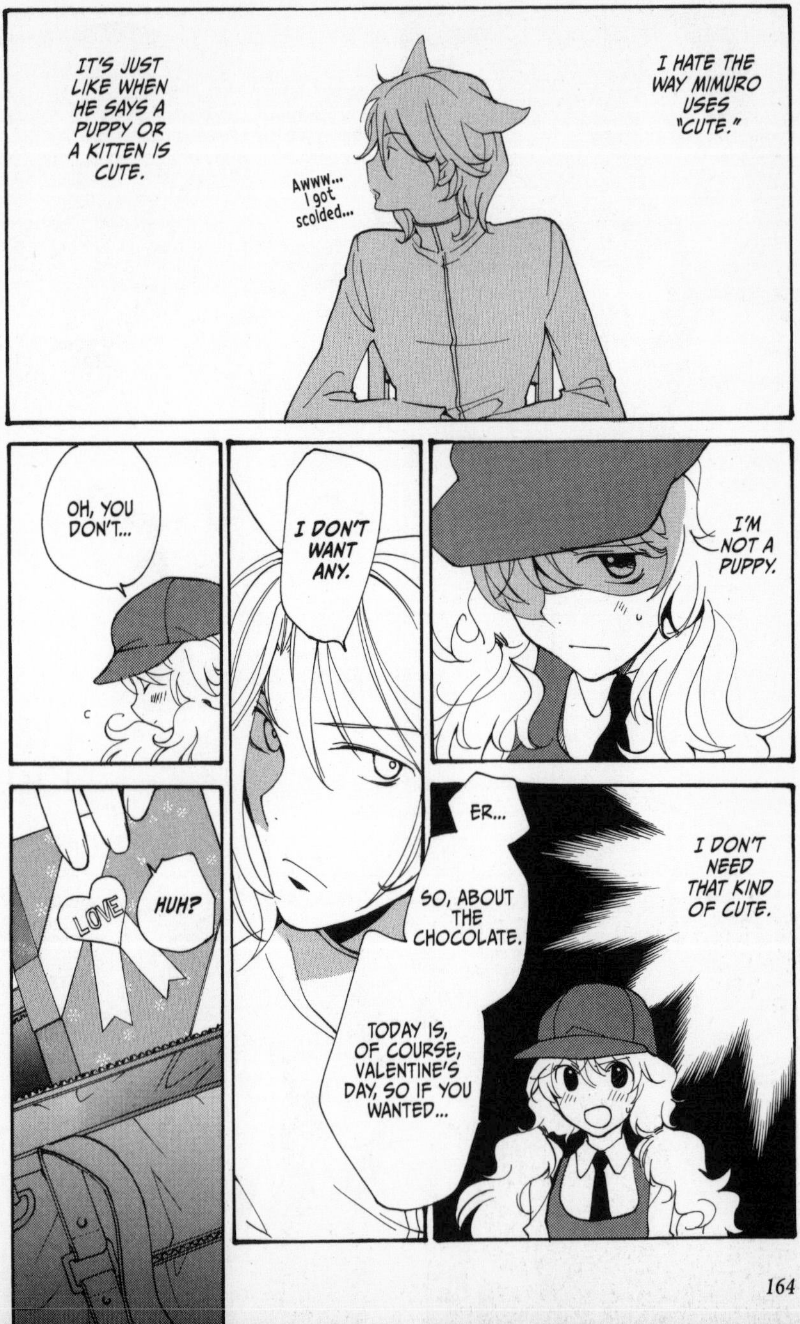
I HATE THE WAY MIMURO USES "CUTE."
Awww... I got scolded...
IT'S JUST LIKE WHEN HE SAYS A PUPPY OR A KITTEN IS CUTE.
I'M NOT A PUPPY.
I DON'T NEED THAT KIND OF CUTE.
ER...
SO, ABOUT THE CHOCOLATE.
TODAY IS, OF COURSE, VALENTINE'S DAY, SO IF YOU WANTED...
I DON'T WANT ANY.
OH, YOU DON'T...
HUH?
LOVE

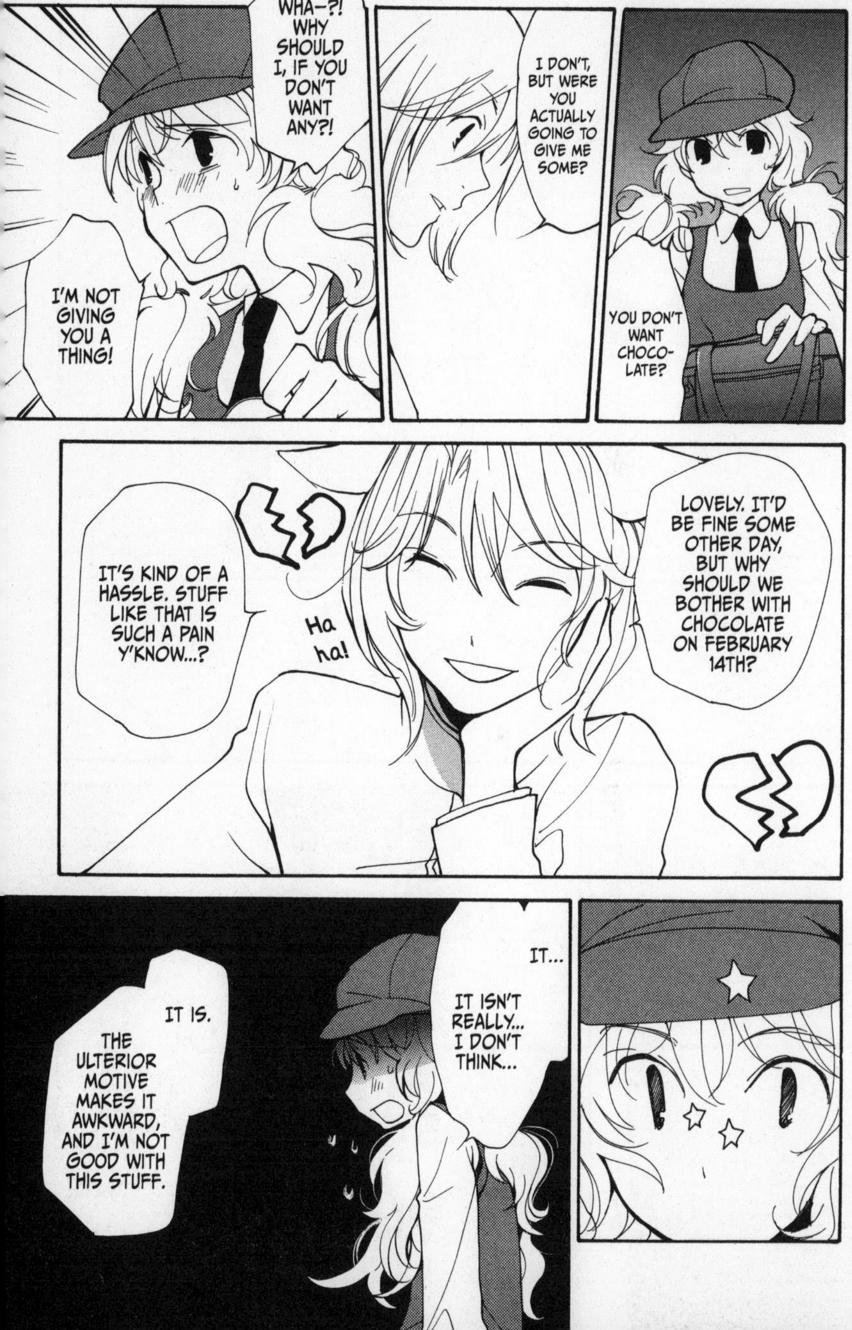
YOU DON'T WANT CHOCOLATE?
I DON'T, BUT WERE YOU ACTUALLY GOING TO GIVE ME SOME?
WHA-?! WHY SHOULD I, IF YOU DON'T WANT ANY?!
I'M NOT GIVING YOU A THING!
LOVELY. IT'D BE FINE SOME OTHER DAY, BUT WHY SHOULD WE BOTHER WITH CHOCOLATE ON FEBRUARY 14TH?
Ha ha!
IT'S KIND OF A HASSLE. STUFF LIKE THAT IS SUCH A PAIN Y'KNOW...?
IT...
IT ISN'T REALLY... I DON'T THINK...
IT IS.
THE ULTERIOR MOTIVE MAKES IT AWKWARD, AND I'M NOT GOOD WITH THIS STUFF.

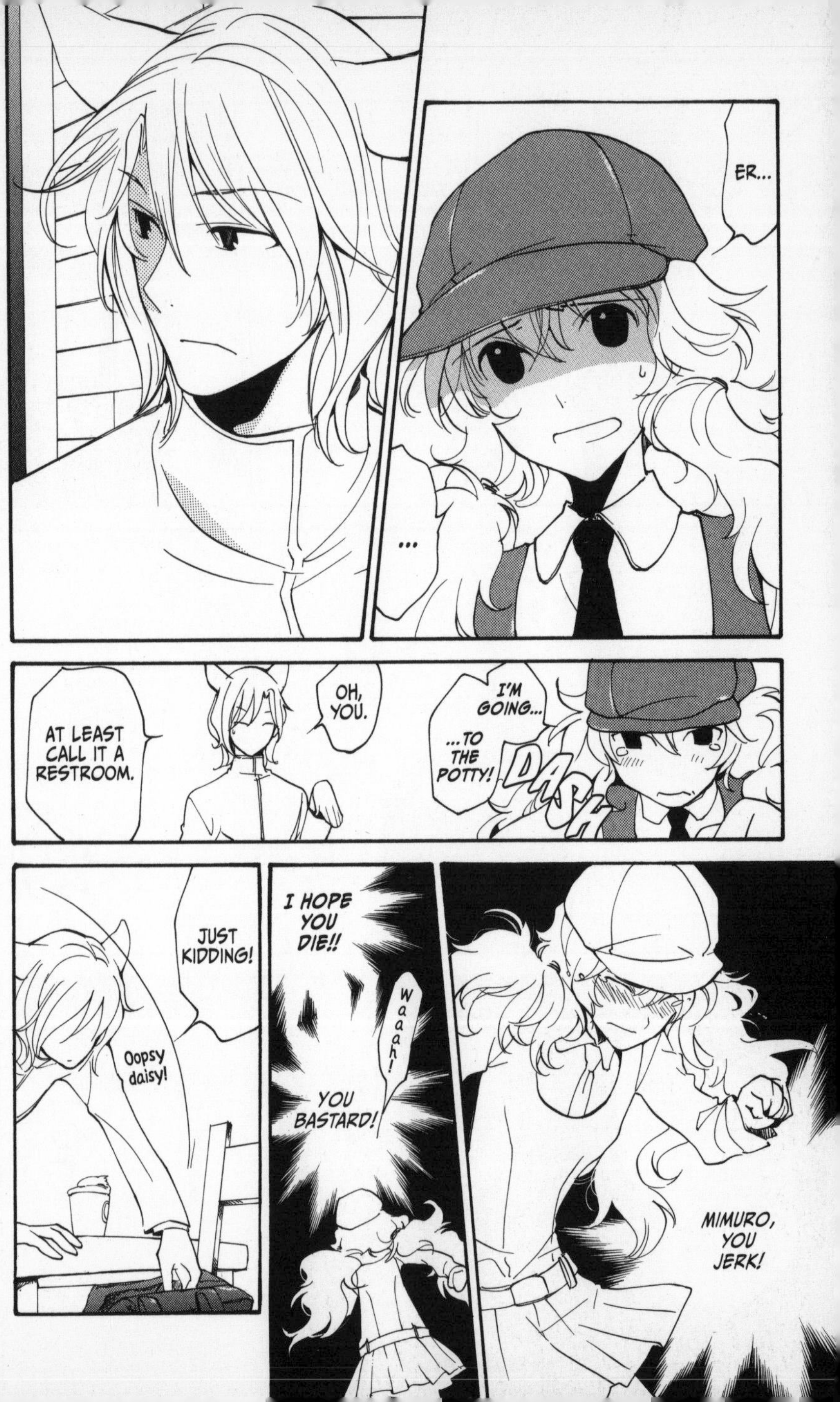
ER...
...
I'M GOING...
...TO THE POTTY!
DASH
OH, YOU.
AT LEAST CALL IT A RESTROOM.
MIMURO, YOU JERK!
I HOPE YOU DIE!!
Waaah!
YOU BASTARD!
JUST KIDDING!
Oopsy daisy!

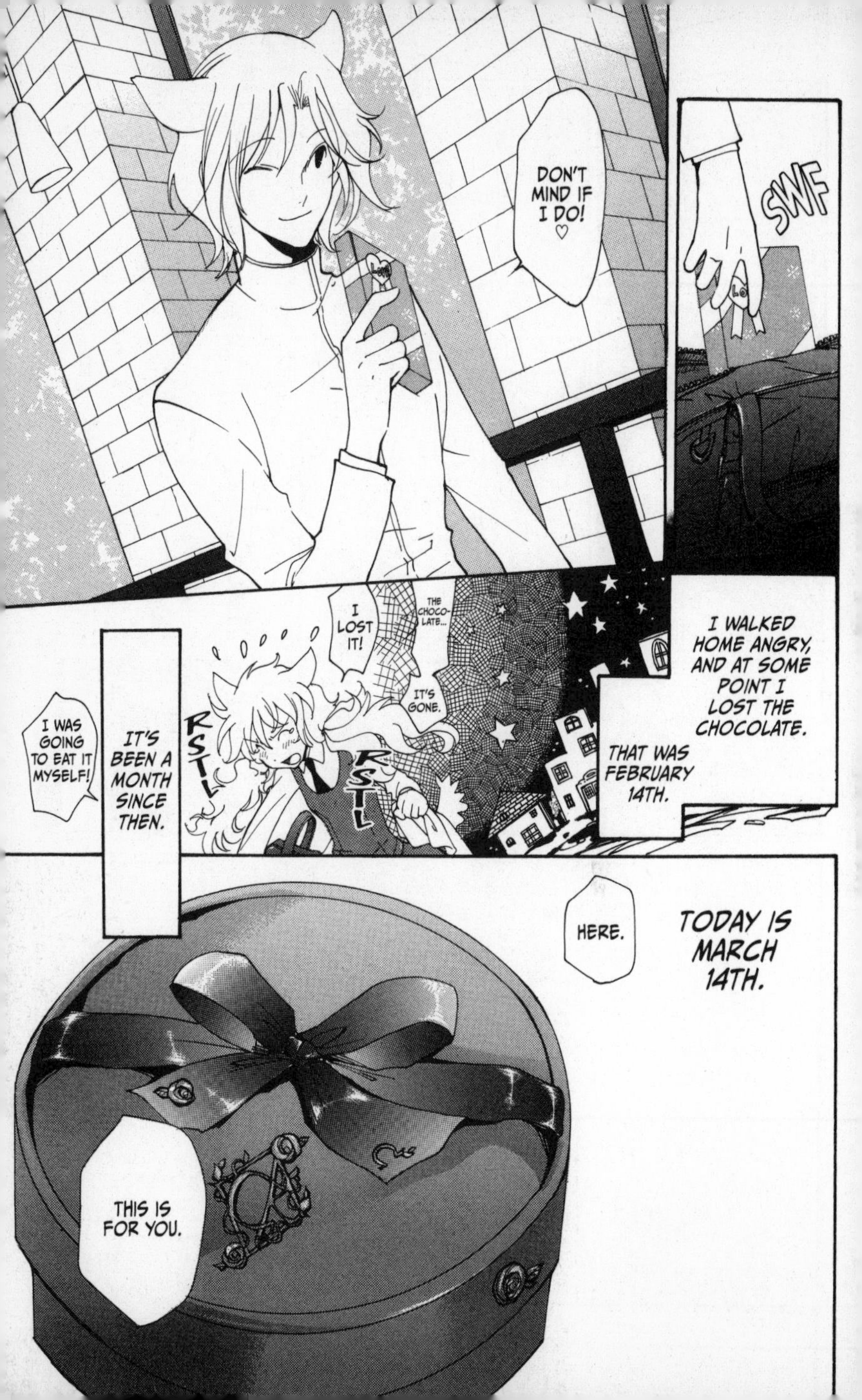

SWF
DON'T MIND IF I DO! ♡
I WALKED HOME ANGRY, AND AT SOME POINT I LOST THE CHOCOLATE.
THAT WAS FEBRUARY 14TH.
THE CHOCOLATE...
I LOST IT!
IT'S GONE.
RSTL
RSTL
IT'S BEEN A MONTH SINCE THEN.
I WAS GOING TO EAT IT MYSELF!
TODAY IS MARCH 14TH.
HERE.
THIS IS FOR YOU.

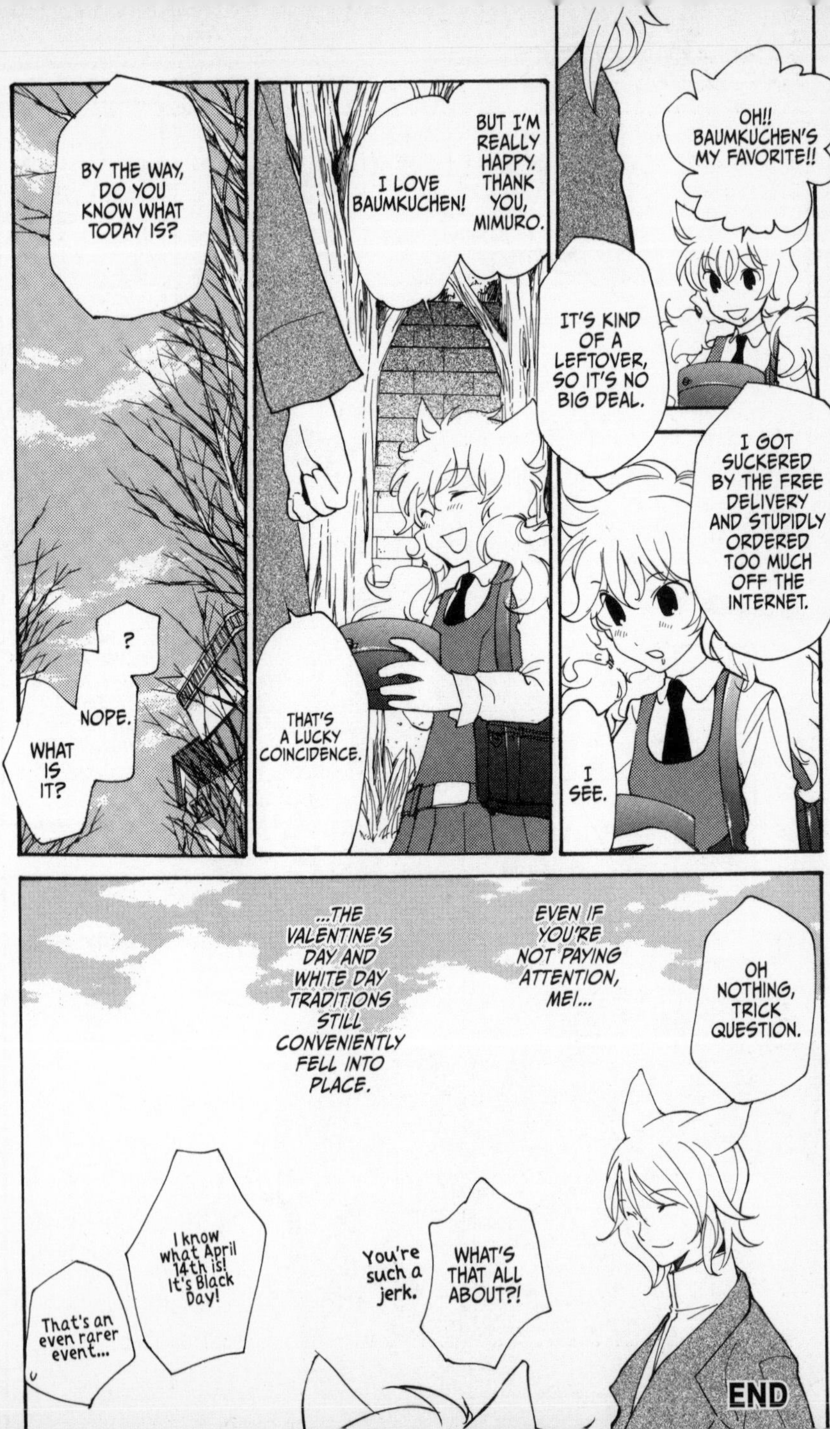
OH!! BAUMKUCHEN'S MY FAVORITE!!
IT'S KIND OF A LEFTOVER, SO IT'S NO BIG DEAL.
I GOT SUCKERED BY THE FREE DELIVERY AND STUPIDLY ORDERED TOO MUCH OFF THE INTERNET.
I SEE.
BUT I'M REALLY HAPPY. THANK YOU, MIMURO.
I LOVE BAUMKUCHEN!
THAT'S A LUCKY COINCIDENCE.
BY THE WAY, DO YOU KNOW WHAT TODAY IS?
?
NOPE.
WHAT IS IT?
OH NOTHING, TRICK QUESTION.
EVEN IF YOU'RE NOT PAYING ATTENTION, MEI...
...THE VALENTINE'S DAY AND WHITE DAY TRADITIONS STILL CONVENIENTLY FELL INTO PLACE.
WHAT'S THAT ALL ABOUT?!
You're such a jerk.
I know what April 14th is! It's Black Day!
That's an even rarer event...
END

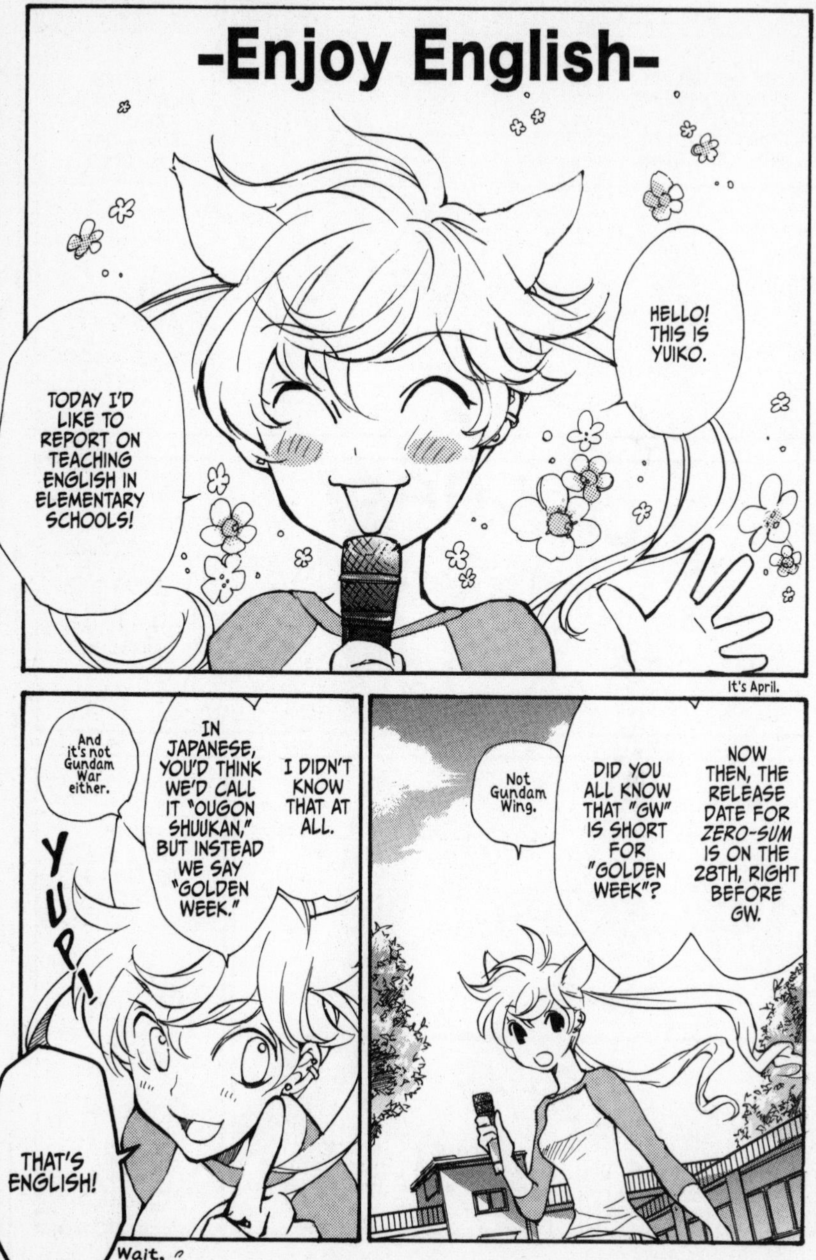
-Enjoy English-
HELLO! THIS IS YUIKO.
TODAY I'D LIKE TO REPORT ON TEACHING ENGLISH IN ELEMENTARY SCHOOLS!
It's April.
NOW THEN, THE RELEASE DATE FOR *ZERO-SUM* IS ON THE 28TH, RIGHT BEFORE GW.
DID YOU ALL KNOW THAT "GW" IS SHORT FOR "GOLDEN WEEK"?
Not Gundam Wing.
I DIDN'T KNOW THAT AT ALL.
IN JAPANESE, YOU'D THINK WE'D CALL IT "OUGON SHUUKAN," BUT INSTEAD WE SAY "GOLDEN WEEK."
And it's not Gundam War either.
YUP!
THAT'S ENGLISH!
Wait, really?

According to the new government guidelines for teaching, it appears that beginning in 2011, English will be a compulsory subject in elementary schools. (As of November 25, 2009.)

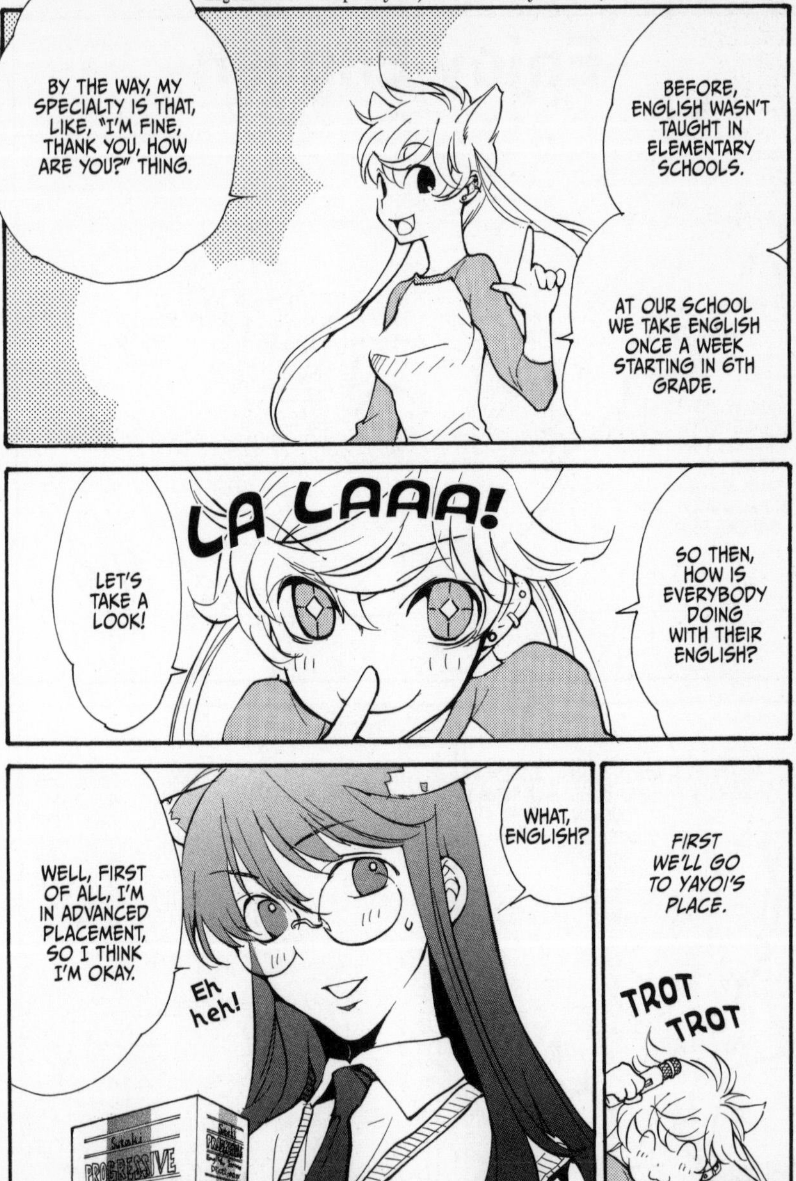
BEFORE, ENGLISH WASN'T TAUGHT IN ELEMENTARY SCHOOLS.
AT OUR SCHOOL WE TAKE ENGLISH ONCE A WEEK STARTING IN 6TH GRADE.
BY THE WAY, MY SPECIALTY IS THAT, LIKE, "I'M FINE, THANK YOU, HOW ARE YOU?" THING.
SO THEN, HOW IS EVERYBODY DOING WITH THEIR ENGLISH?
LA LAAA!
LET'S TAKE A LOOK!
FIRST WE'LL GO TO YAYOI'S PLACE.
TROT TROT
WHAT, ENGLISH?
WELL, FIRST OF ALL, I'M IN ADVANCED PLACEMENT, SO I THINK I'M OKAY.
Eh heh!
PROGRESSIVE
English-Japanese Dictionary

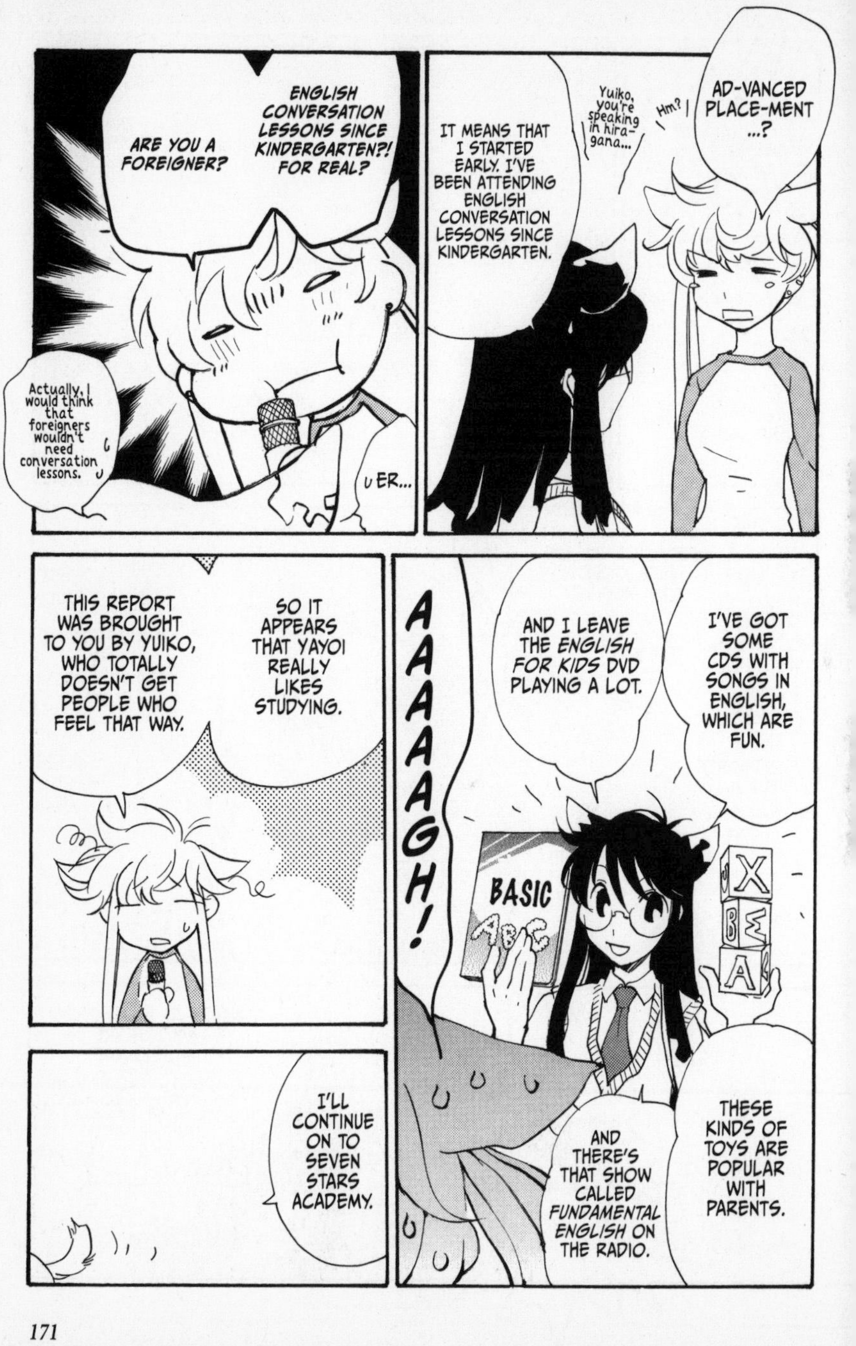
AD-VANCED PLACE-MENT ...?
Hm?
Yuiko, you're speaking in hira-gana...
IT MEANS THAT I STARTED EARLY. I'VE BEEN ATTENDING ENGLISH CONVERSATION LESSONS SINCE KINDERGARTEN.
ENGLISH CONVERSATION LESSONS SINCE KINDERGARTEN?! FOR REAL?
ARE YOU A FOREIGNER?
ER...
Actually, I would think that foreigners wouldn't need conversation lessons.
I'VE GOT SOME CDS WITH SONGS IN ENGLISH, WHICH ARE FUN.
AND I LEAVE THE *ENGLISH FOR KIDS* DVD PLAYING A LOT.
AAAAAAAGH!
BASIC
THESE KINDS OF TOYS ARE POPULAR WITH PARENTS.
AND THERE'S THAT SHOW CALLED *FUNDAMENTAL ENGLISH* ON THE RADIO.
SO IT APPEARS THAT YAYOI REALLY LIKES STUDYING.
THIS REPORT WAS BROUGHT TO YOU BY YUIKO, WHO TOTALLY DOESN'T GET PEOPLE WHO FEEL THAT WAY.
I'LL CONTINUE ON TO SEVEN STARS ACADEMY.

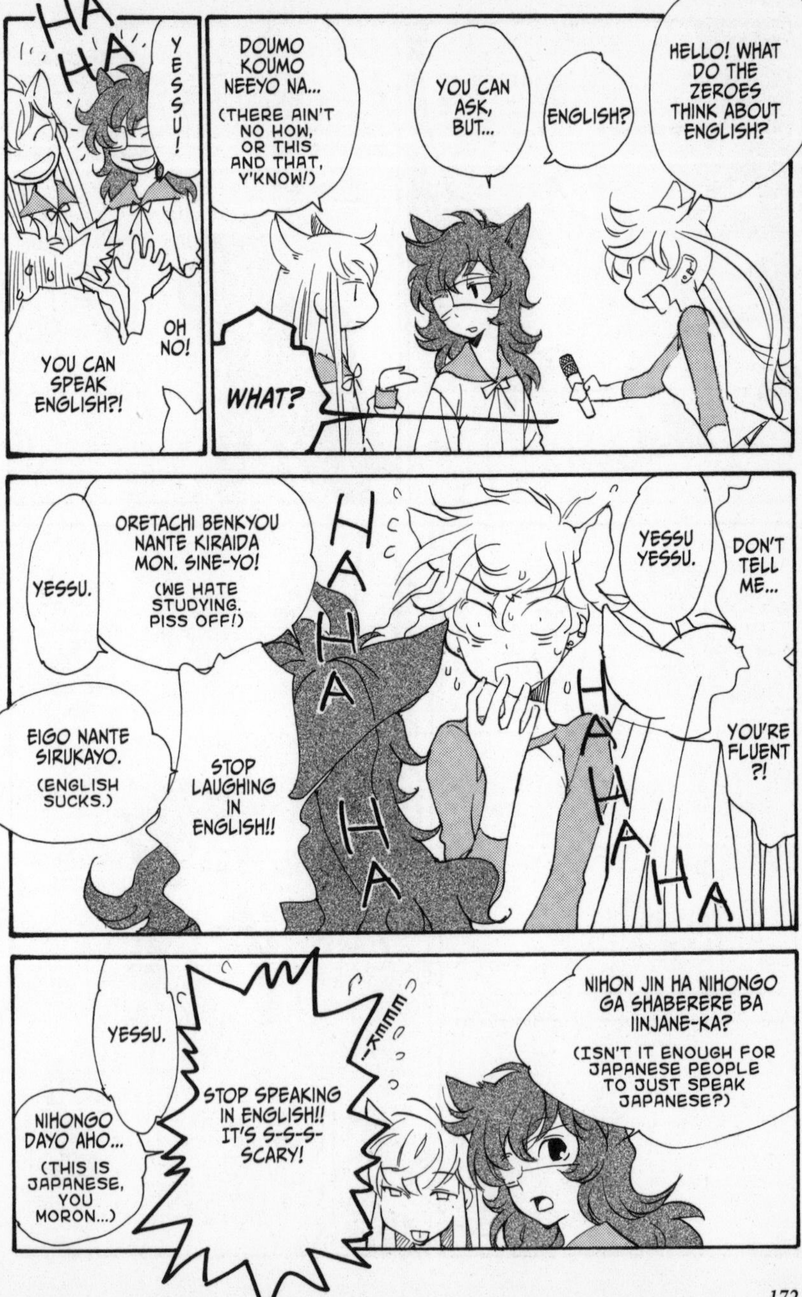
HELLO! WHAT DO THE ZEROES THINK ABOUT ENGLISH?
ENGLISH?
YOU CAN ASK, BUT...
DOUMO KOUMO NEEYO NA... (THERE AIN'T NO HOW, OR THIS AND THAT, Y'KNOW!)
WHAT?
YESSU!
HA HA
OH NO!
YOU CAN SPEAK ENGLISH?!
DON'T TELL ME...
YESSU YESSU.
YOU'RE FLUENT?!
HAHAHAHA
HAHAHAHA
ORETACHI BENKYOU NANTE KIRAIDA MON. SINE-YO! (WE HATE STUDYING. PISS OFF!)
YESSU.
STOP LAUGHING IN ENGLISH!!
EIGO NANTE SIRUKAYO. (ENGLISH SUCKS.)
NIHON JIN HA NIHONGO GA SHABERERE BA IINJANE-KA? (ISN'T IT ENOUGH FOR JAPANESE PEOPLE TO JUST SPEAK JAPANESE?)
EEEEK—!
STOP SPEAKING IN ENGLISH!! IT'S S-S-S-SCARY!
YESSU.
NIHONGO DAYO AHO... (THIS IS JAPANESE, YOU MORON...)

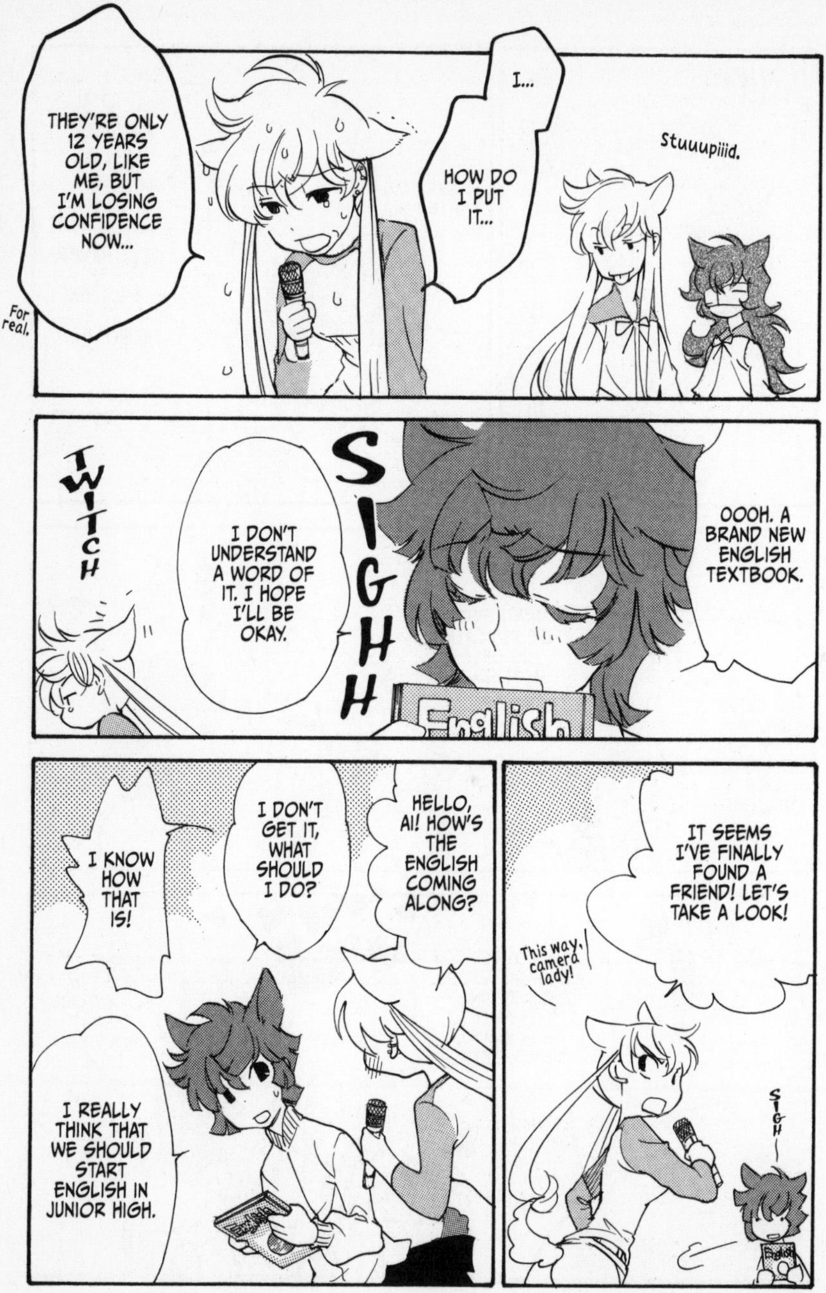
I...
HOW DO I PUT IT...
Stuuupiiid.
THEY'RE ONLY 12 YEARS OLD, LIKE ME, BUT I'M LOSING CONFIDENCE NOW...
For real.
OOOH. A BRAND NEW ENGLISH TEXTBOOK.
SIGHH
I DON'T UNDERSTAND A WORD OF IT. I HOPE I'LL BE OKAY.
TWITCH
English
IT SEEMS I'VE FINALLY FOUND A FRIEND! LET'S TAKE A LOOK!
This way, camera lady!
SIGH
HELLO, AI! HOW'S THE ENGLISH COMING ALONG?
I DON'T GET IT, WHAT SHOULD I DO?
I KNOW HOW THAT IS!
I REALLY THINK THAT WE SHOULD START ENGLISH IN JUNIOR HIGH.

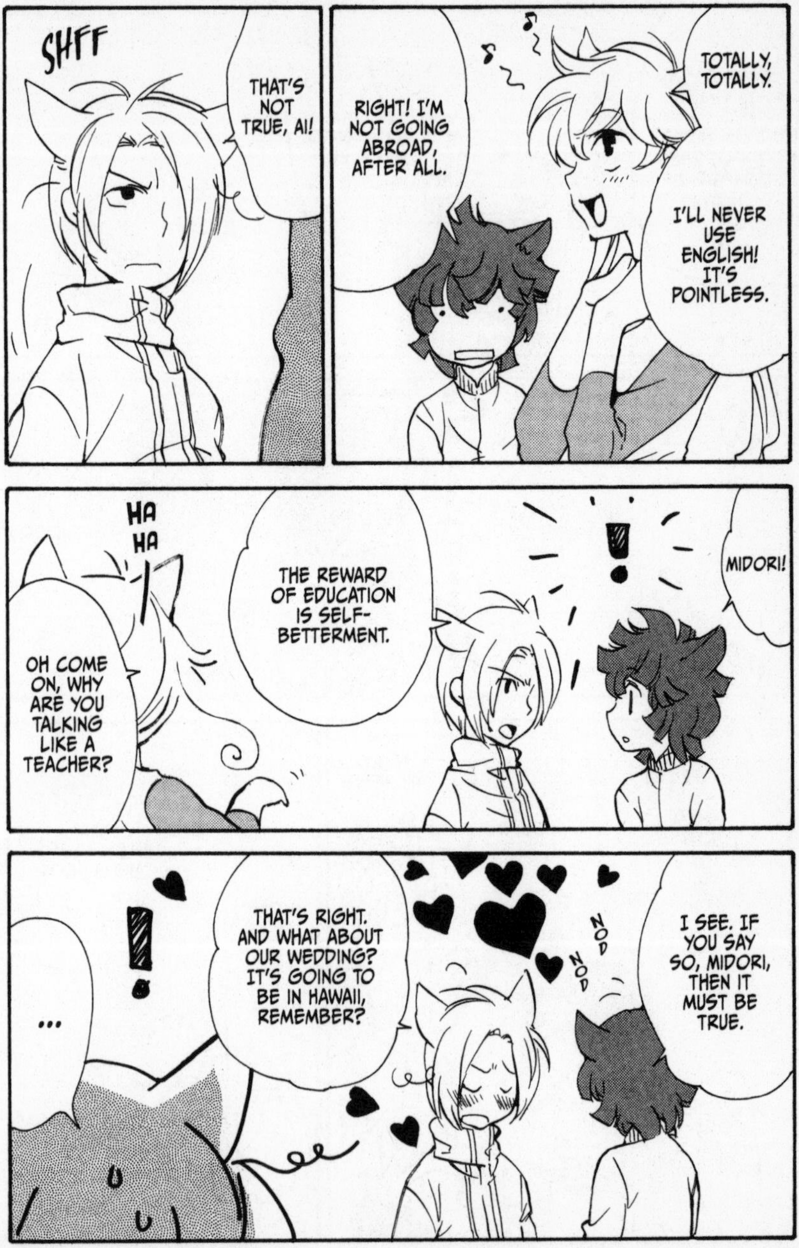
TOTALLY, TOTALLY.
I'LL NEVER USE ENGLISH! IT'S POINTLESS.
RIGHT! I'M NOT GOING ABROAD, AFTER ALL.
THAT'S NOT TRUE, AI!
SHFF
MIDORI!
THE REWARD OF EDUCATION IS SELF-BETTERMENT.
HA HA
OH COME ON, WHY ARE YOU TALKING LIKE A TEACHER?
I SEE. IF YOU SAY SO, MIDORI, THEN IT MUST BE TRUE.
NOD NOD
THAT'S RIGHT. AND WHAT ABOUT OUR WEDDING? IT'S GOING TO BE IN HAWAII, REMEMBER?
...

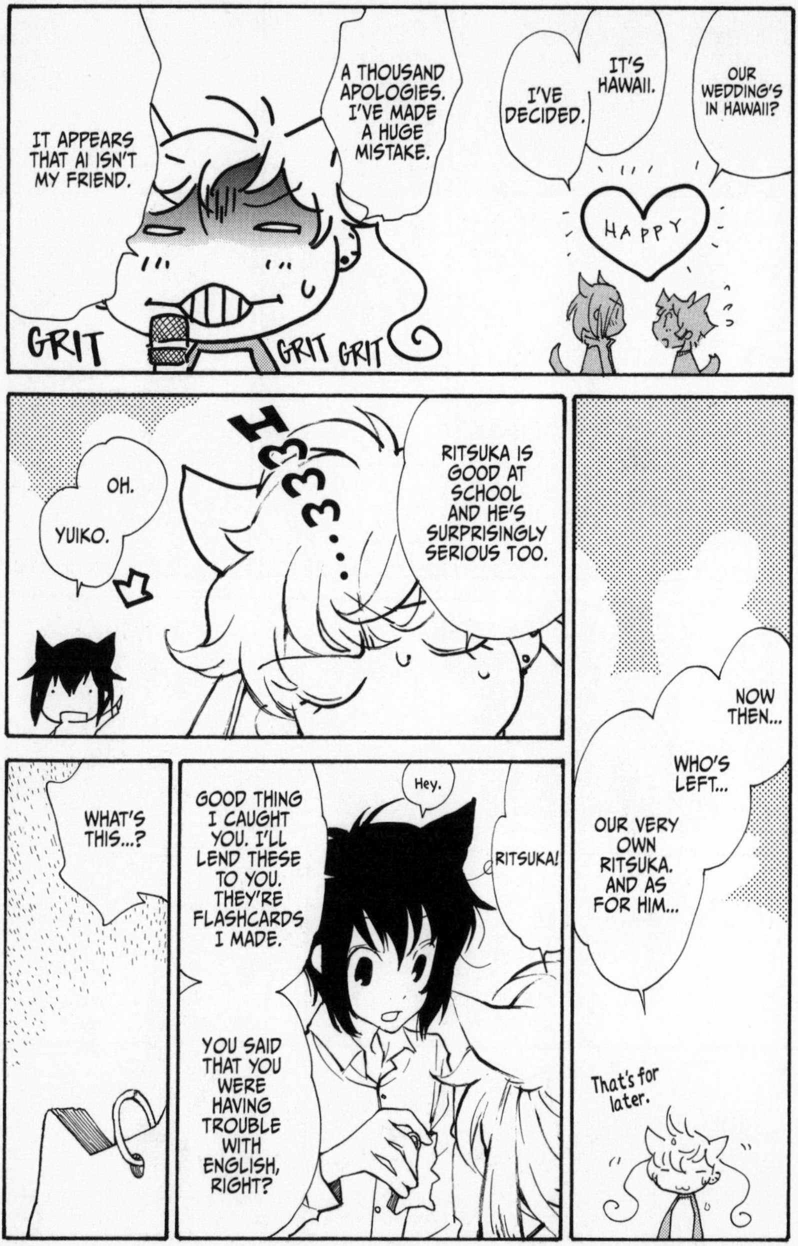
OUR WEDDING'S IN HAWAII?
IT'S HAWAII.
I'VE DECIDED.
HAPPY
A THOUSAND APOLOGIES. I'VE MADE A HUGE MISTAKE.
IT APPEARS THAT AI ISN'T MY FRIEND.
GRIT GRIT
GRIT
NOW THEN...
WHO'S LEFT...
OUR VERY OWN RITSUKA. AND AS FOR HIM...
That's for later.
RITSUKA IS GOOD AT SCHOOL AND HE'S SURPRISINGLY SERIOUS TOO.
H333...
OH.
YUIKO.
Hey.
RITSUKA!
GOOD THING I CAUGHT YOU. I'LL LEND THESE TO YOU. THEY'RE FLASHCARDS I MADE.
YOU SAID THAT YOU WERE HAVING TROUBLE WITH ENGLISH, RIGHT?
WHAT'S THIS...?

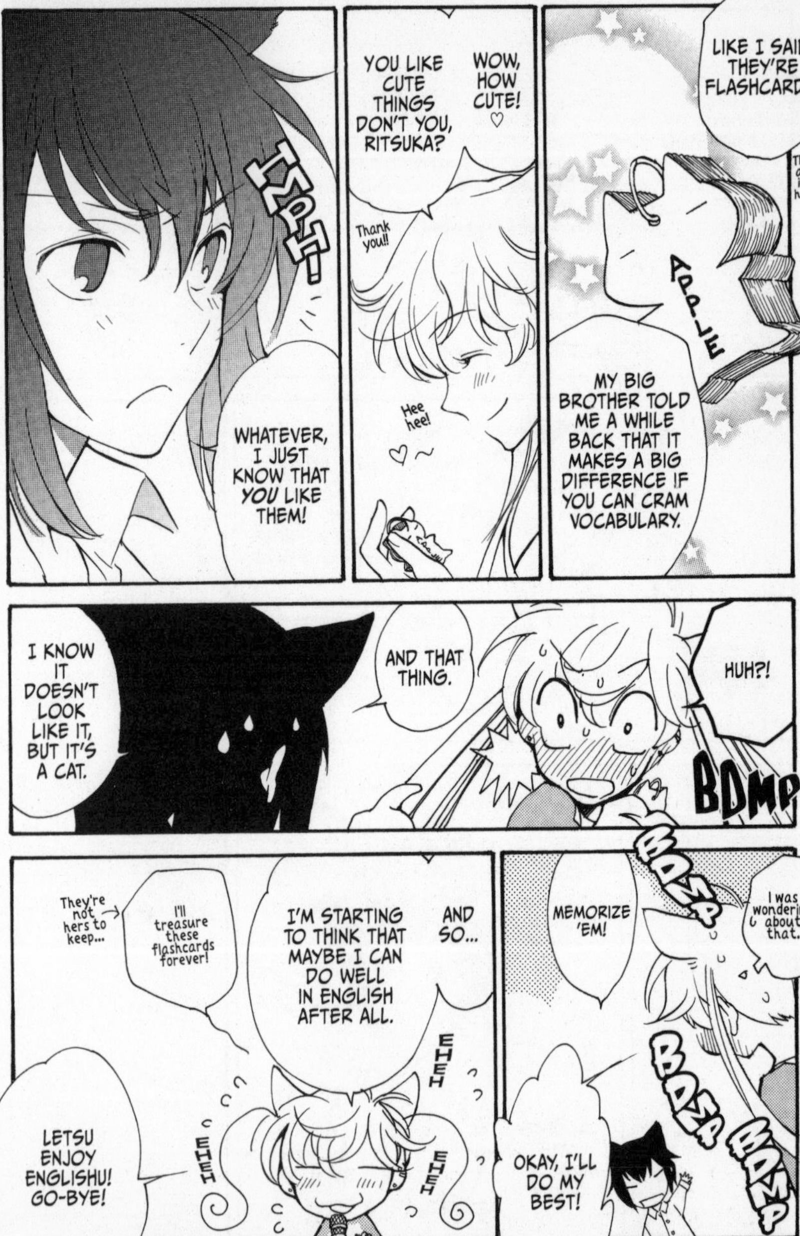
LIKE I SAID, THEY'RE FLASHCARDS.
There's a hole in his head...
APPLE
MY BIG BROTHER TOLD ME A WHILE BACK THAT IT MAKES A BIG DIFFERENCE IF YOU CAN CRAM VOCABULARY.
WOW, HOW CUTE! ♡
YOU LIKE CUTE THINGS DON'T YOU, RITSUKA?
Thank you!!
Hee hee! ♡~
IMPH!
WHATEVER, I JUST KNOW THAT YOU LIKE THEM!
HUH?!
BDMP
AND THAT THING.
I KNOW IT DOESN'T LOOK LIKE IT, BUT IT'S A CAT.
I was wondering about that.
MEMORIZE 'EM!
BDMP
BDMP
BDMP
BDMP
OKAY, I'LL DO MY BEST!
AND SO...
I'M STARTING TO THINK THAT MAYBE I CAN DO WELL IN ENGLISH AFTER ALL.
I'll treasure these flashcards forever!
They're not hers to keep...
EHEH
EHEH
EHEH
LETSU ENJOY ENGLISHU! GO-BYE!
END

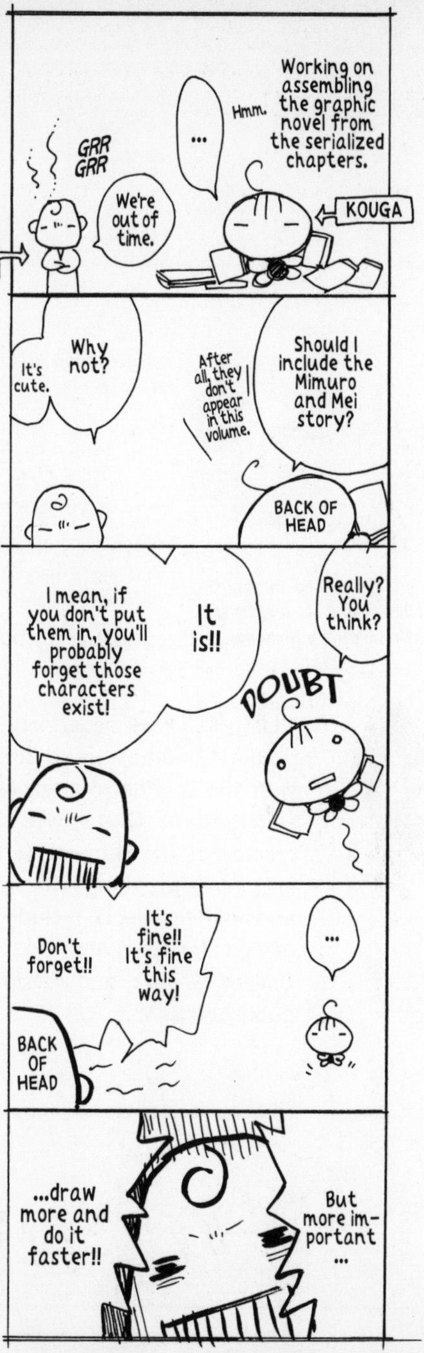
Working on assembling the graphic novel from the serialized chapters.
Hmm.
...
KOUGA
GRR GRR
We're out of time.
EDITOR S
Should I include the Mimuro and Mei story?
After all, they don't appear in this volume.
Why not?
It's cute.
BACK OF HEAD
Really? You think?
It is!!
I mean, if you don't put them in, you'll probably forget those characters exist!
DOUBT
...
It's fine!! It's fine this way!
Don't forget!!
BACK OF HEAD
But more im-portant ...
...draw more and do it faster!!

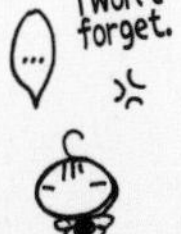
I won't forget.
...

I dedicate volume 9 to everyone who waited for it for so long. Thank you very much!!

When you flip this illustration horizontally, it's kind of...suggestive. I swear that wasn't intentional.

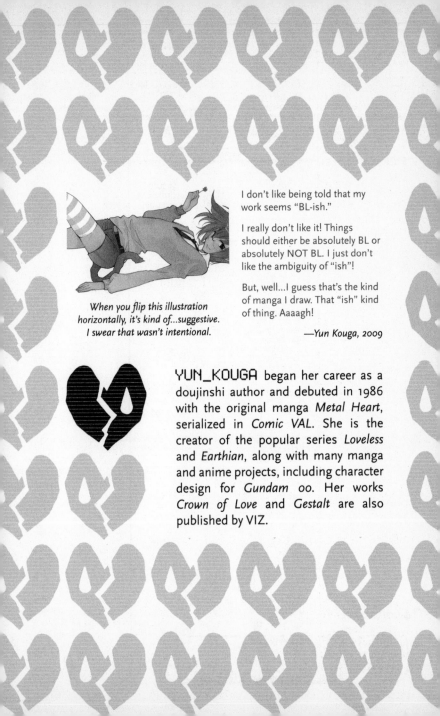

I don't like being told that my work seems "BL-ish."

I really don't like it! Things should either be absolutely BL or absolutely NOT BL. I just don't like the ambiguity of "ish"!

But, well...I guess that's the kind of manga I draw. That "ish" kind of thing. Aaaagh!

—*Yun Kouga, 2009*

YUN_KOUGA began her career as a doujinshi author and debuted in 1986 with the original manga *Metal Heart*, serialized in *Comic VAL*. She is the creator of the popular series *Loveless* and *Earthian*, along with many manga and anime projects, including character design for *Gundam 00*. Her works *Crown of Love* and *Gestalt* are also published by VIZ.

Loveless

Volume 9
VIZ Media Edition

Story and Art by YUN KOUGA

Translation // RAY YOSHIMOTO
English Adaptation // LILLIAN DIAZ-PRYZBYL
Touch-Up Art + Lettering // ERIC ERBES
Design // FAWN LAU
Editor // HOPE DONOVAN

Loveless © 2009 by Yun Kouga
All rights reserved.
Original Japanese edition published by ICHIJINSHA, INC., Tokyo.
English translation rights arranged with ICHIJINSHA, INC.

Printed in the U.S.A.

Published by VIZ Media, LLC
P.O. Box 77010
San Francisco, CA 94107

10 9 8 7 6 5 4 3 2 1
First printing, September 2012

PARENTAL ADVISORY
LOVELESS is rated T for Teen and is recommended for ages 13 and up. This volume contains adult situations.
ratings.viz.com

www.viz.com

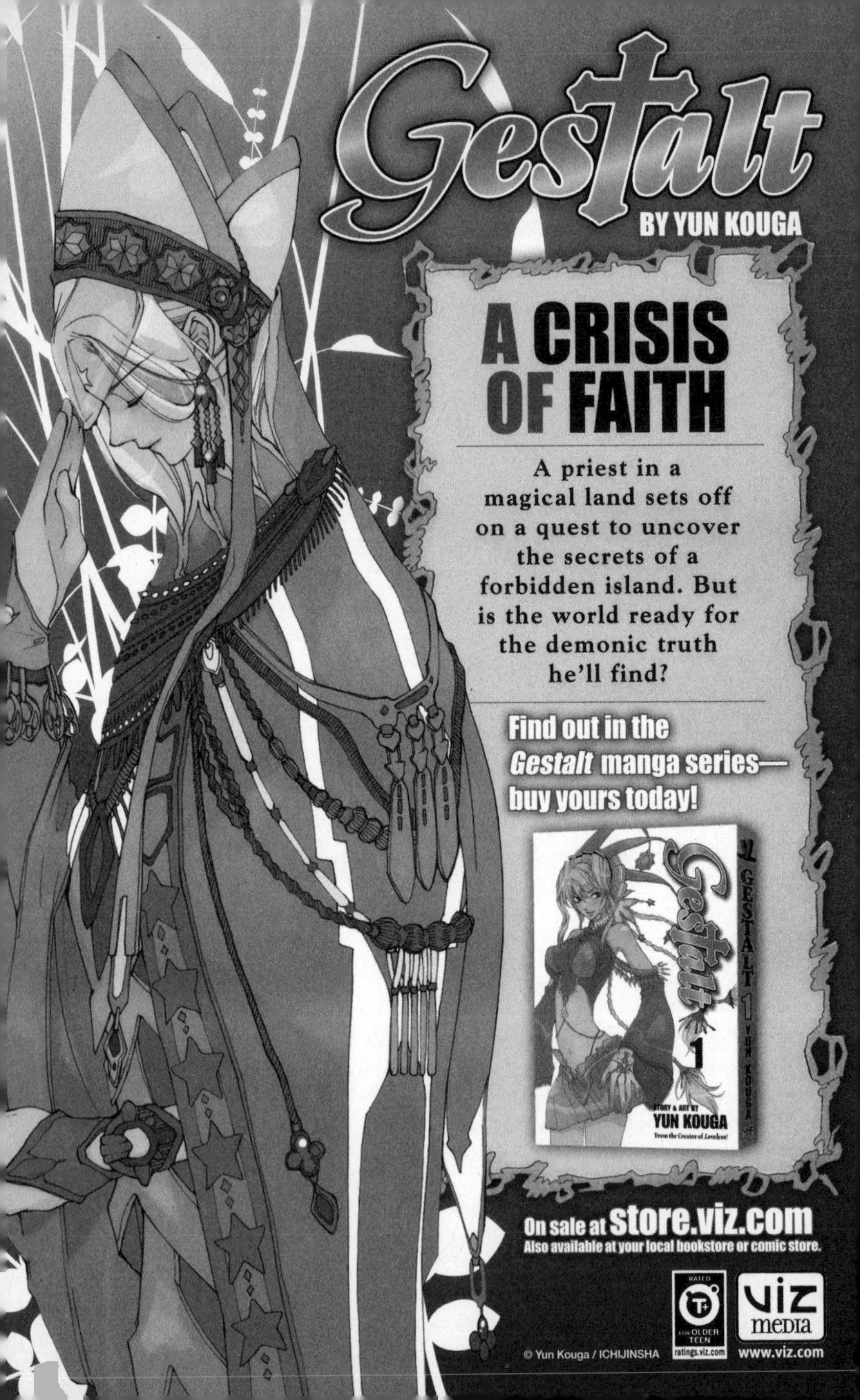

Gestalt
BY YUN KOUGA
A CRISIS OF FAITH
A priest in a magical land sets off on a quest to uncover the secrets of a forbidden island. But is the world ready for the demonic truth he'll find?
Find out in the Gestalt manga series—buy yours today!
Gestalt
GESTALT 1 YUN KOUGA
1
STORY & ART BY
YUN KOUGA
From the Creator of Loveless!
On sale at store.viz.com
Also available at your local bookstore or comic store.
RATED T+ FOR OLDER TEEN
ratings.viz.com
viz media
www.viz.com
© Yun Kouga / ICHIJINSHA

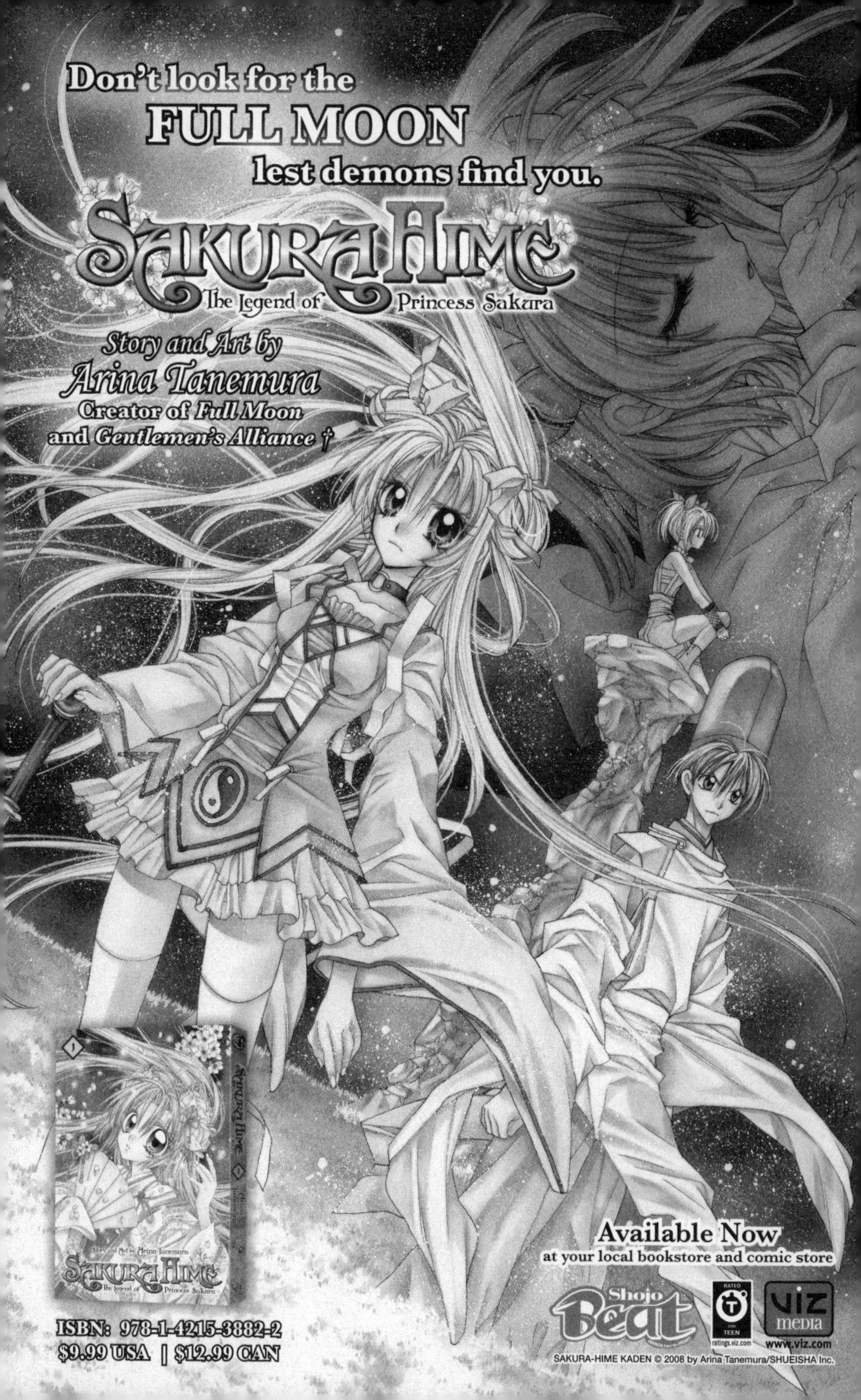
Don't look for the
FULL MOON
lest demons find you.
SAKURA HIME
The Legend of Princess Sakura
Story and Art by
Arina Tanemura
Creator of Full Moon
and Gentlemen's Alliance †
ISBN: 978-1-4215-3882-2
$9.99 USA | $12.99 CAN
Available Now
at your local bookstore and comic store
Shojo Beat
RATED T TEEN
ratings.viz.com
VIZ media
www.viz.com
SAKURA-HIME KADEN © 2008 by Arina Tanemura/SHUEISHA Inc.

Five Leaves

Complete Series Premium Edition

This beautiful box set features the complete two-volume, twelve-episode DVD set of the acclaimed anime series and features the original Japanese audio with English subtitles, as well as a sturdy slipcase and full-color hardcover art book.

House of Five Leaves Complete Series Premium Edition comes with a hardcover art book (full-color, 30+ pages), featuring character information, episode guides, artwork, behind-the-scenes storyboards, draft designs, concept art, and even a glossary of terms for insight on the culture of feudal Japan.

House of Five Leaves
Complete Series Premium Edition
12 episodes • approx. 274 minutes • color
Bonus Content:
Clean Opening and Ending, Japanese Trailer

For more information, visit
NISAmerica.com